Tourism and Hospitality Education and Training in the Caribbean

To my friend, Gabor,
with best wishes

Chandi
6/3/03.

Tourism and Hospitality Education and Training in the Caribbean

Edited by

Chandana Jayawardena

For
The Hotel and Catering International
Management Association – Jamaica Group
and
The Council of Caribbean Hospitality Schools

With a foreword by Rex V. Nettleford

THE UNIVERSITY OF THE WEST INDIES PRESS

Barbados • Jamaica • Trinidad and Tobago

University of the West Indies Press
1A Aqueduct Flats   Mona
Kingston 7   Jamaica

06 05 04 03 02   5 4 3 2 1

CATALOGUING IN PUBLICATION DATA

Tourism and hospitality education and training in the
Caribbean / edited by Chandana Jayawardena; with a foreword
by Professor Rex Nettleford.
p. cm.
Includes bibliographical references.
ISBN: 976-640-119-5

1. Tourism – Study and teaching (Higher) – Caribbean Area.
2. Hospitality industry – Study and teaching (Higher) –
Caribbean Area. 3. Leisure industry – Study and teaching
(Higher) – Caribbean Area. 4. Hotel management – Study and
teaching (Higher) – Caribbean Area. I. Jayawardena,
Chandana.

G155.C27T68 2002   338.4'791729

Cover: Chef photo courtesy of Grace Kitchens.
Cover design by Robert Harris.
Book design by Roy Barnhill.

Printed in the United States of America.

Contents

SECTION ONE:
INSTITUTIONAL AND SPECIAL PROJECT CASE STUDIES

Foreword

The University of the West Indies is pleased with the emphasis that is now being placed on the tourism and hospitality sector in the Caribbean which it serves and, in particular, the recognition being given the need for education and training in this most important bridgehead of the region's economy. As a lynchpin of development the tourist industry has gained a priority place in the checklist of policy options among governments throughout the entire region.

Half a century or more ago, the region was able to exist, and indeed flourish, at least in the minds of many observers, on the strength of its beautiful beaches, the ever-present glow of the sun, the tranquility of country life, and the fact that those who had access to travel were more limited in number. Consequently, the region dealt with a small, if elite, cohort of travellers.

Things have changed dramatically since those halcyon days. The succeeding decades have had island resorts transformed from beaches into *countries* tenanted by citizens who now claim ownership of former colonial-dependent spaces and who are energetically shaping new societies into feisty self-determining and by no means docile aggregations of souls. And as air travel and access to leisure funds by the democratized and more prosperous many of the North Atlantic have brought about a dramatic increase in the numbers that now frequent Caribbean shores, the competition among travel destinations for market share has intensified. The need for education and training for those who service the industry has increased accordingly.

Visitors now need to have a greater knowledge of the country that is being visited; the history that has brought the region to its present-day existence needs to be transmitted to avoid too great a culture-shock; and the rich, diverse and textured culture that helps to make the region the "tourist attraction" it has become in the minds of millions, demands of each visitor much understanding and empathy.

By "culture", one must refer to all that encapsulates the region's form and substance in the food it eats, the art, dance, music, theatre and festival arts it produces, the religions it practices, the creole languages and linguae francae it speaks and the family patterns by which it lives. One must further ponder on where and how such items of Caribbean civilization originated and the many strands that have gone into the Antillean weave following on five centuries of encounters between diverse cultures from the Old Worlds of Europe, Africa and Asia and they in turn engaging with the Old World civilizations of the Americas whose ancestral tenants discovered Columbus (arguably the region's first tourist) and his crew on the beach at Watling Island.

Indeed, part of the greater professionalism needed in this service industry must be a deeper understanding of the socio-economic, cultural and political realities of the Caribbean today, so that those who interface with the travelling clientele are able to answer questions about the different destinations in the region with a degree of intelligence and honesty and yet with a sensitivity that ensures that the person asking the question gets the kind of response that will bring clarity to some of the difficult questions that often and inevitably arise in a society that has changed so dramatically over recent years and continues to change as the wider world itself is doing.

So education and training in the Caribbean, if it is to be successful, needs to take into account the new Caribbean in all its complexity – a Caribbean that is no longer the backwater of "primitive in innocence" that it was deemed to be a half a century or less ago. And those who have decided to make the industry their profession themselves need to understand the challenges that now face a developing region required to function in a twenty-first century "globalized" world order. They should be able to grasp and be comfortably poised to emphasize the positive dimensions of the heritage and all the things that would serve to justify the region's tenacious hold on the imagination of travellers to vacation destinations.

All of these factors demand serious thought when preparing a curriculum for the kind of training that the new situation requires; and the University of the West Indies is pleased to be a part of this "re-think" which is so essential if the Caribbean region is to keep itself on the list of preferred places that the foreigner wants to visit. And it must be able to do this without fear of losing dignity or of endangering its patrimony.

It is good that the Hotel and Catering International Management Association and the Council of Heads of Caribbean Hospitality Schools have seen the need to assess the education syllabus by taking all these factors into consideration and are prepared to support both content and future direction on the basis of serious research. Such assurance, evident in the offerings by the many contributors to this volume, is most welcome if only because it is so timely.

Professor, the Honourable Rex Nettleford, OM, FIJ,
BA (UWI), MPhil (Oxon), Hon DLitt, LLD, LDH
Vice Chancellor
University of the West Indies

Messages

FROM THE FORMER CHIEF EXECUTIVE OFFICER, HOTEL AND CATERING INTERNATIONAL MANAGEMENT ASSOCIATION

The Caribbean is one of the jewels in the world's tourism destination crown, requiring the highest standards of hospitality and tourism education and training in order to maximize its visitor potential.

Since our formation in 1971, the promotion of best management practice has always been a priority concern for us at the Hotel and Catering International Management Association (HCIMA). This excellent book edited by Chandana Jayawardena fulfils that objective admirably; and the HCIMA's Jamaica International Group and the Council of Caribbean Hospitality Schools (CHOCHS) are to be congratulated on producing such an invaluable industry aid that will undoubtedly help to enhance standards of education and training throughout the Caribbean.

It is fitting that the book should be published at this time, when the HCIMA has recently celebrated its thirtieth anniversary (in 2001) as the professional association for hospitality managers worldwide. This publication reflects our steadily growing influence internationally. In June 2000, for example, Malta became the first country outside the UK to adopt our highly successful, definitive Hospitality Assured standard for delivering customer service excellence. Within six months of the standard's launch on the island, over sixty organizations were demonstrating a firm interest in signing up to the standard – fired by the Malta Tourism Authority (MTA), with whom the Hospitality Assured programme in Malta is being undertaken. In November 2000, the first-ever international Hospitality Assured accreditation was awarded to the five-star, deluxe 252-bedroom Radisson SAS Bay Point Resort Malta, situated in St George's Bay.

At the time of writing, the Hospitality Assured standard is being piloted in the province of Ontario, Canada. And that's not all. Hospitality Assured is currently in negotiation – at government and national tourism association levels – in Chile, Greece and Cyprus over the possible adoption of the standard by these countries. The scope for international growth of the standard is enormous.

Further information on Hospitality Assured can be found on our Web site (www.hcima.org.uk), currently attracting over 7,500 hits per day – one third of which are from overseas. The site includes details on all the HCIMA's other major initiatives, including the Corpus of Management Excellence – our comprehensive analysis of management expertise, providing both the framework for the HCIMA's own accreditation activities and a common currency for educators, industry trainers and individual managers worldwide to chart and plan for professional development.

The HCIMA Web site was given its new look and upgraded to give it more utilities for exchanging information across the globe, making it an even more user-friendly and invaluable industry resource to industry members and educationalists in the Caribbean. This is a crucial factor, given the growing importance of Continuing Professional Development (CPD), with individual managers becoming increasingly responsible for their own CPD in a business climate where lifelong learning is the order of the day. Hence, one of the main challenges currently facing the HCIMA is the development of CPD and its role as part of the future criteria for HCIMA membership.

The redesigned site provides HCIMA members with even greater and easier access to the association's information services. The HCIMA's highly acclaimed WHATT (Worldwide Hospitality and Tourism Trends) CD-Rom is no longer in CD format but has gone fully on-line, enabling Internet users to gain access to its three databases: Current Awareness Bulletin (CAB), World Trends, and International Research Register. CAB provides access to 200 English language periodicals relating to the hospitality and tourism industries; World Trends contains précis of carefully selected journal articles; and the International Research Register comprises information in extract format from government and industry publications, as well as research projects completed or in progress across the globe.

As with many of the HCIMA services on the newly designed Web site – such as its library catalogue – users can search by using keywords, significantly enhancing the efficiency and speed of the search process.

The redesigned WWW Hospitality Gateway – the association's catalogue of hospitality-related Internet resources – can also now be searched by keyword as well as browsed by subject, greatly assisting the site visitor.

Other bonuses for HCIMA overseas members include full access to the texts of all the association's technical briefing documents; up-to-date on-line directories on key aspects of the industry such as UK hotel groups, and organizations based outside the UK; as well as catalogues of, and links to, industry-related Internet sites.

Developments in information technology (IT) are drawing our global family of HCIMA international groups and members ever closer together. We greatly value this relationship and will continue to do everything in our power to provide the necessary support to promote best management practice internationally wherever practicable. The initiative shown by the HCIMA Jamaica International Group and CHOCHS in publishing *Tourism and Hospitality Education and Training in the Caribbean* is to be loudly applauded. I know it will prove to be a book of incalculable value to its readers, as well as an inspiration for our members and international groups across the globe to undertake projects of similar importance to the prosperity of our major growth industry.

David Wood, FHCIMA, MIPD, FTS, MBA, Hon DBA
London, England
March 2002

FROM THE CHAIRMAN, COUNCIL OF CARIBBEAN HOSPITALITY SCHOOLS

Tourism has never been more important to the Caribbean region than today, and this publication most definitely emphasizes this. The stress of modern-day employment environments has made travel and leisure an essential must in the life of most working people. With the violence and threats of violence in so many parts of our world, the Caribbean, where safety is still the order of the day, has become an increasingly desirable place for that much needed repose from the stress of work.

This book is a significant contribution to our efforts to keep tourism the most important occupation for our region. As the authors reflect on the past and chart their views of the future, it is obvious that we look forward to an ever increasing need for more quality tourism education and careful attention to quality service at all levels.

The caliber of the material and the wisdom with which each author writes is a reflection of the quality of tourism business we have supported and promoted for more than forty years, and an indication of what we can expect in the future.

The Council of Caribbean Hotel Schools (CHOCHS) is extremely proud to be a part of this very significant publication, no doubt an enormous undertaking destined to have a lasting impact on the future of Caribbean tourism. CHOCHS supports the unification of efforts among hospitality schools and hospitality educators in our region, and considers this book a tremendous tool in fostering that objective. We congratulate the editor on succeeding in bringing together so many of the best minds of our region to make this publication possible.

May this be only the first of several publications produced by our regional leaders and on behalf of our diverse and tourism-rich Caribbean.

Tony A.D. Green, BSc, MS, PhD
Aruba
March 2002

FROM THE SECRETARY GENERAL, THE CARIBBEAN TOURISM ORGANISATION

Some Key Challenges Facing Caribbean Tourism Educators[1]

This event is billed as a three-day intensive workshop for Caribbean tourism educators at the post-secondary level, with the purpose of "updating their knowledge of the tourism/hospitality sector globally, with special emphasis on the Caribbean region, and to prepare them for some of the changes and challenges the industry will face, moving into the twenty-first century".

We hope that at the end of this forum educators will be in an even better position to impart up-to-date information to their students, will be *au fait* with the latest international developments and trends in key aspects of the industry, and will have shared with us and each other, the vast store of knowledge they already possess and the mechanisms they wish to suggest for dealing effectively with the challenges identified.

I am not aware that such a forum has ever been held before at any level in the Caribbean. And yet it makes such good sense that those who are charged with both training and educating the region's children about the most important economic activity in the region should come together to share ideas, sharpen their skills and deepen their knowledge in an area in which the only constant is change itself.

We begin our discussions on this occasion at the post-secondary level, where much has already been done with respect to developing tourism educational institutions, curricula and certification. We are conscious, however, that at secondary and primary levels, we have hardly begun to meet the challenge within our formal educational systems, of imparting to a wide audience even a basic understanding of what tourism is and does.

The Caribbean Tourism Human Resource Council (CTHRC), under the auspices of which this forum is being held, realizes the size of the challenge and has created a multifaceted programme of action designed to transform the status of Caribbean tourism education.

We are already aware that the teaching profession generally has lost much of the esteem in which it was formerly held in our society. Teachers of tourism, however, have additional and very special problems. At the primary and secondary levels there is a dearth of material with which to teach, which is probably a function of a resistance to

---

[1] From the opening address to the first Caribbean Tourism Educators Forum, Barbados, 2000.

establishing it as one of the core disciplines in the education and examinations systems of schools. The textbooks available in the secondary schools for teaching tourism as part of the optional social studies programme seem, for the most part, to have been created by external authors. Some are not only of little relevance to real present-day Caribbean realities, but do more to denigrate Caribbean people and the tourism industry than to inculcate knowledge. The question must be asked and answered: Whose business is it to create the appropriate material for the teaching of tourism in this region? Certainly it is unusual for this task to be foisted onto the industry that is being studied.

Part of the problem may very well be that at a policy level it is not always clear that the importance of tourism in our socio-economic development is accepted by some of the education authorities. Not so long ago a minister of education in a Caribbean country was heard to express the view that tourism people are always exaggerating the importance of tourism to the economy. In response I would suggest that there are at least two examples of Caribbean countries where, once the thriving tourism industry came under enormous pressure due to external circumstances, almost instantly the entire economy of those countries began to die. It was then that they came to understand not only what role tourism played directly in the economy, but its many linkages, formal and informal, with other sectors of the economy. Creative strategies were needed by those countries to develop new markets and the political directorate found itself involved in aggressive campaigns to sell the idea to its own people that tourism was the very lifeblood of the country's communities.

At the faculty level tourism teachers sometimes have to contend with the view expressed by their colleagues that tourism is somewhat of a mindless activity and a soft option. This derives largely from ignorance of what is involved at a strategic policy level in creating a sustainable tourism industry. So often the end product, which is the enjoyment of the vacation experience, prevents people from understanding the skills and the multifaceted disciplines needed to produce a tourism product. So few people understand the complexity of creating a comprehensive tourism master plan, which can involve anything from anticipating the impacts of climate change, to land use policies and sewage systems, to architectural design, legal frameworks and marketing strategies. During the Gulf War in 1991, which caused a significant fall in tourism flows to Britain, Prime Minister Margaret Thatcher learnt a salutary lesson about the importance of tourism to Britain's economy, and had the good sense to become personally involved in promoting Britain as a tourism destination. We would prefer not to have to rely on such dramatic circumstances as embargoes, advisories or war as painful lessons to teach us what, by now, should be obvious even to the casual observer, that the success of tourism is highly correlated with quality of life in the Caribbean.

One of the by-products of our failure to deal adequately with tourism at an early point of our formal education system is that far too few students have enough information about the industry to see tourism studies later on as an option. Ultimately, therefore, there is not a wide enough cadre of high quality persons coming through to the tertiary level to provide the pool of Caribbean excellence we need at the top, to transform an industry which we are all agreed could benefit from change in important ways.

The industry is often accused, and sometimes rightly so, of importing foreign skills at the upper end of the managerial scale. But it is equally true that the Caribbean at both the public and private sector levels has invested too little in tourism human resource development, as was documented by a recent Caribbean Tourism Organisation (CTO) study on Caribbean human resource needs. People seeking employment often are academically qualified, but not necessarily qualified to perform the task in question. And while they are trainable, and arrangements must be made to train them, they must not expect to begin at the top.

If we are to create a more fertile environment in which tourism is to flourish, we have several challenges:

- We must educate the wider public about the industry and its impacts.
- We must somehow do a better job of sensitizing our public sector at both the political and bureaucratic levels about the intricate nature of this industry and its interrelationship with all the other ministries for which the Cabinet is responsible.
- Policy decisions must be made with some urgency about if and how we will teach tourism in our schools and the manner in which it will be examined and certified.
- We must equip our hospitality schools to provide the technical skills needed to provide quality service.

- We must, at university and other tertiary levels, invest the resources needed to provide cadres of excellence.
- Our private establishments must recognize the importance of training and be able to see that the giving of quality service to the customer is closely connected with providing the employee with training, certification and a career ladder that gives him or her job satisfaction.

There is no suggestion here that none of this is being done in some countries.

In planning this forum we could not in three days attempt to deal with all the major issues that confront the industry. We see this meeting as a first step in a long journey, as the first in many such forums where tourism teachers meet to strategize.

There are some issues, however, which I hope can be addressed, even if they are not all formally placed on the agenda. One of these is the redefinition of what we mean by "tourism success" and how it is to be measured. We are our own worst enemies when we simply play the numbers game. Another is, how can we give meaning to the statement that we now live in a world in which, for many of us, tourism and other services are the present and future realistic options for development? Certainly it must be more than a recognition that the old policies of export agriculture and import substitution have a bleak future. The answer does not lie simply in providing a larger budget for tourism marketing. Surely, changing the paradigm must involve some structural changes needed to execute new kinds of policy, and the time may have come for retraining the traditional advisers.

In that context, how prepared are we for dealing with the intricacies of the General Agreement on Trade in Services? How aware are we that the developed countries will seek to take from us whatever advantages in services we have been able to obtain to diversify our struggling economies?

Do we really understand what sustainable tourism development is about and do we have in place a programme to achieve it?

Today we are dealing with the problem of public access to beaches. Tomorrow we may be dealing with the problem of beaches lost entirely through lack of planning or understanding of the ravages of climate change – all because some of us thought that tourism was simply about putting people in beds.

Do we understand what will be the impact of the imposition of external quality standards on our industry? We live in a small global village in which international quality standards are being imposed by the marketplace. In no industry is this more true than in tourism, which has become the world's largest international business. Our industry has no option but to measure up to these standards. What steps are we taking as a region to achieve these objectives?

How prepared are we for meeting the technological challenges that confront us? We are involved in an industry that operates on the cutting edge of information technology. We know that the Internet and e-commerce, at several levels, have already begun to transform our lives in many ways. A clear grasp of the technology and investment in the software and hardware required as tools of the trade is critical to being any kind of player in our business and to maintaining our competitive edge.

The CTO is seeking to play its part in the business of transforming the industry through its own programme of tourism education and training. Our Work Plan includes a varied and multifaceted programme in human resource development. We have launched a CTO Foundation dedicated to scholarship. We have begun to implement our mandate to create the Caribbean Tourism Human Resource Council and to launch its specific programme.

We have launched some components of our sustainable tourism development programme in which we seek to establish some quality standards in key areas. We are on the point of launching a new and revamped Internet strategy, which speaks to the technological needs of our membership.

However, the job of shaping the future, of broadening the horizons of knowledge, of developing skills and changing behaviours, belongs, as it always has, to educators.

This is what this forum is really about. We hope that we can, in some small way, help you to fulfil your own objectives.

Jean Holder, MVO, BA, MA, Hon LLD (UWI)

Preface

This volume, published on behalf of the Council of Caribbean Hospitality Schools (CHOCHS) and the Hotel and Catering International Management Association (HCIMA)–Jamaica group, represents a milestone in Caribbean tourism research. The main objective of this publication is to "record, investigate and analyse significant initiatives, practices, trends and challenges in education and training in tourism and hospitality sector within the Caribbean region". The book taps into the vast knowledge on tourism and hospitality education that exists within the Caribbean and packages it in a manner that will edify the members of the Caribbean community on the past, present and future of tourism and hospitality education and training in the region. Contributions to this volume have been made by twenty-eight academics and industry practitioners from thirteen Caribbean countries who provide insight, share experiences, and discuss initiatives to improve the current state of tourism and hospitality education in the Caribbean region.

This book revolves around the central theme of "tourism and hospitality education and training in the Caribbean" and is divided into three sections of eight chapters each:

- Section 1: Institutional and Special Project Case Studies
- Section 2: Country Case Studies
- Section 3: Present and Future challenges.

TOURISM IN THE CARIBBEAN

The tourism sector in the Caribbean has assumed prominence as a result of consistent stagnation in the traditional economic sectors. As such, the region is often referred to as the most tourism dependent region in the world. Tourism earnings account for approximately 25% of the region's gross domestic product. The Caribbean, as a single destination, usually ranks sixth in the world in terms of tourist receipts. In 1999, the Caribbean region (thirty-two countries and two destinations in Mexico) recorded US$17,733 million in tourism receipts, with 20.32 million tourist arrivals and 3.14 million cruise passenger arrivals (CTO, 2001).

Table 1   Visitor Expenditure of Top Ten Caribbean Destinations
in US$ Millions

Destination	1995 Tourism Receipts	1999 Tourism Receipts	Increase %	1995 Rank	1999 Rank
Dominican Republic	1,568	2,483	58.35	2	1
Puerto Rico	1,842	2,326	26.28	1	2
Cancun	1,371	2,144	56.38	3	3
Cuba	977	1,714	75.43	6	4
The Bahamas	1,346	1,583	17.61	4	5
Jamaica	1,068	1,279	19.76	5	6
US Virgin Islands	822	955	16.18	7	7
Aruba	521	773	48.37	9	8
Barbados	612	677	10.62	8	9
Bermuda	488	479	(1.84)	10	10
Total of Top 10 Destinations	10,615	14,413	35.78	–	–
Total of Other 24 Destinations	3,258	3,320	1.90	–	–
Total of all 34 Destinations	13,873	17,733	27.82	–	–
% of Top 10 Destinations	76.52	81.29	–	–	–

In 1999, the Caribbean attracted 3.1% of tourist arrivals in the world. The benefits of tourism are not, however, evenly distributed among the thirty-four countries and destinations in the Caribbean. For example, in 1999 the top ten destinations in the Caribbean accounted for over 81% of the tourism receipts in the region (Jayawardena, 2001b). Five years ago, these ten countries accounted for 77% of total tourism receipts in the region. Phenomenal growth in tourism receipts over the last five years in Cuba (75%), the Dominican Republic (58%), Cancun (56%) and Aruba (48%) have contributed to the increase of the market share of the top ten Caribbean destinations, as shown in Table 1.

The top ten destinations have not changed over the last five years. However, slight changes in the ranks (based on tourism receipts) have been observed over the five years. Barbados, Jamaica, the Bahamas and Puerto Rico have slid one position each. Cancun, the US Virgin Islands and Bermuda remain in the same position held in 1995. The Dominican Republic and Aruba have advanced one position. Cuba is the only country in the top ten that has advanced by two positions.

The tourism sector also contributes to Caribbean economies by providing employment for 25% of the region's labour market. Success of tourism in the Caribbean, in general, has not been a planned

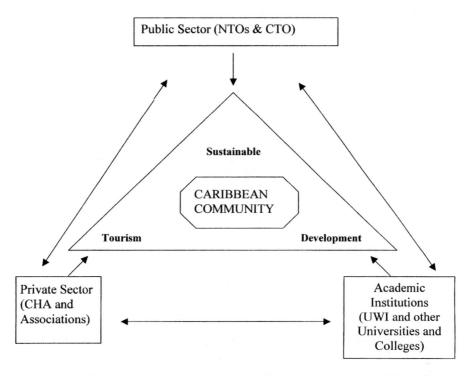

Figure 1   Model of sustainable tourism development for the Caribbean

achievement or a strategic option. In a majority of countries, tourism has emerged accidentally as an economic saviour. The future of tourism in the Caribbean will be dependent, however, on a more structured and less spontaneous approach to tourism development. According to Holder (1999), in light of the current deep troubles faced by export agriculture and many of the infant Caribbean industries, tourism's premier place as the development vehicle for the region has to be recognized. This would necessitate a paradigm shift in the manner in which the industry is managed in order to achieve the ultimate goal of a sustainable tourism industry.

   Figure 1 shows a model of sustainable tourism development for the Caribbean region that recognizes the need for partnership, cooperation and collaboration among the main stakeholders in the industry, such as local communities, universities and the academic community, the private sector Caribbean Hotel Association (CHA), the public sector Caribbean Tourism Organisation (CTO) and CARICOM (Jayawardena, 2000).

Critical areas such as destination marketing, product promotion and marketing, customer service, and guest safety and security are also areas that should be addressed. Nevertheless, the successful future of Caribbean tourism lies ultimately in teamwork, communication and a united effort by all main stakeholders. During the twelve months after the terrorist attacks in New York City on September 11, 2001, the Caribbean faced the worst challenge in fifty-five years. In this context the teamwork by all stakeholders in tourism in the Caribbean was no longer a luxury. It was, is and will be essential for survival and growth of the sector.

EDUCATION AND TRAINING

During the last decade there have been a number of changes that have affected the tourism and hospitality sector, and will continue to affect this sector in the twenty-first century. Some of these changes include greater environmental awareness among travellers and industry operators, the technological revolution that has affected the way the tourism product is marketed and the way in which plants are operated, and the move towards a more sustainable tourism industry. These have challenged academia to revise and revisit the approach used to tourism and hospitality education and training in the Caribbean.

Education, therefore, is identified as a key component in ensuring the sustainability of tourism. This volume reflects academia's efforts to improve and upgrade the programmes offered to adequately anticipate the needs of the industry and the needs of its students. The need exists, however, for a more structured approach to tourism education. Based on the findings of chapters presented in this volume, there clearly has to be a more concerted effort in education and training, with assistance from the private sector and regional governments to enable educational institutions to offer a better service to the tourism industry. Overwhelmingly, the lack of funding and adequately trained staff was cited as challenges faced by these institutions. This is unacceptable considering the importance of tourism to the region. The type of tourists visiting the Caribbean region is changing. Therefore, employees should be adequately trained and prepared to meet the needs of tourists. This is critical since the region faces competition from other destination that are actively improving the quality of their human resources to meet and exceed the needs of tourists.

Educational institutions in the Caribbean have to employ a more creative and proactive approach to training and education to lead and not follow the industry. The current approach taken to tourism and hospitality training may be a reflection of the degree of importance attached to the industry by regional governments. Initiatives such as the creation of the Association of Caribbean Tertiary Institutions (ACTI) are steps in the right direction. The University of the West Indies has also expressed the desire and demonstrated the ability and will to assume a more active role in tourism education and training in the Caribbean. Many proposals to improve the offering by institutions in the regions are also discussed in this volume. The time has come to act on these proposals.

While tourism earnings are increasing in most destinations, the adoption of a "laid-back" attitude to the industry's development and growth will auger ill for the Caribbean. The quality of the tourism product and the quality of the visitor experience ultimately depend on the quality of the human resource base in the region. Providing high quality education and training is, therefore, the most critical component in the future growth and development of the tourism industry in the Caribbean.

From the outline provided in the contents page, the reader will see that *Tourism and Hospitality Education and Training in the Caribbean* is a collection of authoritative and worthwhile contributions by experts in this field with wide ranging experiences in the Caribbean. The twenty-four chapters provide new concepts, philosophies and ideas to be explored by further research.

REFERENCES

CTO (Caribbean Tourism Organisation). (2001). *1999 Statistical Report*, CTO, Barbados.

Holder, J. (1999). *Perspectives for Caribbean Tourism in a Changing Environment*, Caribbean Tourism Organisation, Barbados, pp. 1–10.

Jayawardena, C. (1999). "Tourism Trends in the World and the Caribbean", paper presented at the Millennium Tourism Trends Conference, Centre for Adult Education, North-East of Finland.

Jayawardena, C. (2000). "An Analysis of Tourism in the Caribbean", *Worldwide Hospitality and Tourism Trends*, 1 (no. 3), Hotel and Catering International Management Association, London, pp. 122–136.

Jayawardena, C. (2001b). "Recent Research on Tourism and Hospitality Education and Training in the Caribbean", *Journal of Education and Development in the Caribbean* 5 (no. 1): 259–266.

Jayawardena, C. (2002). "Emerging Trends in Tourism and Likely Impact on Jamaica",
    paper presented at Professional Development Seminar on the Future of Tourism
    in Jamaica, Jamaica Institute of Planners, Kingston, Jamaica.

Jayawardena, C. (2002a). "Future Challenges for Tourism in the Caribbean", *Social
    and Economic Studies* 51 (no. 1): 1–25.

Jayawardena, C. (2002b). "Mastering Caribbean Tourism", *International Journal of
    Contemporary Hospitality Management* 14 (no. 2): 88–93.

Acknowledgements

This text would not have been possible without the dedication and hard work of many professionals. I am deeply indebted to the twenty-eight authors for their contributions and to the Ford Foundation, USA for providing a research grant towards this book project. I thank Professor, the Honourable Rex Nettleford, vice chancellor of the University of the West Indies (UWI) for writing the foreword, Dr David Wood, chief executive officer of the Hotel and Catering International Management Association (HCIMA) and Dr Tony Green, chairman of the Council of Caribbean Hospitality Schools (CHOCHS) for their messages, and Dr Jean Holder, secretary general of the Caribbean Tourism Organisation for his permission to include his address to the first Caribbean Tourism Educators Forum (2000) in the book.

I also thank all members of the HCIMA–Jamaica Group, CHOCHS–Jamaica Chapter and the Department of Management Studies, UWI, Mona campus, Jamaica, for their support and encouragement during this book project.

I am grateful to the following colleagues from the UWI for their professional inputs as chapter reviewers: Dr Ian Boxill, Dr Anne P. Crick, Dr Michael Haughton, Dr Hilton McDavid and Professor Alvin Wint. I am also grateful to Professor Richard Kotas, an external examiner of UWI, and Professor Richard Teare, principal, University of Action Learning at Boulder, Colorado (UALB), for their inputs as my advisors and mentors.

My special thanks are due to my administrative assistant, Mrs Allison Atkinson and my colleague Mr Samuel Bandara for providing project support over a period of eighteen months. Finally, I am indebted to my research assistant, Ms Eritha Huntley for her patience and hard work, without which this textbook would not have become a reality.

Abbreviations

ACF	American Culinary Federation
ACS	Association of Caribbean States
ACTI	Association of Caribbean Tertiary Institutions
ADP	Adolescent Development Programme
ASC	Antigua State College
AT	Alternative tourism
BAS	Belize Audubon Society
BCC	Bahamas Community College
BCC	Barbados Community College
BHTC	The Bahamas Hotel Training College
BIM	Belize Institute of Management
BTB	Belize Tourism Board
BTC	Belize Technical College
BTIA	Belize Tourism Industry Association
CAPE	Caribbean Advanced Proficiency Examination
CARICOM	Caribbean Community
CARIFORUM	CARICOM and the Dominican Republic
CAST	College of Arts, Science and Technology, Jamaica
CDB	Caribbean Development Bank
CET	Centre for Employment Training
CHA	Caribbean Hotel Association
CHOCHS	Council of Caribbean Hospitality Schools
CHRIE	Council on Hotel, Restaurant, Institution Education
CHT	Certified Hospitality Trainer
CHTI	Caribbean Hotel Training Institute
CHTM	Centre for Hotel and Tourism Management (UWI), the Bahamas
CIDA	Canadian International Development Agency
CMT	Conventional mass tourism
COB	College of the Bahamas
COE	Council on Occupational Education
CPEC	Caribbean Programme for Economic Competitiveness
CSTHM	Caribbean School of Tourism and Hospitality Management
CTEC	Caribbean Tourism and Education Council
CTO	Caribbean Tourism Organisation
CULP	Caribbean University Level Programme
EAST	Environmental Audit for Sustainable Tourism, Jamaica
ECDPM	European Centre for Development Policy Management
EMS	Environmental management systems
EU	European Union

FCCA	Florida Caribbean Cruise Association
GCE	General Certificate of Education
GDP	Gross domestic product
GEI	"Getting Education into Industry"
GIE	"Getting Industry into Education"
GOB	Government of Belize
GPE	General Proficiency Examination
GPS	Global positioning system
HCIMA	Hotel and Catering International Management Association
HEART/NTA	Human Employment and Resource Training Trust/National-Training Agency, Jamaica
HRD	Human resource development
HRM	Human resource management
HRMIS	Human resource management information system
IDB	Inter-American Development Bank
IH&RA	International Hotel and Restaurant Association
ILO	International Labour Organization
IOB	Institute of Business, Trinidad and Tobago
IPCC	Intergovernmental Panel on Climate Change
ISO	International Standards Organization
JAMAL	Jamaican Movement for the Advancement of Literacy
JHTA	Jamaica Hotel and Tourist Association
JMA	Jamaica Manufacturers Association
KSA	Knowledge, skills and attitudes
LCI	Learner-controlled instruction
LRQA	Lloyd's Registered Quality Assurance
MIF	Multilateral Investment Fund
MOU	Memorandum of understanding
MSB	Mona School of Business, Jamaica
NCTVET	National Council on Technical and Vocational Education and Training
NDC	National Development Corporation
NEWLO	New Life Organisation
NIHERST	National Institute of Higher Education, Research, Science and Technology
NISE	Nature Island Standards of Excellence
NRCA	Natural Resources Conservation Authority
OAS	Organization of American States
OASIs	Office of Administrative and Special Initiatives, University of the West Indies
OBUS	Office of the Board for Undergraduate Studies, University of the West Indies
OECS	Organisation of Eastern Caribbean States
OJT	On-the-job training

PEP	Primary Education Project
PEU	Project Execution Unit
PFB	Programme for Belize
RRTM	Resort, recreation and tourism management
STEs	Small tourism entities
TAMCC	T.A. Marryshow Community College, Grenada
TCIs	Turks and Caicos Islands
TETI	Tourism education training institute
TIDE	Toledo Institute for Development and the Environment, Belize
TPDCo	Tourism Product Development Company, Jamaica
TTHTI	Trinidad and Tobago Hotel and Training Institute
UALB	University of Action Learning at Boulder
UCB	University College of Belize
UNCED	United Nations Conference on Environment and Development
UNEP	United Nations Environment Programme
UTech	University of Technology, Jamaica
UWI	University of the West Indies
UWICED	University of the West Indies Centre for Environment and Development
UWIDEC	University of the West Indies Distant Education Centre
UWIDITE	University of the West Indies Distance Teaching Experiment
WCED	World Commission on Environment and Development
WFDC	Work Force Development Consortium
WTO	World Tourism Organization
WTTC	World Travel and Tourism Council
YES CORP	Youth Environmental Services Corps

INSTITUTIONAL AND SPECIAL PROJECT CASE STUDIES

Educational institutions in the Caribbean are continuously creating and recreating tourism and hospitality programmes geared to equipping men and women with the requisite skills and knowledge necessary to develop and manage the industry. Within the industry, there are also a number of initiatives that require the training of employees to master new processes and procedures. Section 1 of the book, comprising eight chapters, is devoted to examining a number of case studies from the industry and academia.

Chapter 1 by Kenneth O. Hall and Chandana Jayawardena examines the challenges that face educations in the Caribbean and summarizes the plans and visions of the University of the West Indies (UWI) in terms of tourism and hospitality education. The past, present and future role of the university is also examined with recommendations to enhance the institution's offering in the areas of tourism and hospitality education and training. The University of Technology, Jamaica (UTech) is also assessed by Rae Davis and Ava Sewell who examine the accomplishments and initiatives employed at UTech to proved relevant and appropriate training for persons within the industry, or desirous of entering the tourism and hospitality industry.

Chandana Jayawardena and Marcia Taylor-Cooke then examine the joint degree initiative between the UWI and UTech. The implementation process for the Joint Degree Programme in Tourism and Hospitality Management is outlined, along with the challenges faced in creating this programme. In chapter 4, Jayawardena also shares his experiences in creating the first Tourism and Hospitality Management master's degree in the Caribbean. The author recognizes that the successes and failures of educational programmes in the region are seldom recorded, analysed or investigated. The primary purpose of this chapter, therefore, is to record the process by which the programme was designed, developed and managed. He concludes by making recommendations that would ensure the sustainabiltiy of the master's degree.

Anthony Hall and Ayanna Young, in chapter 5, discuss the implementing of a human resource management system in Jamaica. The authors also examine the objectives and expectation of this initiative prior to the implementation of the project, and the challenges and opportunities experienced during operation. The project was developed in collaboration with a number of agencies including the Jamaica Hotel and Tourist Association (JHTA), the Inter-American Development Bank, and the National Council on Technical and Vocational Education and Training. The JHTA has also been involved in the Jamaica EAST Project, along with the US Agency for International Development. Hugh Cresser discusses this project in a study that demonstrates the importance of becoming an environmentally friendly hotel through the adopting of an Environmental Management System. He also identifies new opportunities for hospitality education and training in the Caribbean region by incorporating environmental "best practices" into the training curricula of education and training institutes. Chandana Jayawardena and Maxine Campbell present a case study of the efforts from the leading business hotel in Jamaica to attain ISO 9002 certification. The approach to employee training for ISO 9002 is assessed in the backdrop of redundancies, prolonging Union negotiations, increasing competition, decreasing profits and a re-branding process. The training efforts, along with the commitment from management and staff resulted in the Le Meridien Jamaica Pegasus becoming the first hotel in the Caribbean and the Americas to achieve ISO 9002 certification.

The final chapter in this section is presented by Kwame Charles who discusses the future human resource development needs for the tourism and hospitality industry in the Caribbean. The author recognizes that there are new global realities and changing requirements for the future tourism personnel. He then identifies the urgent need for the industry to adapt to these changes to remain competitiv. Most importantly the industry must be able to attract, motivate and retain and best personnel in order for the industry to be sustainable.

CHAPTER 1

PAST, PRESENT AND FUTURE ROLE OF THE UNIVERSITY OF THE WEST INDIES IN TOURISM AND HOSPITALITY EDUCATION IN THE CARIBBEAN

Kenneth O. Hall and Chandana Jayawardena

Abstract

This chapter critically assesses the role of the University of the West Indies (UWI) as the leading tourism and hospitality educator in the Caribbean. The authors discuss initiatives by the UWI to meet the needs of the most important sector in the region. One of the early achievements is the creation of the Centre for Hotel and Tourism Management, Nassau, the Bahamas. They also examine the current challenges that the UWI faces, mainly as a result of the technological revolution. The possibility of providing Internet-based tourism and hospitality educational programmes is explored. The chapter also reports on a recent UWI Review workshop on Tourism Education at which UWI's programmes were assessed with the view of making them more relevant to the needs of the industry. The authors conclude by making recommendations and suggesting a vision for 2003.

INTRODUCTION

Tourism has been recognized by most Caribbean governments and enterprises as an important economic activity for the region in terms of its multiplier effect in numerous areas, namely income generation, foreign-exchange earnings, investment and employment, and especially in related sectors such as agriculture, food processing, light manufacturing, environment and conservation, engineering, telecommunications, art and handicrafts.

This chapter examines some of the issues facing educators in the Caribbean when considering the development of education and training

3

programmes in the tourism and hospitality fields. The chapter also summarizes some of the current plans and vision of the University of the West Indies (UWI), particularly the Mona campus, towards tourism's future impact and growth in the region, especially in the direction of new trends and technologies.

According to InterEd (1999), the productivity of organizations in new knowledge societies lies increasingly in its intellectual and knowledge systems, as intellectual capital can be leveraged in ways that material capital cannot. Since increased leverage translates into competitive advantage, it is very important for the Caribbean region to recognize that most companies, including those in the tourism industry, should be redesigning their fundamental organizational structures to support their intellectual resources.

One of these redesign strategies is that which moves corporate education from its historical position as a marginal function to that of a core business activity. When this move is combined with efficient organizational structures, it is believed that education can move intellect both horizontally (within organizational levels) and vertically (across organizational levels) throughout the organization (InterEd, 1999).

The overriding assumption behind this and in fact all reasons for investing in corporate education, is that the education programme will be the right kind, will be offered to the right people, and will be available at the right time. This assumption sets the premise to explore the new and critical roles needed between the UWI and the tourism and hospitality sector in the Caribbean.

THE UNIVERSITY OF THE WEST INDIES

The UWI is an autonomous regional institution supported by and serving fourteen different countries in the West Indies – Antigua and Barbuda, Barbados, Belize, the British Virgin Islands, the Cayman Islands, Dominica, Grenada, Jamaica, Montserrat, St Kitts and Nevis, St Lucia, St Vincent and the Grenadines, and Trinidad and Tobago. In addition, Guyana is a full participant in the Faculty of Law and, by agreement, has a limited number of students in the other professional faculties. The university has long been recognized for its scholarship and has been a significant force in the political, economic and cultural development of the Caribbean region.

The UWI was founded in 1948 at the Mona campus (Jamaica) as a university college with a special relationship to the University of London and achieved university status in 1962. The St Augustine campus (Trinidad and Tobago), which was formerly the Imperial College of Tropical Agriculture, was started in 1960. The Cave Hill campus (Barbados) was founded in 1963. At present, UWI has a student population of 23,000. The Queen of England is the visitor of UWI and Sir Shridath Ramphal is the current chancellor.

Mission and Vision

The UWI's mission is to unlock the West Indian potential for economic and cultural growth by high quality teaching and research aimed at meeting critical regional needs, by providing West Indian communities with distinguished centre of research and teaching in the Caribbean and overseas.

Professor, the Honourable Rex Nettleford, vice chancellor of the UWI observes that

> The vision of the University as an instrument of growth and an institution of development is itself a challenge to the tyranny of distance; and the urgent search over the past two decades to find appropriate weapons of struggle and modalities of action to defeat the tyranny of distance . . . is partly what has been driving the University to relevance and greater usefulness in fulfilling its mandate in the service of our people throughout this region. (Nettleford, 1999)

Traditional challenges to the archipelago of Caribbean islands include the separation of the region's land resources by the sea. Physical separation by water from each other has indeed created certain unique difficulties in terms of intercountry travel by the people. It has contributed to what the vice chancellor calls "the tyranny of distance", which places the Caribbean in the extraordinary place of being separate and sovereign within one geographic region, but naturally divided by water.

Evidence of the university's regional role in redefining itself over the years to provide a regional institutional framework to facilitate greater access to tertiary education and training to Caribbean people (and to reduce and eliminate this tyranny of distance) can be seen in the institution's expanding reach, as illustrated in Table 1.1.

THE PAST

The relationship between the regional academic and tourism industrial sectors was formalized in May 1971 when the UWI obtained

Table 1.1   The University of the West Indies (1948–1999)

1948–1960	1960s	1970–1980 University Centres in Non-Campus Countries	1976–1996 Further Education Colleges (Continuing Studies)	1982–1999 UWIDITE/ UWIDEC Sites
Main Campus	Main Campuses			
Mona, Jamaica	Cave Hill, Barbados	Organization of Eastern Caribbean States	The Bahamas	Jamaica, Barbados, Trinidad and Tobago, Dominica, St Lucia, Antigua and Barbuda, Grenada, St Kitts and Nevis, St Vincent and the Grenadines, Montserrat, the British Virgin Islands, Belize, the Cayman Islands, the Bahamas
	St Augustine, Trinidad and Tobago	The Bahamas	St Lucia	
	Mona, Jamaica	Belize	Antigua and Barbuda St Kitts and Nevis St Vincent and the Grenadines	

financial assistance from the Inter-American Development Bank (IDB) to conduct feasibility studies to explore areas of education and training, including that of tourism and hotel management. The appointed committee for the latter programme recognized that:

> The UWI has a responsibility to contribute towards meeting the needs for skilled personnel in the countries that it serves and the importance of tourism to most Caribbean countries points strongly to a role for the University in this area of education and training. The University's role is not entirely vocational and the justification for university studies in tourism and hotel management rests as much on their educational value as on the vocational need for such training. (UWI, 1971)

The committee also recommended that education and training in tourism and hotel management should be a multidisciplinary exercise, embracing social and environmental studies, management principles, technical areas of study and foreign language skills. All these offerings should then be bound by courses designed to develop analytical and decision-making abilities, articulated expressions and the communication of oral and written ideas by students who intended to successfully enter the regional tourism industry.

In addition to the primary objective of training West Indians for senior positions in the industry, it was projected that a university programme would stimulate greater research activity into aspects and implications of Caribbean tourism. These would include work in agricultural development and land use, architecture and engineering, preservation and development of natural resource facilities and cultural activities and historical sites.

Some of the recommendations made by this early committee were implemented by the university, including the establishment of the Centre for Hotel and Tourism Management (CHTM) within the Faculty of Social Sciences at the Mona campus. Located in Nassau, the Bahamas, the CHTM offers courses towards the BSc degree in Hotel Management and Tourism Management, as well as a diploma programme in Hotel Management for graduates from other fields (Charles, 1990). The efforts of CHTM are examined in detail in chapter 23.

THE PRESENT

Along with its gradual expansion of geographic academic bridges, the UWI's ongoing mission is to become what is broadly defined as a partnership university. The institution is working to forge deeper links with regional social partners to provide comprehensive programme delivery, graduate work with a focus on economic development, and the development of other tertiary institutions. UWI has responsibility for quality graduate programmes and areas of specialized and relevant research, and the application of that research to address national and regional needs.

As a partnership institution, the UWI has positioned itself to forge ties through the organization that it founded, that is, the Association of Caribbean Tertiary Institutions (ACTI), which links the institution with other colleges and other universities. Affiliated university colleges are working with UWI to take on the responsibility for mass education as well as the equitable distribution of education institutions throughout the region. Over time, these institutions are expected to be upgraded to include faculties, as well as to expand their programmes.

The Office of Administration and Special Initiatives (OASIs) and the Office of the Board for Undergraduate Studies (OBUS) at the UWI are the offices that are primarily responsible for coordinating the development of the Regional Tourism (Undergraduate) Programme. This programme was established in 1998, and it was intended to improve the human resource base for the Caribbean tourism sector. The CHTM is the university arm that is responsible for the implementation of this programme in the region.

The UWI has been sensitive to the criticisms levelled against it by the Caribbean tourism and hospitality industry, and as such, has made major efforts to design and implement relevant programmes, and to deliver courses that meet the need for more flexible and accessible modes of training for the industry.

As a partnership institution, the UWI has positioned itself to forge ties through ACTI with other regional colleges and other universities. One of the set outputs of this association is to make new product offerings in tourism education and training available to the people of the Caribbean region into 2000 and onwards. OBUS has outlined some of these new offerings in five areas of specialization, whereby it is planned to grow the graduate pool with joint degrees being offered between the UWI and other regional educational institutions.

OBUS indicates that to complement the programme's academic component, the region's tourism sector has agreed in principle to assist with the placement and internships of trainee personnel in all language groupings. It is anticipated that they will be placed in a variety of facilities, including parks, protected areas, heritage sites and unique communities and sites. From the tourism employer's point of view, the emphasis that the university will place on work-based projects will make this initiative particularly valuable. This balance between academic rigour/learning and direct relevance to the learner's job in the industry is the key to the university's programme.

Current Programmes in Tourism and Hospitality Management

In summary, some of the current tourism and hospitality offerings now available from the UWI include:

- The MSc degree programme in Hospitality and Tourism Management, Mona campus. The European Union (EU) funded the programme for two years. Chapter 4 of this book provides detailed information on this master's degree (Jayawardena, 2002b). The programme commenced in 1999.

- Two MBA programmes with concentration in tourism management were offered by UWI's Mona School of Business in Jamaica (MSB) and UWI's Institute of Business (IOB) in Trinidad and Tobago, with around 20% tourism-related courses. After the introduction of the MSc in Tourism and Hospitality Management, the MBA programme in Jamaica was stopped but the programme in Trinidad and Tobago continues.
- A conversion diploma programme in Hotel and Tourism Management for graduates from other fields. This programme is delivered at CHTM with the undergraduate courses.
- A three-year degree programme in Hotel and Tourism Management at CHTM in Nassau, which accepts students with A levels. The first year is in the Faculty of Social Sciences on any of the three UWI campuses, and the second and third years are in CHTM. The programme commenced in 1978.
- A four-year joint degree programme in Hospitality and Tourism Management delivered by UWI, Mona and the University of Technology (UTech), Jamaica. It also includes a 2+2 arrangement to accommodate students from Montego Bay Community College and the Knox Community College. Chapter 3 of this book provides detailed information on this joint degree (Jayawardena and Taylor-Cooke, 2002). This programme was fully accredited in 2000 by the world's largest association in hospitality management, the Hotel and Catering International Management Association (HCIMA). This was the first occasion on which the HCIMA has fully accredited an educational programme in the Caribbean and South America. The programme commenced in 1998.
- A four-year joint degree programme with specialization in Hotel Catering and Institutional Operations, Culinary Arts and Tourism and Travel (with an emphasis on travel agency and tour management) with the Barbados Community College (BCC) and the UWI's Cave Hill campus. The programme is delivered in two parts. The BCC's Hospitality Institute delivers the first two years at the end of which students receive an associates degree from the Barbados Community College and then proceed to UWI, if they wish. The Faculty of Social Sciences delivers the management component in the final two years of the programme. Students are accepted with five CXCs. The programme commenced in 1999.

- Antigua State College delivers the first two years of a UWI degree programme with the students having an option, at the end of that period, to pursue specializations in traditional tourism courses now offered at CHTM or one of three non-traditional specializations to be offered at St Augustine. These areas of specialization are Events and Entertainment Management (designed to focus on Caribbean culture and heritage and community development issues), Tourism Product Management (focused on biodiversity and environmental issues) and Eco-Site Management (designed to focus on ecotourism, including its links with the community and agriculture). Those students who opt for the traditional courses will, however, be required to take electives in either environmental issues or agriculture. Students are accepted with five CXCs. The programme commenced in 1998.
- Trinidad and Tobago Hotel and Training Institute (TTHTI) and the UWI's St Augustine campus have a 2+2 arrangement similar to that of the Barbados Community College. The programme commenced in 2000.
- A diploma programme in Supervisory Management (Internet-based). The EU funded this programme with objectives "to increase the coverage of training for Supervisors and Managers in the region's tourism industry at the least possible cost and to develop permanent distance/open learning capacity through the piloting of a model programme". UWI's first proposal for a regional distance/open learning programme in the tourism sector, which conceptualized the programme, was submitted in 1999 (Jayawardena, 1999). This proposal was fine-tuned with various inputs from members of CHTM, and was implemented in 2001.

Distance Education and the Potential of the Internet

Distance learning programmes have been available in many areas of education for years, including at UWI over the past twenty years. It all began with a Challenge Examination Scheme in the early 1970s, through to teleconferencing via the UWI's Distance Teaching Experiment (UWIDITE) and now videoconferencing and other modern distance programmes through our current UWI Distance Education Centres (UWIDEC), located on all three main campuses.

The EU is building capacity of the UWI's distance education programme, via the Internet and a Web-based instructional environment. According to the EU:

> Graduate programmes by distance allow the working professional to retain employment and complete the programme on a part-time basis. This approach widens the market for these programmes and will ensure the sustainability of the programme after Lomé funding ends . . . Some of these programmes will offer a complete degree in the distance mode with short summer residency requirements, while others will offer non-degree distance programmes consisting of particular sets of courses targeted to identified special needs in the region. (Moore, 1998)

Some of the components of this EU upgrade will include the establishment of ten workstation computer labs at each site, significantly improved voice quality, ability to send and receive real-time video, Internet access, concurrent teleconferencing activities and regional computer application sharing. Teare (1998) reports that

> The rapid development of new communications technologies is revolutionizing the delivery of learning experiences. As lifelong learning is increasingly becoming recognised as the route to personal effectiveness and, within learning organisations, mechanisms, to organisational effectiveness, emerging virtual university models look set to be key to their delivery. Access to global domains of knowledge is now a reality and the Internet brings the generators, brokers and users of knowledge closer together than ever before.

The primary concern in the Caribbean is not the inherent value of the Internet for education and training, but the accessibility and affordability of this technology across the region. One of the many recommendations of the 1999 report done for the Caribbean Tourism Organisation (CTO) by Quality Consultants was that

> Given the geographically dispersed nature of the Caribbean, new and emerging technologies should be used to bring training to the industry rather than bringing the industry to the training. For example, Internet technology can be used to deliver in part or in whole, many . . . training modules and courses. With the increased use of information and communication technologies, access to distance learning

opportunities will also increase. This could give industry workers the opportunity to learn "anywhere and anytime" and at ever-reducing cost as the technology reduces. Local and regional training institutions can also be used as on-site training and assessment centres for centrally-coordinated training and certification programmes. (Quality Consultants, 1999)

Nonetheless, it is often suggested that, although technological deficiencies exist in the region, capabilities are to be found in promoting further use of distance education and can be strengthened by training and collaboration, especially between the private and education sectors for the advancement of an educated workforce.

This expanded UWIDEC network will allow increased and rapid connections to the three Caribbean University Level Programme (CULP) universities in the Dominican Republic and another in Haiti, which will create a common Web site that will facilitate sharing audio and video teleconferences among all the sites. A "virtual library" containing reference material will also be developed within this Web-based instructional environment.

With the EU upgrade of UWIDEC's teleconferencing network, some of the benefits inherent will enable more Caribbean students and faculty who may be dispersed geographically across the region to reduce the "tyranny of distance" that has been the traditional scourge affecting access to regional higher education. This new workplace learning programme should soon enable more managers and supervisors in the hospitality industry to gain academic awards through courses tailored to meet the needs of the industry. The UWI will be able to join with other regional universities to deliver more economical programmes and also will become a dual-mode institution with both on-campus classrooms and distance delivery programmes.

However, the rapid proliferation and popularity of the Internet has reshaped the way in which much educational material is offered and distributed. In more developed countries, distance learning in higher education is now dependent on personal computers, sophisticated (and expensive) software and efficient telecommunication networks to permit interaction of student and teacher while separated by both time and distance. Other effective (and more affordable) means of distance education still exist, however, including correspondence courses and other delivery media such radio, audio tapes, video tapes, teleconferencing, and so on (Dong, 1997).

It is also important to remember that distance or Internet education is not for everyone. Studies have shown that successful distant education students have certain characteristics that will determine their success. The successful individuals in these programmes are commonly ones who are motivated, goal-directed, highly disciplined and, generally, more mature degree-seeking students (Dessinger et al., 1998).

The UWI recognizes that there is a growing sophistication of higher education and skills training which can be delivered through the Internet to enhance the education and training of our tourism industry's labour force. In addition to requiring strong interpersonal and customer service skills, most segments of the tourism industry are information intensive, requiring workers, from front-line personnel to managers, to be adept in all forms of communications technology. So Internet proponents could argue that technology-driven distance education could be the platform for reinforcing skills in this area.

THE FUTURE

The time has now come to alter radically the philosophical foundations of tertiary education in the region. Current indicators suggest that the limited number of programmes and students in the UWI system is inadequate for the region's future development. Broad access would seem to require a system of mass tertiary education providing for wide access at different points in the system, and articulation of programmes between institutions with specified missions located geographically and utilizing the benefits of modern technology to provide tertiary education for the region. This is even more true of education and training of human capital within the regional tourism industry.

Since the beginning of the 1990s, dramatic changes in lifestyles have been witnessed. The prevailing common denominator of these changes has been global information and communications technology, which have had tremendous impact across all industries. Spivack and Chermck (1999) point out that within the tourism and hospitality industry, technological changes appear to be moving the whole industry towards globalization from both the supply side as well as demand side. Improved telecommunication systems are now allowing a rapidly growing number of clients and potential travellers easy access to every type of information needed to facilitate travel.

In today's technical world, it is becoming standard practice for many travellers to electronically inspect their hotel rooms before making a reservation, or to "virtually" visit a potential vacation destination on a Web site before selecting their next holiday. It is now possible for travellers to shop for and seek the best prices for airfares and hotel rooms by using the Internet. The technology itself has not only helped to open thousands of new destinations worldwide through new communication systems, but at the same time, improved transportation systems have reduced the time and stress involved with travel, and increased travellers' safety.

The new global positioning satellite (GPS) navigation systems are not only improving travel globally through improved efficiency and safety of air traffic control, but are making it almost impossible for travellers to be lost, whether they are trekking through a South American rain forest or exploring a glacier on the South Pole.

The above examples are but a few of the thousands that exist of how technological developments are changing the travel landscape for both the consumer and the travel industry. It is projected that guided computer-controlled cars and buses, self-controlled airport trains, trains that travel 300 miles per hour, alternatives to fossil fuels such as photovoltaics and biomass for inexpensive travel, trips to outer space and trips to amusement parks on the ocean's floor will become commonplace travel experiences in the near future (Spivack and Chermck, 1999).

For the Caribbean, this underscores the importance of keeping ahead of the needs of visitors, as they expect more and become more sophisticated, and as they choose their destinations much more efficiently and travel choices become more personal.

The Challenge of the University of the West Indies

The vice chancellor has challenged his colleagues to remember that, while the inevitable changes in modern educational technology are welcomed, the emphasis remains on education, rather than just the adoption of the technology. He implores his colleagues to understand that:

> access to information . . . of Internet and Web-sites does not necessarily mean access to education in the interactive, creative, mind-developing sense and so the use of the technology becomes an important factor in the push towards the greater use of educational technology

> . . . to prepare the well rounded, integrated and textured West Indian who will be needed for grappling with the unruly phenomena of the 21st century. (Nettleford, 1999)

At the same time, given all these global developments in travel budding on the doorsteps, there is growing concern among industry professionals that this labour-intensive industry will face severe staff shortages in the coming years. This concern is worldwide, and is of even more import to the region and in the respective Caribbean countries as well.

It appears that, worldwide, there is an inverse relationship between the steady increase in consumer demand for travel products and services, and the labour pool to fill jobs in tourism (Spivack and Chermck, 1999). While in industrialized countries this decrease is attributed to lower fertility or birth rates, that is, fewer persons being available to fill key positions, leaders and managers in the Caribbean have identified inadequate quality of human resource rather than quantity, as the problem. Education and training are therefore primary areas of focus in tourism for this century.

Although there are myriad opportunities for those who are preparing for international careers in this field, there are concerns which have to be addressed. Many pay lip service to the knowledge that the tourism industry is a highly competitive, service-based industry. At the same time, they seem to be doing a great many things that do not "key in" to the many changes occurring in the industry due to the technology and special needs of the twenty-first-century traveller. No matter who runs it or where they are located, many tourism enterprises will soon close unless they have educated and trained personnel to deliver the quality service that has come to be expected by customers throughout the service sector.

Now, in order for the people of the region to take full advantage of the career opportunities that await tourism and hospitality students today and in the very near future, these students must be well educated and have excellent technical, personal and interpersonal skills. It is imperative that they understand the nuances of marketing, from multilevel marketing to niche marketing. At the same time, they must be able to understand the basics of a business, such as whether a hotel room is clean and habitable.

Students will need to have, within their basic management training, a working knowledge of numerous software programmes for improving the performance of their business. A good working knowledge of

software programmes for manipulating spreadsheets, database management, statistical analysis, graphics design, desktop publishing,
Web publishing, and others will become standards for anyone want-
ing a mid- or upper-level management job in tourism. In summary
then, the tourism and hospitality manager for tomorrow must be
prepared to wear many hats, with the most important one being that
of a "continuing" or "knowledge-driven" student.

No one institution or business can provide, in a single programme,
all of the skills, knowledge and training needed to work for a lifetime
in the international tourism marketplace. What this will require is a
change in the educational focus at the post-secondary level, from
"just-in-case" learning to "just-in-time" and "anyplace, anytime"
learning (Spivack and Chermck, 1999).

Identified Training Needs of the Tourism Industry in the Region

The Caribbean Tourism Organisation (CTO) publication, *Tourism
Training for the New Millennium* (Quality Consultants, 1999), indicates
that, in the conduct of the research, it was found that the critical skills
deficiencies in the general training needs category across the Caribbean tourism industry, as of 1999, include:

- Customer relations
- Communication
- Computer literacy
- Foreign languages
  (especially Spanish, French, German and English)
- Marketing
- Leadership
- Human resource management
- Financial/accounting skills

All of these areas, in addition to major technical training needs,
including culinary, tour guiding, food and beverage, and mainte-
nance-related skills, have to be addressed by institutions such as the
UWI in its mission to provide relevant education and training for
West Indian people.

Initiative to Form Tourism Educators Association in Jamaica

In addition to developing and delivering education programmes to
suit the changing needs of the region, the education sector expects

the UWI to play a vital leadership role in uplifting the educational standards of the whole region. The following initiative from Jamaica is an example that reflects this role.

In September 2000 a number of Jamaican tourism and hospitality educators and trainers were invited to an informal meeting initiated by the Department of Management Studies of the UWI, Mona campus. The guest speaker at that meeting was world-renowned hospitality management consultant and author, Professor Richard Kotas from the UK. Encouraged by the positive outcomes from that meeting, those present decided to meet again. At the second meeting, hosted in Ocho Rios by the Tourism Product Development Company (TPDCo), it was decided to form an association of Jamaican Tourism Educators. At the third meeting, hosted by the Northern Caribbean University in February 2001, it was agreed to name the association "CHOCHS–Jamaica Chapter" and the constitution was formally adopted. The representative of UWI was elected as the first president.

The Council of Caribbean Hospitality Schools (CHOCHS) was formed in 1990 with heads of twenty-three member institutions from twelve Caribbean countries, and with the UWI as a founding member. In 2001 CHOCHS–Jamaica became its first national chapter. Depending on the success in Jamaica, the rest of the Caribbean is expected to follow. Almost all Jamaican educational institutions offering master's, bachelor's, associate degrees, diplomas and certificate programmes in tourism and hospitality management have joined CHOCHS–Jamaica Chapter. Its eleven founding member institutions are:

- The University of the West Indies
- The University of Technology
- The Northern Caribbean University
- The Tourism Product Development Company
- Bethlehem Moravian College
- Brown's Town Community College
- Montego Bay Community College
- Excelsior Community College
- St Andrew Community college
- Moneague College
- Runaway Bay HEART Hotel and Training Institute

Entrenching Partnerships in Caribbean Tourism Education and Training

In consideration of the rapidly changing technology environment and the need to provide continuing education for those who are currently employed within the tourism and hospitality sector, as well as to those who are current students, there exists a growing need to reaffirm our partnerships within the industry. The UWI intends to continue its plan to provide effective education programmes for the diverse regional tourism and hospitality sector in the first critical years of the new century.

However, by a pooling of resources between all of the education and training institutions, much of the diverse needs of the industry in terms of human resource provision would be better served. This move is supported by recent studies, which have pointed to an overwhelming need for education and training institutions to focus on the development of interpersonal skills in order to meet the needs of the tourism sector in all industry segments (TEDQUAL, 1997).

Many in higher education stand willing to assist students, teachers and tourism industry professionals in the region with the provision of basic information that will be helpful in optimizing the time they have for adding content to their respective curricula, especially in tourism education. In many respects these institutions are already personally engaged in additional education, training and learning appropriate to improving the tourism products.

Clearly, further development and implementation of programmes for tourism and hospitality education hold great promise. That promise, and its attendant expectations, must be tempered with a realistic assessment of the costs and benefits. Expansion into the Americas and the Caribbean can be accomplished effectively with adequate planning, coordination and funding.

Establishing a cooperative endeavour between respective international and the regional tourism organizations would be helpful. These could include bodies such as:

- The World Tourism Organization (WTO)
- The World Travel and Tourism Council (WTTC)
- The Hotel and Catering International Management Association (HCIMA)

- The Council on Hotel, Restaurant, Institution Education (CHRIE)
- The Pan American Federation of Hotel and Tourism Schools (CONPHET)
- The Caribbean Tourism Organisation (CTO)

If the UWI does not establish a solid educational foundation the region, as a whole, may be precluded from expanding its presence in the competitive, technologically driven, international tourism marketplace. The quality of a country's or a region's educational system will largely determine whether or not there will be a sufficient supply of workers who can deliver the types of service that will allow destinations to effectively compete.

It is also unlikely that any one institution or one business can single-handedly provide the total education and training required to equip students for a lifelong career in tourism in a technology-evolving society such as our own. Distance education and the Internet may be one of the most important elements in improving the current education infrastructure to better meet the current and future needs of tourism employers in the region.

However, while not diminishing the importance of the new technology, the academics and industry must continue to work together to focus on the all-important task of improving the quality of tourism education and training. New methodological insights must be developed and provided to standardize the analysis of tourism education and training quality gaps, in order to better match the needs of tourism employers with the training options offered to tourism students.

Review Workshop on Tourism Education

In March 2001, the Graduate School of the Faculty of Social Sciences, Mona campus and the Office of Administration and Special Initiatives, UWI hosted a review workshop. The UWI utilized part of a research fund from the Ford Foundation, USA to cover the expenses of this workshop. Most of the industries and segments of the tourism and hospitality sector were present at this workshop. The main objective of the workshop was for the UWI to be proactive and consult major players and industries in the tourism sector to determine the strategic steps the UWI should take to prepare a long-term plan in tourism and hospitality education.

One of the papers tabled at the workshop states:

Fortunately, there is within the region a growing awareness by all stakeholders of the need for a coherent strategic plan and implementation
strategy. There is also a recognition that the world is not waiting on the
region to adjust to the requirements of a rapidly changing global economy. It is therefore absolutely imperative that all stakeholders, investors,
workers (intellectuals, hands-on players, managers), and policy makers
be brought together to determine a plan and strategy for development
of the region's tourism and hospitality industry. (Alleyne, 2001)

After the welcome and general presentations, participants (over
fifty) were grouped to review the following areas:

- Culture and people
- Arts and crafts
- Health tourism
- Sports tourism
- Events and entertainment
- Site and attraction management
- Public sector management
- Hospitality management
- Eco-systems
- Innovation
- Investment
- Information technology

Outcomes from the Workshop

It was generally accepted that people whose lives are touched by
tourism must be consulted in ensuring the sustainability of tourism
development in the Caribbean. Some of the key thoughts from the
workshop are summarized below:

- The relationship of the UWI with the tourism industry is
  somewhat ad hoc and it must become seamless by improving communication.
- Potential in sports tourism is vast in the Caribbean. The UWI
  should pay more attention to this area.
- Small operators in tourism and hospitality should benefit
  from specific training and educational programmes.
- The UWI should offer multidisciplinary tourism degrees.

- Information technology education must blend with behavioural and tourism business issues.
- The UWI should set up a Caribbean Institute of Tourism Research.
- The UWI should help and advise the region's governments to develop national policies on heritage tourism.
- The UWI's Mona campus can also be used as a historic attraction.
- Research students should be trained to solve industry problems.
- Training of chefs should be done with 50% on coordinated and well-monitored internships. Partnerships with hotels and catering companies should be sought.
- Professionals from the industry should be used as part-time faculty at the UWI.
- "Best practices" case studies from the Caribbean should be developed by the UWI.
- Graduate-level education should be customized to industry professionals.

Post-Workshop Analytical Meeting

The following day a selected group of UWI academics and administrators further analysed the outcome of the workshop. The occasion was used to analyse the findings of a review of the CHTM arranged by the Quality Assurance Unit of the Board for Undergraduate Studies. It was strongly felt at this meeting that CHTM needed reorganizing to ensure that its programmes respond to the needs of the industry. It was decided to prepare a report in advance of a forthcoming summit of the CARICOM Heads of State/Government.

The following recommendations were made during and soon after this meeting and are expected to be included in the strategic plan for tourism and hospitality education of the UWI:

- CHTM degrees to be expanded as four-year programmes with the entire third year involving monitored industry experience completed with a six-credit project report.
- The selection of elective courses in degree programmes to be made wider with more options for majors and minors.
- A high level board of advisors with all relevant industry representation.

- Programmes to be developed in keeping with the actual demand for specializations. As an example, approximately 80% of the tourism sector managers and workers are employed in the hotel industry, which required more focused education and training. Tourism education with various electives is important, but the demand for such graduates is usually limited compared to hotel/hospitality management specialists.
- Accreditation of the UWI's degree to be sought using the UWI/Utech Joint BSc degree accreditation by HCIMA as a good example.
- Previously carried out surveys and research on human resource development for tourism in the Caribbean to be used in the decision-making process of the UWI.
- Mobilize, marry and redirect UWI resources towards tourism and hospitality management education.
- UWI to be more focused on tourism research and this to be the driving force of tourism education within UWI.
- More 2+2 degrees to be set up.
- More part-time lecturers from the industry to be used in the delivery of courses.
- Cross-campus and cross-faculty multidisciplinary master's degrees, for example a joint MSc in Environmental Management with emphasis on tourism with the Department of Geography, UWI. Twenty-five percent of the credits will be allocated for courses developed for the MSc in tourism and hospitality management.
- An Internet-based MBA (two-year part-time programme with three face-to-face interactive sessions) in hospitality management for senior managers in the Caribbean.
- A selected repertoire of MSc courses to be open for limited number of senior industry practitioners as certificate courses. This may be done as modules gaining credits towards the award of the MSc in Tourism and Hospitality Management.
- A summer (twelve weeks over two years) programme for experienced middle managers, using some of the MSc courses.
- An MPhil/PhD programme in tourism management. A Caribbean journal of tourism management to be launched and

doctoral students' research papers to be considered for publishing regularly in the proposed journal. Experienced and senior practitioners and well-known academics with knowledge of tourism and hospitality business in the Caribbean to be invited to contribute.

CONCLUSION

It is proposed that the UWI sets up a "Caribbean School of Tourism and Hospitality Management"(CSTHM) (Jayawardena, 2000). It is hoped that various other current programmes and initiatives by the UWI to be placed under this new school, in addition to the new programmes suggested above. CSTHM ideally should have cross-campus and cross-faculty responsibility and authority to be the main umbrella organization for advanced tourism and hospitality education in the English-speaking Caribbean. The proposed structure is shown in Figure 1.1.

The other current programmes and institutions referred to in the figure are:

- Two degree programmes offered by CHTM, UWI, in the Bahamas.
- Distance/open learning programmes for middle managers and supervisors in tourism and hospitality sector being finalized by CHTM, UWI in the Bahamas.
- Joint degree in hospitality and tourism management, Cave Hill campus, UWI, Barbados and the Barbados Community College.
- Joint degree in hospitality and tourism management, UWI and UTech.
- Joint degree in hospitality and tourism management, by St Augustine campus, UWI, Trinidad and the Trinidad and Tobago Hospitality and Training Institute (TTHTI).
- Other joint programmes between CHTM and schools in Antigua, St Lucia, etc.

In planning and setting up such a regional school a great deal will depend on the partnerships between academia and public and private sector organizations representing the whole region. It is proposed, therefore, that the UWI as the initiator should seek support, funding

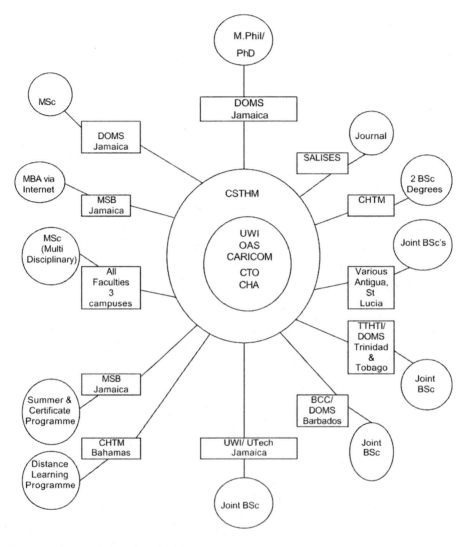

Figure 1.1   Vision for 2003

and advice from the following key regional organizations as active
partners in this endeavour: CARICOM, the Organization of American
States, the CTO (representing the public sector) and the Caribbean
Hotel Association (representing the private sector). This initiative for
the future development of the tourism and hospitality sector in the
Caribbean is referred to as "Vision for 2003".

REFERENCES

Alleyne, F. (2001). "Training and Research – Priorities in Development of Programmes to Respond to the Needs of the Tourism and Hospitality Industry", paper presented at the Tourism Workshop, University of the West Indies, Mona, Jamaica.

CTO (Caribbean Tourism Organisation). (1999). *A Guide to Tourism Career, Education and Training in the Caribbean*, Caribbean Tourism Organisation, Barbados.

Charles, K.R. (1990). "Career Orientation and Individual Perceptions of Caribbean Tourism and Tourism Management Students", in *Tourism Education and Human Resource Development for the Decade of the 1990s.* Proceedings from the First Caribbean Conference on Tourism Education, University of the West Indies, Centre for Hotel and Tourism Management, Nassau, Bahamas.

Chute, A., Thompson, M. et al. (1999). *Handbook of Distance Learning*, McGraw-Hill, New York.

Critchlow-Earle, B.C. (1990). "Opportunities for Employment in Tourism and Career Paths", in *Tourism Education and Human Resource Development for the Decade of the 1990s.* Proceedings from the First Caribbean Conference on Tourism Education, University of the West Indies, Centre for Hotel and Tourism Management, Nassau, Bahamas.

Dessinger, J.C., Brown, K.G. et al. (1998). "Measuring Attitudes to Assess Training: The Interactive Distance Learning Group Looks at Learning and Transfer from Satellite Training", in *Distance Training: How Innovative Organizations Are Using Technology to Maximize Learning and Meet Business Objectives*, edited by D.A. Schreiber and Z. Berge, Jossey-Bass Publishers, San Francisco.

Dong, F.H. (1997). "Technology and Teachers", in the Proceedings of Improving University Learning and Teaching International Conference, Vol. 2, Rio de Janeiro, Brazil.

Hall, K.O. (1999). "Implementing New Higher Education Programmes for the Caribbean Tourism and Hospitality Sector at the University of the West Indies", paper presented at the Caribbean Tourism Organisation Annual Conference, Dominican Republic.

Hayle, C. (1999). "Status of Tourism Programmes", unpublished document, University of the West Indies Office of Administrative and Special Initiatives, Mona, Jamaica.

InterEd. (1999). http://www.intered.com.

Jayawardena, C. (1999). "Consultancy Report – Caribbean Regional Tourism Sector Programme: Post Graduate Training and Distance/Open Learning Programmes", University of the West Indies/European Union, Mona, Jamaica, pp. 7, 115–125.

Jayawardena, C. (2000). "Creating Advanced Tourism and Hospitality Management Educational Programmes in Developing Countries", DPhil thesis, International Management Centres, Oxford, UK, pp. 158–161.

Jayawardena, C. (2002a). "Creating Hospitality Management Educational Programmes in Developing Countries", *International Journal of Contemporary Hospitality Management* 13 (no. 5): 259–266.

Jayawardena, C. (2002b). "Developing, Managing and Sustaining the First Tourism and Hospitality Management Degree in the Caribbean", chapter 4 in this volume.

Jayawardena, C. and Taylor-Cooke, M. (2002). "Challenges in Implementing Tourism and Hospitality Joint Degrees: The Case of the University of the West Indies and University of Technology, Jamaica", chapter 3 in this volume.

Moore, J. (1998). "Lomé Supports Development of New Internet Technology for Education", in *Caribbean Waves*, Newsletter, issue no. 4, University of the West Indies Distance Education Centre, Bridgetown, Barbados.

Ministry of Education and Culture. (1998). *Information and Technology Policy: Framework for Use in the Education System – Draft Policy on Information Technology in Education*, Ministry of Education and Culture, Kingston, Jamaica (December).

Nettleford, R. (1999). "Technology and the Tyranny of Distance", *UWI St Augustine News* 8 (no. 5).

Office of the Board for Undergraduate Studies. (1998). *New Directions in Tourism Education: A Rationale*, Office of the Board for Undergraduate Studies, University of the West Indies, Mona, Jamaica.

Quality Consultants. (1999). *Tourism Training for the New Millennium: A Study of Tourism Education and Training Needs in the Caribbean*, Caribbean Tourism Organisation, Barbados.

Richardson, A.G. (1990). "Curriculum Development Teaching and Assessment", in *Tourism Education and Human Resource Development for the Decade of the 1990s*, Proceedings of the First Caribbean Conference on Tourism Education, University of the West Indies, Centre for Hotel and Tourism Management, Nassau, Bahamas.

Shafer, E.L.D. and Zeigler, J.F. (1990). "Linking Tourism with Education", in *Tourism Education and Human Resource Development for the Decade of the 1990s*, Proceedings of the First Caribbean Conference on Tourism Education, University of the West Indies, Centre for Hotel and Tourism Management, Nassau, Bahamas.

Spivack, S.E. and Chermck, W.N. (1999). "Distance Learning: Assessing its Potential in Higher Education for the Tourism and Hospitality Sector", Proceedings of the First Pan-American Conference on Latin American Tourism in the Next Millennium, Panama.

Teare, R. (1998). "Editorial" in *Journal of Workplace Learning: Employee Counselling Today* 10 (no. 2): 55–57.

TEDQUAL. (1997). "Quality in Tourism Education", in *Tourism Education Quality*, World Tourism Organization, Madrid, Spain.

University of the West Indies. (1971). Report of the Special Committee on Education and Training in Tourism and Hotel Management, University of the West Indies, Mona, Jamaica.

University of the West Indies. (1997). *Strategic Plan for UWI 1997–2002*, Canoe Press, Mona, Jamaica.

CHAPTER 2

PAST, PRESENT AND FUTURE ROLE OF THE UNIVERSITY OF TECHNOLOGY IN TOURISM AND HOSPITALITY EDUCATION IN JAMAICA

Rae Davis and Ava Sewell

Abstract

This chapter outlines the past, present and future role of the University of Technology (UTech) in tourism and hospitality education in Jamaica. It traces the historical development of the School of Hospitality and Tourism Management at UTech, examining the different guises under which it has operated, the various programmes offered at different stages and the different needs that the programmes have met within the society. Some of the current changes are also outlined, together with details of UTech's plans for the future of tourism education.

INTRODUCTION

The University of Technology (UTech) was initially established as the Kingston Technical College, then renamed the Jamaica Institute of Technology in 1958 and the College of Arts, Science and Technology in 1959. University status was accorded in 1995. Inheriting the site of the Jamaica Farm School, UTech has grown dramatically over the years and is now a respected and very relevant Caribbean institution.

The introduction of UTech as Jamaica's first national university has enhanced the Jamaican society. It demonstrates Jamaica's level of commitment to tertiary education. Moreover, Jamaicans now have a wider choice of higher educational programmes.

The growth and impact of UTech over the past forty-four years can be seen in many different ways. Some of these are:

1. The growth in student numbers from 50 to over 7,000.
2. The growth in number of courses from 4 to over 70.
3. The impact of the institution on the skilled manpower requirements of the country.
4. The innovative directions and educational leadership that the institution has given in many areas, such as work oriented modular courses, part-time degree programmes and interinstitutional linkages both at home and abroad.

PROGRAMMES OFFERED

The Hospitality and Food Science Department (now the School of Hospitality and Tourism Management) was started in 1958 as an Institutional Management programme. At that time there were a mere six resident female students pursuing a two-year certificate programme in General Catering and Management. This programme prepared them for supervisory positions in the hotel and food service industry. In 1975, the unit was granted full departmental status, which reflected its growth and development. Sensitive to the demand for training and the increased job opportunities, the department reviewed and restructured its programme. A name change to the Institutional and Food Science Department reflected the range of subjects offered in food service and dietetics/nutrition.

With the aim of making its graduates more proficient in their chosen field the two-year certificate was upgraded to a three-year diploma. It offered a common core in the first year and the opportunity for on-the-job training, which has become an integral part of all the programmes offered by the School of Hospitality and Tourism Management. This innovation in the training of hospitality/tourism students at UTech highlights the practical orientation to human resource development, a concept on which the university has placed much emphasis over the years. It is also a requirement of the university that students participate in the Community Service Programme.

In response to industry demands for graduates with baking expertise, UTech officially opened its Baking School in July 1991. In September the then College of Arts, Science and Technology began the one-year certificate programme in Baking Technology. In November 1991, the school's first baking seminar was held.

A day release course in general catering is now offered to upgrade the skills of those in the catering trade. This programme has met the needs of those persons in industry requiring more professional staff members in this area. It also serves to raise the standard of service offered in many catering establishments.

The demand for shorter courses led to the development of the summer school. These include Advanced Cake Decorating, Basic Pastry Making, Techniques in Food Preparation, Chef's Upgrading, Pattern Drafting, Clothing and Fashion and Children's Culinary Adventure. These courses suit the needs of children and adults who are available during the summer break.

The diploma in Food and Beverage Management was launched in 1990. The course was developed after much planning with a very vibrant, dedicated Advisory Committee comprised of representatives of the Jamaica Hotel and Tourist Association, Jamaica Tourist Board, the Ministries of Tourism and Education, Versair In-Flite Services, representatives of restaurants of Jamaica and staff.

Through a variety of part-time, short or modular courses and workshops, service continues to be offered to individuals in the community who wish to upgrade their knowledge and skills for personal development or for wider service in the community. These programmes cover areas such as clothing and fashion, hospitality and tourism, general catering and baking technology.

Factors Responsible for the Introduction of the Programmes

In September 1990, the two-year day release course in Baking Technology began through the request and cooperation of the Bakers Association of Jamaica. US Wheats and the US Department of Agriculture were among those requesting development of this programme, with the latter providing funds for construction of the Baking School. The Baking School project received a special grant under the PL 480 Food Programme.

Over the years the School of Hospitality and Tourism Management has remained fully aware of its role as a training institution and has sought to keep pace with trends in the industry and produce graduates capable of satisfying the industry's human resource needs. This has led to the establishment of the Baking School, the introduction of the Hospitality/Tourism Diploma Programme and the opening of Lillian's, a training restaurant on the university campus at Papine.

Between 1991 and 1993, with assistance from the Canadian International Development Agency (CIDA), a project was funded to facilitate three other hospitality programmes: Hotel and Resort Management, Tourism Management and Culinary Management. The School of Hospitality and Tourism Management was to be assisted in the implementation of these programmes by the Association of Canadian Community Colleges.

In June 1996 the school launched its second post-diploma/degree programme: Hotel Restaurant and Tourism Management. This was a major achievement, as it endeavoured to fulfil part of its mission to provide students with the opportunity to improve their educational status and provide the industry with more competent employees.

In December 1997 a memorandum of understanding was signed by UTech and the University of the West Indies (UWI), Mona to offer a joint Hospitality and Tourism Management four-year degree. Extensive preparation by both institutions led to the acceptance of the first batch of sixty-nine students in September 1998. Students registered in this programme attend classes simultaneously on both campuses (Utech and UWI) and are required to complete a two-year course in foreign languages. This cooperation marks a milestone for the school.

The year 1999 saw the start of the new BSc degree in Food Service Management. Extensive preparation and consultation with the advisory committee led to development of this programme, which answers the needs of today's food service industry.

Programmes currently offered by the School of Hospitality and Tourism Management are:

Degrees	**Certificates**
Tourism Management	Clothing and Fashion
Hotel and Restaurant	Baking Technology (full-time)
Management	Baking Technology (part-time)
Culinary Management	Pastry Making
Food and Beverage	Food Service Organization and
Management	Supervision
Food Service Management	General Catering

Internship Opportunities

With the advent of globalization and cultural diversity there was an increasing need for students to gain international exposure and experience an alternative work ethic. This need was addressed through international internships. The process was formalized through the establishment of links with international companies.

Students from the School of Hospitality and Tourism Management took part in their first overseas internship in the United States:

- Eighteen students were successfully placed at Walt Disney Corporation in Orlando, Florida.
- Forty students were placed with Resort, Recreation and Tourism Management (RRTM), an International Hospitality Programme. Four of the students who took part in the RRTM Programme received the top awards given to interns from all over the world.
- Two students went to Santo Domingo under the Lomé Programme.

To date the overseas internship programmes have proven largely successful, with students emerging with excellent recommendations and appraisals.

Seminars and Expositions

During 1998 the School of Hospitality and Tourism Management hosted food and beverage seminars at Jamaica Grande Renaissance and Le Meridien Jamaica Pegasus. The seminars, which were well supported, were made possible by the sponsorship of the Jamaica Hotel and Tourist Association, British Airways, Le Meridien Jamaica Pegasus, Renaissance Jamaica Grande and Nestle Jamaica Limited. Professor Gianfranco Nobis from the United Kingdom and Dr Chandi Jayawardena from UWI were the presenters. The seminars enhanced the school's visibility and fostered awareness of its role as a chief tourism educator.

The need to generate further public interest and awareness of the importance of tourism and tourism education was addressed through the launch of the first Tourism Exposition in 1988. The exposition successfully brought together a wide cross section of public and private sector companies that service the tourist industry. Approximately fifteen companies were represented. The three-day exposition, which also included seminars and workshops, was open to, and well attended by, the general public.

In keeping with the process of restructuring of the institution from a college to university status and the changes that arise, members of staff are presently upgrading their qualifications to the master's level so as to meet the new requirements. This will create a workforce better equipped to meet the demands of its stakeholders in the twenty-first century.

The School of Hospitality and Tourism Management now operates under the auspices of the Faculty of Business and Management. The school provides hands-on experience in food preparation and service, as well as small quantity and commercial baking. UTech is now a four-year degree granting institution. This enables the institution to develop better-qualified managers for the industry. Admissions criteria include five GCE O levels A, B and C or CXC General Proficiency I and II. For other programmes, admissions requirements vary.

PROCESSES THROUGH WHICH CHALLENGES WERE ADDRESSED

In an effort to facilitate an outreach programme, the School of Hospitality and Tourism Management worked jointly with the Montego Bay Community College and Knox College in the Food and Beverage Management programme. After two years of study at the Community Colleges students were then transferred to UTech for completion of the final year of the programme, at the end of which they were awarded a diploma. Such collaboration addressed the need for hospitality programmes to be made more widely available across the island.

Lillian's, the training restaurant in the School of Hospitality and Tourism Management, was officially opened on November 4, 1992. It was severely damaged by Hurricane Gilbert but through assistance from local and international agencies UTech was able to restructure the building and so address that challenge. It is located in a beautifully renovated Georgian building on campus and is open to the public Mondays to Fridays for lunch. The restaurant also caters for special functions. Lillian's Restaurant offers international cuisine as a part of the training programme. The restaurant is a required training facility for Hospitality and Tourism students and provides the necessary platform for students to gain practical experience in fulfilment of the hospitality programme requirements.

Through the process of establishing linkages with industry, UTech has been able to develop its programmes and other offerings. The School of Hospitality and Tourism Management worked closely with an advisory committee in developing Lillian's. The committee also assisted the school in its fundraising efforts. The response was encouraging and contributions have been made to the project by SuperClubs,

Appliance Traders Limited, Sandals International, Versair In-flite Services Limited, the Jamaica Broilers Group, Swept Away Resorts, the Jamaica Pegasus Hotel, Caterair International and George Brown College in Canada.

Strong links have been forged with industry through membership in professional associations and the establishment of advisory committees, which monitor and endorse the curricula. The programmes offered prepare graduates to fill positions at the middle management level in hotels, restaurants, bakeries, cafeterias, pastry shops, hospitals, hostels, tourist attractions and related areas of employment.

During 1998 a unique partnership agreement was also forged between Grace Kennedy and Company Limited and the school. Contributions of goods and services to the value of J$1 million were offered during the academic year. This addressed some of the school's financial needs. Students also gained experience through conducting "taste panels" for products during Grace Kennedy's marketing campaigns.

The school continues to enjoy linkage with the Conrad N. Hilton College of Hotel, Restaurant Management, Houston University. The college provided a graduate assistantship for a member of the academic staff. This facilitated the process of upgrading of qualifications for the staff member.

PUBLIC RESPONSE TO UTech AND ITS PROGRAMMES

The development of Lillian's has been viewed by many as a delightful example of private sector involvement in educational projects.

The School of Hospitality and Tourism Management continues to be oversubscribed, receiving over eight hundred applications for one hundred full-time places. In fact most of UTech's programmes are oversubscribed, which indicates their overwhelming popularity. Industries welcome the fact that the institution's graduates possess strong technical skills in addition to sound theoretical knowledge.

THE FUTURE

In order to continue to address the needs of its stakeholders in the future, the School of Hospitality and Tourism Management continues to work with an advisory committee whose members give valuable advice on industry matters.

The school maintains the strongest connections with the tourism industry and other tourism education bodies through the advisory board, the Community Service Programme, other universities and colleges. The Work Experience Programme, the establishment of Lillian's Restaurant and the practical nature of the programmes offered by the school ensure that graduates acquire hands-on experience in tourism education and the tourist industry.

Continuous self-development is a mandate and goal for all faculty. Attendance at conferences, trade shows, exhibitions and seminars both locally and abroad is an ongoing requirement for faculty. New ways are constantly being sought to foster the symbiotic relationship between the school and the tourism industry. A food bank, a recycling programme, and the development of short courses for business are currently being planned. Not least significant is the planned expansion of the international Work Experience Programme that aims to provide students with a more global perspective of tourism education and the tourist industry.

UTech is constantly reviewing the content and delivery of its programmes to ensure the advancement of the institution. UTech is exploring the use of alternative media for the delivery of its courses and programmes. Coaches from each school or department are being trained in the design of distance learning programmes. The intention is to offer courses through the Internet, thereby permitting distance learners to enrol with the institution. This will allow UTech to become more competitive as its programmes become available to a wider cross section of persons. This strategy also opens the door for UTech to become known at the international level.

UTech continually upgrades its programmes so as to maintain its position as one of the better tourism and hospitality educators in Jamaica and in the Caribbean region.

LESSONS TO BE LEARNED

The growth of UTech over the years is evidenced not merely in the increased numbers of students, but also in the increased number of programmes, the improved methods of delivery, the institution's visibility and its links with industry. These improvements have not happened by chance. UTech is a university in transition – the process is ongoing. The appropriate structures have been implemented to facilitate the process. Academic staff members have readily sought to upgrade their qualifications and standards, and the institution has sought the expertise of its stakeholders to aid in devising its programmes. Moreover, change in the institution has happened because of a united effort by all stakeholders.

REFERENCES

UTech. (1988). "A Sense of History", *Cast Review* 12, University of Technology, Kingston, Jamaica, p. 2.

UTech. (1993). "Lillian's – New Training Restaurant Opens at Cast", *Cast Review* 15, University of Technology, Kingston, Jamaica, p. 44.

UTech. (1995/96). Departmental Report for the Hospitality and Food Science Department, University of Technology, Kingston, Jamaica.

UTech. (1996/97). Departmental Report, Hospitality and Food Science, University of Technology, Kingston, Jamaica.

UTech. (1996/97). Hospitality and Food Science Department Report, University of Technology, Kingston, Jamaica.

UTech. (1997/98). Departmental Report, Hospitality and Food Science, University of Technology, Kingston, Jamaica.

UTech. (1998/99). Report – School of Hospitality and Tourism Management, University of Technology, Kingston, Jamaica.

CHAPTER

CHALLENGES IN IMPLEMENTING TOURISM AND HOSPITALITY JOINT DEGREES: THE CASE OF THE UNIVERSITY OF THE WEST INDIES AND UNIVERSITY OF TECHNOLOGY, JAMAICA

Chandana Jayawardena and Marcia Taylor-Cooke

Abstract

The University of the West Indies has been the only regional university in the Caribbean over the last 54 years. The University of Technology has been a pioneer in technological education in Jamaica over the last 44 years. In 1998 the two universities pooled their resources and joined in developing a four-year joint degree in Hospitality and Tourism Management. This chapter analyses the implementing process of this joint degree programme during the last three years. The programme has attracted 249 young men and women from Jamaica who joined the first three cohorts since 1998. The chapter also identifies challenges faced by the programme implementers owing to the different cultures, traditions and practices of the two universities. Finally it draws conclusions and suggests a model for creating and implementing such joint degrees in developing countries.

INTRODUCTION

This chapter chronicles the process that resulted in the creation and introduction of the joint degree in Tourism and Hospitality Management by the University of the West Indies (UWI) and the University of Technology (UTech). An analysis of different tourism and hospitality management degrees is presented first. The authors then examine the development of joint degree programmes, with special emphasis on those in developing countries. Many partnerships have been entered into among universities in developing countries and universities in developed countries. Care should be taken, however, in introducing these programmes because of differences that may exist in culture and the needs of the students and the local tourism and hospitality industry. There are also the challenges of funding these programmes and finding adequately qualified staff to teach in them.

The primary focus of this chapter is the four-year bachelor's degree programme in Tourism and Hospitality Management introduced in 1998. The remainder of the chapter examines the structure of the two universities involved in this joint venture, the general course structure, its objectives and management. The authors outline the process of programme development and identify a number of challenges that are currently faced by the programme. Recommendations are then made on possible ways to improve the overall quality and delivery of this programme.

HOSPITALITY AND TOURISM MANAGEMENT DEGREES

Degree Titles

Hospitality and tourism are certainly two of the most widely used words in the fields of hotels, restaurants, travel and related areas. They are used independently or in combination with other words, such as hospitality industry or tourism industry. As prevalent as these words are in conversations and in literature, they are used broadly, loosely, interchangeably and erroneously, according to Keiser (1998).

In a study of four-year educational programme titles in the United States, Bloomquist and Morero (1997) refer to the lack of clarity among titles in tourism/hospitality programmes. A wide variety of programme titles with different words representing purposes of schools was noted. Some use "hospitality" and others use "hotel and restaurant" to identify similar programmes. Meanwhile, some departments commonly use "tourism" and others "travel" to identify similar programmes. During a survey by the authors, schools were asked to indicate words that would be preferred if the field were to adopt a common title for all the programmes. According to the survey, the titles that were popular among academics are (listed in order of popularity):

1. Hospitality
2. Management
3. Tourism

4. Hotel
5. Restaurant
6. Institution
7. Travel

Growth of Hospitality Management Degrees

In the United States alone there are over 150 institutions offering four-year hospitality management degrees, with an annual enrolment of approximately 30,000. Considering that in 1960 there were only 15 institutions offering such degrees, this is seen as phenomenal growth. The hospitality industry and hospitality institutions are experiencing tremendous growth. Will this result in a trend towards professional schools with four-year programmes that combine the best of technical skills with management and business education? If they can create a curriculum that fuses the technical skills of a good culinary programme with the management and business skills of a good hospitality management programme, then their graduates may become more attractive to prospective employers (Rappole, 2000). The traditional focus of hospitality education is being challenged by the rapidly changing needs of the hospitality industry for more general managerial skills and interpersonal competencies. This may represent a fundamental shift in the hospitality industry's definition of the optimal balance between what is generally applicable and what constitutes specific training (Ashley et al., 1995).

Joint Degrees

Joint ventures in international business training can offer educational institutions many possibilities for expanding their programmes. Such linkages can provide particular benefits (International Trade Forum, 1987). Joint degrees between traditional universities with a good reputation in management and social science studies and institutions with a good reputation for technical education can be seen as a good answer to some of the education offerings–industry expectations gaps. Joint degrees can offer universities and colleges, in both developed and developing countries, mutual benefits in such partnerships. Some of the more common benefits are:

- Expansion of markets
- Exporting of programmes
- Expanding subject knowledge base

DEVELOPED COUNTRIES

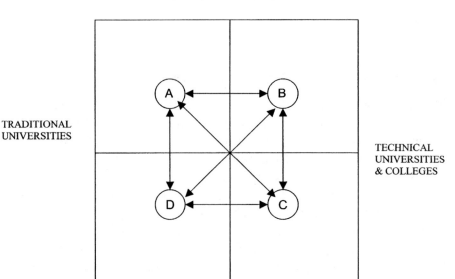

TRADITIONAL
UNIVERSITIES

TECHNICAL
UNIVERSITIES
& COLLEGES

DEVELOPING COUNTRIES

Figure 3.1   Joint degree partnership mix.

- Exchange of information and learning from each other
- Joint research
- Faculty exchanges
- Student exchanges
- Joint consultancies
- Reduction of overhead costs
- Economies of scale (use of laboratories, kitchens, restaurants, libraries, computer laboratories and other facilities)

As indicated in Figure 3.1, joint degree programmes can be developed between institutional partners of different academic standings and countries in different stages of the macro-developmental cycle. Educational institutions are broadly categorized as:

A. Traditional universities in developed countries
B. Technical universities/colleges in developed countries
C. Technical universities/colleges in developing countries
D. Traditional universities in developing countries

Six different combinations of partnerships among these institutions to deliver joint hospitality and tourism degrees are identified:

1. A and B
2. B and C
3. C and D
4. D and A
5. A and C
6. B and D

Joint Degree Programmes in Developing Countries

Developing countries at times can provide partnerships that are extremely interesting and beneficial to their partners in developed countries. As an example, the popularity of the Caribbean for numerous joint degrees initiated by universities in the United States and the United Kingdom can be indicated.

It is evident that joint degrees between traditional universities and other educational institutions (colleges, polytechnics and new universities) focused on technological education are becoming common. As an example, the University of the West Indies (UWI) has developed a number of joint degrees with technical universities and colleges in Jamaica, Barbados, the Bahamas, Antigua, St Lucia and Trinidad and Tobago during recent years. It is also noted that many universities in developed countries seek educational partnerships with reputed educational institutions in developing countries. Some universities now seek franchises, affiliations, formation of consortia for mutual benefit, as well as virtual university linkages. In a changing horizon in developing countries such strategies often prove to be useful in networking and rapid expansions. Credentialling and accreditation also seem to be useful tools for educational institutions in developing countries to gain recognition and improve the marketability of their programmes.

The host population must also be educated in the requirements of their target market to sustain a thriving tourism industry. As stated by Caothup (1999, 69):

> The more aware our target market becomes, the more necessary it is for the destination to match this component of international travel. It can be seen that education, both at the market source and at the destination, must be included as one of the major players in international tourism. Without an educated international population, the desire to travel diminishes and, without an educated host population, the ability to satisfy the visitor declines.

In keeping with the growing importance of leadership skills and the changing developmental needs of middle managers, a change in hospitality education is imperative.

According to Umbreit (1992, 71):

> Hospitality educators must understand that these changes are permanent and that graduates from their schools will need a different set of skills to succeed in a restructured business environment. Hotel and restaurant firms are already learning that their survival is predicated on taking a fundamentally different approach to the way they manage their operations.

"Understanding of the latest trends and problems faced by the industry is extremely relevant to the universities offering tourism and hospitality degree programmes. More and more managers are required to assume more diverse responsibilities" (Williams and Demicco, 1998). The evolution of multidepartmental management is due mainly to organizational downsizing and consolidation of support service management.

ACADEMIC CHALLENGES IN DEVELOPING COUNTRIES

Some educational institutes in developing countries attempt to create and design educational programmes simply by copying popular programmes from developed countries. In doing so, most of these institutions aim to take shortcuts in introducing academically accepted programmes, but as a consequence they lack industry and market orientation. In creating tourism and hospitality management degrees in developing countries, it is important to learn from the experience of the developed countries, benchmark and maintain high academic standards.

It is equally important, though, to identify and analyse current and anticipated future needs of the tourism and hospitality industry of the respective developing countries or region.

> A number of important issues have been discussed by tourism and hospitality educators in recent years. The value of hands-on, industrial experience has now been generally recognised, and few hospitality management schools would dare not to include it in their curriculum. A matter which is still the subject of considerable controversy is: should

we teach industry specific skills or general management competencies? (Kotas et al., 1996, xxiii)

Lower Skill Levels

In a paper on "Skills Improvement in Hotels: The Case of Sri Lanka", Jayawardena and Edrisinha (1993) report that only 13% of the work force of about 17,500 in Sri Lankan hotels has had vocational training. Similar situations are noted in many other developing countries. Surprisingly the hotel skills situation is not extremely positive in some of the developed countries either. The general business journals and trade press report that "the current work force in the United States is not adequately skilled or educated to meet the technological needs of the next decade. If those findings are valid in the hospitality industry, there is reason to question hospitality education as it is being provided today" (Pavesic, 1993). In educating hospitality managers of the future, it is important that sufficient operational skills and trainer skills are developed. These skills will be very useful especially during the early years of management careers when on- and off-the-job training of junior employees are seen as important routine tasks of supervisors and middle managers.

Expectations and Needs

Meeting both industry and student expectations of hospitality/tourism education is an ongoing challenge, which may best be met by further stakeholder involvement in the design and improvement of course curricula (Hing, 1997). In addition, hospitality/tourism education needs in the Asia Pacific region provide both challenges and opportunities for education and training providers. Hospitality/tourism curricula are also implicit in a framework developed by Ritchie (1995) for designing and developing tourism/hospitality management programmes. Criteria emphasized include sensitivity to industry needs, balance between economic development and environmental protection, building on and developing skills of faculty members, location where tourism is a significant component of the local economy, and a balance of conceptual material and practical experience. Echtner (1995) examined the challenges facing developing nations when designing tourism programmes. She concluded by advocating a three-pronged approach: professional education, vocational training and entrepreneurial development.

Lack of Funds

To raise the standards of both hotel management and operations within the hotel industry in China, there is a great need for better hospitality education. However, given the lack of funds available to build quality educational institutions and staff them, it is necessary to explore alternative ways of achieving the same end (Huyton and Ingold, 1999). Owing to lack of funds, often the facilities such as training kitchens, training restaurants, libraries and computer laboratories of hospitality schools in developing countries are inferior to their competitors in developed countries. Developed nations such as the United States, Canada, Japan and some of the European Union countries often assist developing countries with generous funding. Charles (2001) argues that the challenge is to forge and sustain the collaboration, cooperation, partnership and participation of all the major stakeholders of Caribbean tourism – the public and private sectors, the education and training institutions, the representative organizations and associations, the trade unions, the media, the people of the region – in the development of the industry and the people in it. Imagination and creativity are essential ingredients in developing new educational programmes in developing countries. This is so, as often developing countries are handicapped in terms of technical expertise and equipment.

Changes in Student Demographics

In implementing tourism and hospitality management degrees, one should be aware of changes in of demographic trends of the target student population. According to Pavesic (1993), in the United States, the average age of the hospitality student is rising, and women will soon outnumber men in programme enrolment by a 2 to 1 ratio. This demographic change will have an impact on teaching specific courses, the level of content of the courses and teaching methods. Too much is taught from the front of the class now, and lectures will be replaced by student-directed learning. The female perspective will replace the male perspective in the way the material is presented. In the Caribbean, female dominance over males in student numbers has been quite common for many years in tourism and hospitality, as well as most other disciplines. Education has been identified as the factor which, in the framework of existing social structures, will be most influential in determining the achievement of most of the other objectives identified for women's development. Many women recognize that they have been using education to facilitate their more active participation in the workforce and this has had, and continues to have, an impact on society in a number of ways (Leo-Rhynie, 1995). In September 1999, when UWI commenced the Caribbean region's first master's degree in tourism and hospitality management, 77% of the students who enrolled in this new programme were women.

Negative Attitudes

Owing to unpleasant memories from the colonial past, negative attitudes towards service still linger in some developing countries. In the Caribbean, where the forefathers of many citizens were captured and forcibly shipped as slaves across oceans to unknown lands, the problem of negative attitudes towards service is quite common. Service to "white" tourists sometimes is seen as going back to the plantation era in the Caribbean. The result of this is difficulty in attracting higher quality staff to tourism and hospitality jobs and students to tourism and hospitality management programmes in the Caribbean. This situation is different in most other developing countries where the slave trade never took place. Notably, in most Asian countries, hospitality and service seem far more culturally deep-rooted compared to the Caribbean. This means that tourism and hospitality educators operating in the Caribbean have to be sensitive to this common feeling. Certain adjustments have to be made to curricula and delivery methods. Even terms common in the global hospitality business such as "bus boy", "bell boy", or "room maid" are considered bad words in most Caribbean countries. A hotel general manager was once told by a union leader in Jamaica that the staff refused to wear certain types of uniforms. These were designed by a top French designer for employees of Le Meridien hotels worldwide to maintain uniformity and general standards. The reason given by the union leader and employees for this refusal was "these uniforms remind us of the colonial past". Instead of considering this as an act of insubordination by the staff, this general manager changed the uniform design in order to maintain industrial harmony.

Regional Needs

To ensure the sustainability of tourism in the Caribbean it is seen as essential to improve communication and teamwork, and to strengthen the links between regional organizations such as the public sector-funded Caribbean Tourism Organisation (CTO), the private

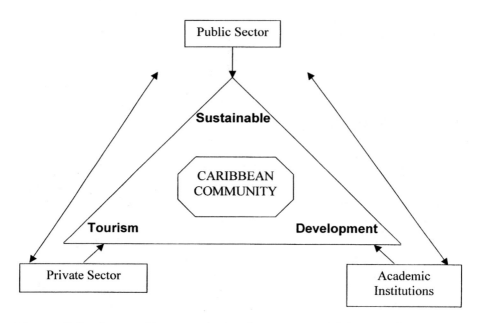

Figure 3.2   Sustainable tourism development model for the Caribbean.

sector-funded Caribbean Hotel Association (CHA), national tourism organizations, national tourism and hotel associations and other academic institutions, as shown in Figure 3.2.

A regional consulting firm was commissioned by CTO to conduct a study of tourism training needs in twenty-five Caribbean countries. The study was carried out in 1998. A total of 1,112 private and public sector organizations participated in the study. Responses to a question regarding the degree of difficulty (very difficult, difficult, fairly difficult) in filling job vacancies for the various staff categories, can be summarized as:

- ■ Unskilled   12%
- ■ Skilled/semiskilled   40%
- ■ Professionals   45%
- ■ Managers   50%

An analysis of responses when participants were asked to indicate all current major training needs among managerial staff is as follows (Quality Consultants, 1999):

Table 3.1   Stopover Visitors by Region/Country of Origin (in Thousands)

Region/Country	1996	1997	1998	1999	1999 Share (%)
United States	774	804	829	870	69.7
Europe	208	211	213	209	16.7
Canada	102	99	110	100	8.0
Caribbean	31	35	37	38	3.0
Japan	22	16	11	8	0.7
Other countries	25	27	26	23	1.8
Total	1,162	1,192	1,226	1,248	100.0
U.S. share (%)	66.6	67.5	67.7	69.7	–

- Marketing   42%
- Leadership   41%
- Human resource management   39%
- Computer literacy   33%
- Customer relations   32%
- Finance and accounting   31%
- Communications   31%

Needs in Jamaica

In the 1980s when the world prices of Jamaica's traditional exports of bauxite/alumina and agricultural products fell, tourism became the country's major foreign exchange earner. Currently the hotel sector employs over 30,000 workers, an average of 1.3 per room. Table 3.1 gives tourist arrival figures during the last four years (Jayawardena and Crick, 2000).

In addition to approximately 1,250,000 annual tourist arrivals, Jamaica attracts approximately 750,000 cruise passengers annually, bringing the total visitor arrivals to 2 million a year. In a recent study conducted by the CTO, Tourism Training for the New Millennium, the level of employee training and development, as well as the major training needs in Jamaican hotels, were identified for different levels of staff ranging from management to skilled and unskilled staff. The findings of the study revealed that there was a training deficiency in the areas of marketing, customer relations, computer literacy and foreign languages, particularly German (Quality Consultants, 1999).

THE UNIVERSITY OF THE WEST INDIES

The UWI is a unique university funded by fourteen governments, the first such regional institution in the world. At present, UWI has a student population of 23,000 on campuses in Jamaica, Trinidad and Tobago, Barbados and a centre in the Bahamas. Sir Shridath Ramphal is the current chancellor of UWI. The university was founded in 1948 at the Mona campus (Jamaica) as a university college with a special relationship to the University of London, and achieved university status in 1962. The St Augustine campus (Trinidad and Tobago), which was formerly the Imperial College of Tropical Agriculture, was started in 1960. The Cave Hill campus (Barbados) was founded in 1963. The UWI is an autonomous regional institution supported by and serving fourteen different countries in the West Indies: Antigua and Barbuda, the Bahamas, Barbados, Belize, the British Virgin Islands, the Cayman Islands, Dominica, Grenada, Jamaica, Monserrat, St Kitts and Nevis, St Lucia, St Vincent and the Grenadines, and the Republic of Trinidad and Tobago. In addition, Guyana is a full participant in the Faculty of Law, and by agreement has a limited number of students in the other professional faculties.

Hospitality and Tourism Management Degrees at UWI

In 1977 a degree programme in Hotel Management was established in the UWI Centre for Hospitality and Tourism Management in the Bahamas. Part one of the programme is being taught at the campuses and, by special arrangement, at the College of the Bahamas. A separate Tourism Management degree was introduced in 1983. The joint degree in Tourism and Hospitality Management between the UWI and UTech was launched in 1998 in recognition of the growing value of the tourism industry to the region's economic development, and the need to strengthen relations between the UWI and other tertiary level institutions. Other collaborative initiatives in the same field have since been undertaken by the UWI with the Barbados Community College and the Antigua State College in addition to the programmes in the Bahamas.

THE UNIVERSITY OF TECHNOLOGY

UTech was established in 1958 as the Jamaican Institute of Technology. In 1959, it became the College of Arts, Science and Technology (CAST) and in 1986 was accredited to grant degrees. The institution was formally accorded university status in 1995, and its name was changed to the University of Technology, Jamaica (UTech). Its academic offerings and development have been modelled on the British polytechnic system with emphasis on flexibility of approach, work-based learning and professional linkages.

The student population has grown rapidly from the first 56 students in 1958 to over 7,000 today. About 40% of the students are employed. The gender ratio is 45% male and 55% female. Full-time courses account for 42% of total enrolment with 58% being part-time. Approximately 3% of students are from other Caribbean countries. UTech has a full-time staff complement of approximately 540. Academic staff both full-time and part-time, totals 531, resulting in a teacher–student ratio of 1:13.

The School of Hospitality and Tourism Management

The School of Hospitality and Tourism Management (formerly the Hospitality and Food Science Department) began in 1958 as an Institutional Management programme. In 1975, the unit was granted full departmental status, which reflected its growth and development.

Strong links have been forged with industry through membership in professional associations and the establishment of advisory committees, which monitor and endorse the curricula. The programmes offered prepare graduates to fill positions at the supervisory and middle management levels in hotels, restaurants, bakeries, cafeterias, pastry shops, hospitals, hostels and tourism attractions.

THE FOUR-YEAR JOINT BSc DEGREE IN HOSPITALITY AND TOURISM MANAGEMENT

General

The bachelor of science degree in Hospitality and Tourism Management is offered jointly by the University of the West Indies (Mona campus) and the University of Technology, Jamaica. This is a four-year programme, which is designed to meet the needs of the tourism industry and covers courses in sciences and culture as well as courses specific to the hospitality and tourism industry, such as finance, marketing, human resource management and operations management. The goal of this programme is to develop specific competitiveness appropriate for careers in the industry.

Curriculum

The curriculum for this degree emphasizes the business and technical skills needed for a career in the industry, combining both theory and practice by involving industry professionals in the programme. Students are required to complete foundation courses from both institutions and core courses specific to the industry in the first two years of study. In addition, practical training will be provided through the internship programme. At the end of the second year, students may choose from four areas of specialization (listed below). A critical component in the programme is the development of a language competency through regularly scheduled language courses as well as an intensive language programme to be taken in the summer of the first year. A list of course offerings is provided as Table 3.2.

Internship Programme

While classroom lectures are important to any subject area, actual work experience in the field is critical to hospitality and tourism training. Students enrolled in the programme are required to complete two summers (ten weeks each summer) of internship at organizations within the industry. The internship is used as a way for students to apply their knowledge and gain professional experience. The internship may begin at the end of the first year and must be completed before the start of the fourth year.

"The concept of co-operative work-study programme was pioneered by the University of Cincinnati in 1906" (Breiter, 1991). "Recent research shows that collegiate students have increasingly relied on internships to differentiate themselves from the non-participating counterparts in different business careers" (Cannon and Arnold, 1998). The support of the advisory committee and the well-established industry network by the School of Hospitality and Tourism Management was useful in arranging internships for all students. Some students complained of the significant difference in payment of different organizations during internships.

Programme Purpose and Rationale

Students enrolled in the programme may choose from four areas of specialization:

Table 3.2   Course Offerings

Year I	**Year II**
HTM 100 – Introduction to Hospitality and Tourism	HTM 200 – Principles of Hospitality Management
HTM 101 – Sanitation and Nutrition	HTM 213 – Baking I
HTM Culinary Arts I	HTM 212 – A la Carte I
English for Academic Purposes (Foundation)	Introduction to Statistics
Introduction to Microeconomics	Introduction to Psychology
HTM105 – Introduction to Computers	HTM 210 – Food and Beverage Management
Foreign Languages I	HTM 220 – Hotel Operations
Foreign Languages II	HTM 230 – Tourism Management
Maths for the Management Sciences	HTM 201 – Business Communications
Sociology for the Caribbean	Introduction to Financial Accounting
Introduction to Macroeconomics	Foreign Language III
	Foreign Language IV
Total credits: 33	Total credits: 36
Year III	**Year IV**
HTM 306 – Hospitality Law	HTM 407 – Research Methods in Hospitality and Tourism
Introduction to Cost Accounting	HTM 406 – Hospitality Financial Management
Human Resource Management	HTM 450 – Entrepreneurial Development
Foundation Course	
4 Specialization Courses	HTM 402 – Cultural Diversity
HTM 308 – Hospitality Marketing and Sales	HTM 455 – Strategic Management in the Hospitality Industry (Capstone)
HTM 302 – Facilities Design/Maintenance Engineering	4 Specialized Courses
HTM 300 – Ethics in the Hospitality Industry	HTM 450 – Computer Applications in the Hospitality Industry
Elective	Elective
Total credits: 36	Total credits: 33

- Hotel and resort management
- Food and beverage management
- Tourism management
- Culinary management

At a faculty review meeting at the UWI Centre for Hotel and Tourism Management in the Bahamas, the following needs for concentrated training and education were identified:

- Senior management – "industry needs well-rounded, highly educated graduates who have been exposed throughout their careers to the details of the operations of hotel and other entities in the industry" along with hands-on experience in the industry, exposure to sociology, psychology and international business.
- An extreme shortage of hotel engineers and maintenance personnel. So far no current programme looks at this.
- Food and beverage marketing. This area has not kept up with the competitive nature of the market.
- An extreme shortage of international executive chefs trained in the Caribbean.
- Tourism marketing strategies – insufficient to deal with developing new products, refreshing old markets, finding new ones, and penetrating other markets.
- Lack in product development skills.
- Insufficient language and cultural exposure. Market requires that the tourism professional be culturally aware and fluent in at least one major language, in addition to English. The courses now offered do not provide for operational fluency or even basic conversation. Cultural awareness is lacking. There appears to be little tolerance and/or knowledge of alternative cultures. It needs to be broadened/appreciated.
- Hotel and tourism management as a field of study is too isolated. It needs to have a more multi/interdisciplinary approach, one which emphasizes and understands its interconnectedness with social development, environmentalism, culture (in both directions), business, etc.
- Very little research on an ongoing basis in the industry.
- Access to continuing education opportunities as well as short-term skills development and upgrading programmes.

In recognition of the needs of Jamaica as well as the English-speaking West Indies, for management to be equipped with the proper analytical tools and management skills, the Hospitality and Tourism Management degree programme combines a comprehensive curriculum with valuable work experience to produce highly qualified managers capable of making significant contributions within the workplace.

Programme Goals

The goal of the Hotel and Tourism Management programme is to prepare students who have chosen hospitality/tourism as their career for entry-level management positions, leadership roles and life.

This will be accomplished through a commitment to student learning and development marked by high expectations and standards of conduct and performance, excellence in scholarship and instruction, exposure to the industry and successful industry professionals, training and experience in the student's chosen area in the industry.

The programme is designed to meet the needs of the hospitality and tourism market and aim at producing graduates who have:

- Immediate functional competencies
- An entrepreneurial and innovative attitude to work
- A good overall knowledge of the business and competitive environments in the industry
- Language and cultural sophistication, awareness and appreciation
- A strong sense of social obligations and environmental responsibilities of the industry
- Strong people skills
- Strong self-learning orientation
- Respect for vocational work
- A self-conscious identification with the industry (problems and solutions)

Target Population Matriculation Requirements

Before registration and before beginning courses in the joint degree programme the candidate must have satisfied the following minimum requirements for entry to both universities:

- Five Caribbean Examination Council (CXC) subject passes at the general proficiency level 1, 2, or 3 (or equivalent), including English Language and Mathematics
- All applicants are required to sit the UWI English Proficiency Test. Only those achieving a pass will be considered for acceptance into the programme.
- Short-listed applicants are required to face a selection interview. Based on academic achievements only, one cannot

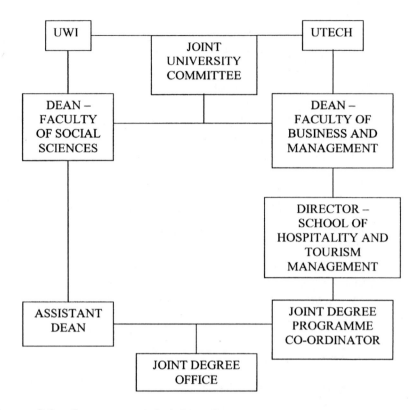

Figure 3.3   Programme administration

objectively decide on the suitability of the future leaders of the hospitality and tourism sector. This is an industry that demands prerequisites and attributes such as outgoing personality, social skills and high emotional intelligence.

Programme Management

A joint office located within UTech is used for the administration of the programme. Twenty percent of the fees collected are utilized to operate this office. The remaining 80% is distributed equally to the two universities. The coordinator of the programme (an employee of UTech) works very closely with the assistant dean of the Faculty of Social Sciences, UWI, Mona, who is responsible for the day to day running of the programme at the UWI. Two deans from the respective institutions work closely together and are responsible for programme policy. The organizational structure is shown in Figure 3.3.

Programme Franchising

The joint degree programme has been extended to two colleges in different parishes of Jamaica, which are authorized to deliver the first two years of the programme. These institutions face a number of constraints in their efforts to deliver the programme, which are reflected in the administrative processes. Among these are:

- Difficulty in obtaining information on a timely basis
- Problems with delivery of examination papers
- Limited number of courses which can be offered
- Inability to attract staff to teach foreign languages
- Problems with staff liaising with UWI counterparts

Notwithstanding the above, the coordinators are making every effort to manage the programme in a way that ensures quality is maintained and standards observed. It was suggested that special efforts were to be made to meet with the coordinators on a regular basis to ensure smooth communication flows (Cruikshank, 2000).

QUALITY ASSURANCE

The main components of the programme that constitute internal inputs are:

- Programme structure
- Programme content
- Programme recruits (students)
- Programme delivery (lecturing staff)
- Programme management

However, internal inputs are not sufficient for an academic programme to maintain quality in the context of changing environments of academic, professional and industrial standards and needs. In this context, for quality assurance of the joint degree programme a few key semi-external inputs are ensured periodically from:

- Joint University Committee
- Board of Advisors
- Student bodies
- Accreditation bodies

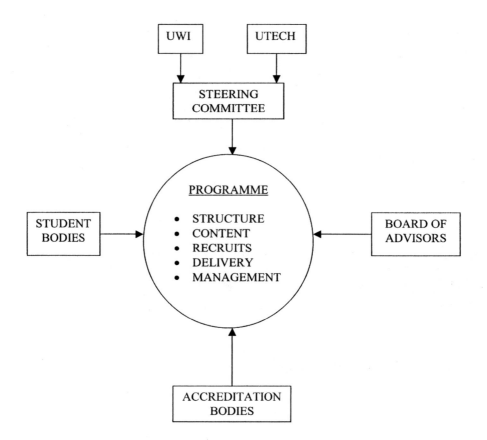

Figure 3.4 Quality assurance.

These are shown in Figure 3.4.

Steering Committee

During the development stages this committee was referred to as the Joint Degree Planning Committee. For both universities this was an extremely important and unique development. Although there are many joint educational programmes between universities and colleges around different parts of the world, joint degrees where students are educated equally in two universities are uncommon. Certainly, in the Caribbean this was the first such university degree, jointly owned, delivered and awarded by two universities located in the same city and same country.

Table 3.3   Steering Committee

UWI	UTech
Deputy principal	Vice president
Dean – Faculty of Social Sciences	Dean – Faculty of Business and Management
Project officer – Board for Undergraduate Studies	Director of Curriculum Development and Evaluation
Academic director – MSc in Tourism and Hospitality Management	Director – School of Hospitality and Tourism Management
Assistant dean – Faculty of Social Sciences	Joint Degree Programme coordinator

For this reason, a well-balanced committee with equal representation from both universities representing administrative, academic and operational leadership was required. Once the programme was implemented, the name of the committee was changed to Steering Committee of the Joint Degree Programme. Currently, the committee consists of ten members, as shown in Table 3.3.

The deans chair the committee meetings during alternate years. The meetings are held in both campuses during alternate years. The committee usually meets six times a year. Occasionally, subcommittees with a few committee members and co-opted employees (representing the bursaries, registries, libraries and departments) from both universities are appointed on anassignment basis to report on specific issues to the steering committee.

Board of Advisors

A study of 108 two- and four-year hospitality programmes reveals that advisory boards function primarily in matters pertaining to the curriculum. Specifically, they act as advisers to programme administrators and teachers. Board members also play a crucial role in developing and promoting the programme as well as generating financial aid. The hospitality industry's perception of the programme is also determined not only by the quality of the programme's graduates but also by its relationship with the board members (Conroy et al., 1996).

The School of Hospitality and Tourism Management of UTech has a twenty-member Board of Advisors to the Joint Degree Programme. This committee has representations from the following subsectors and groups:

- National tourism organizations (public sector)
- National hotel and tourist associations (private sector)

- Non-governmental organizations (such as UNESCO)
- The education sector
- Hotels (representing business hotels, all-inclusive hotels and small hotels)
- Catering (representing quick service restaurants, airport catering and bakeries)
- Alumni and others

This board is currently chaired by the executive director of the Jamaica Hotel and Tourist Association (JHTA). Meetings of the board are held each quarter.

Accreditation Bodies

As the programme matures the joint committee will seek local, regional and international accreditation. The first such accreditation was awarded by the Hotel and Catering International Management Association (HCIMA) in November 2000. HCIMA was established in 1971 and has its headquarters in London. It is the world's largest association for professionals in the hotel and catering industry. Today it has 23,000 members in 100 countries. In addition to branches in the United Kingdom, there are overseas chapters or international groups in eighteen countries, including Jamaica.

The HCIMA accreditation of the joint degree is the first to be granted to a degree programme in tourism and hospitality management in the Caribbean and South America. Full accreditation means that all quality criteria and the programme content criteria are met at the level set by HCIMA for benchmarking. This programme has now become one of the HCIMA accredited educational programmes offered by 110 universities/colleges (65 in the United Kingdom and 45 in 25 other countries). Full accreditation also means that graduates of this programme are eligible to become associate members and use the professional title AHCIMA after their names, thus giving them a unique degree awarded by two universities as well as a highly sought after professional qualification at the same time. Students will have to apply for HCIMA membership individually with a copy of their degree certificate if they wish to obtain AHCIMA qualification.

Student Bodies

Feedback from students is received primarily through:

Table 3.4 Applicants and Students

Academic Year	1998/ 1999	1999/ 2000	2000/ 2001	3-Year Total	Annual Average	%
Applications received	382	337	376	1,095	365	100.0
Applicants interviewed	179	206	212	597	199	55.0
Applicants selected	79	77	93	249	83	23.0
Students retained up to 2001/1/1	74	75	88	237	79	22.0
Students retained as a % of applications received	19%	22%	23%	22%	22%	–

- The student union at UWI
- The student union at UTech
- Student focus groups from the joint degree
- Cohort representatives
- Course representatives

In addition, informal feedback is used to ensure consideration of students' views.

STUDENTS

Most of the students who have applied to the programme have been Jamaicans, with only a few other Caribbean nationals attracted to the programme so far. On average, the programme received 365 applicants; interviewed 199; selected 83 and retained 79 students a year (shown in Table 3.4).

Of the total of 237 students, 177 (average of 59 per cohort) joined the programme in Kingston. The target set was 195 students or 65 a year and the actual number is behind the target by 9%. Other students commenced their studies in franchise institutions. Around 50% of the students who applied had passed the advanced level (GCE) examinations.

Over the last three years only twelve students have left the programme. This is 5% of the students selected. The main reasons for leaving have been financial difficulties, low academic performance and migration.

As is common in most university level programmes in Jamaica, the female students outnumber the male students in this programme. Actual numbers are given in Table 3.5. Eighty-five percent is a much

Table 3.5 Mix of Female and Male Students

Gender	Students	% of All	Average Age When Joining
Female	201	85.0	18 years and 7 months
Male	36	15.0	19 years and 8 months
All	237	100.0	18 years and 10 months

higher percentage of female students in comparison to similar programmes.

So far, 72 students (average of 26 a year) or 29% of the student
population of the programme are from the franchise institutions.
Owing to quality assurance concerns, the steering committee decided
to postpone considering requests from colleges that were identified
as potential franchisees. After a full cycle of four years, in 2002 this
expansion option will be reviewed to increase the number of students
from different parts of Jamaica. This joint degree is now the second
largest degree programme in tourism and hospitality management in
the English-speaking West Indies.

PROGRAMME CHALLENGES

Creating a unique joint degree between two universities with different
philosophies, academic levels and culture is a complex endeavour.
The following are some of the key challenges of the programme:

- A major difference in marking and grading philosophies
  between the two universities was identified. Frequent observation was that the courses taught at UWI were marked
  more strictly compared to courses taught at UTech.
- Logistical problems involving lack of space in training kitchens and restaurants of UTech owing to practical sessions of
  the number of students from other programmes.
- Delays in student registration mainly owing to late transfer
  of information across both universities.
- There still exists a lack of ownership of the programme by
  a number of individuals and units on the campuses. This is
  particularly the case with UWI where the programme is
  most often than not referred to as the UTech programme.
  There needs to be a sensitizing programme to get all staff
  involved in all aspects of the programme delivery and

administration fully aware of the importance of the programme. The reality is that this programme poses special difficulties for the systems of both institutions but the answer cannot be to treat it as a "stepsister", but rather it must become an integral part of the operations (Cruikshank, 2000).

- Duplication of simple tasks such as each student having to get two identity cards is common owing to the bureaucracy of each university.
- Time tabling problems resulting in students spending long hours between campuses.
- Inadequate public and university arranged transportation between the two campuses for students. On many days students have to travel from one campus to the other. Although the distance between the two universities is about a mile, at times tight scheduling results in student delays. In attending lectures during bad weather, this problem worsens.
- UTech had established a grade point average (GPA) system which is now fully operational. On the other hand, the UWI is reviewing various proposals to consider implementing a GPA system. However, it will be difficult to iron out this problem in the near future as the letter grades relate to different percentages in each university.
- At the UWI uniforms are not worn by students. At the UTech, students wear uniforms and are at times ridiculed by other students when joint degree students visit UWI to attend lectures or to use the library facilities. UWI courses are delivered in large classrooms with as many as 500 students in each class, representing different majors. On the other hand, at UTech class sizes are small and lectures are delivered to small batches of students, which allows personal attention to each student by the teaching faculty.

CONCLUSION

In analysing the performance during the last three years, many strengths were identified and recorded in the early sections of this paper. Those students who will graduate in 2002 and after will receive a unique joint award signed by the vice chancellor of UWI and the president of UTech.

Four-year joint degree programme students are seen by many other students of both universities as superior to other students.

Recommendations

- Rethinking the administration process in both universities.
- Frequent meetings of faculty teaching courses from both universities.
- Review space available for use as training kitchens and restaurants and embark on expansions.
- Coordination of online registration in both universities.
- Internal public relations and marketing in both universities to increase awareness among faculty members and to improve feeling of "ownership".
- Rescheduling semesters so that each semester will be spent on one campus on an alternate basis. Changing the mode of delivery is expected to sort out some of the key problems.
- A full programme review to be done at the end of 2001/2002 with inputs from the students, faculty and the external evaluators.
- A qualitative assessment system to be built in to enhance the current quantitative assessment method of student evaluations.
- More student focus groups to be used to identify problems and to "brainstorm" on possible solutions.
- Induction of students to be expanded, thus giving an overall idea of both universities and the programme.
- Exit interview system to be introduced to capture student views at the end of the programme.

Joint Degree Programme Creation

Based on the "action learning" from the UWI–UTech case, the following are suggested for those educational institutions that may want to embark on joint degree programmes in hospitality and tourism management.

- Research should be done to determine the level of past, present and future educational programmes of competitor institutes.
- The availability of full- and part-time lecturers needs to be determined well in advance.

- Appointing a few well-known practitioners and academics in tourism and hospitality management (at local, regional and international levels) to a board of advisors is normally useful.
- A strategic approach should be taken in creating, developing, implementing, managing and reviewing educational programmes.
- Steps should be taken to ensure the long-run economic viability of the programme.
- Medium-term and current needs of the industry should be given special attention.
- Desired accreditation should be kept in focus throughout the programme development process.
- Industry partnership should be sought where possible.
- Ideal mix of full-time lecturers and practising managers as part-time lecturers should be decided.
- Blend of practical and theory to suit the needs of the industry, the level of programme and the type of students should be ensured.
- Career planning skills and trainer skills should be installed in all programmes. "Live" case studies should be included where relevant.
- International business ethics, practices and management topics should be included in advanced programmes.
- Preparing the students for the next level job should be a primary objective.
- Previous academic achievements are important and must be considered, but this should not be the only main criterion in selection to the programme.
- Students with suitable aptitude, attitude and personality should be considered.

It is important to analyse current and anticipated future needs of the tourism and hospitality industry of the respective country or region. The contention here is that a well-balanced approach is required to create practical and academically accepted advanced education programmes. In developing a model for this purpose, one has to think "outside the box". Imagination and creativity are seen as essential ingredients. Of course these have to be blended with the learning outcomes and information gathered through desk and field research. Arising from current research findings a new strategic model is proposed, which can be used in creating joint degree programmes

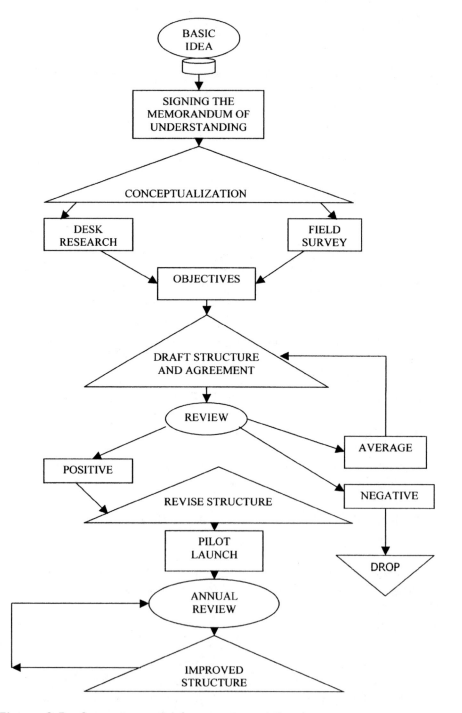

Figure 3.5   Strategic model for creating a joint degree.

in tourism and hospitality management (Jayawardena, 2000b). This model is shown as Figure 3.5.

REFERENCES

Ashley, R.A., Bach, S.A. et al. (1995). "A Customer-Based Approach to Hospitality Education", *Cornell Hotel and Restaurant Administration Quarterly* 36 (no. 6): 76.

Bloomquist, P. and Morero, P.J. (1997). "What's in a Name? An Exploration of Program Names in the Field of Hospitality Education", *Journal of Hospitality and Tourism Education* 9 (no. 2): 10–15.

Breiter, D. (1991). "The Value of Co-operative Education", *Hospitality and Tourism Educator* 4 (no. 1): 31–33.

Cannon, J.A. and Arnold, M.J. (1998). "Student Expectations of Collegiate Internship Programs in Business: A 10-Year Update", *Journal of Education for Business* (March/April): 202–205.

Charles, K.R. (2002). "Future HRD Needs of the Caribbean Tourism Industry", chapter 8 in this volume.

Coathup, D.C. (1999). "Dominant Actors in International Tourism", *International Journal of Contemporary Hospitality Management* 11 (no. 2/3): 69–72.

Conroy, P.A., Lefever, M.M., and Withian, G. (1996). "The Value of College Advisory Boards", *Cornell Hotel and Restaurant Administration Quarterly* 37 (no. 4): 85.

Cruikshank, I. (2000). "The Report to the Steering Committee", Faculty of Social Sciences, University of the West Indies, Mona, Jamaica.

Echtner, C.M. (1995). "Tourism Education in Developing Nations: A Three Pronged Approach", *Tourism Recreation Research* 20 (no. 2): 75–79.

Hing, N. (1997). "A Review of Hospitality Research in the Asia Pacific: A Thematic Perspective", *International Journal of Contemporary Hospitality Management* 9 (no. 1): 5–12.

Huyton, J. and Ingold, A. (1999). "A Commentary by Chinese Hotel Workers on the Value of Vocational Education", *Journal of European Industrial Training* 23 (no. 1): 16–24.

International Trade Forum (1987). "Training Joint Ventures: A Means to Expand Educational Programmes", International Trade Forum, Geneva, pp. 1–7.

Jayawardena, C. (2000a). "An Analysis of Tourism in the Caribbean", *Worldwide Hospitality and Tourism Trends* 1 (no. 3): 122–136.

Jayawawrdena, C. (2000b). "Creating Advanced Tourism and Hospitality Management Educational Programmes in Developing Countries", DPhil thesis, International Management Centres, Oxford, UK, pp. 158–161.

Jayawardena, C. and Crick, A. (2000). "Human Resource Management in Jamaica: Responding to Challenging Times", pp. 113–128 in Hofmann, S.M., Johnson, C., and Lefever, M.K. (eds.), *International Human Resource Management in the Hospitality Industry*, American Hotel and Lodging Association, New York.

Jayawardena, C. and Edrisinha, E. (1993). "Human Resource Development: The Case of the Hotel Industry", *The Hotelier*, Ceylon Hotel School Graduates Association, Sri Lanka, pp. 6–9.

Jayawardena, C. and Taylor-Cooke, M. (2001). "Implementing Tourism and Hospitality Joint Degree Programmes in Developing Countries: The Case of Jamaica", paper presented at the International Hospitality Industry Evolution 2001 Conference in China, Cornell University and Chinese University of Hong Kong.

Keiser, J.D. (1998). "Hospitality and Tourism: A Rhetorical Analysis and Conceptual Framework for Identifying Industry Meanings", *Journal of Hospitality and Tourism Research* 22 (no. 2): 115–128.

Kotas, R., Teare, R., Logie, J., Jayawardena, C., and Bowen, J. (1996). *The International Hospitality Business*, Hotel and Catering International Management Association and Cassell, London, pp. xxiii–xxx.

Leo-Rhynie, E. (1995). "The Education of Women: Provision Participation and Impact", pp. 181–190 in Cowell, N.M. and Boxill, I. (eds.), *Human Resource Management: A Caribbean Perspective*, Canoe Press, Mona, Jamaica.

Pavesic, D.V. (1993). "Hospitality Education 2005: Curricular and Programmatic Trends", *Hospitality Research Journal* 17 (no. 1): 285–294.

Quality Consultants Ltd. (1999). "Tourism Training for the New Millennium", Caribbean Tourism Organisation, Barbados, pp. 7, 31.

Rappole, C.L. (2000). "Update of the Chronological Development, Enrolment Patterns, and Education Models of Four-Year, Masters, and Doctoral Hospitality Programmes in the United States", *Journal of Hospitality and Tourism Education* 12 (no. 3): 24–27.

Ritchie, J.R.B. (1995). "Design and Development of Tourism Hospitality Management Curriculum", *Tourism Recreation Research* 20 (no. 2): 7–13.

Umbreit, W.T. (1992). "In Search of Hospitality Curriculum Relevance for the 1990's", *Hospitality and Tourism Educator* 5 (no. 1): 71–74.

Williams, J.A. and Demicco, F.J. (1998). "The Challenge of Multi-Departmental Management for Future Hospitality Graduates", *Journal of Hospitality and Tourism Education* 10 (no. 1): 13–17.

CHAPTER 4

DEVELOPING, MANAGING AND SUSTAINING THE FIRST TOURISM AND HOSPITALITY MANAGEMENT MASTER'S DEGREE IN THE CARIBBEAN

Chandana Jayawardena

Abstract

Recording, investigating and analysing the success or failure of tourism and hospitality management educational programmes is somewhat lacking in the Caribbean. This chapter aims to record the development stages and analyse the structure and management of the first master's degree in tourism and hospitality management in the Caribbean. The methodology used by the researcher in his capacity as consultant to the funding agency, the European Union, in developing the programme is described. The researcher inter-viewed 123 respondents from 17 countries. The experience gained between 1999 and 2001 as implementor of the programme on behalf of the University of the West Indies is shared. Methods for evaluating the programme are explained. Finally, recommendations are made for future improvements to ensure the sustainability of the programme.

INTRODUCTION

The focal point of this chapter is the master's degree in Tourism and Hospitality Management, funded under the European Union (EU)–Lomé IV Convention, and launched at the University of the West Indies (UWI), Mona campus in September 1999. The process by which the programme was developed, the methodologies used to accomplish this task, as well as the findings of consultation work conducted are examined. The creation of the programme is also anal-ysed and attention is given to the delivery, objectives, philosophy, prerequisites and management of the MSc degree in Tourism and Hospitality Management.

A critical assessment of the first year of the master's programme is presented, identifying some of the strengths and weaknesses of the programme as well as areas for improvement. The need to sustain the master's programme after initial funding from the European Union is exhausted is then underscored. Since tourism is such a critical sector of the economy of the Caribbean, it is imperative that efforts to educate and train Caribbean nationals in tourism and hospitality management are continued and sustained.

TOURISM AND HOSPITALITY EDUCATION IN THE CARIBBEAN

The Caribbean region is the most tourism-dependent region in the world (Jayawardena, 2000). Over the years, the Caribbean has been fortunate to have a few well-developed and successful educational programmes in tourism and hospitality management. However, the recording, investigating, and analysing of the reasons for the success or failure of educational programmes is somewhat lacking. As a result, valuable opportunities for learning from programmes developed in the past to enhance new programmes are often lost.

The First Caribbean Conference on Tourism Education – 1990

The Caribbean Tourism Organisation (CTO) and Organization of American States (OAS), with the support of the European Union and the Government of Barbados, organized the first Caribbean Conference on Tourism Education in Barbados. "There needs to be an integrated approach to tourism training, incorporating relevant public and private sector entities and interests" (Hall et al., 1990).

The West Indian Commission – 1992

The report of the West Indian Commission, *Time for Action,* noted that "it will be necessary to sustain and promote human resource in tourism at the level of entrepreneurship, at the level of public sector planning and co-ordination, in the areas of marketing and promotion of overall hotel management" (West Indian Commission, 1992).

The Vice Chancellor's Committee – 1993 to 1995

In 1993 the previous vice chancellor of the UWI established a high calibre committee to advise on needs for training in hotel and tourism management in the region. The report was submitted in 1995 with the following recommendations:

- The establishment of a coherent training system closely integrated with the industry and offering higher quality and more sophisticated education/training from vocational to graduate levels.
- A system of graduate education and research should be established (Brice, 1995).

Caribbean Tourism Training Need Assessment Study – 1999

Consultants to the CTO conducted a study of tourism training needs in twenty-five Caribbean countries in 1998. A total of 1,112 private and public sector organizations participated in this study. The study identified current major training needs among managerial staff as follows (Quality Consultants, 1999):

1. Marketing   42%
2. Leadership   41%
3. Human resource management   39%
4. Computer literacy   33%
5. Customer relations   32%
6. Finance and accounting   31%
7. Communications   31%

MASTER'S DEGREE PROGRAMME DEVELOPMENT

The UWI was the implementing agency for the postgraduate training programme (a master's level programme) funded by the European Union (EU) under Lomé IV – Caribbean Regional Tourism Sector Programme. The programme is open to nationals of CARIFORUM (the fourteen English-speaking West Indies countries, as well as the Dominican Republic, Haiti, Suriname), the Netherlands Antilles (Curaçao, Bonaire, St Maarten, Saba and St Eustatius), and Aruba.

Consultancy

The researcher was invited by the deputy regional authorizing officer for the EU/pro vice chancellor and dean, School for Graduate Studies and Research in the University of the West Indies, to participate in a three-month consultancy to undertake the tasks of evaluating tertiary level programmes in tourism in the Caribbean and proposing a design for a master's degree in Tourism and Hospitality Management.

Scope of Work

During a total period not exceeding three months, the researcher was expected to:

- Evaluate regional tertiary level academic programmes in tourism and hospitality management.
- Identify regional trends in tourism and hospitality services and the outlook for the industry over the medium term (i.e., five to seven years).
- Identify the strategic planning and management skill requirements of the tourism and hospitality industry.
- Identify gaps in the expected demand for and supply of academic/nonacademic training of management personnel.
- Propose a programme design for the UWI master's degree in Tourism and Hospitality Management.

METHODOLOGY FOR PROGRAMME DEVELOPMENT

Full-time consultancy work began in January 1, 1999. Information collected during preliminary desk research and a few meetings to test ideas during the later part of 1998 became useful to the researcher to plan his work for the next twelve weeks. At the end of twelve weeks (sixty working days) the work was completed and a 209-page report was submitted. The following were the main steps taken in preparing this report.

1. Desk research: All key reports done on the subject matter were read and analysed. (5 person-days)
2. Industry contacts: Many previously developed contacts were used and, where required, new useful contacts were established to lay a strong foundation for the field research as well

Table 4.1   Profile of Respondents

Category	No.	%
Public policy maker/implementor	10	8.0
Chairman/president/CEO/group director/MD/VP/GM	27	22.0
Director/manager/executive	16	13.0
Association official/executive	15	12.0
Academic	25	20.0
Consultant/advisor	11	9.0
Training specialist	10	8.0
Student	9	7.0
Total	123	99.0

as for future industry support and promotion for the pro-grammes. (5 person-days)

3. Field research: Field research was carried out in Barbados, the Dominican Republic, Haiti, Jamaica, Puerto Rico, and the Bahamas. There were 123 respondents from 17 Caribbean countries. The profile of the respondents is given in Table 4.1. (25 person-days)

4. Consultation meetings: A series of formal and informal meetings were held at UWI with the dean of the School of Graduate Studies and Research, the programme manager, Faculty of Social Science Committee, the head of the Department of Management Studies, and the executive director of the Mona Institute of Business. Seven meetings with the dean and committee were held by the consultant and seven weekly reports were submitted for discussion purposes during the early part of the consultancy period. (5 person-days)

5. Inputs from other consultants: Brainstorming sessions were held with a tourism consultant identified by the EU and a colleague with expert knowledge of Guyana, invited by the researcher. Many useful inputs were obtained. (5 person-days)

6. Written and verbal communication: Potential academic partners, teaching staff and research supervisors were identified by the researcher and contacted to check availability and seek advice on fine-tuning the proposal. (5 person-days)

7. Writing the report: The report was planned, a draft discussed with relevant persons and the final copy prepared by the end of March 1999. (10 person-days)

FIELD RESEARCH FINDINGS

A simple questionnaire was used for the field research and took the form of "elite-interviews". The key findings regarding planning and management skills required in the industry are summarized below.

- Creative decision-making and risk-taking (entrepreneur type) management skills and ability to manage change.
- Skills in human resource development, training and succession planning as well as skills to improve recruitment, especially to attract better quality, better qualified employees.
- Systematic approach in process management, operations management and planning.
- Trainer skills to improve in all technical areas.
- Strategic approach in planning and coordinating intersector development.
- Long-term "visioning" skills.
- Research skills to help industry to take research driven decisions.
- Productivity improvement planning with unions.
- More marketing skills, especially regional marketing planning to enter new markets and to implement multidestination marketing in the Caribbean.

PROGRAMME CREATION

Based on the findings from desk and field research, the first ever master's (MSc) degree in Tourism and Hospitality Management in the Caribbean was created. The programme was delivered by the Department of Management Studies, UWI, Mona campus, in association with the Mona School of Business (MSB), Jamaica.

Programme Philosophy

This master of science degree programme seeks to provide excellent education in tourism and hospitality management and to train CARIFORUM nationals for high level participation in the management of the region's tourism and hospitality industry, in response to the demands of the industry for well-qualified and capable managers in a dynamic, complex, changing and growing environment. The programme will provide a balance between general education requirements, business administration courses and technical courses relating to the fundamentals of management within the tourism and hospitality industry.

Programme Objectives

Through a mix of taught, research and reflective elements, this programme seeks to provide students with the opportunity to:

- Develop and improve their analytical capacities through rigorous graduate level courses.
- Gain a thorough knowledge of the operating characteristics of the international and Caribbean tourism business.
- Understand the processes through which tourism and hospitality organizations become internationally competitive and thereby enhance the national standards of living and levels of development.
- Gain an in-depth knowledge of the functional activities of tourism and hospitality operations in an international and Caribbean context.
- Gain experience in group and individual research and improve written and verbal communication.
- Learn practical, efficient and professional methods of solving industry problems through a series of case study analyses with the guidance of academic staff and industry experts who will share a wealth of knowledge and experience with the students.
- Appreciate the importance of the strategic approach in ensuring the long term sustainability of tourism in the Caribbean region.
- Be exposed to the "psychology" of tourism and the dynamics affecting the Caribbean tourism worker due to sociohistorical and cultural variables.
- Improve the understanding of the vital role of tourism in the context of the macroeconomic development of the whole Caribbean region.

Entry Requirement

Matriculants are normally expected to have the equivalent of at least an upper-second-class honours degree in Tourism or Hospitality Management. Students with at least an upper-second-class honours degree in another discipline may be accepted if they have more than one year postgraduate experience in a tourism sector industry.

Table 4.2   Programme Structure

Course Type	Courses
Foundation courses	International Business Management and Research
	Operations Management and Quantitative Methods
	Human Resource Management and Industrial Relations
	Financial and Management Accounting
	Management Information Systems and Technology
Common core courses	Tourism and Hospitality Marketing
	Caribbean Tourism Business
	International Hospitality Business
Tourism specialization	Tourism Management
	Sustainable Tourism Development
	Research Course in Strategic Planning and Management in Tourism, with two 6,000-word research papers
Hospitality specialization	Rooms Division Management
	Food and Beverage Management
	Research Course in Strategic Planning and Management in Hospitality, with two 6,000-word research papers

Other Information

- Approximately twenty to thirty students are expected to enrol each year.
- Commencement is in September each year.
- Programme duration is twelve months full-time.
- Courses include ten three-credit courses and one six-credit year-long research course.
- Credits total thirty-six.
- Course duration is thirty-six classroom hours per course.
- Classroom hours average twelve per week.
- Students are given an opportunity of specializing either in Tourism Management or Hospitality Management options.

The programme structure is shown as Table 4.2.

PROGRAMME MANAGEMENT

Administrative Structure

In order to ensure efficiency the structure was kept trim, with clear reporting lines as shown in Figure 4.1. This MSc degree, which is the most advanced tourism and hospitality management study programme

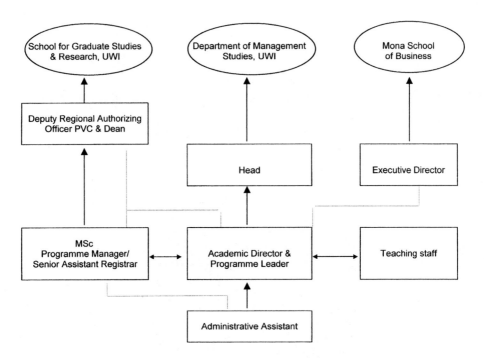

Figure 4.1 Administrative structure of the programme.

in the Caribbean, was developed within nine months. The programme was launched in September 1999.

Student Profile

Including the second cohort, the programme has attracted forty-seven students from fifteen Caribbean countries up to September 2000. The average age of a student in the first and second cohort is thirty-two years. The average number of years experience in the tourism and hospitality sector is six years.

The first degrees of the students are from well-known universities such as Stratsbourg University, France; Thames Valley University, United Kingdom; Ryerson University, Canada; Florida International University, University of Nevada, Colorado State University, University of New Brunswick, University of Miami, United States; University of the Virgin Islands, University of the West Indies, University of Guyana, University of Technology, Jamaica.

In analysing the professional profile of the students, it is noted that in the two cohorts, five students were employed by airlines. There were nine students employed at national tourism organizations in Belize,

Table 4.3 Programme Review

Month	Activity
February 1999	A two-week review of the planning process by an expert from the UK (arranged by EU)
March 1999	Departmental peer review of the draft proposal by the consultant (this was done in a seminar format)
April 1999	Independent committee (on behalf of EU) review of the proposal by the consultant
May 1999	Review by the Faculty of Social Sciences Graduate Studies subcommittee
June 1999	Review by the campus Academic Board
October 1999	Independent review by two experts from France and Germany (arranged by EU)
December 1999	Course evaluation by students
April 2000	Course evaluation by students
July 2000	Programme evaluation by students
August 2000	Teaching staff (of the programme) and supervisor review
September 2000	Visit and full review by special programme evaluator and external examiner

Dominica, the Dominican Republic, Haiti, Jamaica, St Lucia, St Vincent and Suriname. Ten students were lecturers in educational institutions. Fourteen students were employed as managers by hospitality companies, including Le Meridien, SuperClubs and Allegro Resorts.

PROGRAMME ANALYSIS AND SUSTAINABILITY

Programme review was done in various stages, as shown in Table 4.3. In his report the European programme evaluator states that he has formed a very positive opinion of the programme. In his opinion the UWI MSc in Tourism and Hospitality Management programme compares very favourably with master's programmes of the University of Surrey, the Oxford Brookes University and Thames Valley University, UK.

Programme Strengths

The following are noted as the main strengths:

- Industry support and involvement.
- High calibre and diversified panel of lecturers. Owing to the location (Mona is the largest campus of UWI) it was possible

to draw from senior faculty members teaching in MBA programmes and sustainable development programmes.

- Total number of guest lecturers from the industry was forty-six during the first year, and this element was well received by the students.
- Industry supervisors/mentors for the research course.
- Involvement by the national tourism organizations of Jamaica in teaching the tourism management course. Thirty-six hours of lectures were done by eighteen senior tourism experts, including the director general of Tourism in Jamaica.
- A one-week seminar and workshop was held at the end of the year, which was more like a capstone course. Seven group research papers and twenty-six individual research papers (average length of 6,000 words) were presented by the students at the workshop. This proved to be a very beneficial exercise to all students as well as the faculty members. A 225-page seminar and workshop folder included abstracts of these thirty-three papers (Jayawardena, 2001).

It was clearly evident that, in general, the students had blossomed during a very demanding and a highly productive academic year. Twenty-four of twenty-six students who enrolled in the first cohort graduated with MSc degrees in November 2000 at the UWI graduation ceremony. The students graduating from this new programme are expected to make significant contributions to the tourism sector across all countries in the Caribbean for a long time. Three students of the first cohort graduated with distinction.

Programme Weaknesses

- The programme duration of one year (two semesters and the summer session) tended to be too taxing on the students.
- Lack of coordination in course work assignment dates among faculty created a problem in semester one. Learning from this, the researcher suggested staggered due dates for assignments for semester two and year two.
- Commencing a master's level programme in Tourism and Hospitality Management on the Mona campus created the problem of lack of subject expertise. This was due to the fact

Table 4.4 Programme Highlights

Date	Activity
January 1, 1999	Research and industry needs assessment survey with inputs from 123 respondents from 16 Caribbean countries commenced
March 25, 1999	A consultancy report with a proposed design for the MSc programme was submitted
June 30, 1999	The proposal was approved with minor adjustments
July 21, 1999	15 applicants were chosen for scholarships awarded by the funding agency, European Union
September 2, 1999	26 students from 11 Caribbean countries arrived at the Mona campus to join the first cohort
September 13, 1999	Official launch of the programme
February 29, 2000	7 group research papers submitted by the students
March 6, 2000	Field Research Trip I
March 27, 2000	Field Research Trip II
June 30, 2000	26 individual research papers submitted by the students
July 10–14, 2000	Year-end seminar and workshop
July 14, 2000	End of academic year
September 4–12, 2000	Programme evaluation by a European expert
September 5, 2000	21 students from 11 Caribbean countries joined the second cohort (10 on EU scholarships and 3 on Dutch scholarships)
September 27, 2000	Final grades were released; 3 students passed with distinction, 21 passed and 2 were referred
November 4, 2000	24 students of the first cohort graduated

that the Mona campus never had an undergraduate programme in tourism and hospitality management.

- In addition to the lack of specialist lecturers, lack of tourism-
  related books in the library added to the problem. These
  matters are now being resolved. Access to online library
  facilities have been welcomed by the students.
- It was felt that the programme was overly dependent on the
  academic director. For the second cohort, this was sorted
  out by recruiting more specialist faculty members on a full-
  time as well as part-time basis.

CONCLUSION

The highlights of the programme creation, implementation and evaluation between January 1999 and November 2000 are summarized in
Table 4.4.

Some key challenges facing Caribbean tourism educators were discussed at the First Caribbean Tourism Educators Forum organized by the CTO in Barbados in March 2000. In the opening session of this forum, the secretary general of the CTO stated that "The Caribbean Tourism Organisation is seeking to play its part in the business of transforming the industry through its own programme of tourism education and training. But the job of shaping the future, of broadening the horizons of knowledge, of developing skills and changing behaviour, belongs as it always has, to educators" (Holder, 2002).

"Clearly further development and implementation of programmes for tourism and hospitality education holds great promise. That promise, and its attendant expectations, must be tempered with a realistic assessment of the cost and benefits" (Hall and Jayawardena, 2002).

One of the main future challenges in ensuring the sustainability of the MSc programme in tourism and hospitality management of the UWI is that the EU funding was available only up to July 2001. The EU funding was utilized mainly to give twenty-five fully paid scholarships, build the library material and pay the costs associated with visiting lecturers/evaluators from the United Kingdom, Barbados and the Bahamas.

Agreed Adjustments from September 2001

The following suggestions made by the researcher were accepted:

- Discontinue scholarships, unless a few can be funded through other agencies.
- Students will be requested to pay extra for field trips and the year-end one-week workshop and seminar (which is planned as a capstone for the whole programme).
- UWI to bear the expenses of advertising and promotion from the central budget.
- The Department of Management Studies will absorb some indirect overhead expenses.
- Accreditation by the Hotel and Catering International Management Association (HCIMA) to be sought.
- A high profile board of advisors from eight countries will be appointed.
- All local faculty with wide international and regional experiences will be scheduled for programme delivery. This will

result in significant savings on airfares, lodging and incidental expenses of overseas faculty. The only exception will be overseas faculty on semester/academic year faculty exchange programmes. A few of the faculty members who are expected to return to Jamaica with doctoral qualification will be scheduled to lecture in the programme.

- The programme will be offered for part-time students from the industry.
- Individual courses will be offered as certificate courses for industry professionals with entry qualifications similar to graduate students.
- The current annual tuition fee of US$4,000 was increased to US$5,000 for the 2001/2002 academic year and after that will be increased annually based on the local inflation.

With these adjustments, it is aimed that the programme will break even at twenty-four (50% part-time) paying students a year. This is identified as an achievable target if the programme is marketed well. Success of a new programme cannot be measured only by the results during the initial year or the potential income and profits. Success can be measured by the manner in which the programme is sustained over a long period of time and the acceptance level by the industry of its graduates. To achieve such measurable success, periodic reviews, adjustments and improvements to suit the changing needs of a dynamic industry and the people of the region must be ensured.

REFERENCES

Brice, D. (1995). Report of the Committee on Training in Hotel and Tourism Management in the Region, University of the West Indies, Mona, Jamaica.

Charles, K.R. (2002)."Future Human Resource Development Needs of the Caribbean Tourism Industry", chapter 8 in this volume.

Hall, J.A., O'Reilly, A.M., Braithwaite, R., Charles, K.R., Salvaris, C., and Brereton, V. (eds.). (1990). *Tourism in Education and Human Resource Development for the Decade of the 90s: Proceedings of the First Caribbean Conference on Tourism Education*, University of the West Indies, Mona, Jamaica.

Hall, K.O. and Jayawardena, C. (2002)."Past, Present and Future Role of the University of the West Indies in Tourism and Hospitality Education in the Caribbean", chapter 1 in this volume.

Holder, J. (2002). "Some Key Challenges Facing Caribbean Tourism Educators", pp. xv–xix in this volume.

Jayawardena, C. (1999). "Consultancy Report – Caribbean Regional Tourism Sector Programme: Post Graduate Training and Distance/Open Learning Programmes", University of the West Indies/European Union, Mona, Jamaica.

Jayawardena, C. (2000). "An Analysis of Tourism in the Caribbean", *Worldwide Hospitality and Tourism Trends* 1 (no. 3): 122–136.

Jayawardena, C. (2001). "Strategic Planning and Management in Caribbean Tourism: Recent Research by Graduate Students", *Journal of Education and Development in the Caribbean* 5 (no. 2): 129–140.

Quality Consultants Ltd. (1999). "Tourism Training for the New Millennium", Caribbean Tourism Organisation, Barbados, pp. 7, 31.

West Indian Commission (1992). *Time for Action*, The Press, University of the West Indies, Mona, Jamaica.

CHAPTER 5

PLANNING A NATIONAL TOURISM HUMAN RESOURCE DEVELOPMENT PROJECT: A CASE FROM JAMAICA

J. Anthony Hall and Ayanna Young

Abstract

Jamaica has become the beneficiary of a most progressive initiative taken on the part of a number of agencies, including the local private sector organization for tourism, the Jamaica Hotel and Tourist Association (JHTA), the Human Employment and Training Trust/National Training Agency (Heart Trust/NTA) and its National Council on Technical and Vocational Education and Training (NCTVET) subsidiary, as well as the Workforce Development Consortium (WFDC). The project is funded by the Inter American Development Bank (IDB) and the Multilateral Investment Fund (MIF). This chapter outlines the development and implementation of the Human Resources Management System in Jamaica Project. The objectives and expectations of the project are examined in addition to the situation that obtained prior to the implementation of the project. The chapter also addresses the challenges and the opportunities relating to the project and its operations within the tourism sector in Jamaica.

HUMAN RESOURCES MANAGEMENT IN THE TOURISM SECTOR

The economy of Jamaica[1] is based primarily on tourism and other complementary services. The Government of Jamaica has identified the tourism sector as belonging to one of the most important clusters of industry. It is an axial industry, in that it sustains and is, in fact,

---

[1] Jamaica is the largest anglophone Caribbean island.

dependent on the support of a plethora of other major industries. Indeed, the sector continues to be the most significant contributor to the Jamaican economy.[2]

The need has been identified to improve the tourism product in the face of intensifying competition from destinations within and outside the region. These destinations have recognized the need to increase their levels of competitiveness and have therefore opted to de-emphasize traditional marketing segments, such as the sun, sea and sand attractions. They have instead focused on new untapped means of securing competitive advantages. Jamaica, having exhausted the sun, sea and sand product, is now forced to diversify its tourism product. In more recent times, it has become clear that emphasis should be placed on eco-, heritage, health and culture tourism, with a view to increasing tourist arrivals and the related earnings from the sector, while maintaining and enhancing the country's competitive edge.

During the decade of the 1990s, the most significant area of growth in the industry was the "all-inclusive" subsector. Today, this sector accounts for a substantial portion of the island's room count.[3] The gradual expansion of the sector came at the expense of traditional small tourism entities (STEs),[4] as well as the economies of surrounding communities. STEs have experienced losses in market share and a resultant decline in the quality of their product, due mainly to a lack of competitiveness when measured against the all-inclusive properties. The Jamaican government has made several attempts to alleviate this situation, by providing loans (short- and long-term) and incentive programmes for STEs. Nonetheless, the small-entities sector has been hindered by several recalcitrant factors, including the inability to properly train and retain the type of human resources necessary to improve and maintain the quality of service within the sector so as to meet the changing needs and tastes of consumers.

The training and development of tourism human resources, especially in the small hotel sector, has been affected by identifiable factors, such as:

---

[2] Tourist arrivals for the period January to October 1999 amounted to 1,648,142.

[3] The all-inclusive sector accounts for approximately 40% of the tourist sector, whereas small entities account for approximately 50% of the sector.

[4] Small tourism entities (STEs) range in diversity of operations from water sports, heritage sites, mountain-based, river-based, and nature-related activities to small inns and bed-and-breakfast operations.

1. The paucity of reliable, industry-specific labour market information
2. Inadequate education and training programmes at line-staff levels
3. Heavy centralization of education relating to the tourism industry due to poor infrastructure
4. The absence of flexible, customized approaches to education and training, in order to cater to the diverse operations and needs of STEs.

Planners and developers of the tourism industry have not been able to carry out proper and appropriate labour force assessment due to the lack of, or poor, labour market information. In recent years, this dilemma has contributed in part to operational problems that have compromised the efficiency and effectiveness of operations, especially in the small hotel sector, resulting in service deterioration and resultant poor operational standards.

Scant regard has been given to human resources development conditions in the labour market, or the availability of specific sets of skills when new tourism developments are planned. There has been no effective mechanism in place to convert human capital into a productive workforce, neither has there been reliable information concerning candidates' employment history, academic preparation and skill competencies. Indeed, this often resulted in costly employee turnover when newly employed persons were found not to have the required skill competencies, or had exaggerated their qualifications for specific positions.

Education and training programmes in Jamaica are still predominantly conducted in the traditional classroom-based style, structured over archaic academic programmes that emphasize theory as opposed to practical assessment. The industry is in need of programmes that can be delivered via alternative means, such as distance learning, on-the-job training (OJT) or learner-controlled instruction (LCI). Such programmes are now more accessible, easier and cheaper to implement and convenient for employers as well as employees.

THE DEVELOPMENT OF A TOURISM HUMAN RESOURCES MANAGEMENT SYSTEM IN JAMAICA

It is within the context of the above deficiencies that the Tourism Human Resources Management System Project (the Tourism HRM) was conceptualized.[5] The project, a three-year Inter-American Development Bank (IDB), Multilateral Investment Fund (MIF) funded project, was conceived out of a need to increase the competitiveness of the tourism industry in Jamaica, most specifically among the STEs.[6] A corollary to this was the need to increase flexibility, accessibility and relevance of education and training within the hospitality and tourism sectors.

The project was approved in November of 1996. However, it took several months for the Jamaica Hotel and Tourist Association (JHTA) to meet the conditions established in the project's design, before actual commencement of the project. During that period, the JHTA negotiated and established formal partnerships with three key organizations: the Human Employment and Resource Training Trust/National Training Agency (HEART Trust/NTA), the National Council on Technical and Vocational Education and Training (NCTVET) subsidiary, and the Workforce Development Consortium (WFDC).

In a Memorandum of Understanding (MOU) signed on September 3, 1997, the basis for the partnership to execute the project and ensure sustainability after completion of MIF funding was defined. After implementation of the MOU between the partners, it took another six months to complete employment of the Project Execution Unit (PEU) team, consisting of the project director, a project secretary, a systems administrator and four extension officers, subsequently called HRD officers. The official start-up date of the PEU was March 1, 1998. Project disbursements started upon completion of all conditions on May 19, 1998.

Project Adjustments

The time frame for implementation of the Tourism HRM project was, at the outset, inconsistent with the project's overall objectives. More delays in the implementation process were experienced, and a review and subsequent restructuring of the project's implementation to suit the peculiar circumstances of Jamaica proved necessary.

Adjustments were made in several areas of the project's design, reflecting the partnership negotiations and agreements as incorporated in the MOU and a reassessment of the project implementation objectives, relative to the current on-the-ground situation in Jamaica.

---

[5] The duration of the project was intended to be three years.
[6] The project was launched in March of 1998.

Objectives of the Project

The overall goal of the project, as outlined in the MOU, is to increase the competitiveness of the tourism industry in Jamaica, particularly among STEs, by increasing accessibility, flexibility and relevance of education and training. The main objectives and key performance indicators of the Tourism HRM project as outlined in the MOU are shown in Figure 5.1.

The specific aims of the project include the following:

- Development of modular and customized programmes for in-firm and classroom instruction with emphasis on small tourism entities
- Making available a cadre of highly skilled trainers, coaches and mentors for the industry
- Facilitation and coordination of comprehensive and specialized skill training for industry employees and new entrants to the labour market
- Establishment of a registry of workers that would serve as the basis for an industry-based exchange of labour
- Creation of a credentialling system that would afford a framework for the rationalization of tourism education and training
- Improving the technical and organizational capacity within the JHTA to institute action plans that cater to the industry's peculiar human resource development and management needs
- Ensuring a labour market information system that directly links training and current and emerging labour market needs in the tourism industry

The project seeks to address three critical areas of human resource management and development. These are outlined and discussed in the revised framework shown in Figure 5.2.

Extension Services and Training Design

This component seeks to provide extension services to determine the sector's training needs and design appropriate training programmes for STEs. Officers are trained,[7] certified and equipped with laptop

---

[7] Persons are trained with the assistance of a national expert for three months.

Project Development Objectives	Key Performance Indicators
■ To increase the competitiveness of the tourism industry in Jamaica, through accessibility, flexibility and relevance of tourism education and training	■ Increase customer satisfaction and maintain positive guest perception of Jamaica's tourism industry ■ Operators of STEs increase their investments (dollars and time) in training ■ Increase the number and types of education and training programs offered to industry as well as participation of industry operators ■ Increase profitability through rises in occupancy levels
Components	**Key Delivery Performance Indicators**
■ Articulate and rationalize tourism education and training for the industry ■ Strengthen the organizational and technical capabilities of the JHTA to assume responsibility for the human resources development and management of the tourism industry ■ Facilitate the development of modular training programmes and customize training support, with a particular emphasis on STEs ■ Leverage public and private sector resources for HRD and training ■ Lessen the gap that exists between the demand for specialized skills and the supply of high quality training in those skills ■ Develop a state-of-the-art HRD management information system	■ Academic and non-academic educational programmes linked with training and HRD programmes ■ Increase in number and types of education and training institutes offering tourism education programmes as well as tourism entities participating ■ The trade and others perceive the JHTA as the leading source of information on education, training and HRD ■ Customized training through modular training programmes delivered and utilized by STEs ■ Available resources from education and training are maximized to industry's benefit ■ Participation in the registry, certification and credentialling system – volume of job search increases over period

Figure 5.1   Project performance parameters.

computers so as to access the Tourism HRMS, headquartered at the JHTA. Training for the programme entails:

■ Continuous collection of information on the training needs of STEs as well as programmes available through training providers such as HEART/NTA and WFDC

Training and Extension Service

A. Training (Coordinate, Facilitate, Broker)
B. Extension Services (HRD Officers)

**Institutional Support and Strengthening
for JHTA**

A. Association Management System
B. Strategic Planning
C. Cost Recovery Strategy

**Human Resources Management
Information System (HRMIS)**

A. Registry
B. Certification/ Credentialing
C. Tourism Training Providers
D. Skills Matching
E. Operations Management

Figure 5.2　Tourism human resource management framework.

- Use of the human resources management information system that was developed as a component of the project
- Registering and tracking registry participants and management of the credentialling programme
- Career counselling via the reconciliation of individual development needs with the supply of education and training programmes for work-based and classroom instruction.
- Sound business practices and technological applications relevant to STEs

Once the extension officers are furnished with the relevant information and the requisite technology, they embark on a continuous assessment of industry needs. These officers now serve as information brokers (reconciling supply and demand in the training market) as well as provide customized training services to STEs. HRD officers foster strong linkages with HEART/NTA and NCTVET, especially on standards relative to curriculum development.

Officers are trained to provide customized training as well as computer software packages to STEs so as to facilitate their ability to produce business plans and operating budgets, conduct cash flow analyses, implement accounting controls, develop marketing plans and other relevant processes. It is anticipated that they will provide training and technical assistance directly to STEs. Officers are aided in their brokering capacity by receiving technical assistance through the contracting of a certification/credentialling expert to assess continuous education and training programmes in the sector. They are also enabled to work with the lead groups instituted by the NCTVET in the design of curricula specifically tailored to the needs of STEs.

THE HUMAN RESOURCES MANAGEMENT INFORMATION SYSTEM (HRMIS)

This component comprises the following:

1. A registry of workers buttressed by a certification/credentialling component
2. Skills matching, labour exchange and job hotline component
3. Database of education and training providers
4. Registry of hospitality and tourism employers and operators
5. Association management system for the JHTA

The HRMIS is designed to provide technical support to the project, through the components identified earlier. The system's centralized registry and skills matching components will facilitate both the placement of individuals in their quest for employment as well as employers searching for skilled workers.

Registry of workers

This component establishes a registry of workers for the hospitality and tourism sector for a wide range of occupations. The registry was developed from the design and implementation of a state-of-the-art database that records, stores and retrieves information about individuals (potential and industry workers). It includes contact information, previous work experience, educational accomplishments, demonstrated job knowledge, skills and abilities, industry-based certification and credentials awarded, as well as other pertinent information.

The registry interfaces with all other modules except the association management module. It is estimated that approximately 60,000 persons will be listed in the registry once registration is completed, and up to 3,000 searches conducted annually by employers. No fee is payable for employees desirous of having their names in the registry. Employers will be charged a small fee for placing jobs on the job hotline or searching for employees.

Certification/Credentialling

The registry is enhanced by a certification/credentialling process established under the JHTA and carried out by the NCTVET. This component is designed to present a framework for industry recognition of combined academic achievement, non-academic or industry-based training, work-history and skills attainment. The credentialling system guarantees accuracy of the employment-related information submitted to the registry as well as overall quality assurance. A certification/credentialling system generally serves to establish a framework within which industry-based recognition for combined academic achievement, non-academic or industry-based training, employment history and attainment of skills flourish. Such a system also nurtures a close relationship with members of the industry and the association since members receive official recognition of employment and education achievements and therefore become willing to offer greater commitment at higher professional standards. Individuals and education and training providers are charged an application fee[8] to be recognized by the credentialling system.

Matching Employment and Skills Requirements

This process utilizes a state-of-the art system that uses artificial intelligence and natural language processing to match industry workers and potential employee skill sets and other attributes to specific job requirements and specifications established by industry. The system is dependent on the registry's database and interfaces with the NCTVET's third-party certification/credentialling system.

---

[8] Fees for credentialling are determined by the existing government licensing scheme for tourism operators with a net profit margin necessary to sustain the operation and maintenance of the system.

Database of Tourism Education and Training Providers

This database supports the delivery and rationalization of on-the-job training in industry operations as well as traditional education programmes in schools and tertiary level institutions. The system is supported by a state-of-the-art database of education and training providers that records, stores and retrieves information pertinent to tourism and hospitality institutions, such as enrolment procedure, admission and graduation requirements, curricula, accreditations received, past history and date of inception, tuition and other fees, as well as course schedules.

Registry of Hospitality and Tourism Employers/Operations

This component establishes an innovative registry of hospitality and tourism employers or operators. The database records, stores and retrieves information about hotels, restaurants, attractions and travel-related services, including size of business, estimated annual gross revenue, number of years in operation, ownership, management staff, training programmes, staff benefits, purchasing volume and patterns for commodities, supplies, equipment, furnishings and capital improvements, and other relevant information.

INSTITUTIONAL SUPPORT AND STRENGTHENING FOR THE JHTA

Association Management System for the JHTA

This component employs similar cutting-edge database technology linked to the national registry of hospitality and tourism employers. The application records, stores and retrieves information about membership status, key contact information,[9] board and committee participation, meeting registration, exhibition management, subscription management, invoicing for dues payments or products and services, accounts including journal, receivables, payables, purchasing, balance sheet, income statement and any other relevant information. It is important to note that although this component is hosted by HRMIS, it actually constitutes part of the third arm of the project.

---

[9] Key contact information includes name, address, phone, fax, e-mail and Web site address.

Strategic Planning

Under this component, technical assistance is provided through the project to guide and assist the JHTA in the development and preparation of a five-year strategic plan, including plans for the sector's human resources development and direction.

The JHTA has a strong sense of responsibility concerning its role in contributing to the improvement of the tourism product. The association is also aware that in the increasingly and fiercely competitive tourism market, service levels must continuously be raised, hence the decision to establish the HRD unit. The JHTA must now define and establish its future role in human resource management within the tourism sector.

Cost Recovery Strategy

Cost recovery strategies and corresponding sustainability of the systems developed under the project are based on revenues generated from training, consultation fees, the sale of instructional materials, revenue generated through the various components of the HRMIS, donations from industry and other sources.

The proposed cost recovery structure for the project is examined over two time periods. The first is concerned with the strategy to be employed in the short term – that is, during the project's implementation period. The second addresses cost recovery implications (structure and strategy) beyond the completion of the project's implementation stage or during the operational period of the project.

It must be highlighted from the outset that revenue generation during the period of implementation is supported by expenditures from project funds. During the second period, however, all expenses will be paid out of revenue generated by the project. An equitable cost recovery strategy for both periods should consider gross revenues only, as net figures will tend to overstate revenues earned during the implementation period.

Revenue projections for both periods are based on the following areas, which are targeted for income generation.

1. Credentialling fees
2. Credentialling renewal fees
3. Employer job search fees
4. Employers' job posting fees
5. Education and training providers' recognition fees
6. Sale of computer software and training

7. External contributions (from industry)
8. Fees for facilitating, coordinating and brokering training
9. Developing and publishing training materials for sale

CHALLENGES

The implementation of the project has been fashioned by factors relative to the distinguishing characteristics of the Jamaican people, their culture, societal norms and location considerations. Several challenges have already been identified during the process, and more are expected beyond the implementation period. The following challenges have been identified.

- It has been said that STEs generally act as training grounds for their larger counterparts. Persons move from the small entities to larger ones as a graduation to the next tier on the virtual hierarchy existing in the tourism sector. As a result, some STEs have been reluctant to participate in the training programmes. Larger entities, on the other hand, feel that their in-house training satisfies their need, and suspect that the project may be a retrograde step although they have been convinced that they too will ultimately benefit.
- STEs also fear that they may be negatively affected when the information available through the HRMIS is made available to all players in the tourism industry. They feel the only beneficiaries then, will be the larger entities and to a lesser extent the cruise ship sector.
- The inevitable concern about the cost of utilizing the Tourism HRM is also raised. STEs hesitate to expend limited resources on project programmes, the results of which are not always immediately visible.
- Players in the tourism sector are yet to be fully convinced that training of employees is necessary. The industry is viewed essentially as being characterized by a master–servant type of relationship, which requires no training.
- Once training started, it was discovered that some employees were illiterate or barely functionally literate and therefore unable to grasp basic principles.
- HRD officers have found that owners or operators, particularly of STEs, are reluctant to pay for training, especially where it benefits line employees.

- The greatest challenge, however, is the expected response to change, and the understanding that change is never usually accepted until clearly understood.

Nonetheless, it is important to highlight that the very cerebration surrounding the project has effected some degree of change. NCTVET has been given the mandate to develop national occupational standards as these relate to skill sets for sectorial occupations, including the tourism industry. Skills deficiencies can now be easily identified and the employee directed to HEART/NTA or any other training provider to improve and upgrade skill competencies through training. At the time of writing, eight such occupational standards have been developed for the tourism sector and are presently being used in the process of registering employees.

The challenge of illiteracy among some employees has been transformed into an opportunity, in that the project presently collaborates with the Jamaican Movement for the Advancement of Literacy (JAMAL) Workplace Learning Programme to conduct on-site remedial training in the workplace via a four-level process of certification. This, in turn is complemented by the training carried out through the WFDC, which comprises remedial work as well, but at higher levels and includes practical hands-on experience with the use of computers and innovative training for adult workers.

OPPORTUNITIES

The national certification system will allow all employees in the industry to benefit from a system where employers can recruit staff through skills matching with already determined verified competencies and skills. It is expected that the Jamaican tourism workforce will now have easier access to skills training, especially in light of the established standards. The specific directive in relation to the establishment of standards is an ultimate national standard. The project and its HRMIS represent a prototype, which may be extended to and adopted by other jurisdictions in the region.

STATUS OF PROJECT AT MID-TERM ASSESSMENT

At the time of writing, the project was at its mid-term stage. Thus far, a number of successes have been achieved. The following major accomplishments have been identified.

Extension Services and Training Design

The extension services and training design component has resulted in a system in which four HRD officers have been assigned responsibility for specific geographical regions within Jamaica's main tourism product plants. They have been working for eighteen months and form the backbone of the extension services and training delivery. This approach has been one of the major achievements of the project. Each officer has a portfolio of hotels and STE operators with whom he or she works. Although the portfolio includes some large hotel properties, emphasis is placed on the STEs, which are all licensed members of the JHTA.

One major chain resort operating in Jamaica offered and conducted, free of charge, several training programmes in small hotels.

The HRD officers have highlighted the following benchmark achievements in training and extension services:

- Delivery of the numerous training seminars and workshops to over 1,200 STE employees within the country's six tourism product plants
- Teaming with JAMAL to deliver the Workplace Learning Programme to participating hotels throughout Jamaica
- Successfully coordinating the first series of the JHTA/ Johnson and Wales Summer Culinary Institute
- Since the start of the programme the officers have seen an obvious increase in commitment to training, especially on the part of small hotel operators
- Collaborating with the Tourism Product Development Company (TPDCo) to deliver training to employees whose hotels are participating in the Insider Jamaica Marketing programme
- The design and development of an on-the-job training manual and the subsequent delivery of train-the-trainer seminars to in-house change agents and parallel trainers

Following the fielding of the HRD officers, their initial tasks were to introduce the programme, build awareness and trust, and conduct needs assessments. This was completed by the end of the first year of the project.

Key milestones after start-up included:

1. Job registry and data collection: The officers are charged with collecting and assembling data for the job registry. This component is not generally understood by STE managers, who have to be convinced to allow their employees to participate, given the fear that larger hotels will "steal" their qualified employees. On the other hand, industry employees are generally excited about the programme and are enthusiastic about participating in it. The PEU believes that the launch of the HRMIS will help significantly to sensitize both employers and employees to the benefits of the project. The unit embarked on a promotional campaign to introduce and explain the system to employers and employees, prior to an official launch in early 2000, followed by a registration drive.

2. Train-the-trainer for the HRD officers: Two training courses for trainers were offered to the HRD officers to assist them in the delivery of customized training programmes. The first course, Demystifying Marketing, was delivered through the Caribbean Hotel Training Institute (CHTI) and the second was conducted by the Educational Institute of the American Hotel and Motel Association, as a precursor for sitting the Certified Hospitality Trainer (CHT) examination in 2000.

3. On-the-job, train-the-trainer programmes: The PEU developed and published a train-the-trainer manual, designed to address the training needs of on-the-job trainers in Jamaica, employing a system of designated change agents and parallel trainers. The manual is user-friendly and integrated as part of the PEU on-the-job training package. There is a nominal charge for employees participating in the programme. Thus far, the response to the programme has been excellent. The package includes the following components:
   - Provision of train the trainer manuals
   - Train the trainer programmes/certification
   - Assistance in rating customized performance standards for NCTVET
   - Consultation/follow-up
   - Coordination of certification for NCTVET

4. The Workplace Learning Literacy Programmes: Through constant interaction with employees, especially in small

hotels, the HRD officers determined that literacy programmes were an important precursor to the on-the-job
training programmes they were offering. It was also necessary in the development of the job registry, the credentialling
and certification modules. The Workplace Learning Programme was introduced to assist participants in achieving
desired levels (I–IV) of literacy and numeracy, while gain-
fully employed. Participants also have the opportunity to
transfer to the Workforce Development Consortium course
system programme on completion of level IV of the Workplace Learning Programme. This has admittedly slowed the
process of implementation, yet it was considered essential to
the long-term sustainability of the training system.

5. Certification/credentialling: In terms of the development of
industry standards, significant progress has been made by
the NCTVET. To date, they have published occupational
standards for several departments in the tourism/hospitality
industry, seven of which are listed below.
   - Beverage service
   - Food preparation
   - Food service
   - Front office
   - Hotel accounting
   - Housekeeping
   - Reservations

All standards are designed at levels I, II and III and are all performance based. These standards have been established to relate to
the minimum acceptable level and quality of performance outcome.
The occupational standards encompass a variety of jobs in each
departmental area. For example, in the front office the standards cover
a range of positions, including the following:

- Bell captain
- Bell man
- Cashier
- Concierge
- Door man
- Front desk supervisor
- Receptionist

- Reservations clerk
- Telephone operator
- Telephone supervisor
- Valet

The HRD officers use these standards as guidelines when completing the skill-sets of each employee during the registration process. These standards are also used when the officers are assisting the STEs in developing operational standards within their organizations.

Tourism Human Resources Management Information System and Labour Exchange Mechanism

The system was designed on an Oracle platform in database format, with full Internet access. The system is a relational database, except for the Association Management module for the JHTA, which is an off-the-shelf software package. A Canadian firm (Hickling Corporation) was contracted to develop and deliver the entire interactive system. A period of nine months elapsed before the system was developed to the satisfaction of the PEU. The system is now on-line on the Internet at the Web site www.jobsNmore.com. It includes a job registry, a tourism product inventory/profile, a listing of accredited education/training providers, the certification system of NCTVET and a skills-matching module providing access to employers and employees.

Registration for the HRMIS registry has been proceeding slowly, due in part to the attitude constraints encountered by officers. To date, approximately 3,000 employee registrations have been assembled on hard copy, awaiting data entry. At the end of the project period, it is estimated that approximately 10,000 employees will have been registered. The target of 35,000 employees is anticipated within the next five years. The PEU plans to implement two strategies in addition to data collection by the HRD officers: a major promotional effort surrounding the launch of the HRMIS and a "blitz" using piecework contractors to assemble employee registrants.

JHTA Institutional Strengthening

Capacity building at the JHTA takes the form of equipment and systems development, strategic planning support and project sustainability planning. The equipment upgrading has been completed and a full internal network system is in place at the JHTA, which provides an excellent platform for the organization's management. The HRMIS includes provision for an off-the-shelf association management system for the JHTA. Sustainability planning has already begun.

CONCLUSION

After a difficult and slow start to the project's implementation process, the PEU has managed to achieve some positive results in the areas of extension services design and training. Following the launch of the HRMIS in March 2000, with approximately 5,000 employees registered on the system, employers and employees throughout Jamaica, the Caribbean and the world have access to information on Jamaica's tourism labour market trends and the availability of jobs in the sector, as well as the capacity to post and seek tourism-related jobs via the Internet.

Although only at the halfway point of the implementation process, the project has clearly demonstrated that it is in the process of achieving its intended objective. Industry's commitment in support of the project is evident, without which the project would not be able to achieve its goal. The HRD officers and the extension services they offer have helped in building a position of trust and understanding with the various client groups. The foundation the project is building during this period is sound and expectations for future sustainability of the project are high.

REFERENCES

KPMG. (1999). "Mid Term Assessment: MIF Project Cluster on Skills-Based Standards and Certification for the Tourism Sector and Jamaica Tourism Human Resources Management System", ARA Consulting Group, a Division of KPMG Consulting LP, Kingston, Jamaica.

Hickling Corporation. (n.d.). "Jamaica Human Resources Tourism Management Information System: Functional Specifications and Normalised Data Model Version 1", Hickling Corporation, Ottawa, Canada.

Jamaica Hotel and Tourist Association. (1999). "On-the-Job Training Made Easy: A Step-by-Step Guide for Change Agents in the Tourism Industry", Jamaica Hotel and Tourist Association, Human Resources Development Unit, Kingston, Jamaica.

Inter-American Development Bank/Multilateral Investment Fund. (1996). "Support for the Development of a Tourism Human Resource Development System in Jamaica: Project Memorandum, Inter-American Development Bank, Kingston, Jamaica.

CHAPTER 6

ENVIRONMENTAL MANAGEMENT: A NEW DIMENSION TO TOURISM EDUCATION AND TRAINING

Hugh Cresser

Abstract

The Caribbean hotel industry is poised to reinvent itself in a way that improves profitability, enhances guest relations, builds bridges into the local communities and preserves the Caribbean's natural beauty. We therefore need to ask ourselves how capable are we to pilot this new "revolution" and are our training institutions ready and aware of the requirements necessary for this new change? This chapter presents the case of the U.S. Agency for International Development/Jamaica Hotel and Tourist Association Jamaica EAST Project, which demonstrated the power of becoming an environmentally friendly hotel through the adoption of an environmental management system (EMS). It also looks at new opportunities for hospitality education and training by incorporating environmental "best practices" in the curricula in our training institutions.

INTRODUCING ENVIRONMENTAL MANAGEMENT TO THE JAMAICAN HOTEL SECTOR

Unlike tourism, it is difficult to measure the "earnings" from education, although that amount would, in real terms, be classified as priceless as a common factor for both social and economic development. Education is the most important area of focus in Caribbean regional development.

When coupled with tourism, education plays an even more important role, as the dependence on the economic benefits of that sector can only be realized if workers in the sector are properly trained and educated to maintain the total tourism product, and to deliver the quality of service that is demanded worldwide.

Today both in the Caribbean and throughout most tourist destinations worldwide, the word "environment" is becoming synonymous with tourism. This is quite understandable, as tourism, in essence, involves promoting and experiencing a destination's natural environment. Unfortunately in the Caribbean, little attention was paid over the past few decades to the effects tourism has had on the environment. Nevertheless, over the past ten years, and increasingly in the past five or so years, tourism planning and development has not been considered without some thought being given to its environmental and social impact. However, in some instances, developers have proceeded with various tourism projects within the Caribbean while conveniently ignoring the resulting negative environmental and social impacts. One can only assume that these decisions were based only on the monetary considerations without due thought to the environmental and social consequences.

Today this is changing somewhat as we are beginning to realize that our markets are becoming more sophisticated, more educated and environmentally aware, with tourists demanding that the destinations they visit, products they consume and the services they enjoy demonstrate sound environmental practices in their operations. This became clear to the Jamaican hotel sector when tour operators (specifically those originating in Europe) began sending questionnaires to find out if the hotels they were promoting had environmental programmes incorporated in their daily operations. They also indicated that by the year 2001 a majority of the operators would not be sending further business to hotels that did not have such environmental programmes in place.

As a result, in July 1997 the Environmental Audits for Sustainable Tourism (EAST) Project, funded by the United States Agency for International Development (USAID) in partnership with the Jamaica Hotel and Tourist Association (JHTA) and the Jamaica Manufacturers Association (JMA) was launched in Negril, Jamaica. This project, which was implemented by Hagler Bailly, Inc., a US-based environmental consulting firm, was established to demonstrate the benefits of becoming an "environmentally conscious" hotel by adopting an environmental management system (EMS). This is a comprehensive organizational approach that is structured to ensure sound environmental practices in all aspects of the hotel's operations.

The audits, which were designed by Hagler Bailly, Inc., focused on:

- The use of energy
- The use of water
- Generation of wastewater
- Generation of solid waste
- The use of chemicals
- Management and staff practices

On completion of the audits, fourteen hotels were provided with energy saving equipment as identified and recommended in the audit report. An integrated EMS was then designed and implemented within their operations. At the end of the first year the performance of the fourteen hotels was evaluated and the data recorded.

During the first year of the project it was felt that the hotels which had implemented an EMS should seek some international recognition for their efforts. As a result, the consultants, in conjunction with the JHTA and the Office of the Prime Minister – Tourism began investigating both the ISO 14000 and Green Globe certification programmes. It was after various options were investigated that the JHTA and the Caribbean Hotel Association (CHA) agreed to adopt the Green Globe certification. The decision was based on the fact that the programme was designed specifically for the travel and tourism sectors. It adopted the Agenda 21 principles for sustainable tourism development as part of the criteria and, similar to ISO 14001, required the implementation of an EMS.

LESSONS LEARNED FROM THE EAST PROJECT

The EAST Project has been an "eye opener" for the Jamaican hotel sector and hotels regionally. Not only did it demonstrate the economic and social benefits of going "green", but it also demonstrated the need for the sector, and the public in general, to realize the urgency to address environmental issues as they relate to tourism and sustainable development. It further highlighted the fact that, traditionally, environmental concerns were not a part of the Jamaican culture and, therefore, there was an urgent need to begin focusing on environmental education and training.

The results of the survey conducted by the EAST Project indicated that hoteliers, when asked why they choose to become environmentally

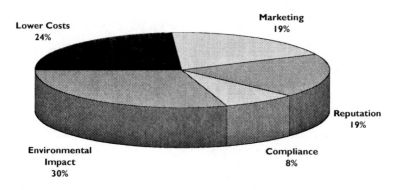

Source: EAST survey of 17 Negril hotels, 1997

Figure 6.1 Top reasons given by hoteliers for making hotels "environmentally friendly".

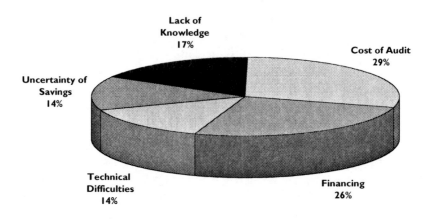

Source: EAST survey of 17 Negril hotels, 1997

Figure 6.2 Top perceived barriers to becoming "environmentally friendly".

friendly, indicated a genuine concern for the impact their operations would have on the physical environment, as shown in Figure 6.1.

When asked what they perceived as barriers to this process, they stated that learning how to make the transition and identifying sources of funding to finance implementation were the main factors, as shown in Figure 6.2. They all felt, however, that becoming "environmentally friendly" could be translated into operating profits.

What was interesting was that government's enforcement of environmental laws and standards ranked the lowest as a reason for becoming "environmentally friendly". This demonstrated to the consultants that the hoteliers were interested in measurable results and that they would respond better to incentives than to government intervention.

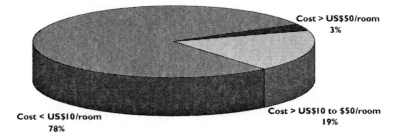

Figure 6.3 Summary of EAST Project audit results for an average Jamaican hotel – breakdown of recommendations by implementation cost.

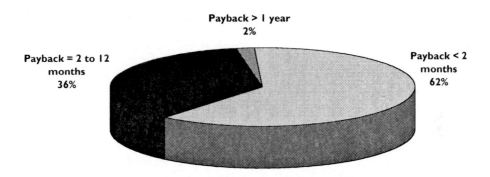
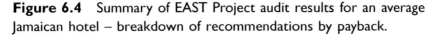

Figure 6.4 Summary of EAST Project audit results for an average Jamaican hotel – breakdown of recommendations by payback.

The project was also able to demystify the illusion that the process of becoming "environmentally friendly" was an expensive one. The audit reports indicated that, of the recommendations made to the hotels to improve performance, over 70% had a cost factor of less than US$10 per room, as indicated in Figure 6.3, and a payback period of less than two months, as shown in Figure 6.4.

The audits further identified the following factors common to the majority of hotels:

- Inefficient use of water. Leaking toilets accounted for 40% of the daily water use in a thirty-five-room hotel.
- Inefficient use of energy. Poor insulation and loose doors and louvres in guest rooms forced air conditioners to work constantly.

- Excessive and unnecessary use of chemicals. One hotel spent over J$240,000 a year on a chemical degreaser to clean the kitchen grease trap instead of doing it manually.
- Excessive solid waste generation. Fifty percent of hotel solid waste can be composted and used on the property, reducing the consumption of plastic garbage bags.
- Staff operating procedures are not followed or enforced. In 90% of cases, housekeepers automatically replaced all used guest towels on properties that had linen reuse programmes.
- Poor (or no) monitoring. Approximately 70% of audited properties had no effective utilities monitoring programmes and management was not aware of department shortfalls.

These six areas indicated the areas in which, and personnel among whom, training should be focused, namely, management and staff, across all the departments of the hotel operations, with some special attention being placed on maintenance.

To further emphasize the economic benefits of going "green" and the importance of sound environmental training, in a report prepared by Bill Meade and Antonio del Monaco (1999) of Hagler Bailly, Inc., the following was observed:

> Based on the findings of the EAST Audits, it was estimated that in Jamaica, the difference between the consumption of water from a tourism sector comprised of "green hotels" and one comprised of average hotels was over 930 million gallons of water per year.

They noted that a green hotel sector would use 77% less water than the average, and 86% less than the inefficient hotel sector. The same simulation was done for energy. The difference between the consumption of electricity for a green hotel sector and that of an average hotel sector was over 47 million kilowatt-hours per year. The green hotel sector using one-third less electricity than the average, and two-thirds less than the inefficient hotel sectors.

The EAST Project clearly demonstrated the fact that environmental management within any operation led to a "win–win" situation. EMS contributes to improving the market share and, at the same time, reducing operating costs. It also demonstrated that adopting environmental best practices was not necessarily an expensive venture, as it had been tried and tested with resounding results. It also made it clear that the tourism and hospitality industry had no choice but to become "green" to ensure sustainability of the businesses. The major challenge now is to find ways and means to change the mindset of managers and workers in the hospitality sector and prepare them to meet these new challenges.

All of these factors arising from the audit reports indicated that the problems in hotels were more operational than they were structural and therefore for any improvements to be made, the focus would have to be primarily on the changing of old working habits and operational practices. The EAST auditors therefore concluded that great environmental and financial benefits could be achieved by more frequent monitoring of utility bills, closer management supervision, improved staff practices, preventative and routine maintenance of water and energy using equipment, and providing incentives for staff to implement programmes. All this clearly indicated the urgent need to place a new focus on education and training.

A NEW FOCUS

A "quiet revolution" is taking place in the Caribbean – one less visible than the construction of new hotel rooms or the construction of new cruise ship piers. Nevertheless, its advent is profoundly changing the nature and shape of the tourism and hospitality sector in every hotel room, housekeeping, laundry, food and beverage, and maintenance facility and in every tourism destination that elects voluntarily to join the environmental movement. This revolution is *environmentally sustainable tourism*. The Caribbean hotel industry, particularly, is positioned to reinvent itself in a way that improves profitability, enhances guest relations, builds bridges into local communities and preserves the natural beauty of the Caribbean. The question is, Where should the tourism and hospitality industry go from here?

The time has come for all subsectors of tourism to be more responsible and accountable for the manner in which they develop, manage and operate. The success or failure of tourism in the region lies, not in the hands of governments or international agencies, but in the hands of the owners, suppliers and users of this entity called the "tourism product" or, in broader terms, the "environment".

There needs to be a focus on the importance of the environment to tourism. Environmental issues should not be viewed as something "other than", somehow unrelated and alien. Each sector of the society and each individual has a responsibility to the environment. Only when this is understood will the true benefits of sustainable development be seen by all.

The lessons learned from the EAST Project are now making the tourism sector refocus on its operational practices and especially on environmental awareness, education and training, as environmental management brings a whole new culture to Jamaica and the Caribbean. Some operators initially are intimidated by the term "environment" or "environmental management systems" and tend to view it as something beyond their reach, something so "scientific" that it could not be understood by the average person. Fortunately, "environmental management", simply translated, means common sense. This opens vast opportunities for education and training programmes, particularly for the tourism sector and specifically for small enterprises within the sector.

THE WAY FORWARD THROUGH EDUCATION AND TRAINING

What has become very clear is that environmental education cannot be left as the sole responsibility of training and educational institutions. Undoubtedly, the major emphasis will have to be on the training institutions; however, some input and close collaboration with other environmental institutions will be required. Environmental concerns do not only relate to saving water and energy but also involve the impacts of climate change, solid waste management, coastal management, etc. Therefore, courses should be developed to address all these issues and the impacts they will have on personal lives as well as the working environment of all.

Providing only one course on environmental management in the curriculum will not be sufficient. Each course offered, whether it is in housekeeping, food and beverage services, maintenance or landscaping, must focus on those "best environmental practices" that will have a positive impact on the environment.

In the past, hospitality training focused mainly on quality of service and attitudes. Today we need to go a step further by incorporating environmental best practices while training how to deliver quality service. Training should not just focus on how we treat our guests but also how we treat ourselves and our environment. Finally, training must target two groups: those entering the training institutions for the first time and those who have already been trained and certified.

Each student leaving a training institution today should be an "environmentalist" and capable of taking his or her knowledge into any area of hospitality service. The tourism sector needs to begin creating a new "mindset" for the younger generation in order for them to become motivators and assist in changing the more mature, moulded attitudes of previous generations.

There is also a need to provide programmes for persons already involved in tourism (and other sectors) who have grown used to the "bad habits" of a "progressive society". The irony is that the more mature minds are most often aware of good "old time" practices but, like in most cultures, as we become more "modern" or "industrialized", we tend to become a bit embarrassed by our "old time ways". For example, many of the products used in households today are harmful to both the environment and persons that come into direct contact with them. However, advertising and marketing campaigns have been successful in convincing us to view these products as the answer to our stressful daily routines. Quantities and varieties of cleaning products purchased for housekeeping and food and beverage departments are also increasing. In most instances the majority of these products could be totally eliminated by using common sense. For example, hotels would not depend on costly heavy chemicals to clean ovens if they were cleaned properly and promptly using milder alternatives, such as baking soda and vinegar, on a more regular basis. It may even be possible to use 50% to 70% less of these harsh chemicals if the proper care of the equipment was initially taken into consideration. The audit results indicate that the general findings in most, if not all instances, related to an operational breakdown rather than a mechanical one. This clearly indicates that a major problem that faces hotels today is directly linked to the level of training and education.

Fortunately, steps are being taken in the right direction. For example, in the third phase of the EAST Project, one of the main areas of focus will be to "green" the Runaway Bay HEART Academy (the training centre for resort skills). The process will include a full environmental audit of the institution, the implementation of an EMS and the Green Globe certification of the hotel school. In addition, Hagler Bailly Inc. will be working with the HEART Trust to develop an environmental component in their curricula.

Further, with the advent of hotels becoming "green", opportunities are being opened for new positions such as hotel environmental officers. Hagler Bailly consultants will be working with the George

Washington University and the University of the West Indies to develop an accredited certification programme for trained hotel personnel to become environmental officers for hotels.

This will all lead to closer ties between training institutions in the region and the HEART Trust, looking at the lessons learned from the EAST Project, and working together on the development of new and revised courses. It will also call for closer links with regional environmental institutions to assist in the preparation and delivery of specific environmental training, research and development programmes.

The need for sharing ideas and experiences now becomes a requirement for sustainability, and no longer can we attempt to tackle the problem or move ahead, individually. Therefore tourism and hospitality education must take on a new dimension to meet the challenges that face the sector and to ensure sustainable tourism development.The way forward for education in the region must encompass the efforts not only of the hospitality sector, but also every other sector in society. It calls for discipline, perseverance and commitment, as well as close collaboration and cooperation among the various tourism organizations, institutions, government agencies and environmental non-governmental organizations in the region. It especially calls for the unification and interaction of all the tourism agencies in the region to drive governments and private sector organizations along the path of sustainable development.

REFERENCE

Meade, B. and Del Monaco, A. (1999). "Report on Sound Environmental Training", Hagler Bailly Inc., Arlington, VA.

CHAPTER 7

TRAINING TO GAIN ISO 9002 CERTIFICATION: A HOTEL CASE STUDY FROM THE CARIBBEAN

Chandana Jayawardena and Maxine Campbell

Abstract

This chapter presents a case study of the efforts from the leading business hotel in Jamaica to attain ISO 9002 certification. The authors discuss the ISO certification in the context of quality assurance in hotels. They emphasize that training and educating employees in this process is critical to its success. The approach to employee training for ISO 9002 is assessed against the backdrop of redundancies, prolonged union negotiations, increasing competition, decreasing profits and a rebranding process. The key to success of training programmes lies in management's commitment and the competence and commitment of employees to making the process work. The training efforts, along with the commitment from management and staff resulted in the Le Meridien Jamaica Pegasus becoming the first hotel in the Caribbean and the Americas to achieve ISO 9002 certification.

INTRODUCTION

Training is an integral part of ISO 9002 implementation in a hotel or any organization. A planned, systematic training process is required, as the skills needed for the development of a quality management system are still new to most service organizations. Sufficient time must be set aside for training in such areas as procedure writing and quality auditing.

Training and orientation should be conducted for new staff (including temporary staff) to provide them with the knowledge and skills necessary for the completion of tasks to specified standards. Training for management and existing staff should be initiated after needs analysis of the organization has been conducted. The organization should define the competence needed for each task that affects the quality of products.

Having well trained people to become members of the working group and to become involved in developing, implementing, using and maintaining the Quality System is vital to the success of the project. This chapter emphasizes the importance of training to gain ISO 9002 certification. The term ISO and 9002 are explained at the beginning and a hotel case study is used at the end to demonstrate the practical method of implementing ISO 9002 standards.

THE INTERNATIONAL ORGANIZATION FOR STANDARDIZATION

The International Organization for Standardization (ISO) is made up of national standards institutes from countries large and small, industrialized and developing, in all regions of the world. ISO develops voluntary technical standards that add value to all types of business operations. These standards contribute to making the development, manufacturing and supply of products and services more efficient, safer and cleaner. "ISO is located in Switzerland and was established in 1947 to develop common international standards. Its members come from the standards bodies in over 135 countries" (www.iso9.com). The ISO technical committee was formed in 1979 to harmonize the increasing international activity in quality management and quality assurance standards.

Organizations Involved with ISO

There are three main types of other organizations that are involved with various aspects of ISO standards. These are:

- Member bodies, the national organizations (or bureaus) of standards in 135 ISO member countries.
- Accreditation bodies, groups responsible for determining that registration groups meet the guidelines for the purpose of granting accreditation to the registrar to issue ISO certificates.
- Registrars, groups that inspect companies for proper adherence to ISO standards and issue ISO certificates to properly qualified companies. Registrars perform thorough registration audits prior to granting an ISO certificate and two surveillance audits each year that the certificates are effective.

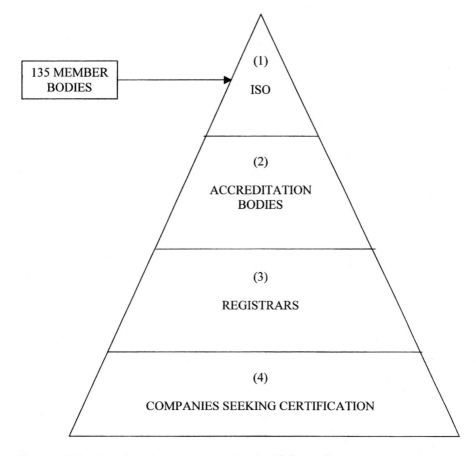

Figure 7.1 Levels of organization in the ISO quality assurance process.

The level of these organizations in the ISO quality assurance process is shown in Figure 7.1.

ISO 9000 and Quality Assurance

ISO 9000 brings together the essential principles common to many different quality management and assurance standards into a single system. The intent of the standard is simply to help a company document and implement a basic quality system so that it has the capability to deliver the quality products and services that its customers request.

The ISO 9000 series covers the entire range of business processes from the moment the order is placed, through the entire production or service development process to the actual delivery of the product or service to the customer. It is important to note that ISO 9000 does not certify products or services or guarantee that quality goods or services will be produced. It simply certifies that a quality system is in place that should enable an organization to meet agreed-upon customer requirements and provide more consistent products or services.

As part of the certification process, an organization implements a quality system based on one of three models relevant to the nature of its operation: ISO 9001, 9002 or 9003. Then a third party (an accredited quality system certification body) audits the company to certify that the system complies with the standard and that the quality system has been implemented. If the organization is found to be in compliance, a certificate is issued bearing the relevant standard.

Benefits

Among internal benefits of implementing the ISO 9002 standard are the following:

- Contributes to improvement through structure and discipline
- Improves efficiency through better documentation and communication
- Reduces rework
- Increases customer satisfaction and therefore reduces customer complaints
- Improves motivation and employee involvement through all levels of the process
- Improves the training process
- Improves positive management control

ISO 9002 in the Caribbean

The eighth cycle of the ISO Survey of ISO 9000, conducted in 1998, revealed that the standards are growing in popularity in the Caribbean and the rest of the world. The Central and South Americas accounted for nearly 2% of the certificates issued worldwide. Forty-seven of these certificates were issued in Caribbean countries. Trinidad and Tobago accounted for approximately one third of these certified organizations. Jamaica came second with six organizations. Antigua and St Lucia received their first certificates in 1998. As has been experienced in the rest of the world, ISO certifications were more common in the manufacturing sectors compared to service sectors.

Up to October 1998 there were no hospitality service organizations achieving this certification in the Caribbean. Considering the importance of the tourism and hospitality industry to the Caribbean, as well as the large stock of hotel rooms in the Caribbean, this is disappointing. At the turn of the century the accommodation stock in the region had risen to around 250,000 rooms and is predicted to approach 400,000 rooms by the year 2020 (Jayawardena, 2000).

Training to Gain ISO 9002

The key to the success of the training process lies in the commitment of management to developing the process. Factors such as organization size, structure, requirements and culture have proven to be very important at the design stage. By involving the end users in the design, planning and implementation of training, it was easy to build the team spirit, a requirement for successful implementation of an ISO 9002 Quality Management System.

Suggested Foundation Training

For organizations that have not yet made a commitment to implementing a quality management system the following training programmes are suggested. This will usually take a total of eight or nine days.

- ISO 9000 Quality Briefing. Examines the fundamental issues and the achievable and measurable benefits of the standard. (1 day)
- Executive Briefing. Provides a clear understanding of the economic benefits and critical success factors for implementing the standards to busy executives who will influence the decision to implement ISO 9000 within their organization. (half a day)
- ISO 9000 Appreciation and Interpretation. Lays the foundation for those individuals directly involved in implementing and maintaining the system. This course is also suitable to provide general quality awareness to all employees of a smaller organization. Maximum benefit will be gained when the employees are encouraged to participate in the setting up of the system. By extending "ownership" of the quality management system to as many people as possible, one can ensure that the system will work well on a day-to-day basis throughout the organization. (1 day)

- ISO 9000 Implementation. Provides sound, practical guidance on how to set about the task of designing and setting up a quality management system and see it through to a successful conclusion. (2 days)
- Documentation/Procedure Writing for ISO 9000. Provides practical guidance in the design, development and implementation of a workable documentation system. Participants will be able to write user-friendly documents, which are effective and suitable for the intended purpose. (1 day)
- Internal Quality Auditing. Provides practical instruction to all employees involved in this process. An additional day may be added for newly trained auditors to put theory into practice by conducting a live audit of the quality system. (2 days)
- Preparing for the Certification Audit. Ensures that the team has clearly understood the prerequisites for a successful assessment and provides guidance on the final preparation and fine-tuning of the quality system. The most common pitfalls – and how to avoid them – will be clearly identified, so that employees will be fully briefed and ready for assessment. (1 day)

The Training Process

ISO 9002:1994 (E) Clause 4.1.2.2 Resources states: "The supplier shall identify resource requirements and provide adequate resources, including the assignment of trained personnel for management, performance of work and verification activities including internal quality audits" (ISO 9002, 1994).

Clause 4.18 Training states: "The supplier shall establish and maintain documented procedures for identifying training needs and provide for the training of all personnel performing activities affecting quality. Personnel performing specific assigned tasks shall be qualified on the basis of appropriate education, training and/or experience, as required. Appropriate records of training shall be maintained" (ISO 9002, 1994).

All organizations implementing the Quality Management System standard (ISO 9002) must have an effective training process in place to satisfy these requirements. Quality and related training and education provide or enhance the knowledge and skills employees need to do their jobs effectively and efficiently. Job enrichment skills are

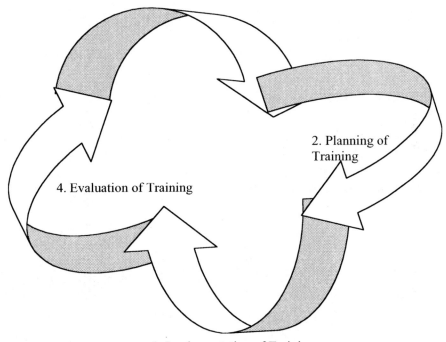

1. Definition of Training Needs

2. Planning of Training

4. Evaluation of Training

3. Implementation of Training

Figure 7.2 The training cycle.

gained and job rotation can occur, thereby enhancing employees' career opportunities.

A planned, systematic training process is instrumental in helping an organization achieve its quality objectives and improve its capabilities. Training can be seen as a four-step process, as shown in Figure 7.2. These four steps are represented in the training cycle, where the output of one stage provides the input for the following stage. Each stage must be monitored with the aim of closing the gap between required and existing competence. Training goals must be established, and later evaluated to determine the extent to which these goals were met. This evaluation process can lead to the identification of new goals, which should be addressed in the design of future training activities.

Definition of Training Needs

The first step in the training process towards ISO 9002 certification involves the conducting of a needs analysis of the organization. There are some useful signs, or symptoms, that may indicate the need for training. These include:

- Dissatisfied customers
- High labour turnover, low morale
- Failure to attain targets on revenue, gross profit and net profit
- High accident, breakage, or wastage rates
- Conflict between departments, such as restaurant and kitchen, housekeeping and reception
- Absence of the skills required for procedure writing or quality auditing
- Absence of formal management review of the quality system.

The organization's strategic goals, quality objectives, training policy, quality management requirements, resource requirements and process design must also be considered when initiating training to ensure that the organization's needs are satisfied. The following activities should also be carried out:

- Define and document the competence needed for each task that affects product or service quality (e.g. management verification activities such as internal quality audits). This is done through job analysis.
- Assess the competence of personnel to perform the task.
- Develop plans to close existing competence gaps.

The training policy stands as a symbol of management's commitment to this important activity. It provides guidance for the planning of training as well as a comprehensive guide on all elements of the training cycle.

The training policy of Le Meridien Jamaica Pegasus is summarized below as an example.

- Policy: It is the policy of Le Meridien Jamaica Pegasus to provide training for new and existing employees, in order to continually improve the workforce skill, product performance and services.

- Scope: This covers all employees involved in delivering service to the hotel's clients.
- Purpose: To ensure that employees are equipped with the appropriate skills to perform their jobs.
- Responsibility: It shall be the responsibility of each departmental manager to ensure that employees have adequate training and experience for the jobs to which they are assigned. The training and quality assurance manager shall be responsible for administering and coordinating the hotel's training plan and activities.
- Procedure: Each employee who performs a service related to the customer, product or administration shall receive training in that area.

Competence requirements once set must be reviewed periodically to ensure that they remain relevant to the operation. A variety of internal and external factors may be used to derive competence requirements:

- Organizational and technological change that impacts the company's product
- Data recorded at training programmes
- The organization's performance appraisal system
- Internal and external certification needed for the performance of specific tasks
- Requests from employees identifying opportunities for personal development
- Legislation, regulations, standards and directives

Planning for Training

The training plan should be developed and documented at this stage. Included in the training plan are the objectives and expected outcomes of the training. All constraints should be determined and listed. Typical constraints encountered in the hospitality industry include labour union requirements, human resource policy, financial considerations, timing and scheduling requirements (especially in a shift system), the availability, motivation and ability of the individuals to be trained. Factors such as the availability of in-house trainers to perform the training or the selection of reputable outside experts must be determined at this stage. The training plan specification is important in establishing a clear understanding of the organization's needs, the training requirements and the training objectives.

Typical items to be considered in an organization's training plan are:

- The organization's objectives and requirements
- Specification for training needs
- Training objectives
- Selected trainees
- Training method and content outline
- Duration, dates and milestones
- Schedule of resources such as training materials and staff
- Financial requirements
- Criteria and methods for the evaluation of training outcomes, such as trainee's on the job performance and satisfaction level of customers

Implementation of Training

It is important that the organization provides the necessary training resources to ensure success of the training process. In addition, the organization must support the trainer and the trainee while monitoring the quality of the training delivered. There will be resource and time constraints during the implementation of an ISO 9002 Quality System. These contraints have to be quantified and allowed for by reassigning work, working extra time, or scheduling extra employees.

Quality system training should address the following:

- Why a formal quality system is being introduced
- Why total participation in the quality system is necessary
- The quality policy of the company
- The documents making up the quality system – quality assurance manuals, procedures, work instructions – and their accessibility to workers.
- Use of forms and other records built into the quality system
- The role of internal auditors
- Corrective and preventive action
- Management review

Evaluation of Training

Evaluation aims to determine the effectiveness of the training process. The organizational and training objectives that were set must be examined to confirm that they have been met. The documents to be examined during the training evaluation are the training specification, training plan and records of the delivery of training.

Training results often cannot be fully analysed and validated until the trainee can be observed and tested on the job. A specified time period (after completion of training) should be agreed within which the evaluations will take place, in order to verify the level of competence achieved.

The evaluation process should include the collection of data and the preparation of an evaluation report analysing the data collected and making recommendations for improvement as required. All training must be documented in training records.

In quality management, reward systems recognize individuals as well as team contributions. A variety of tangible objects may be used to reward superior performance, including days off with pay, badges and medals. Awards functions may be held where recipients are lauded for their achievements. In the hospitality industry benchmarking tours of outstanding properties may be arranged.

The review of the training process should identify any further opportunities for improving the effectiveness of any stage of the training process. A commitment to continuous improvement lies at the heart of a quality management system, modelled from the ISO 9000 Standard.

QUALITY IN HOTELS

Ad hoc training and quality control have been common in hotels for centuries. Systematic training, as explained in the previous section, is a prerequisite to implementing a quality assurance management system. Ad hoc training is merely unplanned training and ad hoc quality control is mostly a post-process checking action. These are not adequate to ensure quality standards to achieve ISO 9002 certification. A few hotels have, in the past, implemented steps to introduce "quality circles", essentially a Japanese concept with proven results in Japanese or similar cultures.

Recent Reviews

Dube et al. (2000) carried out an extensive review of the quality of lodging operations in the United States and noted that functional areas such as human resources, operations, corporate management and marketing receive more attention from management of hotels. They also noted that in the deluxe segment of hotels, the majority of best practices involved operations and human resources. Enz and Siguan (2000) examined thirteen champions in the lodging industry and analysed their best practices. The service-quality "champions" employed a variety of approaches, frequently in combination. Some of the "champions", for example, worked on weaving key tenets into the fabric of the organization in an effort to disseminate service-excellence standards and ingrain employees with them. Others focused on empowering employees to provide whatever service the employee deemed necessary to create guest satisfaction. Ritz-Carlton Hotels, for example, empowers all employees to spend up to US$2,000 to solve a guest problem, if needed (Enz and Siguan, 2000). Although such initiatives are noted from hotels in different parts of the world to ensure quality service to guests, the popularity of ISO 9002 in the global hospitality industry has not been a phenomenal success. Up to late 1998, only 865 ISO 9002 certificates were issued to hotels and restaurants worldwide (ISO, 1998).

Hotel Operations

Maintaining standardization and required quality in the hospitality industry is very complex. A usual hotel has two main operations: rooms division (bell desk, guest services, reception, business centre, telephone switchboard, rooms, suites, laundry, public areas, etc.) and food and beverage operations (kitchen, restaurant, bars, night clubs, banquet and conference facilities, room service, minibars, kitchen stewarding, etc.). The other departments (marketing, finance, human resources, engineering, security, computer systems, etc.) provide essential support services to rooms division and food and beverage operations. It is generally accepted that food and beverage operation is the most complex operation in a hotel. This is because it includes departments and sections where the quality of products and services is more visible, more difficult to maintain and can easily affect a hotel's image.

Apart from the quality of food and beverage products, longer operating hours, better quality linen, cutlery, crockery, glassware, design, wider choice of food and beverage items, better quality print of menu cards and beverage lists, more tasteful décor, better operating equipment, better tailored uniforms and better calibre of staff (in general) can be noticed in restaurants situated in five-star hotels in comparison with hotels of lower grades. The food and beverage service in five-star hotels has become more complex and challenging owing to the important fact that this class of clientele certainly pay much more money and in return expect a different and better service/product.

A survey carried out a few years ago revealed that waiting staff thought that expert serving techniques were the most important features of their work. The customers surveyed, on the other hand, indicated that what they valued most in a waiter was a smiling, agreeable, welcoming blend of social qualities. This does not mean that techniques are not important, since many guests appreciate a high level of practical skills and expect a fully professional service. However, the waiting staff who merchandise a "meal experience" must cultivate friendliness, good manners and the relevant social skills (Kotas and Jayawardena, 1994).

The quality of food and beverage service is a combination of predictions and characteristics on which an individual assesses whether the service will give satisfaction each time it is used, based on the guest's own set of values. A quality standard in food and beverage operations is a combination of characteristics accepted by the consensus of market segments as being appropriate to provide satisfaction for their particular purposes. Therefore, it is important to base policy decisions with regard to quality standards of food and beverage service in a hotel or restaurant on identified and anticipated specific customer needs through research. Hospitality organizations seeking to ensure the continuous quality of their service processes should embark on quality assurance management systems. Only through a systematic process can a hotel achieve a globally accepted quality standard.

Quality Assurance

Terms such as five-star, deluxe, high standards, good service, and fair value for money mean totally different things to different people and are therefore meaningless until they are defined in clear, precise terms. Yet expensive hotel investments and crucial marketing decisions are often described with these phrases. Potential quality can be affected by technical and behavioural factors within organizations and from the environment. It is important to determine the variables that can be manipulated to control these factors, such as design of service process, selection, training, supervision, communication, peer relationships and rewards to ensure sustained quality assurance in hotels.

LE MERIDIEN JAMAICA PEGASUS HOTEL: A CASE STUDY

In October 1998, the largest and premier business hotel in Jamaica, Le Meridien Jamaica Pegasus, became the first hotel in the Caribbean to achieve certification to ISO 9002 Quality Management Standards. This property, referred to as the Pegasus, has 350 rooms and at that time had 400 employees. The organizational structure of the Pegasus is shown as Figure 7.3. A unique characteristic of the hotel is the exceptionally long years of service by many senior employees. In 1998 the average length of service to the Pegasus was sixteen years by the first line managers and nine years by the second line managers.

The hotel has four restaurants, two bars, a large ballroom, nine meeting rooms, a gym, two tennis courts, two swimming pools, a jogging track and a shopping arcade. The Pegasus opened in 1972 and has been managed by the same hotel company, Forte Plc. in the United Kingdom, for the last twenty-nine years. During this period, owing to changes within the managing company, the Pegasus underwent two name changes; in 1992 as "Forte Grand" and in 1997 as "Le Meridien". The second rebranding was more crucial, as to reach Le Meridien standards the hotel had to do considerable upgrading and staff training.

Challenges

In addition to the challenging rebranding process in 1997, the hotel was also faced with a financial problem triggered by an increase of four-star hotel rooms in Kingston by 42% and a decrease of tourist arrivals to Kingston. The occupancy level was around 60% for a few years, but owing to the increase in room capacity in the city, a price war had started. This resulted in the average room rate falling from US$100 to around US$83. Giving in to union demands and agreeing to above-inflation salary increases in the past had resulted in payroll cost (as a percentage of revenue) increasing from 22% in 1995 to 32% in 1997. The bottom line impact of these challenges was that the profitability of the hotel gradually dropped from 22% in 1993 to an alarming 8% in 1997.

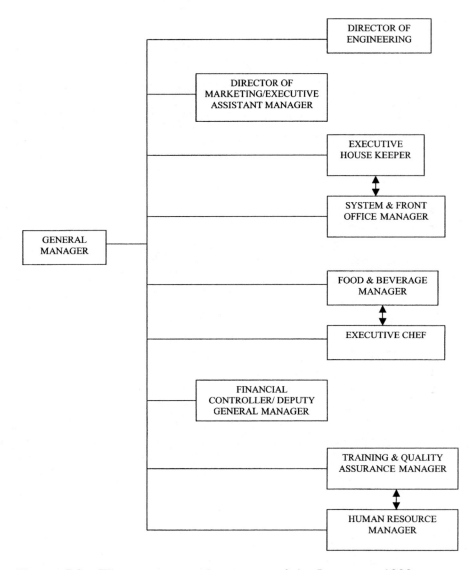

Figure 7.3 The organizational structure of the Pegasus in 1998.

Survival Strategies

As a survival strategy the management was compelled to restructure the operations. While there is nothing new to the downsizing phenomenon, the incidence of organization downsizing has increased considerably in recent years. Commentators warn of the potentially damaging effects of downsizing and redundancy programmes on the survivors and the culture of downsized organizations (Worrall et al.,

2000). The management decided to make 18% of the permanent staff redundant. A bold counterproposal of an unprecedented wage freeze was sent to the union who were demanding a 40% wage increase. The climate was not appropriate for introducing a quality management system that required high labour moral, motivation and commitment. However, the rebranding to Le Meridien and upgrading of the hotel had been committed with the owners. An official launching of "Le Meridien" (by the prime minister of Jamaica) for the end of 1997 had been confirmed. In this context, the management decided to go ahead with the following during the 1997/1998 financial year:

- Redundancy of fifty-one employees
- Not changing the wage freeze stand in union negotiations
- Frequent frank dialogue with the employees with regards to the financial problems faced by the company and working together in "quality circles" to solve operational problems
- Internal marketing and public relations to convince the employees that quality assurance is the key to solving the financial problems
- Implementing the planned product upgrade
- Completion of the rebranding process by the end of 1997
- Introducing the ISO 9002 Quality Management system as a foundation for the future
- Reviewing the possibility of obtaining four-diamond grading by the American Automobile Association (AAA) and the Green Globe Award within three years

A Vision for the Future

The management decided to pay special attention to training and development of a quality culture at the Pegasus. The vision was that this culture would be the backbone of the future quality standards achievements, as shown in Figure 7.4. It was considered important for this backbone to be strengthened with strategic inputs and quality inputs of the desired standards. At the same time this backbone (quality culture) should be strong enough to hold the present (organizational culture) and the future (vision) together.

Quality Policy

The labour dispute at that time arose as a result of the union's refusal to accept a proposal for a moratorium by the management. In spite

Figure 7.4 A vision for the future

of the labour dispute, the management won the support of the employees for the quality vision and 300 employees signed a quality policy, which has been displayed in the lobby of the Pegasus for the last four years. The policy, which was developed with input from the 300 employees, states:

> Le Meridien Jamaica Pegasus is committed to being the best up market business hotel in the Caribbean; by consistently delivering Le Meridien quality product and service standards, satisfying guest expectations, whilst building employee morale and achieving profit objectives.

The agreed slogan is, "The Best Is Getting Better".

Quality Action

The following ten "commandments" related to the quality policy were developed with input from the 300 employees:

1. Make decisions based on findings from internal quality audits, guest surveys, employee surveys and Le Meridien quality audits.
2. Communicate the company policies and business objectives to all employees.
3. Employ skilled, committed and service oriented people with warm and friendly attitudes.
4. Train, develop, empower, reward and facilitate employees to achieve quality objectives.
5. Analyse productivity of the departments and take timely action to improve efficiency and profitability.
6. Satisfy shareholders by increasing the stock value.
7. Implement good public relations with all segments of the community.
8. Hold regular employee meetings to encourage innovative and creative thinking that will challenge conventional thoughts and practices.
9. Ensure that international standards with a European flavour, blended with the local culture, are implemented.
10. Implement ISO 9002 standards, receive and retain certification over the years.

The framed quality policy and quality actions are displayed in each department, section and office of the Pegasus.

Communication

Communication is the key to success in any process of change. For twelve months, quality and ISO 9002 became items on the agenda of many regular meetings, such as:

- Morning briefing (20 minutes – standing) – five times a week with all departmental managers
- Le Meridien/quality meeting (60 minutes) – once a week with departmental managers
- Purchasing/project meeting (40 minutes) – once a week with five executives

Table 7.1   Standard Agenda for Le Meridien/Quality Meetings

Objective
To coordinate the rebranding and quality system and to follow up on delegated tasks.

Attendees
Departmental managers (in their absence, second line managers)

Chair
General manager (GM)

Coordinator
Training and quality assurance manager (TQM)

Day
Tuesday

Time
9:15 a.m. (just after morning briefing)

Duration
60 minutes

Venue
GM's office

Agenda		
Rebranding process – main tasks	–	GM
Main changes/improvements	–	GM
ISO 9000 Quality System	–	TQM
AAA Grading and Green Hotel	–	TQM
Any other business/clarifications	–	All

- All managers meeting (60 minutes) – once a month
- Managers and union delegates meeting (60 minutes) – once a month

The Le Meridien/quality meeting was a new meeting created to coordinate rebranding and implementing ISO 9002 during the 1997/1998 financial year. The standard agenda of this meeting is given as Table 7.1.

Quality Analysis

Qualitative analysis of all corrective action forms (for every guest complaint) has to be done once a month as part of the ISO 9002 system. Corrective action forms are discussed at the morning briefings and with the use of a log, follow-up action is monitored by the general manager. The commitment from the general manager is essential for the system to work effectively and productively. Guest questionnaires, too, are analysed and distributed to all managers and departments once a month. Actual analysis compiled for July 1998 is given as Table 7.2.

Table 7.2 "Moment of Truth" Questionnaire Analysis of Guest Comments Processed During July 1998

Area	Section	Votes				July %
		Outstanding	**Good**	**Average**	**Unacceptable**	
Front office	Doorman	19	27	8	2	73.0
	Bellman	16	29	6	3	72.0
	Front desk	31	24	9	3	77.0
	Reservations in order	26	19	6	1	80.0
	Secure environment	29	30	4	-	82.0
	Directional signage in the hotel	27	30	5	1	79.0
Guest services	Telephone service	15	12	17	10	56.0
	Message service	14	14	10	7	62.0
	Wakeup call	16	20	3	1	78.0
	Cashier	14	18	6	1	74.0
	Laundry and dry cleaning	8	5	3	4	64.0
	Minibar	4	9	6	5	53.0
	Swimming pool	10	12	6	1	72.0
	Fitness centre	6	9	10	1	63.0
	Gift shop	11	12	6	1	73.0
Room	Clean	34	26	3	3	81.0
	Comfortable	26	27	8	1	78.0
	Well equipped	21	24	13	5	74.0
	Adequately lit	30	28	4	2	80.0
	Adequate working space	22	27	9	4	72.0
	Sufficient guest amenities	17	30	12	1	71.0
	Equipment in good working order	17	25	15	6	64.0
Breakfast	Speed of delivery	13	14	11	–	72.0
	Quality	12	20	11	1	69.0
Bars and service	Room service	9	14	4	1	73.0
	Port Royal	9	14	3	3	69.0
	La Brasserie	11	13	6	1	73.0
	Cafe	7	7	2	–	71.0
	Pizza Cellar	4	7	5	–	68.0
	Polo Lounge	4	8	5	–	68.0
	Pool bar	9	8	3	–	79.0
	Banquet meetings	3	4	1	–	78.0

Table 7.2 "Moment of Truth" Questionnaire Analysis of Guest Comments Processed During July 1998 (continued)

		Votes				
Area	**Section**	**Outstanding**	**Good**	**Average**	**Unacceptable**	**July %**
Bars and food quality	Room service	5	12	3	–	73.0
	Port Royal	9	9	7	–	72.0
	La Brasserie	6	11	6	2	62.0
	Cafe	2	9	3	1	63.0
	Pizza Cellar	3	5	2	–	73.0
	Banquet meetings		2	2	–	55.0
Overall opinion	Courteous welcome	27	24	8	1	78.0
	Needs anticipated	19	22	8	5	70.0
	Quick and efficient response	5	2	–	3	64.0
	Overall opinion of hotel	15	23	10	2	70.0
		Yes	No			
	Would you return?	53	5			91.0
	Would you recommend this hotel?	47	9			84.0

Guidelines for Rating %
(Points x no. of votes/highest possible score)

Points	
Outstanding	10
Good	7
Average	4
Unacceptable	0

Questionnaires: 71
Best Rating

1	Room cleanliness	81%
2	Reservations	80%
3	Pool bar	79%

Foundation for the Future

The key hotel activities and external factors that had an impact on the hotel's performance from April 1997 to March 1998 are summarized below.

1. People
   - A Le Meridien trainer from Paris trained thirty employees as on-the-job trainers and a series of training programmes for other employees was conducted by the trainers and management using Le Meridien manuals as guidelines.
   - Twenty-three employees were trained as quality auditors to audit the quality of the operations of other departments.
   - Good relationships were maintained with the union and employees in spite of prolonged wage negotiations and resulting industrial actions.
   - Seven managers underwent brief training/exposure at Le Meridien New Orleans in the United States.
   - Employees of the year were sent to Paris and London to join other employees of the year from seventy-three Le Meridien hotels on an award tour of exposure.
   - The executive chef won an award "For Excellence in Food Preparation, Delivery and Presentation" during 1997, from the *Jamaica Observer* newspaper.
2. Product
   - Le Meridien image, service and product standards were introduced and the hotel was rebranded as Le Meridien Jamaica Pegasus on October 9, 1997 with the prime minister of Jamaica as the guest of honour.
   - Various projects were undertaken to implement the essential upgrading. These included complete refurbishment of two bedroom floors, installation of a new chiller, installation of a new fire alarm system, painting the building exterior, upgrading of tennis courts, upgrading of gardens and public areas, etc.
   - Food and beverage concepts were changed. The coffee shop was upgraded and a section was air-conditioned, the gourmet restaurant concept was fine-tuned to blend with the historic significance of Port Royal and the wine club was transformed into a pizza cellar. All menus were changed.

- The ISO 9002 Quality Management system was intro-duced. The hotel developed a quality policy with input from most of its employees.
- The hotel continued to be the focal point of social activities in Kingston, often being chosen as the location for major banquets. The hotel continued organizing food festivals and other major events, including 101 holiday events dur-ing the last 38 days in 1997.
- The hotel won the *Jamaica Observer* newspaper's first ever "Table Talk" food award for the "Food Event of the Year" (a six-course gastronomic dinner, served in 1997, for the annual induction ceremony of the prestigious association *La Chaine Des Rotisseurs*).
- The Le Meridien mystery guest programme, with a 1,000-point checklist, was introduced by internally arranged monthly mystery guests.

3. Promotions
   - Room reservations, banquet bookings, sales, public rela-tions and advertising were combined and a new marketing department was created with the objective of being more aggressive in marketing.
   - The start of the twenty-fifth year of operations of the hotel was celebrated with the governor general of Jamaica as the guest of honour.
   - Management sales calls to local clients were accelerated.
   - The hotel continued to be the focal point during the Jamaica Carnival. A "wet-fête" was held at the hotel as part of the carnival celebrations.
   - A major wedding expo was held.
   - Le Meridien promoted the hotel in its regional and world-wide publications, sales and advertising campaigns.
   - The hotel continued to be in the limelight through planned public relations and publicity.
   - Familiarization tours were arranged for Le Meridien vice president–sales, sales director, and reservation agents, to Washington, D.C., New York and London.
   - Frequent participation in Le Meridien sales conferences and planned sales trips to North America, South America and Europe.
   - Participation in Le Meridien sales promotion activities.

4. Profit

- Towards the end of the financial year, British Airways reduced the allotment of thirty-four rooms per day to six rooms per day as most crew members were provided accommodation in Montego Bay instead of Kingston.
- The number of rooms in Kingston was increased by 32% and the four-star category rooms were increased by 42% within a year. At the same period, the arrivals to Kingston were reduced by 2%. With the supply of rooms in Kingston greatly exceeding the demand, the hotel experienced revenue problems. The hotel undertook major restructuring and re-engineering, affecting fifty-one job positions (18% of the total permanent workforce), which were made redundant. The hotel spent J$11 million as redundancy payments, but was able to recover this within eight months from the savings on labour cost.
- For seven months, the hotel held its position of a wage freeze against the union demand for a 40% wage increase for year one and a 35% increase for year two, for line employees. After two "sit ins" and a strike, the matter was referred to the Industrial Disputes Tribunal and a 7.5% wage increase for year one and a 7.5% increase for year two was awarded. This is a "landmark" award in the Jamaican hotel industry as salary increases in hotels had been in the range of 30% to 60% for many years prior to this award. As a result of this award, a single-digit wage increase has become the norm in the Jamaican hotel industry today.

SUMMARY OF IMPLEMENTATION

The major building blocks in the implementation of ISO 9002 at the Pegasus are identified below.

Phase 1: Gap Assessment and Organizational Study

- A gap audit and situational analysis was conducted.
- The first task was to plan the implementation project and set the goals of the quality management system. This was done through the formation of a steering committee with members drawn from the first and second line managers.

Once the steering committee was set up, the staff as a whole received training on different aspects of quality management, problem-solving techniques and application of ISO 9002.

Phase 2: Documentation Development and Implementation

- Team members were selected from all areas of the hotel (Housekeeping, Material Management, Kitchen, Restaurants, Marketing, Front Office, Accounts and Engineering) to document their processes.

Phase 3: System Review

- Trained internal auditors carried out internal audits of the quality management system. The auditors were selected from all areas of the hotel. This new activity required cross-functional interaction, since auditors had to be independent of the areas being audited.
- All corrective actions identified were discussed at a management review of the quality system. Decisions were taken to correct problems and systems put in place to prevent their recurrence.

Phase 4: Certification Audit

- Assessment was carried out by Lloyds' Register Quality Assurance (LRQA).

The entire process from gap analysis to implementation and certification was completed in one year.

CONCLUSION

Training is the key to gaining ISO 9002 certification. Undertaking a quality assurance management system in a standard hotel in a developing country poses many challenges. As an example, the concept of ISO 9002 was introduced to a sister hotel, Guyana Pegasus (now Le Meridien), South America in 1995. After three years of hard work, the project was terminated without achieving the certification. Only one other hotel, Le Meridien Dubai, United Arab Emirates, out of 250 hotels in the Forte/Le Meridien chain had achieved this landmark in quality assurance by 1998.

Cowell et al. (2001) suggest that it is appropriate to investigate the approaches firms in developing countries are taking in their efforts to improve the competitiveness of their operations through improved management and worker performances. Many such firms will recognize that movement, in a sustained manner, to levels of operational performance that meet international standards is likely to require a new culture of workplace performance (Cowell et al., 2001). The new culture at the Pegasus was created by introducing the vision for the future indicated in Figure 7.4. Training was the key ingredient in developing the appropriate quality culture at the Pegasus.

The following are the key ingredients for achieving ISO 9002 for a hotel:

- An objective gap assessment
- Appropriate benchmarking
- Systematic training
- External quality consultants
- A full-time internal quality manager
- Understanding of the owners
- Acceptance by the operating/managing company
- Total support of the management team
- Total commitment of the general manager
- Total support of the supervisors
- Appreciation of the benefits by the union
- Motivated employees
- Well-trained quality auditors (employees from all levels)
- Healthy competitiveness among different departments
- Periodic quantitative and qualitative assessment of progress
- Monitoring progress
- Improvements based on the learning outcomes

After achieving the ISO 9002 certification the following steps are suggested:

- Recognizing special contributions by individual employees and teams
- Celebrating the achievement with all employees
- Continuous monitoring of the agreed quality levels of products and services
- Periodic refresher training for employees
- Special training for all newly recruited employees

- Using the achievement for a major public relations effort
- Mentioning certification in selected printed items (e.g. letterheads, brochures, newsletters and all advertisements)

It is hoped that more hotels in the Caribbean region will follow the footsteps of the Pegasus in achieving the most recognized quality assurance certification in the world.

Quality is never an accident, and it has to be visioned, initiated, planned, delivered and monitored. A successful quality assurance system must achieve the goals of boosting employee morale, maximizing guest satisfaction and optimizing long-term profitability.

REFERENCES

Boella, M.J. (1998). *Human Resource Management in the Hospitality Industry*, Stanley Thomas Publishers, London.

Cowell, N.M., Crick, A., and Wint, A.G. (2001). "Managing Workplace Transformation in Pursuit of International Competitiveness: A Developing Country Perspective", research presentation at Research Colloquium, *Enhancing Competitiveness in a Developing Country Environment*, Department of Management Studies, University of the West Indies, Mona, Jamaica, March.

Dube, L., Enz, C.A., Renaghan, M., and Siguan, J. A. (2000). "Managing for Excellence: Conclusions and Challenges from a Study of Best Practices in the US Lodging Industry", *Cornell Hotel and Administration Quarterly* (October): 30–35.

Enz, C.A and Siguan, J.A. (2000). "Best Practices in Service Quality", *Cornell Hotel and Administration Quarterly* (October): 20–29.

Evans, J.R. and Lindsay, W.M. (1996). *The Management and Control of Quality*, West Publishing, New York.

Goldsack, B. (1998). "Putting the Customer First", *LRQ Review*, p. 7.

ISO 9002. (1994). *Quality Systems: Model for Quality Assurance in Production, Installation and Servicing*, International Organization for Standardization, Geneva.

ISO. (1998). *Survey of ISO 9000 Certificates and ISO 14000 Certificates, Eighth Cycle*, ISO, Geneva.

Jayawardena, C. (2000). "An Analysis of Tourism in the Caribbean", *Worldwide Hospitality and Tourism Trends* 1 (no. 2): 122–136.

Kotas, R. and Jayawardena, C. (1994). *Profitable Food and Beverage Management*, Hodder and Stoughton Educational, London, pp. 170–185.

Voehl, F. (1994). *ISO 9000: An Implementation Guide for Small to Mid-Sized Businesses*, St Lucie Press, Boca Raton, FL.

Worrall, L. et al. (2000). "The New Reality for UK Managers: Perpetual Change and Employment Instability", *Work Employment and Society* 14 (no. 4): 647–668.

www.iso9.com

CHAPTER 8

FUTURE HUMAN RESOURCE DEVELOPMENT NEEDS OF THE CARIBBEAN TOURISM INDUSTRY

Kwame R. Charles

Abstract

This chapter discusses the projected future human resource development needs of the Caribbean tourism industry, based on recent quantitative and qualitative research and analysis of global trends. It describes the "new global realities" that will impact Caribbean tourism in the future, as well as some models of the tourism manager and worker of the future. It further identifies some of the new skills and competencies that will be required of these future tourism personnel and emphasizes the urgent need for the industry to adopt new and progressive approaches to managing and developing its human resources. It is suggested that the industry must develop the ability to attract, motivate and retain the brightest and best that the Caribbean can produce in order for Caribbean tourism to be sustainable, and in so doing, become a major player in world tourism.

INTRODUCTION

This chapter attempts to "predict" the future of the Caribbean tourism industry and of the human resource development (HRD) needs of the industry by analysing emerging patterns and trends in global and Caribbean tourism. The chapter addresses the questions: "What new tourism trends can we expect in the future?" "What new demands will tourists make in the future?" "What new competencies and skills will be required of the tourism workers and managers of the future?" The chapter concludes by identifying the "new skills and competencies" required of workers in the Caribbean tourism industry, and making recommendations on how these future HRD needs can be met.

CARIBBEAN TOURISM TODAY

Tourism is the economic mainstay of many Caribbean countries, accounting for as much as 25% of the region's export earnings and an equivalent amount of its gross domestic product. Tourism provides an estimated 2.9 million jobs in the region. One in every five jobs in the Caribbean is said to be a direct or indirect result of tourism (World Travel and Tourism Council, 1997). In 1998, Caribbean destinations received over 30 million visitors, comprising 19.5 million stay-over arrivals and 12.3 million cruise passenger visits. Gross expenditure by all visitors to the Caribbean in 1998 reached an estimated US$17.9 billion, an increase of 7.3% over 1997 (Caribbean Tourism Organisation, 1999). The World Travel and Tourism Council (1997) contends that the Caribbean is one of the highest growth travel destinations in the world. Tourism seems destined to play an even greater role in Caribbean economic development in the future than it now does.

GLOBAL TOURISM TRENDS

The projections for Caribbean tourism are consistent with those for world tourism in general. The World Tourism Organization (WTO) and the World Travel and Tourism Council (WTTC) project that tourism will be a major player in the global economy in this century (World Travel and Tourism Council, 1997). As a part of the fast-growing global service economy, tourism is one of the three "paradigm industries", according to futurist author, John Naisbitt (1994), that will drive service-led economies of the twenty-first century, the others being telecommunications and information technology. In the last twenty-five years the international travel and tourism industry has grown more than 500%. In 1997, tourism demand generated more than 10% of global employment. In the case of the Caribbean, this number was 25%, the highest in the world. Over the next decade, the rate of global employment in tourism is forecast to grow by more than 40%, adding more than 100 million new jobs worldwide. Tourism could well be the leading job creator of the twenty-first century.

THE NEW GLOBAL REALITIES

At the same time that these changes are taking place in world tourism, several emerging trends and new realities are radically transforming the world we live in. The Caribbean and Caribbean tourism are not exempt from the influence of these trends and new realities. As we assess the future HRD needs of the tourism industry in the Caribbean, we must be mindful of these trends, as they will impact significantly on the HRD strategies we employ. Some of these trends and "new realities" are listed below.

- Globalization and international competition. A major trend impacting Caribbean tourism is international competition. Caribbean tourism is operating in an increasingly competitive global environment where the quality and innovation of the goods and services it delivers is going to make the difference between industry success and failure.
- Customer focus. Together with increasing international competition is what some authors are calling the "global customer revolution". Because of the number of choices customers now have, they are becoming more selective and discriminating in those choices and more demanding in their requirements. This is occurring both at the domestic and the international levels. Tourists are no longer willing to accept substandard product and services with the excuse of being "Third World" or a "developing country". There are simply too many choices available to settle for poor quality. The Caribbean tourism industry will have to focus more closely on customer demands as well as the quality of the goods and services it provides for the domestic and international tourist if it is to remain competitive.
- Information technology and knowledge work. A major force for change affecting all aspects of modern life, including tourism, is information technology. Information technology will reshape the way we live, work and play. Caribbean tourism will not be spared the impact of information technology. Already the technology is being used extensively in the operations of the airline industry, the hotel industry and the food and beverage industry, to name just a few. Tourism organizations are increasingly using the Internet and electronic commerce to market and sell the Caribbean as well as to share information and train staff. With the information age comes the era of the *knowledge worker*. By the end of the twenty-first century, all workers, including tourism workers, will be knowledge workers, using information technology to create valuable tourism experiences for the customer.

Knowledge work will not immediately replace the labour-intensive nature of tourism. But it will change how work is done in the industry and, therefore, will require tourism workers to develop a whole range of new information and knowledge skills.

- Environmental issues. A global trend that will continue to impact Caribbean tourism is the growing concern about the environment. According to Goeldner (1992), concern for the environment is a major trend that has not yet peaked. He contends that if tourism is not properly planned, it could create serious environmental degradation in tourist destinations. Environmental issues will have a direct effect on Caribbean tourism as public awareness of the potential negative impacts of over-building, inadequate water and sewage treatment, mass tourism, and host community neglect increases. Caribbean governments will need the competencies to develop policies and regulations to limit tourism capacity, establish planning controls and, in general, protect the environment.

- Rapid change. All of these "new realities" suggest changes in the global and regional tourism landscape. But the pace of change itself has quickened. The world appears to be moving and changing much faster than in the past. It constantly requires us to keep up, lest we fall behind and become uncompetitive. How we manage and lead change is becoming a critical management competence for the future.

FORCES DRIVING CHANGE IN THE GLOBAL HOSPITALITY INDUSTRY

These "new global realities" find empirical support in the ongoing research of the International Hotel and Restaurant Association (IH&RA). The IH&RA is a global network of over 750,000 hospitality operators, associations and suppliers in more than 150 countries. Its mission is to protect, promote and inform the global hospitality industry, which it estimates to comprise over 300,000 hotels and 8 million restaurants, employing 60 million people and contributing US$950 billion to the global economy (International Hotel and Restaurant Association, 1999).

Since 1994, the IH&RA has been conducting research into the major forces that will drive industry change in the future. In research spanning over twenty countries and numerous think tanks, five major forces for change have been identified: concerns for tourist and worker safety and security, technology, asset and capital productivity, the need for new management and issues of capacity control (Olsen and Connolly, 1998). These global forces have been used as the backdrop to further deliberations on the forces specifically impacting Caribbean tourism and the HRD needs arising from them. We return to these issues in the next section.

This, then, is the global and regional context from which the future of Caribbean tourism will flow. These global trends and new realities require new and different skill and competency sets on the part of present and future generations of Caribbean tourism workers. The next two sections look specifically at the new skills and competencies required of the tourism industry in the Caribbean. Two sources of information are used for this purpose: a qualitative source and a quantitative source. The qualitative source is an IH&RA/Caribbean Hotel Association-sponsored Think Tank on Human Resource Management in the Caribbean and the quantitative source is a survey of tourism education and training needs conducted for the Caribbean Tourism Organisation.

THINK TANK ON HOSPITALITY HUMAN RESOURCES

During the last quarter of 1999, the Caribbean Hotel Association, in collaboration with the IH&RA, conducted a "Think Tank on Hospitality Human Resources in the Next Millennium" (Olsen, 1999a). Regional experts on tourism human resource management and development, including this writer, participated in a two-day session to explore the key issues affecting the future of human resource management and development into the next decade. The think tank identified four main needs that will have to be addressed if Caribbean tourism is to continue to be a major player in the global tourism industry. These are the "new worker", the "new manager", competency-based performance and strategic thinking. We will deal specifically with the first two, as the other two are encapsulated in the first two.

The "New Worker"

The think tank recognized that the tourism worker of the future would be very different from one in the past. He or she would be more educated, more independent, more highly skilled and, as a consequence, more marketable, than present or past tourism workers. The HRD consequences of this type of worker for the industry are many. The new worker will require greater variety in his or her job, greater challenge and more learning opportunities. The new worker will not tolerate the traditional "command and control" style of management still prevalent in the industry. They will have more options within and outside the industry, and will be less hesitant than their predecessors to exercise them. They will demand a better balance between their work life and their personal life. They will require a different kind of management and supervision. Indeed, with the use of technology and the move to more knowledge-based systems, they may require no supervision at all, as we know it today. This characterization of the "new worker" has enormous implications for the "new manager".

The "New Manager"

The think tank recognized that the management of the "new worker" would require a different set of skills and competencies of the tourism manager, hence the need for a "new manager". The new manager will require new leadership and motivational skills – team leadership and team building skills, relationship management skills, knowledge management skills, as well as strategic thinking skills. The new manager will be expected to be more of a generalist than a specialist, performing several functions with the aid of available technology. Most of all he or she will be expected to *add value* to the organization in strategic, visionary and entrepreneurial ways. As in the case of the new worker, these new skills and competencies of the new manager will require a different approach to management education and development.

The think tank also recognized that with the new skills and competencies required of the new worker and the new manager, they would desire new competency-based performance and reward systems. With the rapid skills obsolescence that will accompany the twenty-first century and the need to constantly and continuously update and change those skills, workers and managers will expect their rewards to be based on the competencies they acquire in addition to the value they add to the enterprise.

The Think Tank on Hospitality Human Resources in the Caribbean identified a range of issues that should challenge the regional industry to move rapidly into the twenty-first century to be able to compete in the global arena (Olsen, 1999b, 1999c). There are clearly new sets of human resource development needs that will drive Caribbean tourism in the new millennium. The challenge of the industry is to address these needs in an effective and efficient manner.

TOURISM TRAINING FOR THE NEW MILLENNIUM

In recognition of the vital importance of HRD to the development of tourism in the Caribbean, the Caribbean Tourism Organisation (CTO) commissioned a study of the tourism education and training needs of its member countries in 1998. This study was undertaken by Quality Consultants (1999), a regional business research firm, of which this writer is a principal consultant. The main purpose of the study was to analyse the current and future tourism HRD requirements in the Caribbean with a view to helping the CTO and its member countries to prioritize education and training activities and develop appropriate HRD policies and action plans. A total of 1,112 public and private sector organizations operating in nine different sectors of the tourism industry in twenty-five countries participated in the study. A combination of quantitative and qualitative research methods was used to collect the data. The quantitative method used was a survey while the qualitative method was a series of industry stakeholder focus groups and in-depth interviews.

Future Training Needs Identified

Survey respondents were asked, among other things, to identify the future training needs for different categories of staff. The major future training need identified were, in order:

- Customer relations skills
- Communication skills
- Technology/computer literacy skills

With specific reference to the HRD needs of management, respondents identified the following:

- Marketing skills
- Leadership skills
- Human resource management skills
- Technology/computer literacy

Table 8.1   Future Training Needs of the Caribbean Tourism Industry

	Managers	Professionals	Skilled/ Semiskilled	Unskilled
Leadership	18.5%	6.0%	4.2%	0.8%
Human resource management	17.5%	5.1%	2.6%	0.7%
Financial/accounting	13.3%	5.9%	3.8%	0.8%
Marketing	22.7%	9.8%	6.4%	1.0%
Communication	11.6%	11.9%	20.9%	10.6%
Computer literacy	15.1%	9.4%	15.9%	2.9%
Customer relations	11.2%	13.5%	35.8%	19.6%
Foreign languages	9.6%	6.6%	10.9%	3.7%

Source: *Tourism Training for the New Millennium – A Study of Tourism Education and Training Needs in the Caribbean*, Quality Consultants, 1999. Study commissioned by the Caribbean Tourism Organisation, Barbados.

Therefore, from the perspective of the owners and operators of the Caribbean tourism industry, the future HRD needs of the industry centre around customer service skills, interpersonal relations skills and technology. For managers, marketing, people management and technology skills were identified as the key future HRD needs of the industry. Table 8.1 shows the percentage of industry operators and owners identifying the different future training needs for different categories of tourism workers. With reference to *technical and operational* training needs, industry owners and operators overwhelmingly identified *culinary skills* as the most critical training need for the future. This was followed way behind by food and beverage service, tour guiding and housekeeping skills.

The consultants' report concludes that there is a strong need for interpersonal relations and technology training at all levels of the industry, as well as management and supervisory training for persons in those positions. The identification of technology as a training need may reflect the industry's recognition of the important role technology will play in the future, whereas the identification of marketing as a managerial training need suggests that owners and operators are coming to terms with the highly competitive nature of the industry worldwide.

The emphasis on interpersonal or "behavioural" skills such as customer relations and communication is consistent with the idea that customer service and quality will become even more important in the future as customer expectations and choices increase. According to Olsen and Connolly (1998), customer expectations are turning into demands for better service, and this shift toward better service, in turn, requires tourism workers to have higher skill levels, not only in actual service delivery, but in the social/behavioural skills that are needed to meet a more diverse and demanding customer.

THE FUTURE OF CARIBBEAN TOURISM: NEW COMPETENCIES REQUIRED

The new global realities and trends, the trends specific to the global and Caribbean tourism industry, and the findings of the research presented above suggest the need for the following skills and competencies: entrepreneurship, information technology, creativity and innovation, ethics and environmental awareness, new approaches to management and the enhancement of behavioural skills (Charles, 1998).

Entrepreneurship/Intrapreneurship

Future generations of tourism workers will need to be imbued with entrepreneurial and "intrapreneurial" skills and competencies that will prepare them to create business and employment opportunities, either for themselves or for the organizations for which they work. The development of enterprise will be an important competence for the tourism worker and manager of tomorrow.

Creativity and Innovation

Creativity and innovation are important components of entrepreneurship. As international competition increases and customer choices grow, Caribbean tourism will have to develop new and innovative ways of continuing to attract and retain international travellers. The next generation of Caribbean tourism workers will have to continously develop creative ways of retaining and increasing global tourism market share. This will not necessarily be the domain only of the leaders of Caribbean tourism, but as management and leadership approaches become more participative and empowering, all tourism workers will be called upon to use their creativity and innovativeness in the name of Caribbean tourism.

Information Technology

Much has already been said of the role that technology in general and information technology in particular will play in the tourism of the future. The future tourism worker must be "technoliterate" for all levels of jobs: from the room attendant who may be faced with "smart" self-cleaning rooms or hand-held computers to communicate with the stock room or laundry, to the higgler on the beach who may have to accept credit cards as we move toward a cashless world. As has been said before, at some stage during the twenty-first century, all work will be knowledge work and all workers will be knowledge workers, creating and using information and knowledge to produce a better tourist experience. Future tourism workers will have to develop the skills and competencies necessary to work in a "wired world".

Environmental Awareness and Ethics

Within the context of an increasingly competitive world, the next generation of tourism workers will need to have an appreciation of the ethical and environmental issues associated with sustaining Caribbean tourism. As areas like "green" or eco-tourism and cultural tourism emerge as possible alternatives to mass sand, sea and sun tourism, future tourism workers will need both the technical and conceptual skills to work in these emerging areas. Environmental protection, impact assessment, capacity control and policy formulation are just some of the skills that will have to be developed or honed if Caribbean tourism is to be sustained for future generations. The ethical and environmental issues associated with tourism will require particular attention in the development of the future tourism workforce.

New Management Skills and Competencies

We have seen that the future of Caribbean tourism calls for a different approach to managing. The twenty-first century tourism manager will need to have a range of conceptual skills such as systems thinking, environmental scanning, visioning and "futuring" – seeing the future before it happens. He or she will need well developed interpersonal skills, such as coaching and counselling skills and change management skills. He or she will need to be multidisciplinary and multifunctional. Most of all, the future tourism manager should be a learner, constantly updating and upgrading his or her skills and competencies.

Behavioural Skills

Finally, the Caribbean tourism worker of the future will need to have well-developed "behavioural" skills, such as communication, interpersonal relations, and customer service. A positive work attitude and ethic also will be important. In this latter regard, proper selection of future tourism workers will be as critical as proper training and development opportunities.

These new skills and competencies differ from the traditional technical and operational "tourism" skills that we are accustomed to. This is not to say that these latter skills will no longer be important, but many of them will be performed using technology. The broader, conceptual, strategic skills will, therefore, take on a greater significance at all levels of the industry. In order to get to this future, Caribbean tourism itself will need to change. The way the industry manages its human resources will need to be re-examined and more contemporary approaches adopted. Some of these approaches are outlined below.

NEW APPROACHES TO MANAGING AND DEVELOPING HUMAN RESOURCES IN TOURISM

This section draws on the recommendations of the consultants on the tourism training needs assessment conducted for the CTO as discussed earlier (Quality Consultants, 1999). Interestingly, similar recommendations were made more recently in the Annual Congress of the IH&RA in South Africa in October, 1999 (International Hotel and Restaurant Association, 1999).

Tourism as a Career

Tourism operators and managers in the Caribbean need to promote and develop tourism as a viable career option both for potential entrants into the industry and for persons already in the industry – many of whom see tourism in the Caribbean as a transitory job rather than a career. The industry will have to find ways to train, retain and motivate its workforce by providing adequate compensation, incentives and training and promotion opportunities. Given the fact that the majority of establishments in the Caribbean are small or medium-sized family-owned operations, career opportunities are limited and there may be little incentive or motivation for these establishments to develop career opportunities and paths for their workforce. Programmes in entrepreneurship and small business management for the tourism industry should, therefore, be developed to provide workers with career options outside of their immediate place of work.

Holistic Approach to Human Resource Development

Perhaps the most important change that needs to take place in the Caribbean tourism industry is the need for the industry to develop a holistic, "systems" approach to human resource development, that includes the proper recruitment and selection of people for the industry, the appropriate compensation of people in the industry, the use of contemporary management approaches like teamwork, participative leadership and empowerment. Tourism training and education alone will not solve performance problems if people are not properly selected for the industry, if compensation is perceived to be low, if management styles are archaic, if employees see no viable future in tourism and if Caribbean people themselves have a poor perception of the industry. There is need for a total "systems" view of tourism education and training that places it in the wider context of human resource management and tourism development. In general, as the IH&RA Annual Congress concluded, "Human resource management must be radically refocused if the industry is to compete successfully in recruiting and retaining the brightest and the best" (International Hotel and Restaurant Association, 1999). Clearly, these are not uniquely Caribbean challenges.

Education and Training Institutions

Finally, tertiary educational institutions should expand their curricula to include non-traditional courses on entrepreneurship and innovation, creativity and leadership to prepare the future leaders for the industry. Of critical importance is the need to keep current and relevant. Tourism education and training institutes can do this by forming strategic alliances and "smart partnerships" with the industry that they serve and conducting continuous industry-driven needs assessments. In this way, both academia and industry can ensure that the products coming out of the institutions will be well prepared for the industry.

CARIBBEAN TOURISM AT THE BEGINNING OF THE MILLENNIUM

The critical importance of tourism to Caribbean economies now and in the future, the increase in international competitiveness in tourism and the need for tourist destinations like the Caribbean to deliver quality service and products to a more demanding customer, all suggest the need for a well-educated and trained cadre of hospitality and tourism professionals. This, in turn, suggests that education and training in tourism will continue to be central to the development of the industry in the region (Charles, 1997).

The twenty-first century holds much promise for Caribbean tourism as it takes its place in the world tourism industry. The opportunities for the Caribbean to become a major player in world tourism are great. But Caribbean tourism has to be sustainable. An important part of that sustainability is the ability to attract and retain the brightest and the best that the Caribbean can produce. Much work needs to be done if Caribbean tourism is to be sustained by future generations of Caribbean workers, if it is to continue to be an engine of economic growth and prosperity for the Caribbean. As Olsen and Connolly (1998) state, the investment in education must now become a priority in a global environment where knowledge and knowledge workers will be the mainstay of economic development. They go on to suggest that making the tourism worker competitive in the future must become an important policy thrust for industry and government together.

The challenge, therefore, is to forge and sustain the collaboration, cooperation, partnership and participation of all the major stakeholders of Caribbean tourism – the public and private sectors, the education and training institutions, the representative organizations and associations, the trade unions, the media, the people of the region – in the development of the industry and the people in it. The very survival of Caribbean tourism requires no less.

REFERENCES

Caribbean Tourism Organisation. (1999). *1998 Statistical Report*, Caribbean Tourism Organisation, Barbados.

Charles, K.R. (1997). "Tourism Education and Training in the Caribbean: Preparing for the Twenty-first Century", *Progress in Tourism and Hospitality Research* 3 (no. 3): 186–197.

Charles, K.R. (1998). "Preparing Caribbean Youth for Tourism in the Next Millennium", paper presented at the Caribbean Tourism Organisation's Second Annual Conference on Sustainable Tourism Development, Trinidad and Tobago, April.

Goeldner, C.R. (1992). "Trends in North American Tourism", *American Behavioural Scientist* 36 (no. 2): 144–154.

International Hotel and Restaurant Association. (1999). "Industry Must Shake up Human Resource Practices, Says IH&RA Congress", press release, IH&RA, Paris.

Naisbitt, J. (1994). *Global Paradox*, Avon Books, New York.

Olsen, M.D. (1999a). "Think Tank on Hospitality Human Resources in the New Millennium", workshop conducted for the International Hotel and Restaurant Association and the Caribbean Hotel Association, Barbados, September/October.

Olsen, M.D. (1999b). *Executive Summary – Think Tank on New Management in the Caribbean,* International Hotel and Restaurant Association and Caribbean Hotel Association, Paris.

Olsen, M.D. (1999c). "Think Tank on Human Resources", International Hotel and Restaurant Association, Paris.

Olsen, M.D. and Connolly, D.J. (1998). *Forces Driving Change in the Caribbean: A White Paper on the Hospitality Industry,* Caribbean Hotel Association, Puerto Rico.

Quality Consultants. (1999). *Tourism Training for the New Millennium: A Study of Tourism Education and Training Needs in the Caribbean,* Caribbean Tourism Organisation, Barbados.

World Travel and Tourism Council. (1997). *Travel and Tourism: Jobs for the Millennium,* World Travel and Tourism Council, London.

COUNTRY CASE STUDIES

Section 2 presents case studies of various approaches to tourism and hospitality education and training in a number of Caribbean such as Barbados, Belize, Dominica, the Dominican Republic, Grenada, Guyana, the Bahamas, Trinidad and Tobago, and the Turks and Caicos Islands.

It is increasingly being realized that education and training programmes should be tailored to the needs of the industry in order for them to be effective. Sophia Rolle begins by discussing the challenges faced and changes proposed to upgrade the level of tourism and hospitality education currently offered in the Bahamas. The main initiative that serves as the focal point for this chapter is the proposed amalgamation of the College of the Bahamas and the Bahamas Hotel Training College with the ultimate aim of providing relevant industry training to students. Sharret Yearwood then examines the status of training for eco-tourism in Belize. Initiatives of the private sector, the public sector and non-governmental organizations are examined. The author concludes by calling for a more unified effort in eco-tourism training, and for the establishing of long-term strategies for eco-tourism education and training in Belize.

Education is the key ingredient in achieving a sustainable tourism industry. The past, present and future of tourism and hospitality education is therefore examined in Dominica, Grenada, Guyana, and Trinidad and Tobago. In chapter 11, Susan Carter discusses Dominica's attempts to train teachers and prepare youths to participate meaningfully in the industry. She also examines the introduction of two bold initiatives, the Youth Environmental Service Corps and the

Nature Island Standards of Excellence that were designed to prepare youths to one day assume leadership of the industry.

In chapter 12 Guillermo Graglia critically explores hospitality education in the Dominican Republic. He states that academic institutions have failed to realize their potential because they fail to view hospitality education as a business, with the industry and students as the clients. Graglia also identifies academia's need to keep abreast with the changes in the industry in order to offer a better, more desirable product to its customers. Naline Ramdeen-Joseph then assesses the work of the T.A. Marryshow Community College, New Life Organisation and the St George's University in Grenada. She discusses the structures of the programmes and shares some of the challenges and triumphs experienced by these institutions in terms of tourism and hospitality education and training.

In Guyana, one of the newest entrants in Caribbean tourism, efforts have been expended to provide education and training in this field. Donald Sinclair examines the status of programmes offered by the University of Guyana – Tourism Studies Unit, the Carnegie School of Home Economics and the now defunct Pegasus Hotel School. Michelle McLeod gives a similar assessment for the twin island republic of Trinidad and Tobago where the government has recognized the need for a well-trained workforce. As such, two models, the "Getting Industry into Education" and "Getting Education into the Industry" models, included in the Tourism Master Plan, are discussed. This section is concluded with an assessment of the Turks and Caicos Islands compiled by Lindsey Musgrove, John Skippings and Ralph Higgs. The authors disclose that, while the Turks and Caicos Islands government was providing tourism and education programmes for locals, these are not very popular because of negative attitudes of the islanders to employment in the tourism and hospitality industry. This results in the importation of labour. Efforts are underway, however, to reform local attitudes towards the industry, particularly because tourism is the main economic sector for the Turks and Caicos Islands.

CHAPTER

A CASE STUDY ON TOURISM AND HOSPITALITY EDUCATION IN THE BAHAMAS

Sophia A. Rolle

Abstract

The College of the Bahamas (COB) and the Bahamas Hotel Training College (BHTC) were amalgamated in an attempt to enhance post-secondary education in the Bahamas and as a first step towards the creation of a national university. The amalgamation involves the creation of new posts and the upgrading of other posts to mirror positions held in similar institutions internationally. Changes have also been made to the number of credit hours as well as to the general educational requirements, in keeping with the practices of these institutions. It will also involve changes in one of the most important programmes – the Apprentice Cook programme, which will result in the granting of an associate degree rather than a certificate. These changes will not only enhance the earning potential of graduates, but will also make the programme more attractive to the industry.

INTRODUCTION

The Government of the Bahamas felt that national education at the post-secondary level needed some enhancement, thus policy decisions were made regarding the relationship between the College of the Bahamas (COB) and the Bahamas Hotel Training College (BHTC).

In November 1999, the government empanelled a steering committee to devise appropriate strategies for effecting the amalgamation of these institutions. Several findings and recommendations were identified as major activities involved in this exercise. They included the following:

1. Harmonizing the admissions policies and procedures of the institutions

2. Integrating the hospitality and tourism programmes of both institutions
3. Rationalizing the reallocation of material and human resources
4. Devising appropriate compensation for displaced personnel and ensuring that the terms and conditions of service for all categories of absorbed employees are protected after amalgamation
5. Formulating appropriate strategies for financing the operation of the amalgamated institutions and harmonizing accounting mechanisms, procedures and budgets
6. Coordinating an effective physical plant management programme
7. Maintaining and enhancing existing affiliations, accreditation and articulation agreements

The recommended implementation strategy provides for the integration process to extend over a period of up to three years or until the last current student had exited the BHTC programme. An additional reason for the suggested phased approach was the need to allow the general public and clients from both institutions to be properly educated on the process.

The following is taken from the original report, which has not yet been ratified in its entirety by the government; therefore, full disclosure is prohibited. Areas to be discussed in this chapter include the following:

1. Preparation for the task
2. Terms of reference related to programming issues
3. Historical overview
4. The College of the Bahamas
5. The Bahamas Hotel Training College
6. Programming issues

PREPARATION FOR THE TASK

The steering committee divided the thirteen terms of reference into structural organization and human resources issues, programming issues, and student services and related issues. These issues were then framed into tasks and assigned to subcommittees empanelled to examine the potential impact of each issue on the proposed amalgamation process and to recommend appropriate responses for any negatives that might result from the integration exercise.

To aid the completion of their assigned tasks, subcommittees were encouraged to draw on relevant experiences from counterpart institutions in North America and the Caribbean. Five teams were dispatched to colleges and universities in Barbados, Canada and the United States to facilitate the collection and processing of information relevant to the amalgamation exercise.

The team's tasks were specifically to examine structural and programming needs and complexities as they existed in programmes. Administrative nomenclatures were also examined with a view to:

- Determining whether there were any major differences
- What might be adopted, with some modifications
- How best ought certain internal and external procedures to be carried out

In addition to international immersion, subcommittees also held discussions with industry counterparts and potential clients who aided greatly, particularly regarding programme issues (Lopez, 2000).

HISTORICAL OVERVIEW

The need for addressing fragmentation and lack of coordination at the post-secondary level of the national education system has been underscored in every report on higher education produced in the Bahamas since 1964. Between 1991 and 1994, the Government of the Bahamas commissioned three studies on education. Each of the resulting reports, *A Master Plan for Post Secondary Education*, the *Task Force on Education Report*, and the *Una Paul Report*, stressed the need for giving prominence to the development of strategies aimed at addressing fragmentation and lack of coordination, and suggested the creation of a national university as the way forward. The amalgamation process now contemplated gives expression to that suggestion and allows for the process (of amalgamation), which originally gave birth to COB, to continue.

THE COLLEGE OF THE BAHAMAS

COB, a statutory, publicly supported, tertiary-level educational institution, came into being in October 1974 following the amalgamation of the Bahamas Teachers' College, the San Salvador Teachers' College, the C.R. Walker Technical College and the Sixth Form programme of the Government High School. COB admitted its first class in September 1975 and is empowered by the College of the Bahamas Act (1995) to grant degrees, diplomas and certificates and to seek and receive private funding for its operation.

The general responsibility for administration and the formulation of educational policies for COB is vested in an eleven-member College Council comprising the COB president, two public officers, a student, a faculty member, the president of the Alumni Association of COB and five persons representing other relevant sectors of the economy. The Academic Board, subject to the direction of the council, is responsible for the academic administration of the college.

Since 1974, COB has evolved into a national institution operating a main campus and several satellite campuses on New Providence; a campus on Grand Bahama and extension services on several Family Islands, including entities on Exuma, Andros, San Salvador and Eleuthera. The ultimate goal of COB is to establish and maintain a presence in every major population centre throughout the Commonwealth of the Bahamas. Not only has the number of students registering for programmes offered by COB grown over the years, but also the institution's portfolio has been expanded to absorb several fragmented tertiary-level programmes offered by the School of Nursing and Health Services. As a result of this, COB's organizational structure is under constant review and is adjusted when necessary to ensure that the institution remains relevant.

Originally, COB had seven academic units, called divisions. However, as the institution advances toward university status, adjustments now contemplated foreshadow the creation of divisions, faculties, and schools with enhanced capability for coordinating general interest courses and programmes offered by the Continuing Education and Extension Services Centre (Government of the Bahamas, 1974).

THE BAHAMAS HOTEL TRAINING COLLEGE

The BHTC is a statutory quasi-government institution established in 1973 under the conditions of a tripartite agreement between the Bahamas government, the Bahamas Hotel Association and the Bahamas Hotel Catering and Allied Workers Union. The institution began operating in September 1974 with fewer than twenty students. Since its opening, BHTC has attracted a large cohort of students from the

Caribbean, Europe, Asia and several African countries, with the bulk of its population being drawn from the Bahamas.

BHTC is governed by an eight-member council, which parallels its counterpart at COB. It derives its funding from contributions made by each of its three founding partners and also from student fees, which are pro-rated and based on an agreed formula. The BHTC funding strategy is in stark contrast to that of COB, which is almost totally dependent on government subventions.

Because of the highly specific nature of the BHTC programme offerings, the institution only operates a main campus on New Providence and a campus on Grand Bahama. These two communities represent the major economic centres of the Bahamas and serve as hubs of the local hospitality industry. The main objective of BHTC is to develop human resources for national and international tourism, hospitality and allied industries by providing quality vocational training and applied academic education. The institution is an accredited member of the Council on Occupational Education (COE); maintains articulation agreements with Florida International University, Johnson and Wales University and Kendall College, among others, and is also affiliated with the American Culinary Federation (ACF).

OVERVIEW OF EXISTING PROGRAMMES

BHTC attracts 80% of its students directly from high school and 20% from the hospitality industry workplace. When compared with counterpart institutions in North America and the Caribbean, BHTC functions at the level of a community or junior college, and, as is the norm in such institutions, the highest degree offered at BHTC is the applied associate degree, which is usually a two-year programme. BHTC's applied associate degrees are offered in Hospitality Operations and Culinary Arts. In addition to the applied associate degrees, BHTC offers a variety of one-year certificate programmes and short non-credit skills training programmes for clients in the hospitality industry under its Industry Training programme.

The management certificate programmes offered are Food and Beverage Management, Travel and Tourism Management, Bookkeeping and Accounting Management and Supervisory Management. A number of the courses that make up these programmes have been extracted from the applied associate degree programmes. The certificate programmes offered are Bakery Skills, Housekeeping Skills, Front Office Skills, Food Service Skills and Culinary Skills.

At COB, the Department of Tourism Studies offers a joint bachelor of science degree in Hospitality and Tourism Management. Candidates pursuing a degree in Hospitality and Tourism Management can select from concentrations in the areas of Tourism Management, Hotel and Resort Management, Culinary Sciences and Food and Beverage Management. This degree programme is approved by COB's Academic Board and offered jointly by COB, the University of the West Indies and BHTC.

The Continuing Education and Extension Services Centre may facilitate general interest courses connected with programmes offered by the Department of Tourism Studies, for continuing education and extension services at COB.

PROGRAMME ADJUSTMENTS

COB has recently gone through a restructuring exercise that parallels the amalgamation exercises between BHTC and COB. Within the Faculty of Business, Hospitality and Tourism Studies there will be the School of Hospitality and Tourism. The new structure is shown in Figure 9.1.

The committee underwent a fact-finding exercise prior to making any changes to this stalwart programme. Based on this information the committee felt that the Apprentice Chefs programme, as it presently stood, needed to be modified to meet current industry standards globally. One of the major concerns expressed was the actual amount of practical work hours performed by the students in a three-year programme that only netted them a certificate on successful completion of the programme. The graduates would often end up not commanding key entry positions in the industry or earning adequate salaries comparative to other graduates from colleges or universities abroad with a degree designation, who more often than not, had done far less work to attain their degrees. The designation of an applied associate degree would rectify these concerns. The committee also felt that the basic level of Math and English needed to increase slightly above what was currently being taught.

The Apprentice Pastry Cook programme is fairly new in that, although it has always been an option, it was never fully subscribed to by students. Where only a few courses existed, the team took those along with others (some of which have not yet been written) and created the degree. Courses such as Advanced Cake Decorating, Caribbean Cuisine, Chocolate and Sugar Artistry and Show Pieces, Hot

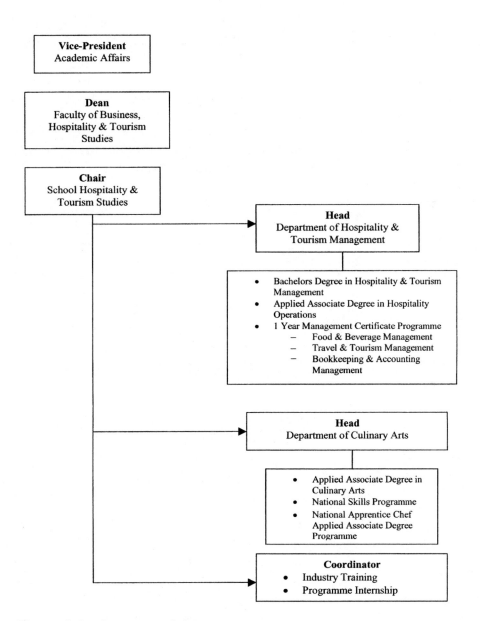

Figure 9.1 Structure of the main campus.

and Cold Dessert Presentations, Computers for Culinary Management and Supervision and Management Studies, have been included as specifically requested by the industry. The first year of these speciality areas parallel each other and students begin specialization in years two and three.

The committee felt strongly that the industry training coordinator, who will also serve as head, should remain in the School of Hospitality and Tourism Studies. The person with responsibility for this area must work closely with the school in terms of coordination of internship activities for students but, above all, must have the flexibility to meet the specific needs of the industry in a timely manner.

All hospitality and tourism certificate programmes that are shorter in duration and do not have as many credited courses will be organized through the Centre for Continuing Education and Extension Services. The industry training coordinator will act as the school's liaison person with respect to these programmes.

The Northern Bahamas campus will have a slightly different structure in comparison to the main campus. This structure is shown as Figure 9.2.

Among some of the concerns expressed by many of the academicians between the two institutions was the number of credit hours offered in the applied associate degree programme offered at BHTC. A specific mission of the various teams that visited international institutions was to ascertain the average number of credit hours offered in associate degree programmes. The findings suggested that between sixty and seventy-five credit hours were the norms. The subcommittees was then given the task to "trim without losing" some of the courses in the two applied associate degree programmes. Our task was also to strengthen the general education requirements of all programmes.

What ensued was a unanimous decision to replace several of the current general requirements (i.e. English, Math, etc.) with those offered by COB. The committee also added the Library Orientation and Student Development non-credit courses to the programme. After careful evaluation and examination of some courses, the committee came away with what they felt was a well-balanced seventy-eight-credit course programme, a step down from the ninety-three-credit programme that originally existed. Upon completion of these programmes, students who wish to can pursue the bachelor degree programme in the school.

ACCREDITATION

The Council on Occupational Education (COE) currently accredits the BHTC. BHTC's status will only be maintained if it remains a separate entity. Once integrated with COB it will lose its COE accreditation

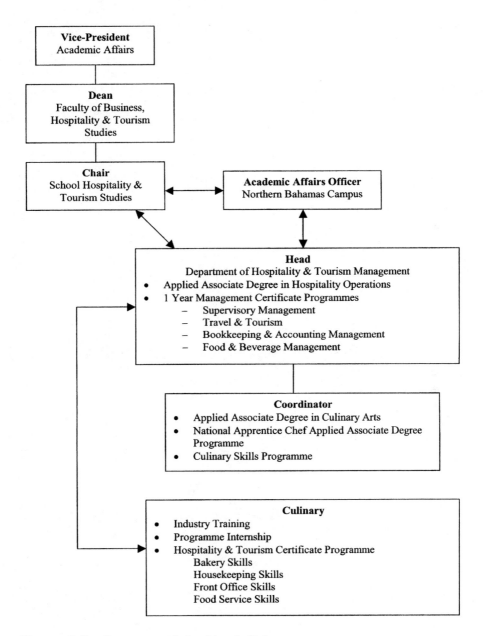

Figure 9.2 Structure of the North Bahamas campus.

status. There is a possibility of extending this status to the School of Hospitality and Tourism Studies at a later date.

Articulation agreements, on the other hand, are maintained with a number of institutions locally and internationally. This integration exercise can only expand current opportunities for students.

REFERENCES

Lopez, K. (2000). "Amalgamating the Bahamas Hotel Training College and the College of the Bahamas", unpublished report, Nassau, Bahamas.

Government of the Bahamas. (1974). The College of the Bahamas Act, Government Printers, Nassau, Bahamas.

CHAPTER

THE ROLE OF TRAINING FOR ECO-TOURISM IN BELIZE

Sharret Yearwood

Abstract

Eco-tourism has great potential for Belize and the government has placed a high priority on protection of the environment and conservation. The National Development Plan explains the government's commitment to the efficient management and utilization of the nations' resources. In order to attain these goals, the country must have proper management of human resources. This chapter explores the present and future education and training needs in eco-tourism for the country of Belize. The government, nongovernmental organizations, private sector and local communities are examined to assess their roles in executing education and training. Local training institutions are also analysed to find out what type of training they provide. The linkages among these entities are also examined to see how much unity exists, assuming that they are all working towards the same goal. The study concludes by making recommendations from the findings with the hope that they will be considered by those involved in eco-tourism education and training.

INTRODUCTION

As Belize becomes more involved in the tourism business, it becomes more apparent that those responsible are still trying to define the key tourism product. "Eco-tourism", the popular word presently used to describe many Caribbean products, is one of Belize's key focuses to market the destination. Tourism is one of the industries heavily dependent on labour. This brings to the fore the issue of education and training for eco-tourism in Belize.

Since the tourism industry is very service-oriented, it is imperative that education and training continue to be updated as the various aspects of tourism evolve. Nettleford (1999) states that "education's role must not only teach people to make a living, it must also teach them how to live". This is certainly something that any country that plans to become involved, or is currently involved, in eco-tourism needs to consider.

The community has to be educated and trained in how to protect its environment while simultaneously attaining maximum economic benefits from its resources. One such example is the use of cultural resources. As Nettleford (1999) suggests about cultural tourism:

> It must, therefore, enjoy logical priority over the satisfaction of others in search of surface titillation though there should be a willingness to share that inheritance which will have been passed down from generation to generation and organically assimilated by that self. What better approach than to nurture one's culture for oneself and welcome our guests in to share it with us?

This chapter seeks to accomplish the following:

- To determine what form of eco-tourism education and training is being conducted
- To analyse what segments of the community are targeted for eco-tourism education and training
- To explore what types of linkage exist in delivering eco-tourism education and training
- To examine the role of government in education and training for eco-tourism
- To analyse the role of non-governmental organizations in education and training
- To identify the present and potential eco-tourism development that can be achieved through proper education and training initiatives

Information for this chapter was obtained during field research interviews that the author conducted with members selected from government, private, non-governmental and community groups in Belize in the year 2000. The researcher distributed questionnaires and conducted interviews via the Internet and telephone, as well as face to face.

ECO-TOURISM IN BELIZE

Belize's underpopulated and fairly undisturbed 8,867 square miles has a diverse flora and fauna. More than 4,000 species of flora, including orchids, are found in Belize's subtropical jungle. A variety of wildlife, including over 500 species of birds, large numbers of howler monkeys, tapirs, pumas and many other species that are either endangered or extinct in other parts of the world, is also found in Belize.

After the country gained its independence in September 1981, one of the first acts passed in November of that year was the National Park System Act. It provides the legal framework "for the preservation and protection of highly important natural and cultural features, for the regulation of the scientific, educational and recreational use of the same and for all matters connected therewith or incidental thereto" (Government of Belize, 1991a). The act paved the way for the creation of national parks and reserves. The country began to focus on conservation, and the exploitation of natural resources became a major concern. This, of course, did not occur in isolation because at the same time the country was experiencing difficulty with the traditional agriculture export as the leading export earner. As stated by the government in 1989, "with the traditional export sector (agriculture) facing problems, Belize was forced to re-evaluate its development strategies with a view to finding alternative sources of foreign exchange earnings". The government shifted its economic growth strategy to emphasize tourism, particularly eco-tourism. The Government of Belize defines eco-tourism as "the careful husbanding of Belize's natural resources . . . for controlled tourism with a specific sensitivity to possible harm or effect to those resources" (Government of Belize, 1991b).

The Belizean government has a written commitment to ensure that the country receives maximum benefits from tourism. Of course, education should be one of the vital means of accomplishing this. However, this is not realized in many countries. However, there is still much work to be done on eco-tourism, as many people still hold varying definitions of eco-tourism. An important component of Belize's tourism is its archaeological assets. The country is also very culturally diverse, with each ethnic group clinging to its customs and beliefs, yet unified as a people. The 1998 statistics showed that 29.8% of the population is Creole (of African descent), 43.6% Mestizo (Spanish and Maya mix), 11.1% Maya, 8.9% of European, East Indian and Chinese and 6.6% Garifuna. This rich mix of cultures representing different communities in Belize plays a vital role in eco-tourism and hence the population needs to be properly educated if it is to success-fully impart this value to visitors.

Much care needs to be taken in the way the country develops eco-tourism. The country must attract visitors who are environmentally conscious of the potential negative consequences that their behaviour can have on the environment, threatening it for future generations. Therefore, there must be a balance between sustainable development and protection of the environment and this can be achieved through education.

ECO-TOURISM TRAINING AND EDUCATION

Only limited research has been conducted on education and training in eco-tourism in Belize. It cannot be assumed that local communities will automatically acquire conservation values. Instead, programmes should be developed that incorporate the local community, govern-ment and non-governmental organizations so that people do not only become aware of conserving natural resources, but also how to be actively involved in the management of these resources.

In a study carried out by the Blackstone Corporation (1998) it was observed that, "a very large number of stakeholders have noted the need for improved training of all kinds with respect to the tourism industry in Belize, to improve service levels at all levels, from man-agement to basic support services." In the study, it was also noted that even though training courses were offered for the tourism sector, those involved claimed that they were often inaccessible. This was because training was centralized and many were unable to participate.

Blackstone also recognized the need for specific training of many small operators who make up a significant part of the industry. They identified several areas that were lacking in training, including man-agement, staff training, marketing and planning and design. They also stressed the importance of building public awareness levels and attitudes of local people:

> Perhaps the key issue with respect to improving service levels within the tourism industry in Belize is associated with the need to improve attitudes and raise awareness about the importance of the industry. To develop a friendly, warm and welcoming environment for visitors throughout the country, to enhance their appreciation of our country and encourage the repeat visits and good word-of-mouth that are critical to a successful industry.

A tourism training needs study conducted by the Caribbean Tourism Organisation (CTO) in 1999 indicates that many tourism organizations in Belize train their staff "as required". Only about a quarter of these institutions have a trainer on staff, since they do not see training as a priority. Most respondents (72.9%) stated that on-the-job training was the strategy they used to train all levels of staff. Only a few of these organizations pay for outside trainers. Many do not even include training in their budgets.

At present, some of the stakeholders in the hospitality industry are not utilizing the training being offered. Some claim that the locations are inconvenient and, thus, inaccessible to them. Some claim that training is offered at the wrong time of the year (during high season) and they cannot sacrifice their staff. Others claim that the training costs too much.

Training institutions offer courses varying from food and beverage to hotel management. However, the CTO study indicates that the country still lacks training in culinary skills, housekeeping and water sports. The CTO study also identified several skill deficiencies at the managerial level. Marketing headed the list, with 44.3% of the organizations showing this deficiency, and human resources management followed closely behind, with 42.9% of organizations deficient in this area.

The study also revealed training challenges faced by organizations and these included (Caribbean Tourism Organisation, 1999):

- Environmental protection
- Community participation in tourism
- The cost of training
- Small staff, small operations/time for training

Training

Training in this context can be defined as any activity that prepares a person for employment in travel, tourism and recreation. "Training of people in the industry, awareness of the importance of the industry by government and local people, and positive attitudes of the host population towards tourists are key elements of any successful tourism industry" (Blackstone, 1998).

"Given the enormous and growing importance of tourism to the Caribbean economics there is no evidence that Caribbean governments have singled out Tourism Education and Training as a major priority in the national planning process" (Caribbean Tourism Organisation, 1990). This statement can be directed to the Government of Belize. Even though tourism is now the number one income earner for the country, the government still is not doing enough to assist in fostering the growth of education and training in the industry.

Human resources play a critical role in tourism, be it eco-tourism or any other sector. Training individuals who come in direct contact with visitors is essential as this will assist in determining repeat visitors, service quality as perceived by the customers, and marketing through customers who are satisfied with services provided. Training of individuals who have indirect contact with visitors is also important, since they need to understand how their actions impact the industry.

Some stakeholders still have not recognized the benefits associated with proper training and, therefore, do not include it in their budgets. Pattullo (1996) states that, "until recently, training a well-equipped and finely tuned army of employees has remained a low priority with money more likely to be budgeted for upgrading buildings than people's skills". Blackstone (1998) also points out that "many small tourism businesses throughout Belize are essentially 'mom-and-pop' operations, where the owners have not been trained themselves, and are not necessarily amenable to a new way".

These stakeholders and the government still have not realized the importance of getting well-rounded employees. According to the CTO (1990): "It is noticeable, however, that when seeking to fill such key posts as Director of Tourism, Marketing Director, Hotel Managers and Executive Chefs, to name a few, the region has enormous difficulty in finding the right combination of training, qualification and experience."

Belize has begun addressing its educational and training needs. Several institutions are currently providing education and training for the tourism industry, including:

- The Belize Institute of Management (BIM) – oriented to short-term training
- Belize Technical College (BTC) – hospitality training programme (two-year curriculum)
- The Centre for Employment Training (CET) – hospitality and catering

- The Belize Tourism Industry Association (BTIA) – tour guide training course (a multi-month certification programme)
- The University College of Belize (UCB) – hospitality courses offered as a part of the Natural Resources degree programme
- The Belize Tourism Board (BTB) – certificate programmes, including the training of taxi operators and teachers

COMMUNITY TOURISM AND TRAINING

Community tourism refers to the types of operations that are developed and managed by members of local communities, such that the majority of the economic benefits accrue directly to the people.

Certainly Belize does not want its indigenous peoples to be displaced, as has happened in South America and other regions. They should not feel deprived of their lands and their traditional way of living. Osmany Salas, executive director of the Belize Audubon Society, says, "to save the place, the people have to be involved" (www.belizeaudubon.org). The Belize Audubon Society has recently embarked on a three-year rural project that aims to build management skills for local communities and to build local support for the management of protected areas.

Yves (1991) states that "community involvement generates commitment and pride, it enhances skills and strengthens community institutions, and it establishes local responsibility". He goes on further to say that

> the extent and richness of local knowledge in the natural and cultural environment that constitutes, we all assume, the product that eco-tourism seems to market. If the forests, the buildings, the musical traditions and the mangrove swamps are now part of the product, and if these resources need to be interpreted and presented in an interesting manner, then the creators and caretakers of those resources – the fisher folks, the craftsmen, the artists, the farmers – have much to offer in the enrichment and presentation of that product. They have an intimate knowledge and experience of that environment, which are as well part of the product.

Community tourism does not only mean the training of members of the community to become tour guides. Even when they become tour guides they should not only be able to identify the flora and fauna surrounding them. They should be able to interpret their environment. The local people should benefit economically from a park, reserve, or eco-tourism facility, and local communities should also have a hand in the decision-making concerning development of eco-tourism. Several such community projects lead the way in this regard. One such pioneer project is the Community Baboon Sanctuary, located along the Belize River, some 27 miles away from Belize City. It was established in 1985 and is a cooperative venture involving private landowners (a number of them are subsistence farmers), conservationists, organizations and researchers. Several other community projects are scattered throughout the country of Belize. Many of them initiate these programmes themselves. However, there still remains room for improvement in regards to education and training.

TRAINING AND DEVELOPMENT PRACTICES

The Role of Government

Although tourism is considerably a private sector activity, the government has taken interest in this sector since it is critical to the economy. Training is vital for maintaining and improving service in the tourism industry. "The Belize Tourism Board defined the priorities for the tourism sector as education and training and enforcement of environmental laws" (Government of Belize, 1991b).

The Belize Tourism Board has expressed its recognition of this need through a programme called "Team Belize", which has as its aim to get the entire country involved in tourism through public awareness and training. The Belize Tourism Board usually conducts training on its own, but has now created alliances with other training organizations throughout the country. "Team Belize" will focus on training "all front line individuals throughout the entire country of Belize", according to Anthony Mahler, deputy director, Product Development, Belize Tourism Board (News 5 Belize Web site). The Belize Tourism Board has also placed emphasis on training tour guides and taxi operators since these people usually have first contact with visitors and the first impression should be a "good" as well as a "lasting" one. Tourist Guide Regulations were passed in 1992 requiring that all guides be registered and meet standard levels of professional training and certification (Government of Belize, 1991b).

The Belize Tourism Board has also conducted training courses for the teachers of Belize. These teachers in turn go back to their schools and incorporate what they have learned about tourism into their lessons. It is hoped that the children will learn to value tourism at an early age while at the same time spreading the importance of it to the country.

Even though training is a priority for the Belize Tourism Board, it does not appear too practical, as the staff that is assigned this responsibility is incredibly small. This really poses a doubt as to whether or not the government actually sees this area as important to the development of eco-tourism.

Government plays a major role in proper and effective training activities for eco-tourism. For the most part, government is responsible for formal education and this needs to be a priority if the training is to be effective. As Sinclair (2000) states, "there is the recognition that some aspects of the tourism industry, especially those concerned with nature-based tourism, rely on highly specialised knowledge and training for advancement, and in this regard the services of academia are indispensable".

Sinclair also suggests that there needs to be a balance between industry and academic training, since "industry charges that academia is wasting precious time; academia counters that industry's view of relevance is too narrow". However, he further states that "a very tenuous consensus establishes that formal academic training assumes greater and greater importance as we ascend the occupational and skills hierarchy in the tourism industry". Institutional and community training need to be considered together in order to achieve a balance.

The Role of Non-Governmental Organizations

The Belize Audubon Society is one of Belize's major non-governmental organizations engaged in environmental education. They target communities surrounding protected areas and schools that invite them in for talks. Education is conveyed through lectures, films and slide programmes. The Belize Audubon Society trains wardens of protected areas to promote environmentally sound practices to visitors.

In 2000, one of the many workshops to be conducted for fly-fishing techniques was held. It was a joint venture between Programme for Belize (PFB) and Toledo Institute for Development and the Environment (TIDE) – both non-governmental organizations. Members of the local community of the Belize River Valley were taught techniques of fly-fishing to aid them in benefiting from the tourism industry. Programme for Belize also promotes and organizes eco-tourism and ecology field courses for school groups.

The Attitude of Workers in the Industry

Most of the subjects for the study conduct some form of supervision in their capacity. Workers are sometimes unreceptive to instructions from superiors. One respondent claims that it is difficult to find hard working, dedicated professional employees in the industry. This behaviour can be attributed to the type of people attracted to the industry. Support for this view can be drawn from the CTO study (1999), which concluded that the least trained staff were those at the unskilled level. In Belize, these unskilled workers are not the highest paid and there are no real incentives for them to pursue this path as a career.

Belize's hotel sector is made up primarily of small properties (mom-and-pop type operations) and the owner/manger is usually the human resources manager. Therefore, it can be said that not many establishments have a designated human resources manager, except for the handful of larger properties. However, most managers recognize the importance of creating a positive working environment. Even though it is a challenge, one respondent says that "most people get on-the-job training, and it is not easy to foster an environment of positive attitudes among employees". It can be concluded that management still needs to work on instilling in employees an understanding of the importance of tourism to them, the organization and the country.

TYPES OF EDUCATION AND TRAINING IN ECO-TOURISM

Education in eco-tourism is mostly informal, since there is currently no specific curriculum in place for it to be taught in schools. Whatever is taught is incorporated in some other subject area. The government and non-governmental organizations conduct hands-on training for those involved in eco-tourism. The institutions that offer training tend to focus more on hospitality than tourism and as such tourism ends up being neglected. Eco-tourism is usually geared towards communities surrounding Parks and Protected Areas. Something very outstanding is that many of these communities themselves initiate eco-tourism practices.

People who are qualified in tourism for the most part have achieved this through experience, many as entrepreneurs. Tourism is not a well-recognized field of study for the country of Belize. Those who do get recognized usually do so after returning from study abroad. Even so, women face a greater challenge than men when entering the industry at professional levels. The society still sees women working at the domestic level in the industry. However, this is slowly changing since the Belize Tourism Board is now headed by a female director.

LINKAGES AMONG ORGANIZATIONS

Government and non-governmental organizations work closely to conduct education and training in eco-tourism. Recently, both parties have exercised the recognition of working in partnership. There have been joint venture programmes among non-governmental organizations and government. However, there is not much coordination among private institutions.

The Belize Tourism Board has been very instrumental in the area and earlier this year established ties with other training organizations across the country of Belize, as they begin to recognize the importance of building linkages if the eco-tourism sector is to be successful. The government is now engaged in training immigration and customs officers in dealing with visitors.

RECOMMENDATIONS

- The government and private sector need to work together to develop strong service quality.
- Since training does not solve all problems, proper selection of employees can assist in improved service quality.
- Employers need to encourage input from employees.
- Employees should be given the opportunity to exercise what they have learned in training.
- Managers/supervisors need to support staff in utilizing skills they learn in training.
- Locals need to become more involved in research.
- Training programmes need to be decentralized so that the entire country can have equal access to training programmes.
- Those agencies responsible for eco-tourism development need to work closely with managers so they understand the importance of training staff.

- A long-term training strategy should be developed, including the creation of certification programmes through a national training institution.
- Locals should be encouraged to utilize the Centre for Hotel and Tourism Management programme (CHTM) in Nassau until a national training institution is created in Belize.
- Education about other cultures should be facilitated since the country is so culturally diverse.
- Decision-makers should be educated so that they know how their decisions can impact eco-tourism.
- More cultural events should be developed.
- The government should provide scholarships for degrees in tourism.
- Tourism should be included in the school curriculum, as in Jamaica's Infusion Programme that addresses K-12.
- There should be support and coordination for community-based activities.
- There should be a balance between academic training and field experience.
- Community members should be encouraged to develop entrepreneurial abilities.
- Training should keep pace with the speed of developments in technology.
- There should be continuous evaluation of training programmes.

CONCLUSION

This research has only begun to explore the role of training and education in eco-tourism in Belize. Since the concept of eco-tourism is relatively new to the destination, and not much research has been conducted, there remains much that can be tapped into. It is hoped that fellow researchers will explore this topic and reveal aspects that are still unknown.

This research has unveiled some of the challenges faced in education and training in eco-tourism in Belize. One aspect of eco-tourism, considered vital for its success, is community tourism. It was recognized that many communities in Belize possess the will to initiate eco-tourism practices. However, support from outside influences needs to be built. Often, the actions of community members are a result of their caring for their surroundings and the academic element is not really incorporated. It is hoped that organizations that offer an academic view of eco-tourism will assist in rounding out the knowledge of community members.

Governmental and non-governmental organizations have also been very active in trying to build education and training in eco-tourism. However, much more can be done to make eco-tourism more beneficial. Given Belize's natural, historical and cultural resources, eco-tourism has great potential for the country. However, it is imperative that it be carried out the proper way. Eco-tourism education and training need to be addressed seriously since effective eco-tourism practices cannot be successful if those involved and affected by the industry are not educated about the subject.

REFERENCES

Blackstone Corporation. (1998). Tourism Strategy Plan for Belize, Belmopan, Belize.

Belize Tourism Board. (1999) "Tourism: A National Priority for the Millennium", presented to the Caucus Meeting, July 14, Belize City.

Caribbean Publishing Company. (1999). *Caribbean/Latin America Profile: The Business Profile of the Americas.*

Caribbean Tourism Organisation (1990). "Caribbean Tourism: Igniting the Engine of Growth, Paper III, Human Resources Development", Caribbean Tourism Organisation, Barbados.

Government of Belize (1989). Integrated Tourism Policy and Strategy Statement, Government of Belize, Belmopan, Belize.

Government of Belize (1991a). National Park System Act 1981, Government of Belize, Belmopan, Belize.

Government of Belize (1991b). Integrated Tourism Policy and Strategy Statement, Ministry of Tourism and Environment, Government of Belize, Belmopan, Belize.

Nettleford, R. (1999). "Keynote Address: The Caribbean Artist's Presence and Education for the Third Millennium", *Caribbean Quarterly* 45 (nos. 2 and 3).

Pattullo, P. (1996). *Last Resorts: The Cost of Tourism in the Caribbean,* Ian Randle Publishers, Kingston, Jamaica.

Sinclair, D., (2000) "Books and Aprons: Finding the Balance between Academic and Industrial Training in Tourism in Guyana", presented at the Fourth Annual Conference on Sustainable Caribbean Tourism, Georgetown Guyana, May 19–22.

Quality Consultants (1999). *Tourism Training for the New Millennium: A Study of Tourism Education and Training Needs in the Caribbean,* Caribbean Tourism Organisation, Barbados.

Yves, R. (1991). Caribbean Conference on Eco-Tourism: Strategies for Increasing Community Involvement in Eco-Tourism, Belize City, July 9–12.

www.belizeaudubon.org

www.channel5belize.com

www.planeta.com

CHAPTER 11

TOURISM EDUCATION AND TRAINING IN THE COMMONWEALTH OF DOMINICA: PAST, PRESENT AND FUTURE

Susan M. Carter

Abstract

This chapter explores the current level of tourism and hospitality training and education in Dominica. The author points to a number of initiatives, past and present, that have been taken to provide quality education and training to teachers as well as the youth of Dominica in the areas of tourism and hospitality operations, and the impact of these programmes. Initiatives such as the Nature Island Standards of Excellence (NISE) and the Youth Environmental Service (YES) Corps are also discussed, along with the goals and objectives of these programmes. Education was identified as the key to sustainability and the future development of the tourism and hospitality sector in Dominica.

INTRODUCTION

This chapter provides an update on the status and direction of tourism education and training within the Commonwealth of Dominica. While references to past practices are indicated, elaboration on the present and future initiatives is the primary highlight of this chapter. Tourism education and training are now recognized as primary components in the future success of the tourism industry in the nation, within a highly competitive international marketplace. Dominica has a dazzling and unparalleled natural product and resources with which few nations can compete. However, Dominica recognizes that it cannot fully compete nor reach its potential within the regional and world tourism market without qualified human resources.

The ability of its present and future workforce to meet visitor expectations, perform occupational skills to high standards, and understand how to exploit its unrivalled natural product within a proper development framework can only be accomplished through industry training and formal education. Presently, expansion plans for formal tourism education lag behind those for industry training. Dominica's current thrust focuses on the development of youth as the nation's future tourism leaders and on the development of current industry workers through a national standards and training programme, the Nature Island Standards of Excellence, NISE.

Dominica, the largest of the Windward Islands, is situated at the northern end of the Lesser Antilles, lying between the two French islands of Guadeloupe to the north and Martinique to the south. The island is 29 miles long and 16 miles wide. Volcanic in origin and ruggedly beautiful, with some mountain ranges of nearly 5,000 feet disappearing into a halo of clouds, Dominica is a land of memorable ambience, unique experiences and spectacular nature-oriented activities.

Dominica, unlike traditional holiday destinations, does not offer its visitors the dilatory three Ss (sand, sun and sea) of mass tourist destinations, but rather nature-based and eco-tourism. Dubbed the Nature Island of the Caribbean, Dominica is an unspoiled paradise boasting awe-inspiring scenery, verdant mountains, pristine rivers, the world's largest boiling lake, towering waterfalls, flourishing rainforest, a myriad of endemic flora and fauna, whale watching, spectacular diving and the World Creole Music Festival. In 1997, its Morne Trois Pitons National Park was designated as a World Heritage Site by UNESCO.

For decades tourism was the nation's "other product", agriculture and specifically bananas being the first. Therefore for decades tourism experienced growth. Currently, Dominica is in the early stages of tourism development as compared to other nations within the Caribbean region. Sustainable tourism and, more specifically, nature-based eco-tourism, is Dominica's main tourism thrust as it strives to be the leading eco-tourism destination in the Caribbean.

Of Dominica's estimated population of 71,000, approximately 60% are under thirty years in age. These youth are the future of Dominica's emergent tourism industry. Presently, underemployment or lack of employment plagues Dominica's youth. Lack of customer service knowledge and basic occupational job skills is the primary reason for the current youth employment situation within the tourism industry.

An emerging awareness of the necessity of tourism education and training began in the early 1980s and has been slowly evolving over the course of the past two decades. Since the mid-1990s, more emphasis has been placed on the development of tourism education in the form of conducting tourism-related workshops and basic skills training in the tourism workplace. Additionally, there has been an increase in development and delivery of tourism awareness curricula for primary- and secondary-level students, who will become our future industry workers.

TOURISM EDUCATION

In 1983, a Social Studies Curriculum Guide was introduced in the primary schools of Dominica for grades K to 6. It was developed by a team of Caribbean educators under a Primary Education Project (PEP), funded by the US Agency for International Development. Since 1983 many changes have taken place in our society and the wider world. These changes have evoked the need for ongoing curriculum review and revision. The ongoing curriculum revisions that began in the late 1990s reflect the growing changes within the region, the world and within Dominica, as evidence suggests that increased intolerance, more violence, and an increased misuse of drugs is negatively impacting the tourism industry within the region. Additionally, there appears to be rapid erosion of traditional cultural and personal values. The economies of small island states such as Dominica have become increasingly threatened by these negative impacts.

The revised primary Social Studies Curriculum Guide does not depart fundamentally in structure from the PEP guide. It maintained in essence the spiral structure. It sought, like PEP, to develop an understanding of government at local, national and regional levels and a deepened appreciation of one's cultural heritage by engaging students in decision making and taking responsible actions to improve the human condition. Greater emphasis was placed on tourism, reflecting the movement of the Dominican economy from its banana base to service industry in which tourism is playing an increasingly prominent role.

The primary expectations of the revised curriculum were to promote greater respect for the environment and increased levels of tolerance for persons of all cultures and backgrounds, thus engendering a culture of peace. Within the revised curriculum teachers were invited to use experiential methods and freely modify recommended activities and evaluation exercises to meet the needs of their students. Teachers were given freedom to initiate other activities. Although recommended time elements for each activity and topic were provided, the actual time was open to the teacher's scheme of work and the strategies used in teaching a given topic or area. From all accounts, students have enjoyed the interactive nature of the revised curriculum and its activities while teachers have greatly appreciated the opportunity to add creative input through activities.

The consensus of the Department of Education, teachers and curriculum development specialists is that effective curriculum development, implementation and monitoring are predicated on a partnership between the curriculum unit and the teachers. Future revisions based on feedback and recommendations from teachers will be encouraged.

Current social studies curricula consist of the following themes and topics, using a building block approach from grades K through 6:

- Myself, my family, my school
- Providing for our needs
- Safety and drugs
- Communications
- Tourism perspectives, including work and occupations and the interdependence of world people
- Caribbean community (parts I, II and III) – heritage, people, customs, cultural practices, organizations, leadership roles, environment
- Our island community (parts I and II) – my community, our country, a changing society
- The world community (parts I and II)

Tourism Education Kit

The need for a Tourism Education Kit for teachers was identified in a national survey conducted with teachers in 1993 by the Division of Tourism and the Ministry of Education, under an Organization of American States (OAS)-sponsored Tourism Awareness Programme. The kit became a joint production of the Ministry of Education, Curriculum Development Unit and the Division of Tourism, National Development Corporation (NDC).

The original kit contained the official Ministry of Education tourism unit within the social studies syllabus, step-by-step classroom session modules and teaching aids. The kit was produced as a resource for teachers to enhance the teaching of tourism modules in grades 1 to 7 and was designed as a useful technical tool for teachers at the secondary school level. The kit has been developed with two main sections: tourism education for primary schools and tourism education modules.

Training modules are presented in outline, concept mapping and matrix formats with technical information contained throughout each module. During the kit development stage feedback from teachers indicated that teaching aids such as games, poems, songs, puzzles, essays and a variety of activities would be particularly effective resource tool, so a concerted effort was made to include a variety of teaching aid options throughout the modules. Upon completion the kit did not immediately become part of the curriculum as various ministries felt that revisions to particular modules were needed.

In early 2000 the Division of Tourism's Product Development Unit provided revision to the resource portion of the Tourism Teachers Education Kit by compiling a list of guest speakers and tourism industry resource personnel and making recommendations for field trip activity.

In April 2000 a decision was reached to launch the kit within the schools in September 2000 upon completion of minor revisions and updates to the Tourism Policy contained within the manual. This decision was part of the recommendations formulated at an interactive group meeting with education, curriculum development, the NDC and Division of Tourism officials and officers. At this meeting a plan of action for future revision, to begin in early 2001, was agreed upon.

In examining the Tourism Education Kit for Teachers in its current state, the group felt that although the materials presented were relevant and required, additional emphasis needed to be placed on current regional and world issues affecting the tourism industry in the areas of safety, crime, health and economic impacts. It was also determined that a full section should be devoted to Dominica's unique tourism product, which is primarily nature tourism and eco-tourism. It was also agreed that much more emphasis would be placed on:

- Guest and customer expectations
- How to provide effective customer care
- The major role that the hospitality industry plays within tourism
- Activities that emphasize the concept of hospitality as a service-based industry

The group also concurred that the primary focus of yearly revisions would be directed by the ongoing course and activity evaluation and recommendations provided by the teachers. During the school year 2000 an estimated 3,000 primary school children benefited from the training provided through the Tourism Education Kit.

Secondary Education

In Dominica, tourism education in secondary schools is outlined by the Caribbean Examinations Council (CXC) Syllabus. From form 1 through form 5 it is taught under the geography syllabus. To date, students preparing for the Ordinary level examination must undertake a comparative study between Caribbean tourism and tourism in Switzerland. As of the 2000–2001 academic year, only Caribbean tourism will be taught. Within this curriculum students are exposed to a variety of topics, such as tourism services, sites and attractions and the costs and benefits of tourism. The social studies curriculum also includes tourism topics. However, this subject area is not as widely taught at the secondary level as geography.

At the tertiary level, tourism forms an optional topic under geography as part of the Cambridge General Proficiency Examination (GPE) advanced level syllabus. Under the Caribbean Advanced Proficiency Examinations (CAPE), soon to be introduced at the Clifton Dupigny Community College, the tourism syllabus has expanded to include areas more relevant to the Caribbean situation. The curriculum to meet varied competencies under CAPE will include:

- Evaluation of tourism arrivals in selected developing countries over the past forty years
- Explanation of the social and economic factors accounting for the growth in tourist arrivals globally
- Explanation of the factors influencing the location of island- and non-island-based tourism
- Description of the physical characteristics of major tourist resort landscapes in a Caribbean country and the conflict over the use of the land resources
- Comparison of the pattern of arrival of tourists and the organization of the tourist trade between island- and non-island-based tourism
- Explanation of the development of package tours and all inclusive packages and the conflicts arising within the tourism sector

- Explanation of the success of efforts to protect the physical environment from the harmful effects of tourism in a Caribbean country
- Explanation of the interrelationship of tourism with the agriculture and service sectors in a Caribbean country

Currently there are no tourism vocational training institutes in Dominica, although several initiatives are being reviewed. In June 2000, representatives from the University of Guyana visited Dominica for preliminary discussion and an exchange of ideas with business and education stakeholders regarding establishment of strategic alliances toward the development of vocational training programmes.

Post-Secondary Education

Post-secondary education on tourism has been part of several initiatives throughout the 1990s. Currently, several dozen secondary school students attend tourism degree programmes in various schools in the United States, England, Trinidad and Tobago, Barbados, Canada, and at the University of the West Indies. With the emerging growth of tourism in Dominica and its large population of youth, a growing need and demand for schools offering associate and bachelor's degree tourism programmes will soon exist in Dominica.

In the fall of 1999 a serious effort to design, develop and open a hospitality training institute was initiated jointly by the NDC and the Ministry of Tourism. Stakeholders agreed that programmes should include offerings for certificate, diploma and associate degrees. Eventually a local tourism education consultant was retained to develop the pre-opening and general operating budgets, to define the classroom and laboratory space, to determine the furniture, fixture and equipment needs, to develop textbook and library needs, to analyse staffing needs and evaluate available local expertise, and to evaluate the curriculum for two associate-level hospitality and tourism programmes offered by two regional training institutes. It was agreed by all that the two degree programmes of most value to both the Dominican student and the Dominican hospitality employer would be those focusing on Hospitality Operations and Tourism Management. After the elections in January 2000 this project was placed on temporary hold to be evaluated by the new administration.

In the spring of 2000 another potential initiative was underway as principals from the University of New Orleans in Louisiana came to Dominica to conduct preliminary talks and networking. This university offers a four-year programme in Tourism Management.

TOURISM INDUSTRY TRAINING PROGRAMMES

Human resources development and training within all tourism sectors is one of the major challenges facing the region and certainly facing Dominica. To date training has been conducted using a piecemeal approach, as there has been no cohesive action plan set forth to address training issues.

During the past five years industry training in the form of seminars, workshops and one-off training courses has been conducted using regional training agencies and consultants, such as the Caribbean Tourism Organisation (CTO) and Retreats International. Much of this training has been paid for through the sponsorship of agencies such as the CTO, OAS, ENCORE, Nature Conservancy and American Express, or has been funded through the European Union–Lomé IV. These training programmes have been directly geared to the tourism industry worker and have addressed such topics as:

- Visitor service for tourism information officers
- Food and beverage service and skills training
- Customer service training for tourism taxi drivers
- Destination knowledge for tour guides
- Destination marketing

Within Dominica, the NDC has taken the lead in developing or identifying tourism sector training programmes. The NDC is a statutory body under the Ministry of Tourism, established in 1988 to stimulate, facilitate and undertake the development of tourism, industry and service activities in Dominica. The Division of Tourism is part of the NDC.

Most often the training presented by the NDC has been a collaborative effort in conjunction with the Division of Forestry, the Dominica Hotel and Tourism Association, the Dominica Water Sports Association, Red Cross and other key stakeholders. These training programmes have focused on customer service and skills development for tour guides, vendors, information officers, customs and immigration officers.

Challenges in Training

Dominica is faced with many training constraints and challenges. For instance, during the past few years a trend has been noted among the larger and more established regional hospitality training agencies, which have turned almost exclusively to serving "large hotels" and "large islands", as that is where the greater profitability lies. The training costs and expense fees charged by many of these agencies have become too high to be affordable to the average small tourism operator or small hotel property owner, which is the exclusive case in Dominica. This trend in high cost training has impacted the ability of the average Dominican service provider to afford training for staff.

Another challenge associated with the courses presented to date by off-island training agencies is that most have little built-in sustainability and none provide for the necessary follow up to ensure that a programme's long-term objectives are being met.

Dominica has an additional challenge to overcome due to the nature of its tourism business, particularly lodging establishments, which for the most part are small, independent and locally owned. In general, and basically due to lack of international exposure, Dominica's local tourism ownership does not have the knowledge, experience, or internal capability to develop and implement international standards, nor to train staff to these standards.

Being fairly new to the industry, neither local tourism industry ownership nor their workforce has had exposure to training in cross-cultural communications and tourism awareness. They, therefore, do not have a full understanding of the impact generated by this type of training upon visitor satisfaction and tourism revenue generation.

With an estimated 2,000 workers, most of whom are untrained, within the tourism sector, and recognizing the constraints at hand as well as the critical need for tourism training for current and future tourism workers, the government approved a document in February 1997 endorsing the development and implementation of training, certification, identification, security, licensing and regulations for all tourism sector providers in Dominica. The government decision was an endorsement of the NDC initiative to establish criteria for quality standards, excellence and professionalism and to provide industry training in support of the standards. The government appointed the NDC to be the authorizing agency to establish and implement all standards, training, certification and licensing in conjunction with appropriate ministries and departments.

Development of the NISE Programme

This government mandate was the catalyst for the Nature Island Standards of Excellence (NISE) programme which is currently being developed for the island of Dominica. The NISE programme is a multifaceted national standard and training programme jointly financed through contributions from the NDC and the tourism private sector of Dominica, and through financial contributions from the Caribbean Regional HRD Program for Economic Competitiveness (CPEC), a project funded by the Canadian International Development Agency. The NDC's Division of Tourism – Product Development Division is responsible for the design, development, implementation and management of NISE.

The NISE programme has three stages: development, implementation and follow up, which includes ongoing inspection, evaluation, and quality assurance. In June 2000 the standards development phase of this two-year programme began. The goal of NISE is to implement a sustainable, internationally accepted, and holistically approached HRD programme through development and implementation of customer service standards, supporting legislature, certification and licensing, facility standards, training and a compliance and monitoring system to measure and report results.

Standards development and training for fourteen tourism sectors were completed by 2001. These sectors include public agencies and workers, such as customs and immigration officers, tourism police officers, airport and port personnel, tourism information officers, and park wardens, as well as private sector agencies and workers in the restaurant, lodging, tourism taxi driver, ground tour operations, tour guide, vendor, car rental, travel agent, and dive and water sport industries.

NISE training focuses on customer service skills, tourism awareness, and cross-cultural communications training for all tourism workers, as well as the training and ongoing development of workplace industry trainers. In addition, a Welcome Dominica training programme will become a mandatory component of the certification and licensing requirements for all private sector tourism workers.

The objectives of the NISE programme not only address the industry HRD and training needs of Dominica, but are directly related to the nation's destination marketing and promotion goals as well. As a local company slogan states, "A trained workforce will deliver what an advertising campaign can only promise."

Key NISE programme aims are to address areas where the greatest HRD impact can be made while enhancing Dominica's competitiveness within the regional and international tourism community and while increasing the benefits to the local community.

The development of quality standards in the areas of product (the tangible) and service (the intangible) go hand in hand. Due to lack of international exposure, few tourism sector businesses in Dominica have a complete grasp of the type of international standards in both product and service quality that are required to become competitive or that are expected by visitors.

Dominica's competitive advantage in the tourism industry lies in its ability to offer a nature-based and eco-tourism product. One primary NISE programme goal is to ensure that Dominica reaps the major share of the fast-growing eco-tourist business within the region and internationally. However, in order to gain any competitive edge, Dominica must upgrade its standards to an international level of competitiveness in two focus areas:

- The development one of Dominica's most important tourism resources, its tourism workers, through training to NISE standards is considered a major factor in developing the economic competitiveness of Dominica's tourism industry.
- The development of physical plant/tourism facility requirements in terms of meeting international standards. This upgrading of current and future levels of tangible product and tourism facility must be an essential component of the island's national tourism development. The NISE programme addresses this critical development area through the development of facility standards for the restaurant and lodging industry. These standards will be designed to meet international criteria. Another component of the NISE programme is the development of internationally recognizable and compatible lodging classification and rating systems.

The future progress of the tourism industry in Dominica rests largely in the development, implementation and ongoing results monitoring of these internationally competitive standards for both customer service and facility. Analysis reveals that most training programmes fail due to lack of planning for long-term sustainability. Additionally, monitoring to evaluate results and to ensure programme goals and objects are met is another critical area that most agencies fail to develop and implement fully. The NISE programme addresses these key issues through implementation of a step-by-step approach. Sustainability features include:

1. The establishment of national associations – NDC will facilitate the establishment of the National Industry Trainer Association of Dominica and will serve in an ongoing advisory capacity to industry trainers.
2. NDC will facilitate the establishment of national associations for tourism sectors currently operating at less than optimal levels, such as tour guides and vendors. These national associations will be responsible for the dissemination of information and coordination of membership for ongoing training programmes.
3. The establishment of an ongoing monitoring programme to include inspection by trained quality assurance inspectors as well as auditing by an outside agency which will maintain the programme's high profile and integrity within the tourism sectors.
4. The training of industry on-the-job or workplace trainers from all tourism sectors to ensure that a qualified pool of trainers exists to service the tourism community.
5. Ongoing partnership with Dominica's tourism sector stakeholders and associations.

Dominica boasts a youthful population. Youth are the future of Dominica. Presently, underemployment or lack of employment plagues Dominican youth. This has resulted in a move away from traditional sectors as youth move into tour guiding, vending and other tourism-related activities. These youth need vital knowledge and skills training in the areas of environmental stewardship in order to develop into the future managers of our natural resources.

Development of the YES Corps

In response to this need, the Youth Development Division of Dominica is developing a Youth Environmental Service Corps (YES Corps).

During its pilot year, the goal of the YES Corps programme will be to mobilize a corps of fifty young people to be trained and educated in sustainable development and environment issues and to allow corps members to apply this knowledge by undertaking service activities and projects at the local and national levels. During its first year, trainees will be expected to complete two four-week residential programmes, followed by five eight-week programmes. Training programmes will be supplemented by the Youth Development Division. Objectives to be met through topics under the tourism portion of the programme include:

- To expose participants to the historical, physical and economic factors influencing the growth of tourism in Dominica
- To develop an understanding of the nature of Dominica's tourism product
- To investigate the relationship between tourism and the environment in Dominica
- To deepen the appreciation through field activities of the variety of tourism activities in Dominica and to establish an understanding of the challenges faced within each tourism sector
- To encourage critical thinking and analysis about the future development of tourism in Dominica
- To equip the participants with knowledge and skills that will facilitate their participation in the tourism industry in Dominica
- To develop within participants an appreciation of the global growth of tourism and the position of the Dominica tourism industry both internationally and regionally

Although the YES Corps programme goals primarily address environmental issues and development of knowledge and skills in environmental areas, it will also incorporate an interlinking tourism aspect within training modules and activities. It is fortunate that the programme is developing modules and activities with this emphasis. As Dominica accentuates eco-tourism and nature based tourism as its future, so it is imperative that its future tourism leaders have a full understanding and regard for protecting and conserving the island's resources. Those resources are the island's tourism future.

For the past five years the Youth Development Division has been offering a five-month Hospitality/Tourism programme. The programme is targeted at youth, ages sixteen and older, and provides basic knowledge and training in the areas of front desk, culinary arts and basic housekeeping. Programme facilitators are persons who are trained in the hospitality/tourism industry. Each programme has fifteen trainees and combines classroom learning with two weeks of on the job practicum. There has been a 75% job placement rate on programme completion. The programme is a success for the division, employers and the participants who become employed in the industry. The knowledge and experience gained during the course of the programme enables trainees to be better prepared in their occupations.

In 1999 the Ministry of Tourism developed a one-year pilot apprenticeship programme targeting 300 early school leavers and unemployed individuals between the ages of seventeen and twenty-five years. Trainees receive a stipend while attending the nine-month practicum-based training programme. Current operating programmes, developed in conjunction with the Clifton Dupigny Community College Technical Division, include those for essential building trades.

Currently under development are two tourism units for front office operations and tour guide operations. The goal for the tourism units is to apprentice a minimum of twenty trainees. Industry support and sponsorship has been high, with at least eight local tourism organizations or companies participating. The success of the pilot year will dictate continuation in the future.

CONCLUSION

At present tourism education and, in particular, tourism training are the focus of many initiatives and ongoing programmes. The future of tourism education and training in Dominica lies in the implementation of an integrated approach that links the efforts of the educational community with those of industry workers.

Although it is an industry-driven training and HRD programme, the national standards and training programme, NISE, can readily be integrated into the future education and training initiatives in Dominica. On a national level future initiatives of major benefit to the education community, to industry workers and to the tourism sector employers include the potential use of NISE industry standards as the foundation for:

1. A vocational education curriculum to be utilized for a career path programme for secondary-level students (ages fourteen to eighteen)
2. Workplace internship programme criteria
3. Adult apprenticeship programme criteria (adults, ages seventeen to twenty-seven)
4. A national workplace certification scheme
5. A basic skills-level programme for industry and the educational community

A linkage with these types of vocational education programmes could supply the industry with the workers who will be needed throughout the next decade as the tourism and hospitality industry grows in Dominica. With a four-year career path school and internship programme, Dominica could produce meaningful training and job opportunities at above minimum wage to youth who choose not to attend university as well as supply a work force already trained to existing national industry standards.

Sustainability is a key factor to the future of any industry training programme. Although addressed within NISE, additional sustainability should focus on the ongoing management of training and systems as well as on the follow-up, monitoring, measurement, analysing and utilization of results. This form of sustainability can be obtained through full communications between the newly developed Quality Assurance Division and the NDC Product Development Division.

Through NISE the Quality Assurance Division will be the agency mandated to perform tourism sector inspections and monitoring to ensure compliance with standards and regulations. It will analyse results and trends and report findings to the Minister of Tourism, the Division of Tourism and to stakeholders. It is essential that the unit operate in a transparent and objective manner while also maintaining a balance as a support service and advisory agency for all tourism sectors.

In its support service role, the Quality Assurance Division must provide recommendations for training and upgrading on an ongoing basis to the NDC Product Development Division, and act in a co-advisory capacity with that division in assisting tourism sector stakeholders to achieve national standards and upgrade resources – both natural and human.

12

RESHAPING THE WAY OF DOING BUSINESS IN HOSPITALITY EDUCATION

Guillermo J. Graglia

Abstract

This chapter examines the state of hospitality education in the Dominican Republic, which was identified as having the largest stock of hotel rooms in the Caribbean region. The author explores the view that hospitality institutions have not fully realized their potential because of their inability to view hospitality education as a business. He also speaks to the need for administration to keep abreast with changes in demand within the industry and among their student clientele in order to adjust their programmes to meet these demands. A number of challenges that can affect the future of hospitality education are also addressed and the need for strategies and policies to address these challenges is stated.

INTRODUCTION

In recent years all the sectors of the economy have gone through drastic changes in the way in which they conduct their business. Some earlier than others, almost no economic activity has been exempted from the effects of the political, socio-economic and cultural ups and downs at the end of the twentieth century. Among those in the Caribbean that have had a delayed reaction to this new environment are the institutions of higher learning, the universities.

As a sector of the economy, the hospitality industry is very far from the cooperative environment of *fusion, internationalization, strategy, managerial efficiency, competitive advantages, competition, re-engineering, total quality, revenue management, positioning, social marketing* and so on, concepts that reflect the preoccupations with which every executive must live today. It is difficult to consider the impact that these factors are having in academia if academics do not begin to consider themselves as executives capable of redesigning the way in which they conduct their "businesses" and transform them into competitive companies.

Universities, which are too focused on fulfilling their mission of social development, being a cloister of higher studies, and on the apparent "moral" incompatibility between "business" and "education", have surrounded themselves with an "academic aura" which has not allowed them to detect these changes in the form in which they carry out their mission, in a timely manner. Still today there are academics, both in the Dominican Republic and in other countries, who consider it a blasphemy to talk about "marketing a career" or naming the academic offering as "products" or coping with "aggressive competition". It would seem that universities still have not come to the internal realization that they are in a specific business: the education services business, and, as such, must satisfy a need with a profit – lucrative or not – for the institution. Even under the altruistic assumption of a house of higher learning, these institutions are not exempted from having to generate profits, which allow a certain capacity of reinvestment for the purpose of their growth, institutional development and the satisfaction of the requirements of the employees who work in them.

It is necessary for the actors who participate in this type of institution to set goals to redefine not their mission, but the way in which they should carry it out. If, after a profound analysis, there is a need to modify their methods, then they should set themselves to doing so, in order to play the starring role that universities have always played. Those universities that do not consider this premise as a valid goal in their declaration of objectives are condemned to having their survival dependent on the charity of others and on government subsidies, limiting their capacity to action to the economic availability of their benefactors.

THE CURRENT STATE OF HOSPITALITY EDUCATION IN THE DOMINICAN REPUBLIC

It is surprising, especially considering the size and number of inhabitants, the number of universities in the Dominican Republic that offer specialized programmes for the industry of hospitality at a higher level. There are approximately thirteen institutions that offer programmes of this type. In all, they add up to a population of almost 2,000 students, the majority of whom are concentrated in only five of those institutions. With a wide variety of names and duration, many of the programmes are similar as far as content is concerned. The heterogeneous quality and titles given these programmes is such that President Leonel Fernandez's government (1996–2000), through the Ministry of Tourism, has unsuccessfully tried to determine the basic and minimum contents of the syllabuses in order to standardize the names and contents of the programmes.

The programmes offered are at the bachelor's degree level, with an approximate duration of four years, divided into six-, four- and three-month terms. Almost all require an internship, some of them up to two or three months in length. Outside of the university context, there are a series of technical programmes, formal and informal, private and public (as, for example, the hotel management school in San Cristobal, created recently with the help of the Government of Spain), where students – mainly from the industry – can obtain certificates and diplomas up to technical levels. In addition, INFOTEP (National Institute for Technical and Professional Formation), works in the area of continuous education and skills certification.

Levels of Hospitality Education

Education for the hospitality industry in the Dominican Republic is distributed in the following manner:

- Technical/professional instruction: INFOTEP
- Technical-level education: some universities and vocational training institutes, for example, UNIBE-CATUR (Universidad Iberoamericana), Hotel Management Macorix School at the Howard Johnson Hotel
- University education: Pontificia Universidad Católica Madre y Maestra (PUCMM), UNIBE, Universidad APEC (APEC), Universidad Pedro Henríquez Ureña (UNPHU), and Universidad Católica de Santo Domingo (UCSD)
- Continuous education: local universities and foreign universities with distant learning courses, the Hotel Management School of San Cristobal

In view of such a wide and varied offering, it is not surprising that the professionals coming out of these institutions are also heterogeneous and difficult to compare, not only from the academic point of view, but also for the purposes of incorporating them actively into the industry. Focusing only on the university level, each year students join the labour market with bachelor's degrees in Hotel Management, Management of Tourism Enterprises and Tourism, to name a few.

On the other hand, considering the rapid growth of hotel room stock in the country, which at present amounts to almost 50,000, it would be logical to suppose that all these graduates would easily find work in their areas of specialization. However, this is not so. Approximately half of the graduates in hotel management and associated programmes do not end up working in hotels or in tourism. Of the remaining half of those young graduates, some set up food and beverage businesses of their own, others work in fast-food establishments and hotels.

Demand and Supply Gaps

The hospitality industry is not able to absorb the graduates who are available for employment. The reasons for this situation are varied and include the following:

1. The demand for qualified professional personnel is not geographically located at the points where the graduates live (the demand is concentrated especially in the north and east of the country).
2. The incentives (salaries and others) are not sufficient to motivate relocation.
3. The major hotel chains "import" their managerial personnel, thus limiting in part the possibilities of development of the new local professionals, discouraging their relocation.
4. Lack of facilities – housing, public services, training and other urban infrastructure – in the most important tourist centres, far away from the capital city, make it difficult for employees to carry out a normal social and family life.
5. Inadequacy of study plans to address the new reality and needs of the hospitality industry.

With regard to the last point, for a long time the industry claimed that the universities were not developing the professionals that they required. Numerous efforts were made to have the demand of the industry and the profile of graduates become more compatible.

Among the efforts was the delivery of a seminar called Hospitality Industry's Training Needs Assessment, organized by the Ministry of Tourism in 1998 at PUCMM, where all the professional and union associations of the national hotel/tourism sector were represented. However, this effort was not successful, since it concentrated specifically in the area of continuous education, which presents some special characteristics.

Adjustments to Curricula

It is, therefore, the universities that, individually, must have their own mechanisms to adjust and update their curricula. PUCMM, for example, has increased the proportion of elective courses that deal with current issues, and that allow the institution to react rapidly to the trends of the sector. In this way, in the last few years, subjects such as Operation of All-Inclusive Hotels, Cruise Management, Casino Management and German for Hotels have been created. This makes it necessary to carry out a thorough analysis of the study programmes and, in the case of the PUCMM, the elaboration of a complete reformulation of the bachelor's programme which was carried out in 1996. This change gave the students more freedom to choose the area of study they were most interested in, thus making their placement in the job market easier, and balancing in a better way, the credits assigned to theory and to practice.

On the other hand, the demand for postgraduate and master's studies in this area has increased noticeably. At present, no local university offers a master's degree in Hotel Management. Only PUCMM offers postgraduate studies in Hotel Management, with specialization in the all-inclusive concept.

The industry has stated, for quite some time, the need to offer intermediate studies at the technical level. Even though it is not generally accepted in the Dominican Republic that this is the responsibility of the university, right now, only the Iberoamericana University (UNIBE) has established a para-university department called CATUR which offers short programmes and diplomas in the area of food and beverage, pastry, and front desk. During 1999, PUCMM offered a programme that could be considered at a technical level, consisting of a diploma in Food and Beverages, lasting nine months, and another, Front Office Management, lasting six months. Both programmes were financed by the European Union/Lomé IV–Cariforum and were aimed at students from all the Caribbean countries. This experience has not been repeated basically due to financing restrictions.

There is another important void in the area of continuous education. In spite of numerous attempts by the universities to offer short programmes aimed at updating the management abilities of hoteliers, they have not been as successful as expected in view of the fact that this country has one of the most developed hotel industries in the Caribbean, especially in terms of size. The industry claims that it cannot send its employees to an off-property programme with inflexible schedules. The training is carried out in Santo Domingo, far from the hotel areas.

In particular, PUCMM tried offering courses to improve skills in tourist areas, sending its teaching staff to those areas, and the results were as unsuccessful as they are when they are offered in the city. There must, therefore, be other reasons for the lack of participation from the industry that have not been identified as yet. However, it is worth noting that each year in the summer months a growing number of hotel executives travel to the United States to take short courses, with correspondingly greater costs.

In 1999, the Dominican government, in response to these needs, with the help of the Spanish government, set up a Hotel Management School at the San Cristobal Hotel, in the city of the same name, located at a distance of 30 kilometres from Santo Domingo. This school has focused its attention on continuous education. Even with the presence of European specialists, and costs lower than those of the market, the results have not been, up to now, what was expected.

The Dominican education industry for hotel/tourism is characterized by:

- An excessive number of universities specialized in the area, with little to differentiate one from the other
- Dissimilarity in the programmes and titles
- Lack of a definition by the government of the minimum contents for the profession in order to standardize programmes
- The variety of offerings
- Little response from the tourist/hotel industry to continuous education programmes
- Considerable frustration on the part of students and graduates
- The need to develop mechanisms for permanent adjustment

- The growing trend of interest in postgraduate studies
- The superimposition of roles between the private and public sectors
- Financial restraints

CURRENT CRITICAL FACTORS IN UNIVERSITY EDUCATION FOR THE HOSPITALITY INDUSTRY

Some of the critical factors that education executives in the Dominican Republic face are:

- Cultural orientation
- Teaching staff; recruiting, maintenance and updating of skills
- Ensuring levels of quality
- Job placement after graduation
- Flexibility of curricula
- Financing
- Technology
- Expectations of students

The following is a review of the most important aspects of the above factors.

Cultural Orientation

There is no doubt that this is one of the most critical factors and requires the most drastic attention. It is no longer the day when the dean of a university is that excellent professor who was promoted to dean (or department head, or coordinator) in order to be recognized and rewarded. From that moment on, several management responsibilities became part of the daily work of that person and required managerial skills that, sometimes, he or she lacked. The person responsible for the academic unit can be identified as a manager of the work of the teaching staff and a friendly face to the students.

Then, who carries out the roles of leadership, motivation, creation of champions within the faculty? Who is responsible for the elaboration of performance policies, doing environmental analysis, establishing strategic objectives and elaboration of competitive strategies? Probably no one or, in the best case, a special planning unit that takes years to come up with a "strategic plan", not usable by anyone.

The university business of today is as dynamic as any other and demands a professional who acts as a real corporate manager, whether at the head of a department or of a division. He or she is a manager who takes risks, who has foresight and materializes it into reachable targets and workable policies. He or she is someone who manages existing resources and generates new ones. He or she is, in the management jargon, the real "entrepreneur" who manages the department as if it is his or her own business.

The academic director then becomes a manager of educational services, with the same characteristics described above. The term "manager" describes that person who every day decides the assignment of resources according to a strategic plan, who plans, organizes, coordinates, controls and evaluates permanently in order not to move away from the set course.

This is the new role of university management. Now, it is a real strategic business unit, requiring strategic direction and, therefore, a radical change in the cultural orientation of the university. The university is conceived as a competitive business, that is, a complete set of resources organized towards a determined objective: offering an educational service of the best level of quality.

Expectations of Students

Most hotel management students in the Caribbean think that they will graduate as "hotel managers". This false assumption caused high levels of frustration among the first graduating class who considered that they had invested in a career that prepared them to be general managers. The work to make them realize this was slow, but measures were taken not to create false expectations. Through conferences, orientation from professors and visits from hotel general managers, little by little a change has occurred. A hotel management university graduate is a person with the potential to be manager once his or her abilities have been developed through practice.

Teaching Staff

Today more than ever difficult decisions have to be made to choose between "professional professors" or "professionals who are professors". No one doubts that the optimum choice would be to have a professor who would have the necessary knowledge and experience of a hotel executive or a hotel executive who handled well the techniques of teaching. However, these qualities seldom coincide in one individual.

On the other hand, it is more and more difficult to retain good professors, since the university professional career is not as attractive as others and so they find better working conditions in the industry due to the fact that teaching salaries more often than not are relatively low. Efforts must be made to implement alternatives of professional and financial development for the faculty, so that they can complement their teaching task with an attractive and challenging professional career.

In the case of PUCMM, business units have been created within the department that allow professors not only to complement their income, but also keep themselves up to date and in contact with the industry. For example, a catering company has been created that services the university community and the general market and a unit of Professional Services provides consulting services to the sector.

The development of the teaching staff is another point that is sometimes forgotten. Complications created by the part-time dedication of the faculty, the difficulty in coordinating schedules and the lack of motivation to take these courses are causes for not implementing them. A programme, not isolated courses, must be developed to update the teaching practice and also the teaching skills of professors to ensure the improvement of the faculty, the enrichment of their experiences and the improvement of the quality of teaching in the classrooms. In-house teacher training courses and professional internships are examples of actions that could be taken.

Ensuring Levels of Quality

Maintaining a certain quality standard from the point of view of the client is a permanent issue of every business and, therefore, must also be that of a university. However, defining the concept of quality applied to the university, as well as identifying who the clients are, raises questions with answers that are hard to find, for example: Who is a good teacher? With respect to the market, who is really the client – industry for which we are "producing" professionals, or the student who "pays" for the service?

This is a question to be discussed which exceeds the scope of this chapter, but it is certain that, as in other service businesses, educational institutions must be capable of ensuring a certain uniformity or consistency in the education service and producing a "final product" (the hotel management graduate) to satisfy the needs of the consumer (the industry).

Managerial efforts should also be focused on developing total quality programmes based on:

- Development of a "quality" oriented culture
- Implementation of incentive programmes aimed at continuous improvement
- Development of systems to measure and control key variables
- Development of systems to recognize achievements
- Reformulation of the professor's role as manager of resources within the classroom and of the academic director as the manager of a business unit

All of these issues deserve to be considered separately. Some have already been analysed, but together they are a necessary requirement to set off and keep the spark of total quality going in these organizations.

Job Placement after Graduation

Hundreds of new professionals each year are unable to find employment in the industry, but instead abandon their profession to work in another sector of the economy. The extent to which graduates are placed quickly and preferred by the industry is an indication of the quality of an academic programme. For these reasons, providing assistance in making the transition from the academic world to the business world is more and more the responsibility of the school. Through the creation of career placement programmes, approaches to the industry, recruitment days and professional orientation, the gap can be reduced, making it easier for young professionals to gain entry into the business world.

Flexibility in the Syllabus

As the business environment changes, the syllabus must also change to adapt to the new realities of the hotel business. Through the analysis of trends, observation of the environment and specific requests from the industry, educational institutions can identify these new requirements of the business sector. Educational institutions must be able to adapt their programmes quickly enough to keep the education and training they provide to date. At PUCMM, the curricula are analysed every two years and reforms are proposed. In addition, there are different areas of concentration and a greater selection of elective courses.

Universities that are not capable of designing mechanisms to make themselves flexible and update their syllabuses will soon become obsolete, since they will have a product that nobody wants to consume. In other words, the university must adapt its academic offering proactively to the demand of the industry, anticipating changes.

Financing

In many educational institutions, budgets are used as a means of control "after the fact". The correction time becomes extremely long and the decisions that involve financial resources become bureaucratic and inoperative.

If it is necessary that the university manager develop his or her enterprising spirit to ensure the growth of the business unit, then he or she must also have a budget to suit the approved work plan. It will be the manager's responsibility to implement it, and, just as an estimate of expenses is prepared, he or she should also have an estimate of income, just as it is the practice in any normal commercial activity. Academic directors are often not aware of the economic impact of their decisions. In some cases, reinforced by the non-profit orientation of the institution and the social purpose of the university, the possibility of generating earnings through any academic activity is not given much attention.

Teaching and making profits seem incompatible. The fact that there are institutions that are non-profit should not mean that it is not the manager's responsibility to generate earnings, but simply that the profit made is not distributed at the end of the month and should be reinvested in the operation. It is necessary to change this. The academic director, as the head of a business unit, should have, as one of his or her objectives, a financial profit as well as an operative or strategic one. If not, his or her performance will always be limited by the extent to which the state or other stakeholder – charitable entity or private business – is willing to provide funding, on the basis of its own interests, to ensure the continuity, development and improvement of the department or school.

NEW CHALLENGES

In summary, in order to be successful in the business of university education, academics should be well focused on the following:

- Ensuring and maintaining standards of quality. This implies maintaining a strategic alignment with the needs of the industry.
- The influence of technology in the education process.
- Change in the cultural orientation of the university in the modernization process.
- The reformulation of the role of the academic director into that of general manager of a business unit of education services.

In specific terms, what is happening in our industry? Based on the experience of the PUCMM in the last few years, an institution that has played a leading role since 1981 in university education for the hospitality industry, the following are some of the main trends and new products that have appeared and are influencing daily work.

Growing Emphasis on the Teaching of Languages

Traditionally, the teaching of languages has been associated with hospitality education; however, there is a growing trend related to the variety of languages required in order to graduate. At present, English is still considered a basic requirement – especially for a Spanish-speaking country – but a growing interest is observed in English-speaking Caribbean countries in learning Spanish and other languages, depending on the nationality of the tourists who visit each country. In the case of the Dominican Republic, English is still first, with approximately 1,000 hours of training or the Teaching of English as a Foreign Language (TOEFL) equivalent, but other languages have been added, such as French, German and Italian, all at conversation level and limited to the hotel/tourism environment.

Certification of Skills

A common problem that all hotels in the Dominican Republic have is that a large part of their basic personnel does not have suitable education or academic preparation. In many cases, they have barely finished the lower levels of primary school. This makes the development of in-house training difficult and causes a very wide gap between the requirements of the position and the inventory of academic qualifications of the individual. For this reason, some hotels have requested a process of certification of skills where the university evaluates the employee and determines if he or she is capable or not of carrying out the duties of the position. If the person fulfils the required conditions for the position, he or she is admitted as competent or, if not, the areas in which the employee must develop are identified.

University Consortiums and Interinstitutional Cooperation

Another trend that is already a reality is the establishment of university consortiums, offering joint programmes, in many cases itinerant, resulting in a double certification. In our case, numerous programmes have been developed with these characteristics, the most successful being Global Connections, an alliance between PUCMM, Tompkins Cortland Community College of the New York State University and the Technological Institute of Rochester. This field holds great potential for – and within – the region, in which there are already well-known universities, which could join their efforts towards similar programmes.

More can be accomplished by interinstitutional cooperation. The limitations of human and financial resources force educational institutions to invent new ways of doing things with greater levels of quality and competitiveness. In the region there are different associations that allow them to work together, such as the Council of Caribbean Hospitality Schools (CHOCHS), the Council on Hotel, Restaurant Institution Education (CHRIE), the International Hotel and Restaurant Association (IH&RA), the Pan American Hotel and Tourism Association (CONPEHT) and the Regional Tourism Internship Exchange System (RTIES), the latter created recently. In that respect, our best and most recent experience has been with the Aguadilla campus of the Inter-American University of Puerto Rico, with which PUCMM organizes an International Congress of Hotel Management every year.

Certification of Experience

Many people have "become professionals" after years of working at their jobs – "coming up through the ranks" – and they see their possibilities for professional advancement limited by not being able to do postgraduate studies. PUCMM is developing a programme to recognize the experience of individuals for the purpose of gaining them entry into academic programmes.

Programmes of Tourism Awareness at Technical and Pre-University Levels

There is a tendency in the Dominican Republic not to place much value on studies in the areas of hotel management and tourism. The family often discourages young members as a result of not having enough knowledge about the matter. It is necessary to address this problem by educating high school seniors about the importance of tourism, so that they can see the industry as a possible source of challenging and rewarding professional development.

Every year, PUCMM implements a programme of visits to schools for that purpose, informing and offering orientation to students about the possibilities that exist, widening their horizons about the traditional idea that this profession is limited to a reception desk at a hotel or to the kitchen. By this means PUCMM indirectly reaches the family by providing first-hand information to the student about his or her potential professional career.

Distance Learning Programmes: Virtual Campus and Off-Campus

The appearance of the Internet has completely changed our lives and has given a new twist and life to distance learning programmes. It is necessary for universities to incorporate this technology, which does not limit itself only to posting a text and assignments. An effort is being made to create real virtual campuses, the potential of which is practically unexploited. In the Dominican Republic there does not exist, up to now, any programme at university level run on the Internet and aimed at the hotel/tourism sector. Probably one of the more serious limitations to doing this is the small number of personal computers among hotel employees and the limited access to, and knowledge of, the technology necessary to run virtual courses.

Off-campus distance learning programmes are limited to continuing education. In response to growing demand for continuing education at tourist centres far away from the city, the PUCMM began to offer a postgraduate degree in Hotel Management off-campus, moving instructors and materials to the hotels, concentrating the classes at one geographical location. This experience was successful since there were more than 100 students enrolled in the programme.

Growing Role of the University as a Source of Recruitment

Hotels have changed their recruitment policies and more frequently are requesting the services of the university for the purpose of recruiting personnel. This service, which is free to the industry, makes it necessary to keep updated files of graduates and to have a system of continuous communication with all of them. PUCMM has moved from a "rudimentary" system of job placement for graduates to the launching, in April 2000, of a Web site for graduates where they can find job offers and post their resumés for perusal by the companies.

Regional Training Programmes

The programmes financed by the Lomé IV–Cariforum agreement have opened a range of possibilities and expanded frontiers for the activities of universities in the Dominican Republic. PUCMM has managed all the programmes in the area of tourism, offering in 1998 and 1999 programmes in Language Training (English and Spanish), Methodology in Language Teaching, Certificate in Food and Beverages, Certificate in Front Desk Operations, a cooperative programme with Quisqueya University of Haiti for the establishment of a hotel programme and a programme for the exchange of hotel and tourism internships. All of these programmes ended in 1999 with the participation of more than two hundred citizens from Caribbean countries. The success of this programme prompted the formation of a network of education institutions – RTIES – to ensure continuity in the exchange of internships, both for students as well as for employees of the industry.

Lengthening of Internships

Many hotel chains have requested the extension of student internships. In general, all the universities in the country require students to participate in two internships, lasting from six weeks to three months, in order to graduate. Hotels say this is too little time for interns to get to know the operation of a hotel and that the ideal time would be six months. This has made PUCMM analyse the impact that this would have on the study programmes.

Development of Postgraduate Programmes

In spite of a growing demand for postgraduate studies, no university in the Dominican Republic offers master's-level studies and only the PUCMM offers a postgraduate programme in Hotel Management. One of the obstacles that exists in the development of this type of programme is the lack of professors with the necessary academic qualifications and publication records to give classes at that level. Also, considering that the persons most interested in this activity are executives in hotel operations, the long distances between the university and the hotel areas is an unavoidable hurdle when considering offering this kind of programme.

Certification of Hotel In-House Programmes

Some companies of the sector are interested in having the university certify their internal training programmes. This is why, for example, PUCMM has established agreements of collaboration with two of the most important local hotel chains for the purpose of recognizing academic credits from their own training programmes towards a university degree.

Social Assistance Programmes

Every university must have the social objective of contributing to the development of the community. It should also act as a catalyst for social assistance programmes, bringing together the parties that can help. Based on this principle, PUCMM has taken as a point of reference a programme implemented in Thailand, at the suggestion of the Pan Pacific of Bangkok, that recruits adolescents, especially girls, who are in danger of exploitation and gives them practical training in hotel operations. In this manner they are offered the possibility of a job and an alternative to prostitution or crime. This programme was so successful that today there are many hotels participating, and it has the sponsorship of UNICEF.

At the suggestion of an international aid organization, PUCMM analysed the programme and is developing a proposal for cooperation with UNICEF in the Dominican Republic, as well as one of the major local hotel chains to start the Dominican chapter of this programme this year.

CONCLUSION

What common element is observed in all the programmes presented? What moving forces can be isolated to allow hospitality educational institutions to improve their capacity as university strategists in the business of the hospitality industry? They are as follows:

1. Related to business/organization
   - Strategic approach to the university business
   - Modification of the role of academic director to university manager

- Emphasis on service
- Emphasis on quality – internal and external, organization-wide
2. Related to the academic product mix
   - Flexibility of university curricula
   - Non-traditional educational products
   - Emphasis on quality
   - Non-traditional approaches to the industry
   - Merging of technology in the education services
3. Related to a global character
   - Regional integration
   - Inter-institutional cooperation

Through the serious work of strategic reflection about these forces which are reshaping the way of doing business in the hospitality sector, hospitality educational institutions can ensure that they assume a leading role in the development of society, with the ideal of making the world a better and fairer place, providing equal opportunities for all. This should be the mission and challenge for these institutions.

ACKNOWLEDGEMENT

This chapter was prepared with assistance from Dr María Luz de San Martín and translated into English by Ms Lillian Ramos.

CHAPTER 13

PAST, PRESENT AND FUTURE ROLE OF EDUCATIONAL INSTITUTIONS OFFERING HOSPITALITY TRAINING IN GRENADA

Naline Ramdeen-Joseph

Abstract

Grenada's two hospitality institutions – the T.A. Marryshow Community College (TAMCC) and the New Life Organisation (NEWLO) are examined and discussed in this chapter. Both institutions were born out of a need to provide trained staff for a burgeoning tourism industry. Since their inception, these institutions have trained over five hundred students in various aspects of hotel operations. While both institutions may be described as successful in achieving their stated goals, they face a number of challenges, including limitations of staff, physical facilities and, most significantly, finances. Local and external funding, which have been used to expand the physical facilities and to train trainers, have somewhat alleviated these problems and there are plans to further expand TAMCC and to introduce an associate degree programme. The author notes the planned introduction of a degree programme at St George's University and concludes with recommendations to coordinate and streamline all of the programmes in order to maximize their contribution to the tourism product.

BACKGROUND ON GRENADA

Grenada is the largest of the three islands that make up the tri-island state of Grenada, Carriacou and Petite Martinique. It is the most southerly of the geographical grouping known as the Windward Islands and is located 12 degrees north, 63 degrees west. The island is 21 miles long and 12 miles wide, with a population of around 100,000.

Grenada's geological formation is mainly volcanic, its terrain hilly and interior vegetation lush green. The island is divided into seven parishes. The city of St George's, the capital, is renowned for its picturesque, land-locked harbour. Other attractions include the world-famous Grand Anse Beach and the Grand Etang Forest Reserve, with a crater lake and various waterfalls and historic forts. These features contribute immensely to the popularity of the island as a tourist destination, and visitor arrivals – both cruise ship and stay-over – have recorded increases. This situation has given rise to the need for well-trained personnel in the industry.

This chapter examines the two tertiary educational institutions in Grenada that offer hospitality training programmes, the New Life Organization (NEWLO) and the T.A. Marryshow Community College (TAMCC). The chapter examines programme content as well as the struggles of these institutions to obtain recognition, their successes and the challenges hindering their efforts. An overview of each institution is presented, as well as their present and future role in the shaping of human resources in Grenada. The St George's University also has commenced a degree programme in Hospitality and Resort Management and the future role of the St George's University is also discussed.

THE TOURISM AND HOSPITALITY INDUSTRY IN GRENADA

The tourism industry in Grenada is still very young and its potential is yet to be tapped. The country has always depended on the agricultural industry for its survival but due to problems of fluctuating prices, low yield, declining exports and crop diseases; the tourism industry has taken on added significance. "The government has determined that tourism should be a major element of its economic development and views it as the key to economic survival" (Government of Grenada, 1997).

Over the period 1986 to 1995, stay-over visitor arrivals increased more than 100%, and cruise ship arrivals by some 119%. Growth was particularly strong during 1989 to 1991 and again in 1993 (Grenada Board of Tourism, 1995). The United States is the single most important market for Grenada and visitor arrivals from that country has shown consistent growth over the period. Other important markets are the United Kingdom and the Caribbean, although the latter market has fallen in significance for Grenada since the post-revolutionary period. Grenadian residents abroad also represent a significant proportion of stay-over arrivals and this category has maintained steady growth to date. Although tourism has been identified as the engine for economic growth by past and present governments, words have yet to be significantly translated into action, and the industry faces a number of constraints, including a lack, or inadequate preparation, of human resources.

Educational institutions, both government and private, have been operating without a policy framework from the Ministry of Education and have developed curricula based on their surveys and linkages with the local industry. According to the 1995 *Annual Abstract of Statistics* from the Ministry of Finance in Grenada, "There were a total of 24,650 employable persons in Grenada." Of that amount the tourism industry employed an estimated 3,539 persons or 14% directly. There were a total of 1,497 or 51% in the accommodation sector and the others were engaged in the delivery of a variety of services such as tour operations, vending and water sports operations.

Critical to the development of tourism in Grenada is the provision of education and training. The increase in numbers, the capacity of tourism enterprises and tourist demands for quality goods and services require well-trained personnel for the variety of jobs in the industry. In order to pacify the hoteliers, who continuously demanded trained personnel, the government established a hospitality department within the TAMCC.

THE T.A. MARRYSHOW COMMUNITY COLLEGE

The TAMCC was established in July 1988, following an amalgamation of six educational institutions with varying entry requirements, from the local School Leaving Exams (14+ exams for students failing the Common Entrance Exams) to A levels. One of the institutions incorporated into this new entity was the Domestic Arts Institute, located at Tanteen, St Georges.

Initially, the Home Economics Department at TAMCC was only able to attract students who failed both the Common Entrance and School Leaving Exams. Its main function was to provide basic skills training of six months duration in the following areas: cookery, cake and pastry making, housekeeping, sewing and child care. It provided the only option for students who were described as being "good with their hands and not with their heads".

The transformation of the curriculum took place a year later, moving its focus from Home Economics to Hospitality Studies. The new thrust began with a formal survey of food and beverage and accommodation establishments throughout Grenada in order to determine their needs. The results of the survey indicated that multiskilled personnel were needed, as most hospitality establishments were small and owner-managed. There was also great demand for cooks, wait staff and housekeepers due to a high turnover in these areas. As a result, two programmes, Hotel and Catering Operations and Food and Beverage Operations, were developed and the owners and managers of these establishments were given an opportunity to make contributions and comments on the programme contents.

Hotel and Catering Operations

This two-year programme is composed of six semesters and its target market is the graduates of secondary schools throughout Grenada, with a minimum of two CXC/GCE O level passes. Students enrolled in this programme must be sixteen years and over. The programme equips students with the necessary skills in a number of areas in the hospitality industry. The curriculum includes courses in housekeeping, meal preparation, tourism and social awareness, sanitation and safety, French, Spanish, mathematics, accounts, interpersonal skills and food and beverage service. Introductory courses in supervisory management and entrepreneurship are also included to provide students with a foundation for further career advancement and the opportunity to be self-employed.

The average class size for this programme is fifteen persons. Due to staff limitation, the traditional approach was to operate with one batch at a time so that students would graduate after two years and another batch enrolled. This method of operation was changed in 1996, and students entering this programme are now admitted every year, due to an increase in staff and financial support for the college. Students graduating from this program are employed as cooks, waiters/waitresses, accounting clerks, front-office personnel and housekeepers, among others. Students' chances of upward mobility are greater when compared to students enrolled in the Food and Beverage programme discussed below, due to their higher qualifications and level at which the programme is delivered.

Food and Beverage Operations

This one-year programme consists of three semesters and provides participants with the necessary knowledge and skills to be waiters/waitresses, cooks, chambermaids and tour guides. The programme targets graduates of primary schools who have been successful at the local "school leaving exams" or have passed the Hospitality Department's entrance exam.

The syllabus covers craft training, with an emphasis on the practical areas of housekeeping, meal preparation and service. Other supporting courses offered are interpersonal skills, tourism and social awareness, sanitation and safety, introduction to the hospitality industry, among others. The average class size for this programme is eighteen persons.

Structure of Programmes

The programme at the Department of Hospitality at the TAMCC is a combination of theory and practice. The two-year programme consists of four semesters in-house and two six-week internships at tourism and hospitality establishments throughout the country, while the one-year programme is composed of three semesters at the college and a six-week internship at hotels and restaurants.

The practical exposure offered to students at the college is affected by limited dining room and kitchen facilities, insufficient staff as well as inadequate financial support from government. To address this problem, the curriculum and the timetable are designed to support the academic content by offering practical exposure to students through participation in the following activities:

- Six-week internships at hotels, restaurants, travel agencies and the Grenada Board of Tourism
- Day-release exercises at selected hospitality establishments (students are placed on a day-to-day basis at these establishments to gain an insight into the operations of certain departments)
- Catering to the general public once or twice per month from the dining room facilities at the Department of Hospitality (two classrooms were converted into a dining room in 1990 and can accommodate approximately forty persons)
- Catering to government departments, non-governmental organizations and hosting special functions
- Provide food and beverage service personnel to the public where possible at rates and conditions negotiated by staff of the Department of Hospitality

- Working at local businesses as part-time staff during school vacations, peak periods and special functions
- Day-release exercises on cruise lines (the Princess Lines collaborates with the college to accommodate the students for additional exposure within various departments for the duration of their stay in port – usually eight hours)

At present, the Department of Hospitality lacks a proper food and beverage training facility similar to institutions in the Caribbean, for example, the University of Technology, Jamaica, with its training restaurant facility, Lillian's, and Barbados Community College with its modern hotel facilities, Pommarine. The methods utilized by the TAMCC are therefore necessary especially as it relates to the acquiring of hands-on experience.

Programme Content

The programme content is patterned on what is offered at Bermuda College, the University of Technology, Jamaica and Barbados Community College, with modifications made to suit the needs of the industry locally. In 1991, the entire staff of the Hospitality Department paid a week-long visit to the Barbados Community College to obtain first-hand knowledge of their operations, liaise with staff and upgrade the programme content.

The staff had the opportunity to tour the college and restaurant facilities. Information on the programmes offered at Barbados Community College was shared with TAMCC staff who used these as guidelines to improve programme content and course outlines. Additionally, the programme has benefited from the collective experiences of the present staff who attended various regional and international institutions.

Staffing

The Hospitality Department is part of the Technical Division of TAMCC. Responsibility for this department rest on the shoulders of the dean of Technical Studies. Supporting the dean is a head of the Hospitality Department, who has the overall responsibility for the day-to-day operations.

The teaching staff consists of three full-time persons with formal training in the field, two with bachelor's degrees in Home Economics and Tourism Management, respectively, and the other presently pursuing a bachelor's degree in Tourism. The head of this department recently completed the MSc in Tourism Management at the University of the West Indies, Mona, Jamaica.

Other aspects of the curriculum are handled via the collaborative efforts of the staff from other TAMCC departments along with representatives from local hotels. They cover the support and practical areas of the curriculum, respectively.

Despite its many problems over the years, the programme has been very successful and reports a 75% graduation and employment rate. The annual student population has been predominantly female, with an average ratio of 98% female to 2% male. During the initial stages of the programme only a few establishments participated in the internship programme and were reluctant to hire students upon graduation. This has changed over the years with the total participation of all establishments, including the Grenada Board of Tourism, travel agencies and recently the cruise lines.

At present, the Department of Hospitality of the TAMCC is the principal government training institution offering hospitality studies in Grenada. There has been improvement in numbers and academic level of students who enrol in the programmes. Students are now accepted based on interest and qualification, rather than coercion or as a last option. Upon graduation, at least 75% of the students find employment, the majority, at their place of internship. To date approximately 330 persons have graduated from the programme at the TAMCC.

Challenges

Since its inception, the Hospitality Department of the TAMCC has faced and continues to face a number of challenges. The greatest challenge is the misunderstanding by government and the Ministry of Education of what the institution needs to deliver the programme effectively. Unfortunately, it is still viewed as "a place where someone learns to cook". This attitude is filtered out to the public, and students are perceived as not being able to cope academically.

Second, recognition and support from the industry have been difficult to achieve and extremely slow in coming. Inputs from the industry were not extended beyond the internship level and no contribution was made to programme content or other areas. Other constraints identified by the Government of Grenada (1997) were:

- Inadequate budgetary allocations
- Lack of appropriate facilities and equipment, especially for the delivery of practical training in the areas of housekeeping, meal preparation and food and beverage service

- Inadequate staffing
- Lack of staff development (there has been no emphasis on staff development by government and further education and training is undertaken on the individual's own initiative)

The Future

The Department of Hospitality underwent some major renovation in 2000. The expansion was funded by the European Union (EU) under the Lomé IV agreement. The kitchen facilities were expanded to reflect what is applicable to training institutions of such a nature. In addition, a dining room, two classrooms, office for the head of the department, staff room, shower and changing facilities for students and staff were added. Government provided counterpart funding for equipping the building.

NEW LIFE ORGANISATION (NEWLO)

Background

The other training institution offering hospitality training in Grenada is the New Life Organisation (NEWLO). It is a Catholic vocational and skills training centre for youths, located at Palmiste in the parish of St Johns, Grenada. "The centre caters to disadvantaged young people of all background and religion, facilitating growth and development of the individual in relation to family, the community and the nation" (Government of Grenada, 1997). The aim of the institution is to provide quality vocational skills to students who are over age sixteen, and were not successful in the local School Leaving Exams or who did not have the opportunity to complete their primary school education. Since its inception NEWLO has played a vital role in the education of young Grenadians, providing the only option to acquire marketable skills.

The Programme

The Hospitality Arts programme was introduced in September 1994 out of the need for more skilled people in this field. It is patterned after the SERVOL model in Trinidad and Tobago (a programme providing vocational training to young Trinidadians and Tobagonians), but tailored to suit the needs of Grenada. The programme is designed to accommodate a maximum of twenty students and is run over a six-month period and includes courses in food preparation and menu planning, food and beverage service, social skills, housekeeping operation and cleaning science, purchasing techniques, basic front office skills, mathematics, and communication skills. Prior to enrolment in the hospitality programme, students must complete the Adolescent Development Programme (ADP), which serves to build character and confidence. These courses include self-awareness, public speaking, literacy and numeracy, spirituality, parenting, health and physical education, environmental awareness and social studies.

Industry exposure is a necessary component for the completion of the hospitality curriculum. Students are required to complete a four-week internship at a number of hotels, including Rex (Grenadian), La Source, Flamboyant and Calabash. NEWLO also provides its students with hands-on experience through the operation of its Dove Restaurant, which is open once per week.

The institution is funded primarily by the Catholic Church, non-governmental organizations, international funding agencies, government and private individuals.

Challenges

The major challenges facing NEWLO are:

- Lack of available space to accommodate more students
- Inadequate facilities for the provision of practical training
- Inadequate financial support
- Insufficient and inadequate staffing
- Lack of recognition given to NEWLO certification by the local hospitality industry and institutions of higher-level hospitality studies within the country

ST GEORGE'S UNIVERSITY

Results from a feasibility study conducted in 1995 revealed that there was a demand for trained personnel in the tourism and hospitality industry, especially at the supervisory and managerial levels. There was a need for more hotel managers and professional chefs. As a result, a proposal was put forward by the St George's University to its board of directors to offer a bachelor's degree in Hotel and Resort Management. The institution will focus primarily on meeting the needs identified, as well as offer short-term training in other aspects of the hospitality industry. These will include management skills, bar technology, culinary skills, front office procedures, and foreign languages, among others (Government of Grenada, 1997).

According to Dr Theodore Hollis, coordinator of the hospitality programme at St George's University, "This new programme will be offered jointly by St George's University and the New England Culinary Institute. Its duration would be four years, with students spending two years at St George's University and the remaining two years at New England Culinary Institute." The Hotel and Resort Management degree began in September 2000, and targets students from the Caribbean, including Puerto Rico. During an interview with the author, Dr Hollis further stated that "The programme has received support from the Caribbean Hotel Association, The Grenada Hotel Association and the Government of Grenada and the participation of regional hotels will be solicited for the purpose of the internship programme." If the board accepts the proposal, construction will begin immediately on the kitchen and restaurant facilities.

CONCLUSION

The two tertiary institutions presently offering hospitality training in Grenada, TAMCC and NEWLO, have contributed significantly to the training and development of students in Grenada. Despite the many challenges facing these two institutions, such as inadequate training facilities, lack of trained teachers, insufficient support and involvement from the private sector, and in the case of government, insufficient budgetary allocation, they have provided adequately trained personnel for the industry. Graduates from both institutions are found in most establishments throughout the tri-island state of Grenada, Carriacou and Petite Martinique in various departments and at varied levels.

However, the future of hospitality training institutions in Grenada hinges on the importance that the government attaches to the tourism industry, particularly as it relates to human resource development. The aforementioned problems indicate that there is need for a national policy on human resource development within the tourism industry as recommended by the *Master Plan for the Tourism Sector* (Government of Grenada, 1997), which would encourage students to choose tourism as a career rather than as a last resort. The *Master Plan* indicated that in a survey carried out among the 1998 examination classes at four of the higher profile secondary schools, only 2.1% of the students – out of 426 – had any interest in careers in tourism. It also showed a general lack of understanding of tourism careers, with over 60% listing taxi driver, vendor, tour guide and hotel employee as the four careers in tourism of which they were aware. The result indicated that those who opt for careers in this sector are those who have run out of options. Many of those who end up in the industry are transients, which contributes to the high turnover rate in the industry.

RECOMMENDATIONS

The following recommendations are proposed for the advancement of educational institutions in Grenada and the development of the country's human resources. The policy on human resource development should include:

- Collaboration between the Ministry of Education and The Ministry of Tourism to plan, monitor and control all the programmes that are offered at all training institutions. This will allow the curriculum to be more relevant, structured and acceptable for human resource development in the industry.
- Strategic partnerships between the private sector and government. This is to ensure that government provides the industry with the relevant personnel and the private sector contributes to the general development, thus supporting staff and students.
- Government must engage in internal marketing that would create awareness among the population as to the importance of tourism to Grenada's economic development. Particular emphasis should be placed on educational institutions so those students are informed about career opportunities.

In addition to the above, other recommendations are as follows:

- Government should provide the necessary investment in teacher training and the upgrading of skills for lecturers and instructors in the industry.

- There needs to be linkages between NEWLO and TAMCC. At present they operate in isolation from each other. This matter needs to be addressed to avoid overlap in programmes. NEWLO should increase their credential rating so that their certification can be used as a prerequisite to enter TAMCC.
- There is a need for a proper training facility that will provide adequate practical exposure to students. A training hotel, operated by staff and students from TAMCC, will provide invaluable experience to students.

REFERENCES

Government of Grenada. (1997). *Master Plan for the Tourism Sector,* Government of Grenada/Organization of American States, St George's, Grenada.

Ministry of Finance of Grenada. (1995). *Annual Abstract of Statistics*, Government of Grenada, St George's, Grenada.

Grenada Board of Tourism. (1995). *Annual Compendium of Statistics,* Grenada Board of Tourism, St George's, Grenada.

CHAPTER 14

TOURISM AND HOSPITALITY EDUCATION AND TRAINING IN GUYANA

Donald Sinclair

Abstract

This chapter explores the landscape of tourism and hospitality education and training in Guyana and assesses the efforts and achievements in the field. Developments and initiatives taken by the principal players are explored and discussed against the background of the slowly unfolding picture of national tourism development. There are four major players in this effort – the Ministry of Education, the private sector, the Department of Tourism and the University of Guyana. The chapter examines the function and structure of the programmes offered by the University of Guyana Tourism Studies Unit, the Guyana Pegasus Hotel School and the Carnegie School of Home Economics and the challenges that they face. The author then acknowledges the accomplishments of these institutions and attempts a glance towards the future by critically assessing the potential for tourism and hospitality education in Guyana.

INTRODUCTION

Those who crave the pioneering scenario would derive great excitement from the current status of tourism and hospitality education in Guyana. What exists at the moment is a fertile field of opportunity, and a challenge to the creativity and innovativeness of Guyanese people.

While the tourism industry in Guyana may best be described as emergent, it would be a seriously flawed judgement to downplay the importance of tourism and hospitality education, both for and about the industry, for the hotels, guesthouses, resorts, restaurants and places of entertainment all provide service to a clientele whose needs may be as complex as those in more developed tourism destinations. Guyana's status as a relative newcomer among tourist destinations makes sound planning and careful implementation of tourism and hospitality education significant.

CRITICAL PRINCIPLES

Initiatives and programmes for tourism and hospitality education in Guyana can be said to be informed by two key principles – education for tourism and education about tourism.

Education that is about tourism is perceived as the opportunity to translate tourism into an instrument for the consideration of economic development, of cross-cultural understanding and of the environmental impacts of human activity. This distinction certainly induces reflection upon a dichotomy between tourism education (education about tourism) and tourism training (education for tourism). While training and education are not interchangeable concepts, they overlap and interrelate in significant ways.

Historically, the education-for-tourism mode has been the most manifest in Guyana, as indeed in the entire Caribbean. The emphasis in Guyana has traditionally fallen upon training that has been designed to provide junior functionaries in the industry with the basic reception and kitchen skills that would guarantee efficiencies at the lower end of the skills hierarchy. This emphasis was driven partly by the post-independence phenomenon of larger numbers of school-leavers looking for gainful employment, but primarily by the demands of an expanding urban catering sector in Guyana. Long entrenched notions about which occupations and skills were most appropriate for women created a strong gender imbalance among those pursuing employment in this sector.

Education for higher-end positions in the tourism industry would be a much later phenomenon in tourism education in Guyana. Discussing the more specialized skills required in the modern tourist sector, Stan and Laurel Reid wrote:

> There is need for individuals within the public and private sector who have the managerial skills to design strategies, manage information, implement procedures and policies, develop new products and co-ordinate a variety of resources for effective servicing of tourism. At the same time, trained personnel with specialised skills are required

for delivering special products and ancillary services demanded by niche markets. (Reid and Reid, 1991)

The multiplication in tourism styles and products, in response to an increasingly sophisticated and diverse travel market, has prompted a reassessment and reworking of many of the training assumptions and methodologies that proved workable in the past.

As Guyana attempts to develop a tourism product that is based upon an experience of nature, as it seeks to explore, in sustainable manner, the myriad tourism possibilities inherent in its rainforest resources and ancient cultures, the prescriptions of Stan and Laurel Reid assume key relevance. Attention to training in the higher-end skills and capabilities will be a prerequisite if the Guyana tourism product is to reflect that competitive quality that alone can guarantee fulfilment to the discerning nature traveller.

Education about tourism was a distinct 1990s imperative. The recognition that communities in Guyana need to be aware of the meaning, character, benefits and implications of tourism, has lent a strong "awareness" dimension to programmes organized by the Department of Tourism in the Ministry of Trade, Tourism and Industry and the University of Guyana. With the support, guidance and endorsement of the Caribbean Tourism Organisation this emphasis is likely to strengthen in the future.

The remainder of this chapter will examine and assess this dual emphasis in tourism education in Guyana.

THE CARNEGIE SCHOOL OF HOME ECONOMICS

Guyana's oldest hospitality training establishment, the Carnegie School of Home Economics, began as a trade school rather than as a catering establishment. Founded in 1933 as the Carnegie Trade School, the institution was the recipient of an initial grant from the Carnegie Trustees and later from the United Kingdom funds for unemployment. At the time the colonial administration assumed full responsibility for the school in 1937, its primary focus was more on trade than hospitality. For more than two decades the institution discharged its trade school mandate by producing custom-made female garments and uniforms for government "messengers", as they were then known. Catering on any significant scale was strictly subordinate to this trade function and was done only on request.

In 1958 the trading section was decommissioned and the institution assumed the name that it has today – the Carnegie School of Home Economics. This school continued for decades as a thoroughly mainstream institution that taught its predominantly female student body the skills required to become good homemakers. Its brochure announced that the curriculum "aimed at giving *every girl* an opportunity to learn all the skills and attitudes, which are essential for good home, family and community life" (italics added). That prescription commanded almost universal and unquestioning acceptance in the 1950s and 1960s.

The decade of the 1970s saw a refining of the Carnegie curriculum that placed greater emphasis on food preparation and the specialized skills associated with that subject. The school heightened its profile as a catering institution by establishing a separate catering section that provided the public with relatively low-cost meals of high quality and thoughtful presentation. This move in the direction of specialized catering bore fruit in a number of ways. Not only did it generate more revenue for Carnegie, but it also captured the attention of external funding agencies, notably the Association of Canadian Community Colleges and the Canadian International Development Agency. Between 1988 and 1990 both agencies channelled funds and technical assistance to Carnegie in support of its curriculum.

Today the Carnegie School of Home Economics has strengthened its links with the tourism sector. Students taking the one-year certificate course in Catering are required to spend two weeks in work attachment at a hotel, restaurant or other training establishment during the Easter break. Those pursuing the two-year Household Management course are required to spend three weeks on work attachment. Graduates from the Carnegie School of Home Economics find employment largely in the restaurant and catering sectors, especially in the rapidly expanding fast-food arena. Other graduates find employment in institutions that provide food services – hospitals, prisons, the military and educational institutions. Some of those graduates would have been sent originally by those institutions to learn or strengthen skills in either household management or catering.

Programmes

The Carnegie School of Home Economics offers four kinds of courses:

1. Household Management, a two-year course that covers food and nutrition, clothing and textiles and home economics management.
2. Catering, a one-year course that includes menu planning, kitchen skills and techniques, kitchen organization, introduction to food cost control, introduction to food service techniques and sanitation.
3. Evening classes in select specialized areas. Courses are usually twenty hours in duration and include elementary and advanced cookery, elementary and advanced cakes and pastries, elementary and advanced tailoring, elementary, intermediate and advanced dressmaking, cake decoration, home management, crochet and macramé, and floral arrangement.
4. Ad hoc courses (on request from government ministries or private agencies). These may include courses on etiquette, waiting on tables, housekeeping and front desk management.

Prospects

The cadre of skilled workers produced by the Carnegie School of Home Economics constitute a key resource for restaurants and other catering institutions upon which to draw. But one constraint to the development of the Carnegie School of Home Economics and to the expansion of its role in tourism and hospitality remains that of finance.

Carnegie receives funding from the Ministry of Education. Students enrolled in the regular programmes pay a nominal contingency fee, while evening students pay a proportionately higher fee. Until this finance resource base is considerably enhanced, the Carnegie School of Home Economics cannot realistically define any grander role for itself in the delivery of hospitality education and training. In order for the Carnegie School of Home Economics to be developed into a local hotel school there would need to be a significant infusion of funds which will most likely have to be sought externally.

THE GUYANA PEGASUS HOTEL SCHOOL

Background

The decade of the 1990s was perhaps the decade of the highest degree of awareness and self-consciousness regarding tourism and hospitality matters in Guyana. In 1993 the University of Guyana organized Guyana's First National Conference on Tourism and by the middle of the decade a Tourism Advisory Board had been established. A Tourism Association of Guyana (now the Tourism and Hospitality Association of Guyana) was formed and a National Tourism Development Plan was being formulated. There was increased local investment by the private sector in resort, hotels and restaurants. The year 1996 was designated as Visit Guyana Year and annual tourism awareness programmes were launched.

This activity tended to direct a harsh, critical spotlight upon the industry. In that glare all weaknesses, deficiencies and shortcomings stood out in bold relief. Newspaper editorials, while extolling the country's ineffable natural beauty, drew attention to problems of infrastructure, marketing, security and product development. Some letters to the editor poured scorn on Guyana's efforts to attract tourists, given some of the challenges mentioned earlier. Others, more optimistic in orientation, gave support to a tourism drive, pointing out that some developed tourism destinations posed even greater threats to the security of visitors.

Inevitably there were concerns expressed about Guyana's preparedness for tourism, from the standpoint of perceived weaknesses in attitudes and skills. One consensus was that the mid-1990s stage of tourism development in Guyana warranted a sharp focus on the education for tourism mode in order to equip a cadre of persons with the skills needed at higher-end positions in the tourism sector.

In 1994, therefore, when it was announced that a Guyana Pegasus Hotel School was being established, a large number of would-be (as well as practising) managers and supervisors sought enrolment. On September 20, 1994, the Guyana Pegasus Hotel School opened its doors.

The Guyana Pegasus Hotel School was not a residential institution. When classes started in September 1994, lectures and practical sessions were on location at the Pegasus Hotel, where the programme director and principal of the new school, Chandana Jayawardena, was also the hotel general manager. During the first year, seventy-eight students from twenty-six local organizations were registered in the programme. At graduation sixty-three students were issued with certificates and twenty-three with diplomas. These graduates were drawn from hotels, restaurants, catering establishments, commercial banks, tourist resorts, the police and army. Fourteen lecturers from ten different countries were recruited.

The Curriculum

The curriculum was modular in character, and students earned a diploma in Hotel Management at the end of three years. In the first year three modules were offered, leading to a higher certificate in Hotel Operations. These modules were Food Production (five courses), Food and Beverage Services (five courses) and Accommodation Services (five courses).

The second year of the programme was designed to give students one year of industrial exposure. During that year theories and concepts learned in lectures were to be tested and applied in a real-life industrial setting.

In the third year students would have a number of specializations available, in tourism, management, finance, human resources, food and beverage, rooms division and marketing. Entry requirements at this level were to be more stringent than the three Caribbean Examinations Council (CXC) passes required for entry to the first year. Candidates were expected to be mature students possessing a university degree, or employed as a hotel executive or supervisor with at least three years experience.

Recognition

The Guyana Pegasus Hotel School gained recognition by the Hotel and Catering International Management Association (HCIMA) in January 1995 as the first hotel school of Guyana. The courses recognized by HCIMA were assigned education points which counted towards a grade of membership of HCIMA. Marketing, Finance and Management courses were assigned five education points each. The Tourism course was assigned four points. Students completing all seven courses at the third-year level were therefore eligible for thirty-four education points. This points system recognition served as an incentive to Pegasus Hotel School students to aspire towards possibly full corporate membership in this prestigious organization.

Despite the promise of the Guyana Pegasus Hotel School, operations were suspended after one academic year, following the departure of the hotel's general manager. Although the full academic year of tutoring, to a significant degree, did upgrade the skills of a number of tourism sector employees, the absence of institutional continuity cannot be seen as furthering the goals of hospitality education and training in Guyana.

OTHER TRAINING MODES

In-Service Training

Another route to employment within the tourism sector is via in-service training. Prospective hotel or restaurant employees are hired even though they possess little or no practical experience in the sector. While on the job these persons acquire skills under the guidance and instruction of a manager or supervisor. Some hotel managers have even expressed a preference for the "uncertified" recruit, who is then "seasoned" on the job under their tutelage. The justification for this localized training is that it ensures the acquisition by employees of skills that are directly relevant to the specific work setting. In that scenario managers derive comfort from the thought that their pro-tégés are well schooled in the institutional culture of the particular work site.

Although in-service training remains a common practice in the tourism sector in Guyana, most establishments rely upon a combination of pre- and in-service staff training. Pre-service training, as provided by the Carnegie School of Home Economics, has introduced many skilled and trained employees into the hospitality sector. However, especially in the larger hotel and restaurant establishments, there seems to be a greater confidence in internal training arrangements and mechanisms than in the capacities of agencies external to those large establishments.

Department of Tourism

The Department of Tourism in the Ministry of Trade, Tourism and Industry has also been a key player in facilitating education that has been both for and about tourism. With funding usually from sources external to Guyana (for example the Organization of American States or the Caribbean Tourism Organisation) the Department of Tourism has been able to mount workshops for such target groups as tour guides, taxi drivers or managers of small hotels. The Department of Tourism has also been able to access funds for staff training overseas, mainly from the Inter-American Development Bank.

THE UNIVERSITY OF GUYANA

The most sustained and systematic initiative in the area of tourism and hospitality education and training in Guyana since the Carnegie School of Home Economics, has been the introduction of Tourism Studies in the Faculty of Arts of the University of Guyana.

Background

As early as the mid-1980s tourism-centred research began to flourish in the Division of Caribbean Studies (now the Division of Caribbean and Tourism Studies) in the Faculty of Arts. Papers on tourism were read at faculty seminars and in 1985 the author contributed an article on tourism and technology to the CARICOM Bulletin. The division's clearest indication of its concern for tourism development was its hosting in 1993 of the First National Conference on Tourism in Guyana. A variety of issues relating to the development of tourism in Guyana were aired at that conference. One year later the Division of Caribbean Studies launched certificate and diploma programmes in Tourism Studies which the university later expanded to a full degree programme in Tourism Studies.

The Tourism Studies programme offered by the University of Guyana was conceived against a national background of low levels of awareness and understanding of the meaning, character, operations and potential of a tourism sector in Guyana. Far from being an indictment of any agency or institution, that circumstance owes much to the fact that for many decades Guyana was off the tourist map at a time when other Caribbean territories had been making aggressive efforts to develop their tourism industries. There is even credible evidence to suggest that, especially in the 1960s, the deprioritising of tourism in Guyana enjoyed official endorsement. One political administration preferred to place its faith in the economic trinity of sugar, rice and bauxite, while another harboured strong reservation and unease about the possible social and psychological impacts of tourism on the Guyanese.

Few Guyanese, in the pre-eco-tourism days of the 1960s and early 1970s, ever regarded tourism as having much serious relevance to their country. The blue waters, white sandy beach image was the dominant paradigm in Caribbean tourism; bush and wilderness would gain ascendancy later.

By the 1980s, when severe economic decline inspired a reexamination of economic priorities in Guyana, the development of tourism gained impetus. By 1994, when the first students were admitted to the certificate programme in Tourism Studies, there existed both an awareness and a skills vacuum in Guyana.

Critical Principles

Given the background outlined above the following principles have guided curriculum design in tourism studies:

1. The tourism studies programme should aim at equipping students with the relevant skills and attitudes that will enable them to discharge executive-level functions in the tourism sector.
2. The tourism education of students should include a strong awareness component that provides a thorough understanding of tourism's numerous dimensions and expressions in the local, regional and international contexts.
3. There should be an integration of classroom instruction and practical exposure in order to ground theory and concepts, to sharpen industrial skills, and to strengthen in students an understanding and appreciation of the industrial environment in which they will be operating.
4. The tourism education programme should develop in students a concern for the impacts of tourism especially upon remote communities and fragile environments and should inspire positive behaviours and actions in support of that concern.
5. Tourism education should develop in students an entrepreneurial spirit that promotes initiative and self-activated enterprise.

Programme Structure

Students reading for the diploma in Tourism Studies do a two-year course of study, outlined below.

In year one:
- Use of English (two courses)
- Management
- Man and the Environment
- Introduction to World Tourism
- Eco-Tourism – Principles and Development

- Dimensions of Tourism
- Guyana Studies

In year two:

- Basic Tour Planning
- Tourism Attractions and Management
- Tourism Development
- History and Tourism
- Spanish
- Introduction to Hospitality
- Management
- Computer Studies

Students preparing for the degree in Tourism Studies do two continuing years.

In year three:

- Advanced Geography of Guyana
- Lodging Operations and Management
- Sustainable Tourism
- Nature Conservation and Management
- Organizational Behaviour
- Operations Management in Eco-Tourism
- Operations Analysis in Tourism
- Environmental Issues in the Caribbean

In year four:

- Personnel Management
- Tourism Project Design
- Public Relations
- Culture and Tourism Development
- Private Sector Environment
- Market Research
- Advertising

Programme Features

1. Industrial attachments. In March 2000 the Tourism Studies Unit launched, on a pilot basis, a system of industrial attachments for students in the third year of the degree programme.

Students spent a minimum of eighty hours in an establishment within the tourism sector. The employer's evaluation contributed to the student's final assessment in the third year. This brief period of attachment was designed to formalize the cooperative relationship between the Tourism Studies Unit and the tourism sector. Beginning in 2001 the period of attachment was extended to five months.

2. Tourism outreach. The aim of this initiative is to stimulate product development actions in selected communities and agencies. Execution of this initiative has assumed a variety of forms:

   - An environmental enhancement exercise at a forestry nature trail.
   - Erection of directional signs at one of Guyana's key historical sites.
   - A seminar on "Sugar, Rum and Tourism" that targeted the Guyana Sugar Corporation, Banks Breweries and Demerara Distillers Ltd.
   - A seminar on "Enhancing Tourism at Bartica" conducted by final-year diploma students. The seminar targeted regional officials, tourism operatives and security personnel in Bartica (a town in Guyana long known as the gateway to the interior, and home of the annual speedboat regatta).
   - An interface with residents of St Cuthbert's Mission – an Amerindian community approximately sixty miles up the Mahaica Creek. This meeting explored tourism development possibilities in the community, especially the potential of indigenous art and craft.

THE FUTURE

These exercises have all constituted an integral part of classroom teaching and have served to consolidate that vital institution – community partnership that is pivotal to tourism development.

In 1999 the Tourism Studies Unit began revision and modification of the Tourism Studies programme and invited personnel from the tourism sector to participate in this process. The Caribbean Human Resource Council of the Caribbean Tourism Organisation was also involved. The concerns of industry for quality training, appropriate attitudes and aptitudes, and committed graduates were reflected in the proposals presented to the university bodies for consideration and possible implementation in the year 2000–2001.

The word that should govern all tourism and hospitality education and training initiatives and programmes is "partnerships". Unless there is a perfect coherence of intention and a rationalization of programmes, developments in tourism education run the risk of neither developing tourism nor enhancing education. The regional picture that emerges from this book will point those involved in tourism and hospitality education and training in the region to the areas where greater coherence needs to be attained.

REFERENCES

Bobtail, D. (1993). "Facing the Challenge", in *Tourism Concern*, volume 3, Froebel College, London.

Reid, S. and Reid, L. (1991). "Managing Tourism in the Caribbean Region", *Caribbean Finance and Management* 7 (nos. 1 and 2).

CHAPTER 15

TOURISM AND HOSPITALITY EDUCATION AND TRAINING IN TRINIDAD AND TOBAGO

Michelle McLeod

Abstract

This chapter examines education development and training in Trinidad and Tobago. The twin-island republic is identified as a late entrant in the tourism and hospitality business, but the need for a well-trained human resource base was identified early. A master plan for tourism was drafted which identified education as an important component of tourism development. Model concepts such as "Getting Industry into Education" (GIE) and "Getting Education into Industry" (GEI) included a tourism awareness component and the development of industry standards, respectively. The author also examines tourism and hospitality programmes and training needs at the bachelor's and master's degree levels. The chapter concludes that a new model for tourism and hospitality education in Trinidad and Tobago has evolved in accordance with the Tourism Master Plan.

TOURISM IN TRINIDAD AND TOBAGO

The Government of Trinidad and Tobago is committed to developing the tourism industry to its fullest potential. The industry, by its very nature, has the potential to generate a significant increase in employment opportunities. Thus, there are efforts to innovate in tourism and hospitality education and training, to ensure that the highest levels of tourism education are made available to potential employees and those employees already working in the industry.

Trinidad and Tobago embarked on tourism development after many other Caribbean tourism destinations. Hence, the country's tourism industry is at a stage of infancy. A 1999 tourism performance outlook indicated that visitor expenditure increased to US$210 million per annum, compared to US$200 million in 1998. The tourism industry is estimated to contribute 2% to 3% of the economy's gross domestic product, employs 15,000 persons and receives, on average, 350,000 visitors per year. It is the government's recognition of the industry's potential to increase foreign exchange, create employment and improve the population's standard of living that has resulted in a commitment to facilitate tourism development.

THE TOURISM MASTER PLAN

Recognizing the need to diversify the economy, the Government of Trinidad and Tobago accessed funding from the Inter-American Development Bank to prepare a Tourism Master Plan (TMP). The TMP was completed in August 1995. Tourism awareness was one component of the plan and tourism education and training another. The plan outlined recommendations for a tourism and hospitality education and training model, with three main objectives which together promote the benefits of a career in tourism:

- Coordination of the tourism industry and government in the sharing of resources to meet the sector's education and training needs
- Alleviation of deficiencies in current training delivered in order to cater for the new tourism development plan
- Provision of a structure that offers career opportunities and incentives for all persons involved in the tourism profession

Strategies to reform the delivery of tourism and hospitality education and training were based on these objectives. Hence, an emerging tourism industry is supported by competitive human resources capable of meeting industry requirements. This chapter expounds on these strategies through the development of models.

TOURISM AND HOSPITALITY EDUCATION

The model of tourism and hospitality education and training has a stated principle which is illustrated in the TMP as outlined below and as shown in Figure 15.1. The model conceptualizes the aspect of "Getting Industry into Education" (GIE) which has several strategies and is implemented through education and training institutions from the primary to tertiary levels. The other aspect is "Getting Education

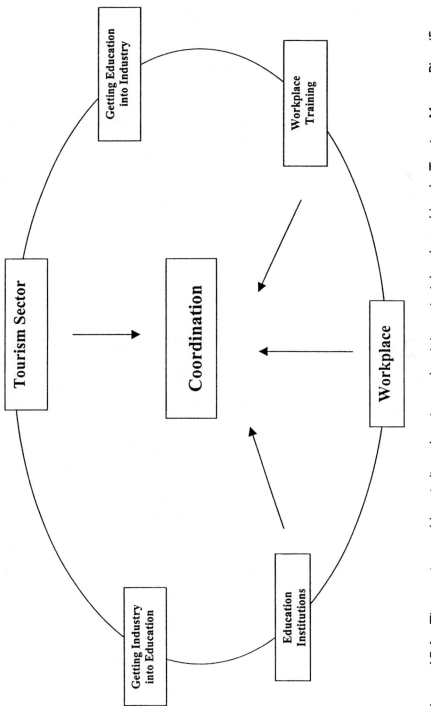

Figure 15.1 The tourism and hospitality education and training principle adopted by the Tourism Master Plan. (From the Tourism Master Plan, Exhibit 16.2, Government of Trinidad and Tobago, Port of Spain.)

into Industry" (GEl) which also has definitive strategies and is implemented through on-the-job training and other similar practices in the
workplace.

Strategies of the "GIE" start with tourism awareness in the school
system. This awareness is further supported with career guidance
initiatives. The tourism and hospitality industry must attract the
brightest minds in order to ensure that it remains competitive in the
global context. Added to this there must be a recruitment exercise
from the earliest stages of the education process.

Lewis (1999) investigated attitudes of secondary school students
towards working in the tourism industry. One of the findings from
the study reveals that secondary school students in Trinidad and
Tobago have positive attitudes towards tourism employment. This
finding gave new insight, since it was previously believed that attitudes towards tourism employment were unfavourable.

TOURISM AWARENESS

A tourism awareness programme is one key strategy that can influence the attitudes of young persons towards embarking upon a tourism career. In fact such programmes at the primary and secondary
school levels give the tourism industry popularity in the minds of
students. Tourism awareness programmes must also take into account
other groups, such as the general public, government agencies and
business communities.

Lynn (1991) conducted a study of tourism awareness programmes
in Trinidad and Tobago and recommended the implementation of a
comprehensive national public programme that shifts from awareness to specific target group information, education and motivation.
Tourism awareness programmes must focus on transforming the attitudes and behaviour of locals. This transformation will also be an
impetus to positive attitudes towards working in the tourism industry.

Essay writing competitions sponsored by the Florida-Caribbean
Cruise Association (FCCA) and Condé Nast Traveler have been
instrumental in creating additional awareness of the nature and
development of the tourism industry. These competitions heighten
interest in the sector and give teachers an opportunity to conduct
research in order to advise their students. Therefore, educating teachers on tourism subject matter becomes essential as the tourism industry gains prominence within the country.

Tourism awareness within the school system involves several methods such as tourism quizzes on television and radio, art and craft exhibitions and educating social studies and geography teachers on the tourism component of the Caribbean Examination Council (CXC) syllabuses. Teacher training has also become a necessary method since there are limited tourism materials and publications for the Caribbean region.

Strategies of the "GEI" are a formidable process involving the formulation of industry standards and performance expectations that will result in favourable outcomes by utilizing several methods, including on-the-job training, in-service or in-plant training and other short-term training exercises. One example of this strategy in action has been the delivery of training programmes, particularly in customer service skills, to front-line public officials. These programmes were funded by several agencies, including the Inter-American Development Bank, the Tourism and Industrial Development Company of Trinidad and Tobago Limited and, recently, VISA International.

Employees in the tourism and hospitality industry, including tour operators, accommodation workers and taxi drivers, have also been trained in customer service and language skills. The University of the West Indies Centre for Environment and Development (UWICED) has also trained eco-tourism operators in the field of environmental management. There are training initiatives on an ongoing basis to ensure all tourism service providers are trained.

ESTABLISHMENT OF THE NATIONAL TRAINING AGENCY

The TMP recommends the establishment of a tourism education training institute to coordinate Trinidad and Tobago's training and education resources in a sustainable manner. The institute would be a partnership of the Ministry of Education, the Ministry of Tourism and the tourism industry.

Until such an institution is created, the National Training Agency (NTA), established in 1999, has a major role in tourism and hospitality education and training delivery in Trinidad and Tobago. The activities of the NTA are modelled after similar organizations in the United Kingdom and New Zealand. The NTA serves to improve overall training standards, accredit training institutions and better match training with the needs of prospective employers. The NTA has established an Industry Training Organization (ITO) to monitor industry training. The organization has formed several lead bodies to develop occupational standards. These standards will form the basis of curriculum design and content.

In addition curriculum development for the tourism and hospitality industry has been guided by an industry-driven needs assessment. This study has been a pivotal point in the provision of appropriate tourism and hospitality education and training. Quality Consultants Limited conducted a study on behalf of the Trinidad and Tobago Hospitality and Tourism Institute (TTHTI) in 1997 to determine industry training requirements. The study, "Industry Driven Hospitality and Tourism Education and Training Needs Assessment and Monitoring System", was based on a survey of eight tourism industry sectors: accommodation, adventure tourism and recreation, attractions, events and conferences, food and beverage, tourism services, transportation and travel trade. One recommendation of the study was to "take industry education and training to the industry rather than bringing the industry to the Institute" (Quality Consultants, 1997). The train-the-trainer programme is one method of achieving this recommendation.

The study also made recommendations to advise curriculum matters. It identified that training is required for managerial and supervisory professions. Other recommendations of the study were related to developing articulation arrangements with other local academic and technical/vocational institutions, developing distance learning opportunities and developing a skills standards and certification process to certify workers at different levels of proficiency.

JOINT EDUCATIONAL PROGRAMMES

In 2000 the University of the West Indies (UWI) and TTHTI joined in offering an innovative first degree collaborative programme in tourism and hospitality management. The programme involves students studying for a two-year period at each institution. The programme is similar to that of the UWI, Cave Hill campus and the Barbados Community College. Both institutions share infrastructure resources through such an agreement and graduates from the TTHTI who meet the approved grade point average will gain entry into the UWI.

The TTHTI offers a range of training options. Tourism industry job seekers may pursue two-year associate degrees in Hospitality and Tourism Management with other specializations in Culinary Arts, Food and Beverage Management and Hotel Operations. The one-year certificate programme offerings include Front Office and Travel Agency Operations, Food and Beverage Supervision, Cooking, and Baking and Pastry Arts.

A report on the update of the needs assessment made additional recommendations on tourism and hospitality education and training (Quality Consultants, 1999a). Recommendations were made to develop an apprenticeship programme for persons interested in pursuing a career in the area of food and beverage, to help students develop appropriate job and industry attitudes before leaving the institute. It was also recommended that the institute develop strategic partnerships with sector and industry associations and stakeholders for curriculum development, funding of training, student scholarships, internships and apprenticeship programmes and general awareness of the institute's offerings.

A tourism and hospitality education and training needs assessment has also been completed at the regional level. A study conducted for the Caribbean Tourism Organisation (CTO) highlights current and future training needs (Quality Consultants, 1999b). Notably, the areas requiring current attention are culinary arts, tour guiding, maintenance and food and beverage service skills. In the future the areas of concentration should be culinary arts, food and beverage service skills, tour guiding and housekeeping. Once again, knowledge of training needs is seen as an important component in the development of hospitality and tourism programmes.

Locally the UWI is expanding its capacity to undertake tourism and hospitality education and training. Its School of Continuing Studies offers a two-year certificate in Tourism Management that meets normal matriculation status. Therefore graduates are given credits for entry into degree programmes. The programme runs on a part-time basis and offers persons interested in the hospitality and tourism industry a work-study option.

POSTGRADUATE PROGRAMME

In addition there are opportunities to further studies at a postgraduate level. The UWI Institute of Business (IOB) in Port of Spain offers an International Master's in Business Administration with a specialization in tourism. The programme runs for a two-year period and offers courses in Human Resource Development, Tourism Marketing, Planning and Policy Analysis. The student completes a series of core courses in the first year, including Organizational Behaviour and

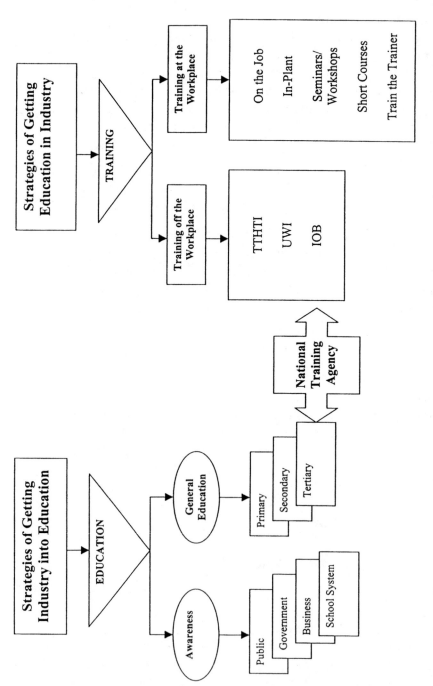

Figure 15.2 The organization of tourism and hospitality education and training in Trinidad and Tobago. (From the Tourism Master Plan, Government of Trinidad and Tobago, Port of Spain.)

Development, Economics of Business and Financial Accounting, and then specializes in tourism subjects during the second year. This programme involves classes after working hours with some workshops and elective courses requiring short periods (three to five days) away from work.

NEW MODEL

Upon examination of the involvement of several agencies in human resource development for the hospitality and tourism industry, a model has evolved based on the two strategies identified in the TMP. This model is shown as Figure 15.2. Strategies of GIE and GEI can be adopted to improve the capability of Caribbean tourism human resources. However, these strategies must be supported by sustained funding and appropriate technology in order to remain effective.

REFERENCES

ARA Consulting Group Inc. (1995). *Trinidad and Tobago Tourism Master Plan*, Part IV, Section 16, pp. 93–95, Port of Spain, Trinidad.

Lewis, A. (1999). *The Attitudes of Secondary School Students Towards Working in the Tourism Industry in Trinidad and Tobago.*

Lynn, W. (1991). *Trinidad and Tobago Tourism Awareness Program: Assessment of Program Needs and Action Plan*, Organization of American States, Department of Regional Development and Environment, Washington, D.C.

National Training Agency. (1999). *National Training Agency at a Glance: Meeting the Challenge for Excellence*, National Training Agency, Port of Spain, Trinidad.

Quality Consultants. (1997). *Industry-Driven Hospitality and Tourism Education and Training Needs Assessment and Monitoring System*, submitted to Trinidad and Tobago Hospitality and Tourism Institute, Port of Spain, Trinidad, p. iii.

Quality Consultants. (1999a). *Report on the Update of the Needs Assessment*, prepared for Trinidad and Tobago Hospitality and Tourism Institute, Port of Spain, Trinidad, pp. iii, iv.

Quality Consultants. (1999b). *Tourism Training for the New Millennium: A Study of Tourism Education and Training Needs in the Caribbean*, for the Caribbean Tourism Organisation, Barbados, p. 10.

CHAPTER 16

TOURISM EDUCATION AND TRAINING IN THE TURKS AND CAICOS ISLANDS

John M. Skippings, Ralph L. Higgs and Lindsey Musgrove

Abstract

This chapter examines the development and growth of tourism in the Turks and Caicos Islands. It notes that, compared to most Caribbean countries, the Turks and Caicos Islands started tourism development late, that is, in the late 1960s. Since then the country has seen a dramatic growth in the sector spurred mainly by foreign investment. Even though hospitality training programmes have been implemented to prepare islanders for work in tourism, there is still a strong reliance on imported labour. While the prognosis for further growth in tourism looks good, there is still the need to find ways of encouraging locals to work in the industry.

THE TOURISM INDUSTRY IN THE TURKS AND CAICOS ISLANDS

For centuries, the Turks and Caicos Islands were among the world's major salt producing countries and its small population had this single export on which to base the economy. In the mid-1960s, that industry disintegrated and without an export product other than the traditional conch and lobster fishery, the economy crumbled. This event was inevitable; it was also fortuitous. It allowed the people of the Turks and Caicos Islands to look around and discover that their greatest asset was simply the environment in which they lived: a benevolent climate, 230 miles of white sand beaches, fabulously clear, aquamarine water, an underwater world teeming with life that continually entices scuba divers and snorkellers from the Western Hemisphere and elsewhere, and nearly 200 square miles of verdant subtropical land mass. They discovered there was more potential in tourism than salt.

Thirty years ago, the Turks and Caicos Islands faced an enormous challenge, having to start from scratch in unfamiliar territory with many competitors. Every other island nation in the region was well ahead of the Turks and Caicos Islands, and they were obliged to launch their adventure into modern tourism with little to offer the visitor in terms of accommodations and man-made attractions.

The first "hotel" was the Turks Head Inn, one of the historic Bermuda-style homes on Grand Turk that was converted into a road-side inn. This was matched with the Admiral's Arm Inn on South Caicos, and Mount Pleasant Guesthouse on Salt Cay. In 1966, two wealthy Americans, Richard du Pont and Fritz Luddington, flew over the islands in private planes and discovered a small cove on Providenciales. With other investors, the "Seven Dwarfs" made an offer to the government – they would build the fourteen-room Third Turtle Inn, an airstrip and a road between them in return for a grant of land. The government accepted and the first "real" hotel in the Turks and Caicos was built. Other properties followed, including the Kittina Hotel on Grand Turk, the Meridian Club on Pine Cay and the Prospect of Whitby on North Caicos, all success stories.

The Turks and Caicos Islands began to attract a particular type of clientele who value an "escape" holiday where they could simply relax, put the pressures of the twentieth-century "rat race" behind them and enjoy surroundings that were pristine and serene. When visitors ventured out, they met friendly people who appreciated the fact that they had chosen to visit their country instead of some better-known destination.

Everyone benefited as an assortment of small properties (fifteen to twenty-five rooms) were built throughout the islands. Then came a large step forward – the Piper family constructed the eighty-room Island Princess on Grace Bay in Providenciales. This was followed by a leap to put the Turks and Caicos Islands on the world's tourism map: in 1984, a Club Med Turquoise was built on Providenciales, in return for which the government extended the airstrip to an 8,000-foot runway, creating the largest airport between Nassau and the Dominican Republic. Other landmarks that followed included the Ramada Turquoise Reef Hotel (Allegro Resort and Casino, 230 rooms), the ultra-luxurious Grace Bay Club, the condominiums suites of Ocean Club and, in 1997, Beaches Resort and Spa, a member of the well-known Sandals all-inclusive family.

During this twenty-year expansion period, tourist arrivals went from a few thousand to almost 125,000, as Americans, Canadians and Europeans began to discover the islands.

Being among the last islands in the Caribbean to be developed has certain distinct advantages. Having much undeveloped land (including East Caicos, the largest uninhabited island remaining in the Caribbean) means the Turks and Caicos Islands possess what other regional destinations can no longer reclaim – space for expansion and room for development well beyond the year 2020.

From the foregoing, it is safe to conclude that tourism is now, and may continue to be, the premier industry of the Turks and Caicos Islands. To substantiate this statement the Caribbean Development Bank reported in its 1996 Annual Report that earnings from tourists exceeded US\$57 million in 1994. In 1995, the Caribbean Tourism Organisation reported that growth in the Turks and Caicos Islands travel sector was the fastest growing in the region and many analysts feel that the Turks and Caicos are a true representation of "sustainable economic development", matching rapid development with strong environmental sensitivity. In 1999 the islands reported record arrivals month after month and led the Caribbean in summer month increases.

TOURISM AND HOSPITALITY EDUCATION AND TRAINING IN THE TURKS AND CAICOS ISLANDS

The Ministry of Tourism of the Turks and Caicos Islands, in its Tourism Policy and Guidelines, clearly states the government's policy in this regard:

> The government shall assume a coordinating role in Human Resource Development, especially educating and training employees in the hospitality and tourism industry with emphasis on the advancement of Turks and Caicos Islanders. . . . It [the government] shall monitor manpower usage, restricting the award of work permits to expatriates in order to ensure that employment opportunities are available for Turks and Caicos Islanders. (Turks and Caicos Islands Tourism Policy and Guidelines, March 19, 1993)

Tourism in the Turks and Caicos Islands is considered the primary industry that fuels the national economy. Presently, it accounts for more than 60% of the gross national product, generates in excess of

US$196 million annually and provides employment for more than 60% of the total workforce.

The industry is very labour intensive and, therefore, workers in the sector must be equipped with the best training and education to help maintain and enhance the benefits to the economy that are derived from tourism. The government plays a vital role in coordinating human resource development and has established the Turks and Caicos Islands Community College and the Turks and Caicos Islands Tourist Board to assist in this area. The Turks and Caicos Islands Community College offers a variety of courses, primarily those that are of a priority need, including a tourism-related course. The course is intended to familiarize students with the industry and its importance and the variety of roles within the industry. Additionally, this course touches on specific areas, such as the operation of the hospitality industry, which is an area in which most graduates seek employment. A significant component of the programme is the work study arrangement, where students are given opportunities to garner much needed on-the-job training prior to securing permanent employment in the industry. The programme has proven to be very fruitful as it has provided many Turks and Caicos Islanders and foreigners with essential skills that are needed in the tourism industry.

Another significant government organization that is mandated to assist government in implementing national policies in the area of training is the Turks and Caicos Islands Tourist Board. This organization plays a principal and rather more specific role in this regard as it provides industry-specific training. In the past, the Tourist Board used to employ, in the slow season, a summer hospitality programme aimed at providing hospitality training for hotel and restaurant staff. The training placed much emphasis on honing customer relations skills and increasing productivity in the individual departments.

To get an international perspective on new training methods and information, experts in the field, including professors from reputable universities such as the University of the West Indies, the Centre for Hotel and Tourism Management and Cornell University, are asked to be guest lecturers at the summer hospitality workshops. The lecturers offer not only specific training but also share valuable experience related to the industry and new trends and concepts employed by competing destinations in the delivery of distinctive customer service.

Ensuring that locals are employed in the tourism industry is another vital responsibility of the government. This is done in many ways, one of which is by monitoring manpower usage and restricting the awarding of work permits to foreigners to increase Turks and Caicos Islanders' chances of obtaining jobs in the tourism industry. Resorts such as Beaches Resort and Spa, Club Med, and Allegro Resort and Casino are allowed to hire foreign labour on the premise that locals will eventually replace them or that there are no locals who are interested in the vacant positions. Additionally, foreign workers are given work permits for a specified period until locals are trained to eventually assume these positions.

The concept does not always work, however, primarily because of the mindset of locals towards the industry and the perception that wages are unattractive. In actuality, the industry still attracts suitably qualified and trained locals, who are highly paid and enjoy working in the tourism industry, which is positive and encouraging.

OUTLOOK FOR THE FUTURE

The new beginning for tourism and hospitality education and training, in the new millennium, spells out the need for specific and innovative training methods. This is essential for all areas of the tourism industry if the Turks and Caicos Islands are to obtain a competitive advantage.

Looking at the future of the industry in the Turks and Caicos Islands, over the next five years growth is inevitable, as tourism accommodation is poised to increase by 60% to match the corresponding increase in tourist arrivals.

Without question, this calls for a qualified and quantified improvement in manpower, which can only be accomplished through changes in attitudes of the populace and new, pragmatic approaches to education and training methods. However, it is imperative that successful case studies of the national policies on tourism education and training of similar countries in the region are explored. This will contribute to the development of a well-trained and qualified workforce that is capable of transforming the Turks and Caicos Islands into an excellent tourist destination.

SECTION III

PRESENT AND FUTURE CHALLENGES

Section 3 deals with specific issues related to tourism and hospitality education. In chapter 17, Allison Atkinson explores the importance of training in customer relations in the Caribbean tourism and hospitality industry. This need is becoming greater as visitors to the region are increasingly becoming more sophisticated, and because of greater competition from other destinations. Service standards have been changing to reflect this change in the customer. Anne Crick examines different approaches used in service training and analyses how they have been used in the hotel industry. The primary approaches discussed are the "McDonaldized" training versus customized training. The author argues that, while customized training is utilized primarily for managers, it may also be appropriate for front-line employees who interact with the sophisticated tourist. The choice of approaches to service training ultimately depends, however, on the organization or the level of contact that the employee has with the tourist.

Training programmes are more readily available for employees of larger hotels, and small hotels in the Caribbean are often unable to take advantage of available expertise because of financial constraints. They are also faced with the challenge of limited physical and human resources. May Hinds assesses the response of these properties to the need for training. She points out that their success in the twenty-first century is dependent on the ability to develop a cadre of professionals who are capable of meeting the needs of the new tourists.

In chapter 20, Anthony Clayton discusses the importance of achieving sustainable development in tourism. Socio-cultural, environmental and economic problems in the region that could affect the future growth of the tourism industry are discussed. Clayton then identifies the urgent need for the clarifying of national strategies for tourism and the development of management strategies to address these challenges. This call is reiterated by Godfrey Pratt, who underscores the necessity of a sustainable approach to tourism development in the Caribbean. Education is identified as a critical element in achieving this goal. It is also identified as a means of preparing Caribbean youths to become the leaders of the industry in the future.

While the problems that affect tourism have been recognized and have been accompanied by efforts at conservation and preservation, Ian Boxill posits that theoretical research on tourism and tourism studies are not seen as a legitimate area of study by regional universities. He challenges academia to conduct further theoretical research on tourism issues. Boxill also recommends that tourism research should draw on the literature of development rather than on hotchpotch theoretical ideas from various disciplines. Ainsley O'Reilly then examines the efforts of the Centre for Hotel and Tourism Management, the Bahamas. He also discusses the revolution of tourism and hospitality education and training in the Caribbean that has challenged the old ways of thinking. Carolyn Hayle reiterates this position and assesses the response of Caribbean governments to tourism and hospitality education and training in the region. Caribbean governments have recognized the need to formalize tourism and hospitality training, which has resulted in the creation of the Caribbean Tourism and Education Council and the Association of Caribbean Tertiary Institutions. The primary focus of these entities is to develop flexible and responsive educational systems and to create a seamless system for education and training for the Caribbean tourism and hospitality industry.

CHAPTER 17

CUSTOMER RELATIONS TRAINING IN THE CONTEXT OF THE CARIBBEAN TOURISM AND HOSPITALITY BUSINESS

Allison Atkinson

Abstract

This chapter explores the importance of training in customer relations to tourism and hospitality management in the Caribbean. It suggests that customer relations is an organization-wide effort and should be practised by all employees. It gives an overview of world tourism and tourism in the Caribbean and provides a timely reminder that service and renewed commitment to service is the underpinning of the industry. Given this, the current deficiencies in levels of training in the Caribbean, the increased sophistication of travellers and major global competition, training in the area of customer relations is critical.

WORLD TOURISM

Tourism is a major contributor to gross domestic product (GDP) in many countries. The number of international tourist arrivals has grown from 69 million in 1960 to 160 million in 1970 and 657 million in 1999 (Jayawardena, 2000). Statistics from *World Hotel Management* show that this industry generated a total gross output of US$3.4 trillion dollars in 1995 and it is predicted that by the year 2005 this figure will climb by 100% to approximately US$7 trillion dollars. In addition to this, the industry was responsible for 231 million jobs, making it the world's number one employer and it contributed 11.5% of GDP to the world economy. In a nutshell, travel outstrips "electronics in Japan, automobiles in America and agriculture in Europe" (Langton, 1997). The World Travel and Tourism Council predicts that by the year 2010, the tourism contribution to GDP will increase to 12.5% and direct and indirect tourism employees will increase to some 328 million worldwide (World Travel and Tourism Council, 1998).

TOURISM IN THE CARIBBEAN

The tourism industry is equally important to the Caribbean. The region as a whole depends heavily on tourism for the following reasons:

1. Earnings from tourism constitute vital components of the balance of payments of the region.
2. It accounts for a large percentage of national income in some countries.
3. It is a labour-intensive industry and generates employment, which is an economic benefit.

The Caribbean region has experienced a 5.5% growth in the number of tourist arrivals during the past decade. In 1998 31.8 million tourists visited the region, including 12.3 million cruise ship passengers. The Caribbean, as a single destination, experienced a higher growth rate than the rest of the world (Caribbean Tourism Organisation, 2000). Tourism has therefore become the leading sector in the Caribbean as the traditional economic sectors such as agriculture experience persistent difficulties as a result of globalization, trade liberalization and changing customer demands. In spite of its significant contribution to the region's economy, tourism as a viable industry receives less than its fair share of attention from the public and private sectors (Jayawardena, 2000). Tourism infrastructure in the Caribbean has failed to keep up with industry needs and the Caribbean tourism industry has fallen short of changing international consumer expectations to a great degree.

The region also faces a number of internal challenges, such as the need for environmental conservation and protection and, subsequently, the sustainability of tourism; coastal pollution; improper solid waste disposal; and tourism harassment in certain countries.

The sun-sea-and-sand cliché is inadequate to fully describe the region and what it has to offer. The Caribbean, as is its peoples, is strikingly diverse. In terms of a product, it offers not only consistent year-round weather patterns and natural beauty, but culture, entertainment and unique destination advantages. In certain parts, the success of the all-inclusive concept has brought about innovative market segmentation approaches. An important boon is the region's proximity to the United States and Canada, where the Caribbean represents an all-important warm weather destination. The Caribbean also attracts the European market, regardless of the fact that it is a long-haul destination, for the reasons of its climate and image of exclusivity.

Despite the challenges, there are substantial opportunities. Emerging buzzwords within industry circles are sports tourism, eco-tourism, health tourism, heritage, attraction, entertainment and cultural tourism. The Caribbean could successfully develop any or all of these products. Further, the region has the potential to capitalize on a great regional strength through the combination of tourism products. By utilizing the proximity of Caribbean islands the region could give tourism options that are seen as complementary rather than competing. The possibilities in this regard are endless, as packages could be based on straight island-to-island or event-to-event combinations, or an island-to-event combination.

There is a caveat in that, in spite of the advantages of tourism, great care must be exercised in making it a primary industry. The region has to ensure that the proper linkages are established between the industry and other economic sectors, to ensure the sustainability of the environment and the prevention of long-term environmental damage, and to clearly delineate whether it is to the region's advantage to target travellers en masse or to attract travellers who have the ability and inclination to spend the type of money the region needs. The region must act responsibly to ensure that whatever development meets the current needs of the region should in no way compromise the ability of future generations to meet theirs.

CUSTOMER RELATIONS

Although referred to as a sector or business, some see tourism as an opportunity for people from different countries to meet each other. It is the ultimate "people" business. In this context, service and customer relations are key words and are prerequisites in tourism. Customer relations falls under the wider umbrella of public relations. Public relations recognizes an organization's reputation as critically important, just as any other corporate asset, and is premised on the basis that the relationship of a subject with its public can be (positively) adjusted as the situation calls for by functioning in part as a damage control mechanism. Unlike public relations, which is a specialist area manned by highly trained persons, customer relations is practised, consciously or unconsciously, by every member of an organization. Whereas public relations is seen as a preventive measure against certain types of public opinion, customer relations in a sense preempts public relations by helping to create favourable or avoid negative public opinion, creating an indelible impression of an organization. In the final analysis it is perceived to be representative of the organization.

Essentially customer relations is the managing of the "moments of truth" in the service encounter and is based on an appropriate attitude and behaviour supported by the interpersonal and communication skills of the service provider or representative. Professor Richard Teare notes that "although systems and procedures provide essential support in achieving service excellence, the real difference lies in the human touch" (Teare, 1998).

Customer relations is critical in ensuring (1) guest satisfaction, (2) the consistency of service delivery and (3) repeat clientele. Training in customer relations becomes not only a reality, but also a necessity as growth and expansion occur within the industry. A premium will be placed on employees with advanced skills and abilities in a variety of areas, including customer relations. The main motivating factor behind this change is the realization that tourism and hospitality are primary industries. Increasing specialization of the field thus requires individuals to be trained beyond the vocational aspects. The increasing sophistication and expectations of travellers also impacts on the necessity for training, as the experienced traveller will immediately know the difference between value for money and a poor substitute.

CUSTOMER RELATIONS IN THE CARIBBEAN

A recent study conducted by the Caribbean Tourism Organisation to assess the training and educational needs in twenty-five member countries gives telling insight into the Caribbean experience (Caribbean Tourism Organisation, 1999). The study revealed that the general training needs identified across staff categories and in descending order were:

1. Customer relations
2. Communication
3. Computer literacy

4. Foreign languages
5. Marketing
6. Leadership
7. Human resource management
8. Financial/accounting skills

The first two needs are interpersonal skills that are central to the provision of service in the tourism industry. There is, thus, an urgent need for interpersonal skills training in customer relations since, first, this is what the industry is all about and, second, as international competition increases, quality service will become a greater competitive advantage.

TRAINING IN THE CARIBBEAN

In general, training has not been a key focus within the tourism and hospitality sector in the Caribbean. Some of the main reasons for this have been that:

1. Training of employees is seen not only as an expensive venture, but also a risky investment, as the rate of staff turnover within the industry is relatively high.
2. Existing hospitality/tourism training institutions are not perceived by the industry as effectively satisfying its training needs.
3. Most organizations recruit their staff from secondary or tertiary institutions depending on the staff level requirement.
4. The industry shows a preference for an on-the-job-training strategy for all levels of staff.
5. There is a practice of hiring staff from the competition.

TECHNIQUES IN CUSTOMER RELATIONS TRAINING

Training in customer relations has been highlighted as critical in the light of the inadequate level of skills currently existing in the industry and the increased complexity of duties an organization's representatives are expected to perform in this area. The key skills being suggested for today's training are:

- Telephone skills
- Problem-solving capabilities

- Maintaining customer satisfaction
- Customer retention

Telephone Skills

In the initial stages customers rarely deal with an organization on a face-to-face basis. In the majority of cases the very first contact is over the telephone. Skills in this area are thus especially required. Training in this area should stress attitude, courtesy, effective listening skills, managing objections and message handling.

Problem-Solving Capabilities

In addition to empathizing with a customer's problem, the employee is now required to develop problem-solving capabilities, with the last resort being that of referring the customer to someone else. Organizations need, therefore, to educate their personnel on the organization's services, policy and practices, products, and to equip them with the necessary tools to solve problems in the most efficient manner.

Maintaining Customer Satisfaction

A main objective of any organization is to provide and maintain customer satisfaction. This can only be achieved through a commitment to service that is not only consistent over time but is imbedded within the culture of the organization. Training of personnel in this area not only helps to develop this commitment but employees can provide fresh perspectives on keeping service consistent from their day-to-day interactions with customers.

Customer Retention

Customer relations and customer retention should be seen as closely linked. Organizations can use customer relations as an effective, inexpensive marketing method to achieve customer retention.

Six methods are recommended to ensure that training really works:

1. Real communication with the training targets prior to developing a training programme. Employee input is essential for a number of reasons – they can help to define a problem and the need for training, they can also identify how they will benefit from training (given the skills they already have) and thus give the training programmes a credibility boost.

2. Training should not be seen as the answer to cover up a problem. Care should be taken not to misdiagnose a problem or, worse, to use training as a quick fix for the symptoms of a problem. The stakeholders involved should be asked how they see the problem and invited to give suggestions on how it might be fixed.
3. The outcomes of training should be measurable.
4. The training effort should keep budgetary and timeframe considerations in focus.
5. Possibly networking among other organizations to see how they handled certain problems.
6. Training follow-through. Encourage reinforcement through ongoing follow-up sessions.

CONCLUSION

In the final analysis, training in customer relations is critical, from the point of view of the employee whose individual achievement and personal satisfaction stems from an environment in which he or she can work to the best of his or her ability, thus ensuring the health of the entire organization, as well as from the point of view of the customer, for as the industry continues to evolve, the opportunity to delight guests through excellent service presents itself at a greater level than previously. When this happens, everybody benefits.

REFERENCES

Caribbean Tourism Organisation. (1999). "Tourism Training for the New Millennium", *Caribbean Tourism Organisation*, May 1999.
Caribbean Tourism Organisation. (2000). *Caribbean Tourism Statistics Report 1998*, Caribbean Tourism Organisation, Barbados, pp. 13–15.
Economist. (1999). *Pocket World in Figures 2000*, Profile Books, London, p. 5.
Jayawardena, C. (2000). "An Analysis of Tourism in the Caribbean", *Worldwide Hospitality and Tourism Trends* 1 (no. 3): 122–136.
Langton, B. (1997). "Small World, Big Business", *World Hotel Management*, Issue 1, pp. 10–11.
Teare, R. (1998). "Interpreting and Responding to Customer Needs", *Journal of Workplace Learning* 10 (no. 2): 1–19.
World Travel and Tourism Council (1998) *The Economic Impact of Travel and Tourism Development*, World Travel and Tourism Council, London, p. 1.

FROM McDONALDIZATION TO CUSTOMIZATION: TRAINING THE FRONT-LINE SERVICE WORKER IN THE NEW ERA

Anne P. Crick

Abstract

Research indicates that today's tourists are increasingly complex and diverse and that service standards have to change to reflect their needs. This paper examines three different approaches that organizations may take to service training and critically analyses how they have been utilized in the hotel industry. Although customized training has been used primarily for managers it may also be appropriate for those employees who deal with the "new tourist", who wants to be treated as an individual. Other forms may be more appropriate when the tourist is less demanding. The paper outlines what a customized training approach for line employees might look like. It concludes with a brief discussion as to when it would be most effectively utilized.

INTRODUCTION

> The thousands of dollars being spent on training in the industry, and on public relations could be spent more productively on changing the culture of the hotels. (Carter, 1997, p. 21)

Carter's comment is based on his finding that, while the vast majority of workers in Jamaica's tourism industry had a positive attitude towards their work, they were very dissatisfied with the way that hotel management treated them. Of particular relevance to this chapter is the finding that one of the major areas of dissatisfaction was the lack of training and development opportunities, which impacted on another area of concern, pay. This dissatisfaction, Carter suggests, may be revealed in worker hostility towards tourists. Dissatisfaction may, of course, lead to other undesirable outcomes, such as low productivity, high absenteeism and sabotage. However, even more interesting than the possible negative consequences is the potential waste implied by his statement. Carter suggests that managers of hotels may be investing heavily and not solving the problem that they intended to solve.

In the Caribbean context, this potential waste may also be experienced at the government level, as many governments invest heavily in tourism training. The question that this chapter examines is whether the limited money that is spent on training is wisely spent and whether there is a better way to allocate resources. The chapter starts by examining the needs of the current clientele and the implications for the workforce. It then examines training options that are used by many institutions, and the logic underlying the choice of option. It concludes by recommending a shift from a standardized approach to one that is more customized and developmentally focused.

TOURIST EXPECTATIONS

Poon (1993) argues that tourism is being driven by new tourists who are more experienced travellers, demanding more variety and more authentic experiences and who are more unpredictable and independent minded. Despite Poon's attempts to categorize, she argues that they cannot be neatly classified and that tourism organizations need to be able to deal with them at the individual level rather than seeing them as part of a market segment. Boorstin (1987) also suggests that these new tourists are more jaded and sophisticated and have to be constantly exposed to new and interesting experiences. Finally, there is the reality that a dramatic increase in tourist options and destinations make it imperative for individual hotels to be innovative and responsive.

At the same time, there are many tourists who do not fit into Poon's category of the new tourist. The majority of tourists to the region continue to come from North America (Jayawardena, 2000) – a market that is not especially noted for its concerns for special-interest tourism. A 1998 report on future trends in tourism also suggested that many of the trends noted by Poon were not likely to be widespread. The report suggested, for example, that the number of

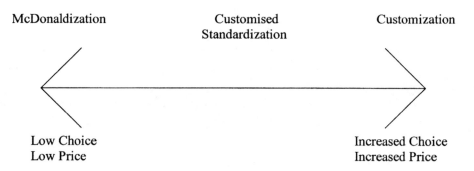

Figure 18.1   Training alternatives.

international hotel chains, tour operators and automobile clubs and motoring organizations were likely to increase in the next five to fifteen years (Obermair, 1998).

The same report showed, however, a market that is demanding more of service providers. Important trends noted by the international panel of experts included demands for better value for money, higher quality of experience and uniqueness, more comfort in travel and accommodation, as well as better and more personalized service.

Tourism entities, therefore, face an increasingly complex and varied market. This puts pressure on the line staff who must deliver what the hotel has advertised and promised and meet the needs of the new and old tourists. Front-line staff must, therefore, be capable of not only doing their main jobs but also responding to these new imperatives. Specifically they must be adaptive, motivated enough to meet customer needs, and skilled enough to know how and when to do so. This creates a new training imperative, one that this paper will suggest has not been taken up by most hotel training.

THE ALTERNATIVES

Training and education are services that may be delivered in various ways. There are innumerable options available to service organizations, but this chapter focuses on just three: McDonaldization, customized standardization and full customization. The three approaches may be imagined as lying on a continuum, as shown in Figure 18.1.

McDonaldized Training

McDonaldization is the term that Ritzer (1995) gives to the standardization of products and services. Like the famous fast-food franchise, organizations that practice McDonaldization highly standardize not only their products but also the way in which they are delivered. This necessitates the standardization of employee behaviour and even of customer behaviour. McDonaldization offers the consumer relatively few choices but it does offer convenience, economy and efficiency, traits that some consumers value more than the opportunity to choose.

This approach to training has the advantage of being relatively cheap and efficient. From the organization's perspective, it is also cost effective because the organization can invest in a particular technology and use it repeatedly until trainees learn the required skills. It is also possible to use this method to train large numbers of trainees at the same time, since the role of trainees is essentially one of watching, listening and demonstrating. Finally, it is also cost effective from the perspective of the trainer, since the organization may take advantage of the minimal variation required and use McDonaldized techniques in training trainers. Like the fast-food franchise, efficiencies of scale may be achieved by utilizing the techniques and information in many different ways and over a long period of time.

McDonaldized training may also mean that the organization selects generic training programmes. A hotel may, for example, invest in a series of customer service training videotapes and make them required viewing for new employees. Alternatively, it may send employees on training programmes offered by someone outside of the organization. In both cases the hotel takes advantage of predesigned programmes and avoids having to use the organization's human resources in conducting the training.

There are, however, disadvantages to McDonaldized training. One disadvantage is that employees trained in this way are relatively rigid and inflexible because they have been so drilled in a particular technique or response. If the need for that technique or response changes the individual may not automatically realize the need to change and may, in fact resist change. Retraining, therefore, requires not only teaching new techniques and attitudes but also unfreezing old ones. A second disadvantage is that McDonaldized training often does not incorporate in trainees the ability to think for themselves. Instead, it is very good at training employees in how to obey and to repeat routines. Over time the trainee will learn, as he or she is expected to, that the way to be seen as a good trainee is to do exactly as the instructor and the instructing mechanism demonstrates.

These disadvantages may be a liability in a rapidly changing environment and in an environment that requires employees to be responsive and quick to change. McDonaldized training produces McDonaldized employees, capable of responding appropriately in a known situation, but it is unlikely to produce employees capable of making some of the on-the-spot decisions that are needed in today's hotels.

McDonaldized training essentially reflects the notion that employees at a particular level do not need-to respond to change but that they can instead be taught ahead of time what it is that they need to do. Ironically, managers often become frustrated when employees who have been McDonaldized fail to show initiative – the one skill that the standardized training has not taught them. Carter in fact finds that 82% of managers of the Jamaican institutions in his study were quick to decry the "attitude" of their employees as being poor – something that most could not define. Perhaps part of "poor" attitude is the inability to act responsively and perhaps this is a function of the training process.

Customized Standardized Training

Customized standardization is the name that Lampel and Mintzberg (1996) give to the middle-of-the-road approach used by many service organizations as they seek to achieve the efficiencies of standardization while, at the same time, providing the customer with increased choice and the feeling that he or she is being treated specially. Customized standardization is the approach to training increasingly taken by large hotels in the Caribbean that have the resources to pay for tailor-made programmes. The Sandals University is one example of this sort of training. Sandals, with its own particular culture and requirements, selects trainers who understand those requirements and has them develop programmes to fit those needs. Organizations adopting this approach typically base training on the needs of the organization and thus training is often specific to a particular issue or problem. The training, if successful, often moves from being a one-time effort to being a part of the regular programme, essentially becoming McDonaldized.

This approach has the advantage of being specific to the organizational needs. Trainees who go through this type of training understand what the organization requires of them and respond accordingly. For the organization it has the benefit of incorporating some aspects of McDonaldization while, at the same time, incorporating some benefits of customization. Organizations adopting this approach, therefore, may benefit from cost efficiencies while at the same time not neglecting the approach that a particular hotel wants.

There are, however, limitations to this approach. Trainees may become insular and limited as they become focused on doing their job in the way that the organization requires at a particular point in time. This may appear to be a benefit to the training organization because it looks as if employees' mobility is limited. On the other hand, this insularity may breed a type of inflexibility to change. The trainee who is taught and socialized to adopt a particular type of culture may come to see this culture as being superior to anything else and may therefore reject change, even needed change. This system that attempts to train participants in a particular mode may limit their understanding of other paradigms and other views of the world and, thus, people who have been trained in this way may not even see the need for change when it occurs.

Finally, it must be noted that standardized customization conducted in this way does not depart much from the standardization previously discussed. The goal in standardized customization is simply to inculcate particular organizational behaviours rather than particular industry behaviours. Essentially, therefore, a good trainee is one who fits the organizational mould in behaviour, speech and appearance. There is little room for individuality and trainees are rewarded for their ability to mimic what their trainer has taught.

Customized Training

Customization is the virtual opposite of McDonaldization, as it offers the consumer a high degree of choice and flexibility. Organizations that practice customization hire service people who are required to work with the customer to produce something that meets the customer's specific needs. For the organization and for the customer, this is the most expensive alternative in terms of cost as well as the time that is required to determine what the customer wants and how to produce it. Customization is not a one-time or one-direction event but is both circular and continuous as the service person develops a better understanding of what is needed and provides it, checks whether the solution is appropriate, refines it, and so on.

Customized training reflects the individual who is being trained as well as the content of the training. Rather than seeing the individual as a sponge ready to soak up information, this approach is one in which the individual is allowed to bring himself or herself to the situation. This is the approach that is used for training managers. Executive management programmes typically take into account some of the skills and the interests that managers have already demonstrated and build upon them. Managers in such programmes are encouraged to take an active part in designing what they want to learn, practising it and even doing further research. Management training also uses a variety of techniques, including on the job practice, role-play, in basket exercises and internships. Throughout the process managers are measured on how well they think on their feet and how well they apply what they have learned rather than on how well they have mastered a particular set of techniques.

The advantage of these techniques is that managers are allowed to practice the skills and attitudes that they are anticipated to need on the job. This type of training also does not put a limitation on what can be learned – rather it sets a minimum standard and allows individuals to build upon it as their interests lie. As a result, trainees are often more interested and committed to the learning process because they are a part of it.

There are, of course, disadvantages. Customized training is expensive and for many organizations it may be an expense that they may not recoup if trainees decide to leave shortly after being trained. It is expensive in other ways. It requires fewer trainees to a trainer and it requires a higher calibre of trainer – someone who can relate to the trainees on an individual basis and help to draw them out. This probably explains why many organizations do not practise this sort of management training and opt instead to select managers who have been McDonaldized. The expense also explains why such training is restricted to only a few handpicked individuals in those hotels that do practise customized training, as shown in Figure 18.2.

Accepting this paradigm, therefore, puts a different spin on the value of training and who should receive the most valuable training. It suggests that by McDonaldizing the training of lower level employees the organisation is limiting the potential of these individuals. This limitation, which implies organizational control, is highly valued by many hotels because employee behaviour is somewhat predictable. There is in this controlled situation little concern that McDonaldized employees will overstep their boundaries because training has inculcated in them the value of rules and compliance with those rules.

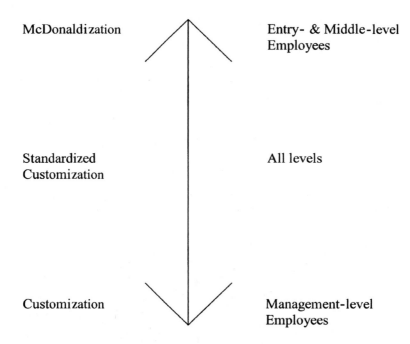

Figure 18.2 Training at various organizational levels.

Unfortunately, there is also little likelihood that they will display initiative and go beyond their roles to delight the customer – something that hotels are increasingly seeking from them. Underlying this decision is a logic that suggests that those employees who are at the bottom of the organization should be trained in the quickest and cheapest way possible, whereas those at the top should be trained more expensively. The cost and effort differential is often justified on the basis of the value of those individuals to the organization. The manager of a hotel or department is seen as having more value to the hotel than a busboy or a receptionist because of the salary that he or she commands as well as the authority wielded. There is, however, a more recent view of value advanced by many service writers who argue that the most valuable people in the organization are those front-line employees who interact with the customers. In this paradigm, the value of managers and support personnel is only as much value as they add to the efforts of the front-line personnel. These are the ones who are actually charged with the responsibility of making sure that the customer is satisfied, delighted and made to feel welcome. These are the individuals who turn dull moments into shining moments for the organization (see, for example, Albrecht, 1988; Albrecht and Zemke, 1985).

Customized training, on the other hand, rewards free thinking and initiative. It rewards individuals who readily absorb the rules and routines but use them only as a preliminary step or as a building block. In customized training individuals are encouraged to be creative, responsive and, most of all, to depend upon their own judgement in situations. This type of training can begin to overcome the all-too-typical responses of many front-line service personnel, of, "I'm not allowed to"; "Let me get my manager"; "We can't"; or, most insulting to the customer, "You can't". These phrases, even politely stated, reflect an individual who has learned the routines so well that they cannot be dislodged by the reality of a needy customer. Organizational attempts at standardized customization, in which employees go through possible scenarios and learn the best response, are simply broadening McDonaldization and do little to bring the employee into the picture.

Introducing customization at the level of non-managerial employees would require organizations to invest significantly more time, effort and money in training than they currently do. The recent survey of tourism training in the Caribbean suggests that training receives minimal attention and funding (Caribbean Tourism Organisation, 1999). The report determined that almost two-thirds of responding organizations provided training to skilled and semiskilled staff "on the job", with less than a quarter reporting the use of in-house classroom training for this category of employees. The report also indicates that this training seldom takes place, with only 9% of the responding organizations reporting that they conducted training for this category three or four times a year. The most popular response given by 43% of the respondents was, in fact, that training was done "as required". In fairness to many hotels that do conduct more training than these figures suggest, it must be noted that the survey is highly skewed towards smaller properties with fewer resources. Many of the larger hotels do spend significant time and effort on training. However, despite this, many of them concentrate much of this effort in the managerial ranks or those ranks in which there is particular need. Many of these hotels may, for example, send cooks to Europe for specialized training while using McDonaldized training for most of the other employees.

Customized training does not take only a few hours; such sessions would probably take several days. In those days, trainers would continue to be focused on transmitting the basic skills and attitudes. They would, however, try to engage trainee interest by putting them through many of the activities traditionally reserved for management personnel. In a training session a group of employees may work on a case, do self-assessment exercises, role-play and even develop their own scenarios. The trainer's job would be to allow them to learn rather than to teach them. In this process, trainees would begin to learn more about themselves, their ability to respond to particular situations and their weak areas. This learning would be strengthened by group work in which peers evaluate one another and provide feedback. Such training moves the trainee's role from a passive to an active one, creates interest and, most importantly, moves from mere training to development. The result is likely to be a front-line employee who not only knows what to do, but knows what he or she is capable of doing and is motivated and challenged to move beyond strict rule compliance into a more responsive and innovative mode.

If this is achieved, organizations have much more to gain than to lose from customized training of all employees. To gain some of these advantages requires a fundamental shift in thinking of trainers. There needs to be the recognition that the traditional method of training people differently at different levels and then pasting on additional training as needed will probably not get the required results. By the time that they get to the top of the organization many of these employees may have become jaded and frustrated and may even have developed a feeling of learned helplessness where they cannot learn. Organizations also have to move from the notion that the ability to respond to developmental training is present in only a few individuals. As the Carter (1997) study showed, the vast majority of Jamaican hotel workers are eager to work hard and enjoy a career in tourism. They do not feel, however, that they have the motivation or the potential to exercise the needed skills.

Customized training may not be for every organization, however, because of its heavy investment in time and money. Some organizations, such as chain hotels that require standardization across the chain, and where customers value predictability, may find that it is not a worthwhile investment. Customized training may also be inappropriate in some sections of the organization where standardization is desired. A coffee shop, for example, keeps its prices low and its turnover high precisely because it limits choices. It may therefore be counterproductive to institute a customized training approach there. Finally, it may be inappropriate in a situation where the organization experiences high turnover of staff and may not recoup its investment in people.

In selecting an approach organizations will, therefore, have to consider the costs and benefits associated with each approach. They may also have to consider more carefully how they utilize trainees who have participated in such training. Engaging in expensive training that promotes self-knowledge and creates a high level of motivation will be totally wasted if the employees are not provided with opportunities to use their new skills.

CONCLUSION

Service training has typically been conducted at different levels with lower level employees being given the most standardized training and senior employees the least. In light of changes in the way that service organizations must operate there is, however, a need to reexamine the logic behind these types of decisions. Some line employees may need to receive training that prepares them not just for the narrow scope of their job, but creates in them the ability to think and innovate in order to meet the needs of customers. McDonaldized training and its variants has traditionally been used in the past but in a new era in which many customers are demanding more personalization, these methods may need to give way to a new, more intense method that will prepare workers to meet these challenges. As Carter (1997) suggests, it also requires a change in the culture of the hotels that employ them.

REFERENCES

Albrecht, K. (1988). *At America's Service: How Corporations Can Revolutionize the Way They Treat Their Customers,* New York, Warner Books.

Albrecht, K. and Zemke, R. (1985). *Service America: Doing Business in the New Economy,* New York, Warner Books

Boorstin, D. J. (1987). *The Image: A Guide to Pseudo-Events in America,* New York, Athenum.

Caribbean Tourism Organisation (1999). *Tourism Training for the New Millennium: A Study of Tourism Education and Training Needs in the Caribbean,* Caribbean Tourism Organisation, Barbados.

Carter, K. (1997). *Why Workers Won't Work: The Worker in a Developing Economy,* London, Macmillan Education, p. 21.

Jayawardena, C. (1999) "Tourism Trends in the World and the Caribbean", paper presented at the Millennium Tourism Trends Conference, Centre for Adult Education, North-East of Finland, October, p. 9.

Jayawardena, C. (2000). "An Analysis of Tourism in the Caribbean", *Worldwide Hospitality and Tourism Trends* 1 (no. 3): 122–136.

Lampel, J. and Mintzberg, H. (1996). "Customizing Customization", *Sloan Management Review* (Fall): 21–30.

Obermair, K. (1998). "AIT Delphi: Study of Future Trends in Tourism", University of Vienna, Austria, pp. 81–91.

Poon, A. (1993) *Tourism, Technology and Competitive Strategies*, CAB International, Wallingford, UK.

Ritzer, G. (1995). *McDonaldization of Society: An Investigation into the Changing Character of Contemporary Social Life*, Pine Forge Press, Thousand Oaks, CA.

CHAPTER 19

CHALLENGES IN TRAINING EMPLOYEES OF SMALL HOTELS IN THE CARIBBEAN

May Hinds

Abstract

Small hotels, which are defined as lodgings with seventy-five or fewer rooms, have unique challenges that must be addressed in the training process. One of the primary issues is management by owners who may not necessarily have the technical and organizational skills of their counterparts in larger hotels. Other challenges include limited financial, physical and human resources, which makes it difficult for them to afford the services of professional trainers or to find the time and space for training. However, with the challenges of the twenty-first century the survival of small hotels is dependent on their ability to develop a cadre of well-trained professional and line staff. Innovative solutions, including cost sharing, bartering and exchanges are proposed to help to overcome some of the limitations identified.

INTRODUCTION

A small hotel within the context of the Caribbean definition is a lodging establishment of seventy-five rooms or less, with wide variability in standards of facilities, amenities and service, where a majority of staff is local and the ownership and management is combined. Most small hotels in the Caribbean have three distinct challenges and characteristics, which are:

- Overdependency on one or two key individuals (usually the owner and/or manager)
- Financial limitations
- Limited physical facilities

In many small hotels the owner-managers personally perform all management functions of the business, resulting in a highly centralized decision making process. Most owner-managers of small hotels in the Caribbean have an inadequate repertoire of managerial skills and training. This makes it difficult for the small hoteliers to implement a smooth transition from start-up to the growth stage of their operations. Such a transition requires a shift, on the part of the small hotelier, to a more managerial style, that is, a more functionally organized management team.

As a consequence of this shortage of managerial training and skills, small hotels also suffer from a lack of strategic planning. This arises primarily because of insufficient knowledge of the planning process and of the expertise needed in the planning process. In addition, detailed planning is generally viewed as too time consuming and, therefore, not essential for a small organization. However, since small hotels are more vulnerable to changes in their operating and remote environments, it is essential that formal, systematic but flexible plans be developed to allow for better management of their limited financial, physical and human resources.

It is recognized that small hotels, particularly those with a room size of twenty rooms and under, are too small to have a full complement of top management staff. The resulting concentration of managerial duties in a very limited number of persons usually leads to very informal organizational structures. Such a practice tends to result in a management team that is not well organized and, therefore, unable to function effectively. However, a small hotel with an organizational structure congruent with its size, objectives, resources and its environment, both internal and external, would allow for a better utilization of limited human resources. The combination of a well-developed strategy and an appropriate organizational structure would assist in utilizing all resources more effectively and efficiently and in being less reactive and more proactive to its environment.

PROFILE OF THE CARIBBEAN SMALL HOTEL SECTOR

The profiles of the entrepreneurs in the Caribbean region who own and manage small hotels are as diverse in backgrounds, professional qualifications and personality as the diverse small hotel subsector of the Caribbean region. Investors in small hotels are usually either nationals of Caribbean countries or have acquired resident status and consider the Caribbean home. Small hotels are usually grouped in three broad categories, as small hotels, apartment hotels and guesthouses.

Small hotels in the Caribbean attract more women than men as full-time and part-time employees. In 1998, 67% of the full-time employees of small hotels in the Caribbean were women, according to a regional survey (Organization of American States, 1998). During this survey, a majority of respondents throughout the region articulated the need for effective delivery of training to employees in operations, financial matters, management, housekeeping and service. Of significance is the clear and region-wide cry for help from the owners who wish to become "better" educated.

MAJOR CHALLENGES OF SMALL HOTELIERS

Major challenges experienced by owners in providing training for employees are lack of finance, the high cost associated with arranging external training and the inability of owners to release their limited staff for off-premises training. Recruiting industry professionals with proven track records in developing and implementing training is also a challenge for small hoteliers in some Caribbean countries. Small hoteliers rely heavily on loans to finance short- and long-term commitments. This places a significant burden on the long-term viability of these properties because of the regular interest payments and cash flow problems as a result of payback responsibility. This can inhibit future growth and development. In addition to inadequate levels of financing, there is the difficulty experienced by small hoteliers in obtaining financing from lending institutions. This is due not only to their small size, lack of adequate collateral and limited profits, but also to the absence of business plans.

NEW CHALLENGES AND OPPORTUNITIES FOR SMALL HOTELIERS

Over the last decade regional and international agencies, in particular the Caribbean Development Bank (CDB)–Caribbean Technological Consultancy Services Network and the Organization of American States (OAS) have provided assistance to Caribbean small hoteliers to strengthen and improve technical and operational capability and reinforce and/or develop the human resource base of the small hotels. Training specialists organized and delivered workshops and trained owner-managers and employees. To complement the training, hands-on consultancy services were provided to the small hotels.

In an ongoing search for a solution to the challenges facing the small hoteliers, the OAS regional small hotels assistance initiative, building on the foundation laid, sought a new approach to address the well-known challenges associated with both the financial constraints and the need for staff to be trained off premises. In 1998, CDB contracted experts from the Caribbean to prepare a series of simple training manuals. These included "Management of Small Hotels", "Accounting and Control Systems" and "Requirements for Establishing a Small Hotel" (Caribbean Development Bank, 1998). In June 1999 a Technology Program for Caribbean Small Hoteliers was launched, which included an electronic library (www.caribbeaninnkeeper.com).

TRAINING EMPLOYEES OF SMALL HOTELS

Training in the hospitality and tourism industry in the Caribbean region, and especially in the small hotel subsector, must focus on long-term human resource development. There is also a need for ongoing monitoring, evaluation and reinforcement from within the establishment and continued financial support. In addressing the challenges in training employees of small hotels in the Caribbean, it is important to first analyse the smaller establishments using three basic criteria – size, structure and standards – to permit analyses of physical facilities, services and human resource requirements. If training is to be cost-effective, beneficial and relevant to management and staff, it must be tailored to meet the needs of an individual establishment. Training must be economically viable, administratively possible and logistically feasible.

The operation, limited as it is by inherent staffing constraints, should not be disrupted due to employee absence, resulting in the delivery of on-site training. This approach allows the employees to maximize the training provided as they work with equipment, systems and in surroundings with which they are familiar. In addition to size, structure and standards the challenges of trainers in the delivery of training programmes to employees of small establishments must take into account the historical and cultural differences of the Caribbean region as well as the stage of tourism development of the countries (mature, transitional and embryonic).

The vast majority of small hotels, twenty rooms and under, is to be found in the guesthouse category, a category in many countries characterized by low and declining standards of facilities, since it is difficult to maintain and upgrade physical plants. In the case where the owner-manager is a mature person, management training is not usually an attractive option. Management, however, should participate in training programmes, since it assures that standards will be maintained, respected, monitored and evaluated after the trainer has departed. A challenge, therefore, surrounds the mobilization of participation of the management in the training process in these hotels. The small hotels with greater room inventory and supervisory level personnel participating in the training at least have a sustainable mechanism in place to monitor and evaluate the training plan.

Language and literacy are other factors to consider in training employees of small hotels. Whereas English is used in the hotels of a majority of Caribbean countries (except Cuba, the Dominican Republic, Guadeloupe, Haiti, Martinique and Venezuela), even in countries such as Suriname, a command of Dutch would create a more meaningful learning environment for the small hoteliers. In Jamaica, for example, literacy is a factor to be determined at the outset, since special attention would be required in the design and delivery of training for employees who are not fully literate.

Careful attention must also be paid to the inclusion of all categories of workers in the training programme, especially when scheduling such modules as customer service strategies. Too many managers earmark front-line personnel (front desk and food and beverage), particularly the restaurant and bar employees, and overlook the security and grounds personnel, who all play a leading role in the delivery of customer service. In small hotels, particularly those with fifty-one to seventy-five rooms, operating as all-inclusive and, to a lesser extent time-share, the security personnel perform a leading role in the "welcome" process.

The challenge in scheduling employees for training is not only confined to getting management to understand the need to include such categories of employees for training, but in convincing the employees themselves of the need to participate as members of the team. Another challenge relates to the fusion of departments by mixing employees of different, though interrelated, departments. This approach is not readily understood, and it is only after the delivery that the employees respect the fusion since employee relationships are improved and staff from different departments are made intimately aware of procedures and practices that are necessary for the efficient operation of the different departments in the establishment.

STAFFING AND QUALIFICATIONS

A relatively small percentage of executives of such hotels in the Caribbean are graduates of universities or hospitality schools. This is not surprising, since the scope for career diversification and advancement in small hotels is minimal, if not non-existent, for graduates of tertiary level institutions. Against this background, a trainer is faced with a demanding task of not only developing and implementing in-service training programmes that will satisfy specific human resources and training needs of the employees of small hotels, but also being familiar with employees' qualifications. This is important in customizing the training programme. Directors and managers should also consult employees in order to gain their support.

THE DELIVERY OF THE TRAINING

In the guesthouse category where training must be conducted on site, the training design must allow employees to engage in practical "hands on" sessions. This will provide a balance of theory and practice that will reinforce the training. In some cases, where human resource development has not kept pace with changes in the physical structure (for example, additional rooms, improved facilities), the trainer must incorporate familiarization of the physical plan for the employees.

Where managers, supervisors and other employees working in small hotels and apartment-type establishments operate and manage the business in a more sophisticated managerial style, a workshop setting may provide the opportunity for properties to "club" together to share the trainer costs. Apart from the financial gain, employees of small hotels benefit from cross-fertilization of ideas, and can pool knowledge and ideas in the group setting. The concept of the club approach for training of employees can extend to purchasing, since the small hoteliers must see the acquisition of training tools such as videotapes, manuals and books as a priority in the promotion of ongoing, multiskilled training.

Small hoteliers may also be required to go on a study tour of similar-sized small hotels that have instituted advanced training and operating procedures. They could spend a fixed amount of time in a selected country at a property considered "best practice". Small hotels may also utilize barter programmes as another feasible and cost effective approach to in-house training. A barter programme envisages that a qualified external trainer will conduct training programmes at a particular property for a period to be agreed upon by trainer and management in exchange for accommodation, meals, laundry and transportation costs.

MOVING TO SUSTAINABILITY

Caribbean countries are at different levels of tourism development, namely

- Embryonic – countries such as Guyana, Suriname and Dominica
- Transitional – countries such as Aruba, Belize, and Trinidad and Tobago
- Mature – countries such as the Bahamas, Barbados and Jamaica

The greatest challenge in training employees of small hotels in the Caribbean is in the countries classified as mature, where care and attention is required to facilitate training without reinventing the wheel while building on existing programmes to avoid duplication. Most of the challenges in training employees of small hotels in the Caribbean region are being addressed. Once the assistance to small hotels is sustained and ongoing pooling of both human and non-human resources in the subsector continues, the long-term viability of this very important subsector, and by extension the tourism industry, in the Caribbean region will move to sustainability.

REFERENCES

Caribbean Development Bank. (1992). *Training Manuals for Small Hotels* (prepared by Brice, R., Critchlow-Earle, B. and Hinds, M.), Caribbean Development Bank, Bridgetown, Barbados.

Caribbean Hospitality Training Institute. (1994). *Caribbean Small Hotel Operators Reference Manuals*, 4th edition, Caribbean Hospitality Training Institute, Puerto Rico.

Organization of American States. (1998). *Caribbean Tourism Competitiveness and Sustainability – Small Hotels: Results of the Regional Survey*, Organization of American States, New York.

www.caribbeaninnkeeper.com

CHAPTER 20

SUSTAINABLE TOURISM: THE AGENDA FOR THE CARIBBEAN

Anthony Clayton

Abstract

Tourism has become a critically important source of foreign revenue for a number of developing countries, including several in the Caribbean region. In some of these countries, however, the industry is being encircled by mounting environmental and social problems that threaten future growth. As a result, there is now a great deal of discussion about sustainable tourism. This resolves into two tasks: to secure the long-term future of the industry and to ensure that it contributes to a wider process of genuinely sustainable development and growth by fostering a more socially and environmentally constructive engagement with other sectors of society. This raises some profound and challenging questions, which indicate an urgent need to clarify national strategies for tourism, assess the performance targets and criteria set by the industry itself, and develop the management strategies needed to address these new challenges.

INTRODUCTION: THE GLOBAL IMPORTANCE OF TRAVEL AND TOURISM

Most international travellers today are tourists, travelling for recreational, cultural or educational purposes. Mass tourism, a relatively modern concept, has grown over the last three decades into one of the world's largest industries, and tourists now outnumber those travelling for business or personal reasons on most routes by a substantial margin. According to World Tourism Organization estimates, international tourist arrivals grew from 69 million in 1960 to

160 million in 1970, and to 594 million in 1996.[1] Between 1980 and 1996, world international tourist arrivals increased by an average of 4.7% annually, while receipts grew from US$103 billion to US$423 billion, an average annual increase of 9.2%, indicating a rapid increase in the number of people travelling and an even more rapid increase in the amount that these people were spending.

Travel and tourism today generate between them a significant percentage – by some accounts 10% – of global gross domestic product (GDP), and probably account for roughly similar proportions of global capital investment and employment.[2] These industries are, obviously, international; they are also extremely *pervasive* in that they affect not just all parts of the world, but also many other sectors (ranging from construction and engineering to a wide range of services) and thereby involve or have implications for almost all levels of society. The livelihood of many millions of people today in all parts of the world depends, directly or indirectly, on the long-term future of the travel and tourism industries.

The travel and tourism sector is currently forecast to grow more rapidly than world GDP over this decade. This is for a range of reasons, including the following:

- There is new demand from the emerging economies.
- There is increased demand from certain expanding sectors (such as affluent retired people).
- Consumers are developing both higher and more sophisticated expectations, which means that the range of tourism options is expanding to include, for example, eco-tourism and adventure tourism.
- The tourism industry is maturing, which itself encourages greater product differentiation in order to maintain competitive edge and profits.
- The high level of competition in the travel industry is helping to keep prices low, which has increased demand.
- The wider process of globalization itself necessitates more business travel as companies increasingly spread their operations over a number of countries.

---

[1] Early estimates suggest that the total for 1999 was around 639 million.
[2] The estimates given in the literature vary widely, in part because of the difficulties involved in estimating the percentage of activity in other economic areas that is directly tourism related.

THE IMPLICATIONS FOR DEVELOPING COUNTRIES

Many developing countries have relatively limited options for eco-nomic development, at least until they have advanced to the point where they have managed to secure one or more positions of com-parative advantage. The sophisticated technology and significant cap-ital investment now required to develop or maintain a competitive position in many secondary or tertiary economic activities present an effective barrier to many potential new entrants. Lack of capacity, in terms of both the administrative and technical skill base, is a serious problem in many developing nations. The lack of expanding eco-nomic opportunities means that graduates from developing nations frequently have to move abroad to seek employment, and the conse-quent lack of a strong professional cadre and ethos is one of the factors that can foster corruption. It has been hard, therefore, for many devel-oping nations to move beyond their traditional economic activity of exporting their natural resources. Many of these natural resources – minerals, for example – are non-renewable; others, such as timber or fish, are renewable but are generally being exploited to exhaustion without any allowance for the time needed for the stock to replenish (Clayton and Radcliffe, 1996). Thus, many developing nations will not be able to pursue these traditional economic activities indefinitely.

Tourism, however, especially tourism based on the attraction of particular natural or social features (such as sunshine, beaches, moun-tains, forests, or a colourful, interesting culture), offers a way to use these resources without necessarily degrading or depleting them. Countries that have been endowed by nature or history with a good range of such features therefore have a genuine comparative advan-tage, which means that the tourism and travel sector has been a lifeline for these countries. Nearly 15 million people visited the Car-ibbean in 1996, for example, of which 71% were tourists and 9% were travelling for business reasons (the remaining 19% were mostly trav-elling for family reasons). This resulted in a total expenditure of US$13.3 billion, and supported 578,000 jobs in the region (Caribbean Tourism Organisation, 1996). For the Caribbean as a whole, tourism now brings in at least one-third of all foreign revenue.

THE CASE OF JAMAICA

While tourism now brings at least one third of all foreign revenue for the region as a whole, there are some countries within the region where the proportion is substantially higher. In Jamaica, for example, tourism now supports about 25% of all jobs, generates some 52% of all foreign revenue (Government of Jamaica, 1996, 1998),[3] accounts for nearly 8% of GDP directly but also the bulk of income from distributive trading, which accounts for about 22% of GDP.

Jamaica's foreign earnings for the export of goods and services is $2.3 billion, equivalent to 34% of GDP (Jamaica's GDP is $6.8 billion).[4] About 93% of this foreign revenue derives from just three sources:

Tourism	$ 1,196 million (52%)
Remittances	$ 611.7 million (26.6%)
Alumina/bauxite	$ 332.7 million (14.4%)[5]
Total	$2,140.4 million (93%)

Thus, Jamaica has become heavily dependent on tourism. This dependence on tourism may become even more extreme in future,[6] as other sectors of the economy currently appear vulnerable. For example: the alumina/bauxite industry is facing lower-cost competition from regions such as Western Australia. Traditional agricultural exports of sugar and bananas currently rely on preferential trade terms given by the European Union. These preferential trade terms have been extended until 2002, but will then come under review with a view to their being gradually phased out and replaced by normal World Trade Organization-compliant bilateral trade relations after 2008 (ECDPM, 1999)[7] or (in the case of sugar and rice) 2009. The production costs for bananas grown in the Caribbean islands are on average about three times higher than the production costs for bananas grown in

---

[3] The estimate given is from Statistical Institute of Jamaica data from 1998. However, estimates vary slightly. For example, the *National Industrial Policy: A Strategic Plan for Growth and Development* (Government of Jamaica, 1996) estimates that tourism generates 45% of all foreign revenue inflows from the productive sectors of the economy (this calculation excludes remittances). There is no disagreement, however, that tourism is by far the main source of foreign revenue.

[4] All figures from 1998 Statistical Institute of Jamaica data, gross figures, in US$.

[5] Calculated as follows: foreign exchange inflow = US$600.7 million (alumina) + US$81.0 (bauxite) = US$681.7 million, of which the share to Jamaica (real return) = levy plus royalty plus local cash inflow = US$332.7 million (14.4%).

[6] The percentage contributed by tourism has continued to climb as other sectors of the economy have under-performed or declined. Preliminary estimates suggest that the total for Jamaica is now in the range 56% to 58%, and may soon pass 60%.

[7] The timetable for the phase-out has been the subject of recent European Union–ACP negotiations. See, for example, ECDPM Lomé 2000 (November 1999). The current convention allows for the extension of current Lomé trade terms until 2002. The period 2002 to 2008 will form a transitional period before the new trading arrangements come into place in 2008. However, some countries will be given longer periods of adjustment.

South America, while the production costs for sugar in Jamaica are now some four to six times the world market price for sugar. These industries will therefore be vulnerable when fully exposed to low-cost competition, world market prices and unprotected trading conditions. Current indications are, therefore, that tourism could account for an even higher percentage of foreign revenue for countries such as Jamaica in future.

Current Concerns

However, there are a number of reasons to be concerned about the growing economic dominance of tourism.

Vulnerability

The fact that a number of countries have become so dependent on tourism is now itself a cause for concern, as it means that these countries will be immediately and severely vulnerable to any downturn in the industry.

Infrastructural Problems

Many developing countries are now realizing that their planning for tourism development has been deficient. Hotels have been built, for example, but public sewage plants have not been sufficiently expanded to cope with the increased flows, which means that inadequately treated sewage is being discharged – sometimes into the same stretch of water used by the tourists. Roads that were not built to take the increased traffic loads are now congested or crumbling and so on.

Similarly, it is clear that some countries are still having problems with certain facilities, including some for food handling, and with the related staff training. A large number of cases of food poisoning among tourists returning from the Dominican Republic in 1997, for example, obliged the UK company Airtours to switch about 10,000 holidays out of the Dominican Republic to other destinations in the Caribbean.

Environmental Impact

A number of countries have found that their tourism industry itself has had a serious environmental impact. The construction of hotels and related facilities (such as golf courses) has generated significant additional demand for construction materials and prime land, the additional flows of sewage have contributed to coral bleaching, the demand for souvenirs has contributed to the decline of certain species (such as conch), and so on.

Social Problems

In some countries, there are serious problems with social issues. As traditional economic sectors in the region decline, the number of people in poverty will tend to increase. Growth in other sectors may provide partial compensation, but there are likely to be severe transitional problems. A redundant sugarcane-cutter, for example, is unlikely to get work in the offshore banking sector. Poverty and desperation can, in some cases, result in harassment, where tourists are aggressively solicited by people attempting to sell them goods or services or simply begging. The tourists are, in some cases, offered legitimate souvenirs, but some are also pressured to buy sex or drugs, or threatened and robbed. This does not, of course, help to create the relaxed atmosphere that many tourists feel is the point of their holiday, and thus serves as a significant deterrent.

Growing Competitive Pressure

There is increasing competition both within the region and externally. The tourism industry in Mexico, for example, has expanded rapidly in recent years – the number of visitors grew by 10% between 1995 and 1996 alone – and offers a concentration of modern facilities and competitive prices in Cancun and Cozumel. As a result, in recent years many tourists from the United States and Canada have switched from the Caribbean islands to Mexico. Further afield, there is growing competition for tourists from states such as Hawaii, Florida and California.

Several of the small island nations of the Caribbean are now, potentially, threatened by the likely reemergence of Cuba as another powerful competitor for the same market segment. The small island nations of the Caribbean were only able to develop their tourism industries after Cuba was embargoed by the United States, and it now seems likely that this embargo will eventually be relaxed. With investment from Europe, Canada and elsewhere, a new generation of resort and leisure facilities is already under construction in Cuba, and many of the facilities in countries, such as Jamaica, which developed their tourism industries at an early stage, and are at a late stage of the product life-cycle. As a result, they could start to lose custom.

The effect of this growing competitive pressure can be already be seen in countries such as Jamaica, where particular subsectors (small hotels[8] in particular) are no longer profitable. This indicates a widening gap between the top tier of the industry (all-inclusive hotels and cruise ships), which continues to be profitable, and the remainder, which is relatively marginal.

This disparity has deep social implications, in that many of the all-inclusive hotels in the region and most of the cruise ships that visit the region are owned by multinational corporations, while the small hotels tend to be locally owned. Jamaica is unusual, in that most of the elite all-inclusives are locally owned, but in the region in general local participation in the industry is becoming increasingly restricted to relatively low-grade service jobs.

Economic Pressures

Increased competition would not necessarily preclude growth in the industry in the Caribbean island nations; the dramatic growth in the size of the tourism industry in recent years has allowed efficient, profitable operators to grow dramatically but has also buoyed up inefficient operators with slender margins. Thus, the industry has not been a zero-sum game. There are a number of factors, however, that may cause the dramatic regional growth rates of recent years to plateau, including:

- A renewed downturn in key global economies, such as Japan, with associated knock-on effects, could cause a decline in levels of disposable income in those countries and a switch from consumption to saving among potential tourists.
- The tourism industry is maturing, which can be seen in the progressive evolution beyond mass tourism to more sophisticated, differentiated tourist products. If the tourism industry follows the same logic of development as other industries, then the increased competitive pressure in the market place will start to generate pressure to cut margins in order to offer a more competitively priced product, thereby focusing attention on the need to improve efficiency and cut costs in order to remain profitable.

---

[8] Small hotels are defined as those having between nine and seventy-five rooms.

Any reduction in the rate of growth, or increased pressure on margins, will start to expose those operators with slender margins and little scope for trimming. Some of these, including many of the small hotel businesses in Jamaica, are already sustaining losses; high utility costs, high costs of debt servicing and heavy discounting are rendering them non-viable.

More Demanding Consumers

Tourists today have an extraordinarily wide choice of potential destinations. Tour operators offer trips into rain forests, to the Arctic, up Everest, across the Kalahari, along mountain trails in Nepal, and into countries that were, until relatively recently, largely inaccessible, such as Tibet.

As the market has become mature – and extraordinarily diverse – the tourists themselves have started to become increasingly sophisticated consumers. There are a number of factors that now make the quality of marketing and the perception that people have of a country as a potential tourist destination critical determinants of choice:

- A very wide range of options is now available.
- Many tourists now shop around and consider a number of options.
- Tourists can switch their intended destinations easily and, at least until the first deposit is paid, without cost.
- Many destination countries have now developed proper tourism marketing strategies, so the competition has become much stronger and more sophisticated.

Tourism is, therefore, a buyer's market in which people are faced with a bewildering choice in terms of both the large number and the diversity of products on offer. This means that perceptions, and the factors that can affect those perceptions, have become critically important.[9]

---

[9] Terrorists, unfortunately, are increasingly aware of this fact, and also that tourism is both economically significant and a very soft target. The murder of seventy tourists at Luxor in 1997 is estimated to have cost Egypt about half of its tourism revenue over the following year, which appears to have been the outcome intended by the terrorist group that perpetrated the atrocity. In a less extreme case, the industry has estimated that the bad publicity generated by the 1999 "gas tax riots" in Jamaica will cost some $60 to $70 million in lost revenue, a 5.4% drop in income. This is equivalent to 2.8% of Jamaica's total foreign revenue.

This gives further grounds for concern about the issues listed above. Beyond a certain point, harassment of tourists starts to create an image of danger, and cases of *E. coli* infections and food poisoning start to create an image of unhygienic conditions, and intending tourists will switch destinations. In countries where tourism is a major source of foreign revenue, even a modest downturn will have a significant and widespread impact.

SUSTAINABLE TOURISM

There is, therefore, a great deal of interest today in the concept of sustainable tourism, and there are now a number of initiatives in pursuit of this new goal. To date, this process has been driven largely by the growing concern over environmental issues. The industry in the Caribbean region, for example, is generally aware that it depends on being able to offer an attractive environment, although much of the actual discussion so far has focused on good housekeeping and internal efficiency rather than on externalized impacts. To date, there has been little discussion of more fundamental issues, such as the sustainability of the utilization of the natural resource base or of the wider social costs and benefits. Nevertheless, there is a good basis of awareness and concern both within the industry and among consumers for a move to a more genuinely sustainable development pathway and for the further evolution of the industry as an instrument of a wider process of sustainable development.

The global association of the industry, the World Travel and Tourism Council (WTTC), for example, has developed a new set of policy priorities in its *Millennium Vision* document (1996), which constitutes a major step towards a more integrated approach to tourism. These policies include:

- Putting tourism at the centre of strategies for economic development and employment
- Pursuing sustainable development
- Eliminating the barriers to growth and addressing the needs for infrastructure improvement
- Human resource development

A combined focus on tourism and sustainable development is now high on the agenda of development institutions such as the World Bank, the European Commission, regional development banks and bilateral aid agencies, partly as a result of the United Nations Conference on Environment and Development (UNCED) in Rio in 1992. At this stage, however, the new agenda has provided little more than a series of studies and some rather unconvincing projects. Some of the development institutions do not yet have a complete grasp of the industry, so they tend to focus on one or two aspects. Some focus on the environmental issues, for example, but may be insufficiently aware of the fundamentally important business aspects – and potential drivers – of the new sustainable tourism/sustainable development paradigm.

A reasonable definition of the implications of Agenda 21 for the travel and tourism industry is that tourism, as an engine of sustainable development, should "improve the quality of human life while living within the carrying capacity of the ecosystems which support life" (UNCED, 1992). The inclusion of both social and economic welfare and environmental concerns suggests that the business, environmental and developmental aspects of tourism need to be subsumed in an integrated strategy that provides for the sustainability and profitability of the industry itself but also uses it as the engine of a wider process of sustainable development for the countries, people and natural resources concerned.

THE TASK

The need, therefore, is to undertake a searching review of the options for the next phase of development of the industry in regions such as the Caribbean. At least for the immediate future, the industry will continue to serve as the main engine of economic development and growth. The task, therefore, is both to secure the long-term future of the industry and to ensure that it contributes to a wider process of genuinely sustainable development and growth by fostering a more socially and environmentally constructive engagement with other sectors of society.

Perhaps the single most important component of this task is to ensure that travel and tourism professionals are themselves made aware of the issues and given the conceptual and practical tools needed to secure the long-term future of the industry which ultimately rests in their hands. This may seem, in essence, a relatively straightforward proposal. Implementation would, however, raise some extremely challenging questions, especially in instances where developments in the industry become entangled in larger issues of global sustainable development.

THE LARGER AGENDA

It now appears that human activity potentially can affect the global ecology in ways and to an extent not previously thought possible. Global warming, ozone depletion, soil erosion, deforestation, desertification, and species extinction are all indicators of the extent to which human activity is now altering the conditions for life on Earth. All of these issues have the potential to alter fundamentally the parameters for the travel and tourism industry. Take global warming as an example.

Global Warming

There are a number of gases that human activity adds to the atmosphere. A small group of these have the capacity to trap heat with varying degrees of efficiency. However, the relative significance of these gases depends on the amount currently present in the atmosphere as well as their efficiency at trapping heat. This is why carbon dioxide, a relatively inefficient greenhouse gas, currently accounts for some 55% of the additional greenhouse effect.

Human activity currently adds some 5 to 6 gigatonnes (billion tonnes, or Gt) of carbon to the atmosphere annually, most of which is due to the combustion of fossilized hydrocarbons (coal, oil and gas). As a result, the carbon dioxide level in the Earth's atmosphere has risen from 275 parts per million (ppm) to 350 ppm since the beginning of industrialization. The Intergovernmental Panel on Climate Change (IPCC) has estimated that emissions could reach some 20 Gt per year by 2050 if current trends are continued, but that with a major shift in a number of relevant policies, additional emissions could be reduced to some 2 Gt per year by 2050. However, as global consumption of fossil fuel is currently rising at some 1.5% per year (varying from 0.5% in the industrialized nations to 6.0% in the developing nations), the low emission scenario currently seems less likely.

Current estimates are that the planet has warmed by 0.5°C over the last century, and that without prompt and effective intervention, the planet will warm by a further 1.5 to 5.5°C within the next 150 years. If carbon dioxide levels double by 2050 or 2100, as they are currently projected to do, then the expected temperature rise will be nearly 6.0°C.

This temperature rise of 6.0°C is currently expected to cause a rise in sea level by 0.3 to 1.2 metres, mostly due to thermal expansion of the ocean. A rise of 1 metre would affect (by inundation, salination and so on) some 5 million km² of land, which is about 3% of the land surface of the Earth. Global weather and tidal systems also may be affected significantly. The changes are likely to cause increasing occurrences of extreme weather such as hurricanes. Current indications are that global rainfall will increase by about 10%, but also that the rise in carbon dioxide levels may change the pattern of precipitation around the globe, so that some regions will become drier. This is likely to have a marked effect on water distribution and supply issues and on agriculture.

Potential Threats to Tourism

- It may be necessary to consider introducing increasingly severe measures to get people to reduce their consumption of fossil fuel. One way to do this would be to introduce or raise taxes on carbon-based fuel. Given that demand for transport is highly elastic, it would be necessary to have relatively high levels of tax on carbon-based fuels in order to achieve the desired rate of reduction in use. Clearly, this would make transport and freight much more expensive. In turn, this would impact severely on the tourism industry, as tourism entails using a great deal of energy to move large numbers of people around the world for what are, after all, non-essential purposes. The impact on particular modes of transport would depend partly on the energy demand per passenger per kilometre, which means that airfares would rise more than comparable ship fares. It is possible, therefore, that cruise ships could take a bigger share of the market in future.
- Sea level rise will affect coastal zones. Some beaches will disappear and others will be formed as currents and erosion patterns change. It is possible, therefore, that some existing coastal resorts will be left without their beaches.
- Any change in the frequency and severity of hurricanes obviously would be particularly serious for regions such as the Caribbean. Increased frequency could cause the tourist season to contract to relatively safe periods of the year.

■ Should rising sea levels make it necessary to construct sea defences for the world's major coastal cities, then the consequent rise in levels of public taxation and expenditure would cause levels of disposable income in many countries to decline, with obvious implications for expenditure on non-essential items such as holidays.

THE IMPLICATIONS FOR TOURISM

It is important to ask, therefore, whether the concept of sustainable tourism makes sense. Does it make sense to consume even more resources by shipping an ever-increasing number of people round the world, largely for non-essential purposes? In the long-term, it may be genuinely difficult to justify any attempt to expand the industry. However, many developing nations are now largely dependent on tourism, so doing without a tourism industry is no longer an option – at least not in the immediate future. The need, therefore, is to develop a real agenda for sustainable tourism. Some of the key issues that must inform that agenda are outlined below.

The first is the need to move the industry beyond the concept of environmental protection to environmental enhancement. Environmental protection is usually taken to involve the defence of current environmental standards and conditions. A number of regional ecologies have, however, been significantly degraded. Programmes of restoration and enhancement will therefore be required, in many cases, to achieve a reasonable level of environmental quality.

The underlying problem is that many people still see the environment only as a constraining or even negative factor – that is, that there is some minimum standard of environmental quality that must be met in order to secure inward investment and continued growth in tourism. This is unfortunate for two reasons. One is that it indicates that the environment is seen as a quality of life issue, and therefore of secondary importance, rather than as an economic development opportunity of primary importance. The second is that it assumes that the environment must be afforded a degree of protection from the adverse consequences of economic development, which in turn implies that environmental and economic needs invariably must conflict. The consequence of this position is, of course, that people will continue to believe that some degree of environmental protection must be sacrificed for economic development.

The need now is to move beyond this conflict and find a new synthesis in which environmental enhancement is fully integrated and compatible with economic development (Clayton et al., 1999). The report of the World Commission on Environment and Development (WCED, 1987) and the Agenda 21 report of the United Nations Conference on Environment and Development (UNCED, 1992) agreed that a new synthesis of this kind will be at the heart of any strategy for sustainable development.

Thus, it is important to ensure that any new developments contribute to both environmental and economic enhancement. This in turn supports the argument introduced earlier, that the strategy for tourism development should be embedded within a larger strategic framework for the social, economic and environmental development of the country.

Vulnerability/Sensitivity Analysis

Issues here include the extent to which the industry would be vulnerable, for example, to carbon taxes that increased the cost of energy-intensive forms of travel, and whether this would result in a displacement within the industry (from air to sea, for example), or an overall slowdown in the industry. Other issues include the possible impact of the projected increase in the occurrence of hurricanes and extreme weather conditions associated with global warming, the beach erosion and relocation associated with coral reef die-back and changing tidal patterns and so on.

Maximizing the Utility of the Flow of Revenue

It is important to ascertain the extent to which the income from tourism could be used to fund investment in other sectors of the economy without weakening the sector itself, and what would be required to channel investment, promote economic diversification, reduce the vulnerability that stems from a disproportionate degree of dependence on tourism, and develop alternatives.

In uncertain situations, diversification is a way to hedge bets and reduce the total exposure to risk. A country with a range of primary, secondary and tertiary sector industries, a reasonable export performance, a healthy financial services sector and a tourism industry can ride out a recession in any one of these areas (especially if the country also has a skilled and flexible workforce who can switch into other activities), because they are unlikely to follow the same market logic or have the same business cycle. A country that depends on any one sector for the bulk of its foreign revenue is one that is intrinsically vulnerable. It would be sensible, therefore, when times are good, to use the income from that one sector, for investment to build up other sectors of the economy and thus reduce the country's vulnerability.

The solution here, of course, is that the government has to have a clear understanding of where tourism fits into its overall economic strategy, and how to use the revenues to:

1. Strengthen the tourism industry itself in order to ensure that the revenues continue flowing.
2. Build up associated economic activity, partly in order to ensure that the benefits are more widely distributed, partly to ensure that the industry can source more of its requirements locally and partly in order to develop the kind of local diversity of options that today's tourists demand.
3. Build up other sectors of the economy to ensure that they too could be in a position to support wider social goals in the future.

CONCLUSION

It is clear, therefore, that the industry has to address some profound and challenging questions. We must consider, for example:

- Is the goal simply to increase the number of people coming to a country, and if so, to what level?
- What are the environmental, infrastructural and social limits to the numbers that can be safely absorbed?
- Has this strategy been properly evaluated and compared with possible alternative strategies?
- Would it make more strategic sense to aim to maximize revenue rather than numbers and move the industry upmarket with a view to taking a higher per capita profit from a smaller number of tourists?
- Does the industry use any indicators of social, economic and environmental impact, and is there a decision-making structure in place that could incorporate these indicators?

These issues indicate an urgent need to clarify the national strategy for tourism, assess the performance targets and criteria set by the industry itself and develop the management strategies needed to take the industry forward through these uncertain times.

No government can safely attempt to answer such questions in isolation. They call for a wider and more inclusive process of discussion involving representatives of the key stakeholder groups in order to ensure that the ensuing strategy is clear and robust. Such a strategy can then be usefully embodied in a national master plan for tourism, with rolling targets and strategies subject to periodic revision and updating in order to allow for the constantly changing environment in which the industry operates.

REFERENCES

Caribbean Tourism Organisation. (1996). *Caribbean Tourism Statistical Report 1996,* Caribbean Tourism Organisation, Barbados.

Clayton, A. (1997). "EU–ACP Relations", briefing paper for the Regional Negotiating Machinery, University of the West Indies, Mona, Jamaica.

Clayton, A. (1998). "Sustainable Tourism", discussion paper, University of the West Indies, Centre for Environment and Development, Mona, Jamaica.

Clayton, A. and Radcliffe, N. (1996). *Sustainability: A Systems Approach,* Earthscan, London.

Clayton, A., Spinardi, G., and Williams, R. (1999). *Cleaner Technology: A New Agenda for Government and Industry,* Earthscan, London.

ECDPM (European Centre for Development Policy Management). (1999). *Lomé 2000 (November),* European Centre for Development Policy Management, Maastricht, The Netherlands.

Government of Jamaica. (1996). *National Industrial Policy: A Strategic Plan for Growth and Development,* Government Printing Office, Kingston, Jamaica.

Government of Jamaica. (1998). Statistical Institute of Jamaica reports, Government Printing Office, Kingston, Jamaica.

UNCED (United Nations Commission on Environment and Development). (1992). *The Report of the United Nations Conference on Environment and Development,* United Nations Commission on Environment and Development, New York.

WCED (World Commission on Environment and Development). (1987). *Our Common Future,* World Commission on Environment and Development, Oxford University Press, Oxford.

WTTC (World Travel and Tourism Council). (1996). *Millennium Vision,* World Travel and Tourism Council, London.

CHAPTER 21

SUSTAINABLE TOURISM DEVELOPMENT IN THE CARIBBEAN: THE ROLE OF EDUCATION

Godfrey A. Pratt

Abstract

This chapter examines environmental, economic and socio-cultural concerns related to tourism development within the Caribbean. More specifically, the author makes clear the need for a sustainable approach to tourism development. Examples from Mexico, Belize and Barbados are cited to demonstrate the issues raised. Education is then identified as a critical element to achieving sustainable tourism development. Such educational programmes should be designed to target private sector operators, public sector officials and agencies and local communities. Education is also identified as a means to prepare Caribbean youths to take leadership in the development of Caribbean tourism in the future.

THE NEED FOR A PEDAGOGY FOR DEVELOPMENT

Conventional mass tourism (CMT) has been a boon to many countries in the Caribbean. As a "smokeless" industry this tool has been much sought after by tourism directors to produce the magical economic benefits associated with the procession of hundreds or thousands of tourists from the major tourist markets in the United States, Europe and South America through their destinations. It is little wonder that this paradigm exists. Within the Caribbean examples abound of nation states and communities that owe much of their growth and development to the tourist dollar. The Bahamas, Jamaica, Puerto Rico, and the US Virgin Islands are in the vanguard of Caribbean destinations that have benefited from CMT and continue to develop this tourism market. At the same time, however, there is considerable concern that the very instrument of prosperity could be the vehicle that sows the seeds of destruction for these destinations. Every tourism planner knows of the deleterious side effects of unchecked CMT on the environment, society and culture of their particular destination.

Increasingly though, the trend in many third world countries worldwide has been to look to "alternative tourism" (AT) as a seemingly benign alternative to uncontrolled mass tourism with all of its negative impacts on the local economy, environment and socio-cultural structure (Cater, 1992). Activities associated with this form of tourism are usually in direct contrast to mass tourism. Development is likely to be on a much smaller scale than with mass tourism. Typically businesses are locally owned and there is less leakage of the business earnings outside the country. Eco-tourism is one variant of AT that has been embraced by many destinations as the answer to traditional mass tourism (Cater, 1992). With this brand of tourism they hope to acquire much needed financial resources, without destroying their natural resources.

Cater (1993), at the University of Reading, Whiteknights, suggests that three major reasons account for this level of interest from many developing countries. First, the benefits accruing locally are likely to be greater than those arising from conventional tourism. Second, as many third world destinations are among the last havens of unspoiled nature they have a distinct advantage over other destinations in attracting the eco-tourist. Third, as the emphasis is on nature, eco-tourism in theory should be an ecologically responsible form of tourism. This (at least theoretically) ensures the conservation and protection of the natural environment. Pioneering efforts of Caribbean nations like Belize, Dominica and others are often examined and presented to tourism planners and the academic community as eminent examples of a new alternative tourism paradigm that promises to confer desired economic benefits to the area while simultaneously protecting its valued natural and community resources.

However, even the most progressive CMT or AT programmes to Caribbean destinations do not guarantee the sustainability of their tourism product. As with any major undertaking, a strategic plan should be undertaken that examines where destinations are with regard to their inventory of tourism products. An assessment of tourism impacts on a destination should be made, whether planners decide to utilize either CMT or AT programmes or a combination of both.

In order to ensure the success of a sustainable tourism action plan, an aggressive education campaign must be undertaken. The subject population to which a sustainable tourism education programme must be directed is varied. The population should be comprised of the following:

- Tourism, hospitality or hotel training schools
- Lodging operators
- Cruise ship companies
- The fishing and boating industry
- Tour operators
- Civic groups
- Entrepreneurs
- Tourists themselves
- All tourism industry workers in the destination

The tourism education campaign must be a part of a sustainable tourism policy that coalesces a cross section of public and private sector partners whose synergistic effort is legitimized by a tourism policy statement. To understand in detail where a sustainable tourism education effort should be directed, we must first examine where the sustainability of the tourism product is threatened. The environmental, economic and socio-cultural climate in the Caribbean is susceptible to degradation and damage from tourism. This chapter examines each of these aspects in detail in order to propose an effective system of education and training to ameliorate or eliminate the damaging effects of tourism. Tourism is only one component of sustainable development. Tourism, as it relates to sustainable development, is tourism that is developed so that the nature, scale, location and manner of development is appropriate and sustainable over time, and where the ability of the environment to support other activities is not damaged, since tourism cannot be isolated from other resource use activities (Wight, 1997). The tourism environment being discussed for sustainability refers to the ecology, economy and social culture of a destination.

ENVIRONMENTAL CONCERNS

With the growth and increased development of tourism in the Caribbean, the marine and terrestrial ecosystems of many tourist destinations have suffered significant, and sometimes irreversible, damage. The very pristine habitats, land and seascapes that originally attract tourists to these destinations are being degraded by human encroachment, either for visits, or for more long-term development. Examples abound within the Caribbean area of the ravages of overfishing, the depletion of marine, plant, and animal life because of human incursion into these areas, with chemicals toxic to the fragile ecosystems. Raw sewage from hotels pumped into harbours in the Caribbean is often the price paid for an influx of visitors that exceeds the carrying capacity of many developing destinations (Government of Antigua and Barbuda, 1998). The use of bleaches, and in some cases explosives, by over-eager fishermen contributes to the killing of coral reefs in this area.

Although a good deal of damage to the reef life in the Caribbean is the result of natural phenomena, humans are in control of the anthropogenic (people induced) threats to this environment. Natural threats to the coral reefs in the Caribbean include:

- Physical breakage and high turbidity due to hurricanes and tropical storms
- Long-term climate changes
- Crowding and substrate takeover by algae
- Predation by other organisms and cannibalism by other corals
- Bleaching, black line disease, white line disease, and related pathogens (Island Resources Foundation, 1997)

Anthropogenic stresses to the reefs include:

- Physical damage from anchoring, boat grounding, and swimmer damage, as well as coral removal
- Substrate takeover by algae in a nutrient-enriched environment
- Nutrient-enriched runoff and biocides (pesticides, herbicides and fungicides – many times vacation homes, guest houses and hotels employ the use of these chemicals, which then often percolate for many miles through porous limestone soil and find their way into reef areas)
- Hydrocarbons and trace elements from terrestrial waste streams and marine products

- Following rainy periods suspended sediment discharge from unstabilized slopes, spoil banks, construction sites, roads, ravines, etc.
- Bleaching, black line disease, stimulated by the damaging effects of chemical runoff, sedimentation, long line fishing, stable or runaway fish traps, cruise ship anchor damage, and additional physical damage committed by divers
- Overfishing (Island Resources Foundation, 1997)

Within the Family Islands of the Bahamas, the above-mentioned ecosystems have experienced an accelerated rate of decline within the past nineteen years, according to a 1994 study done by Ecoplan Net Ltd (McGregor, 1994). Nowhere in the Caribbean are coral reefs considered stable. Professor David Weaver indicates that, based on an extrapolation of current trends, it was estimated that the reefs around Jamaica and Trinidad would be lost within fifteen to twenty-five years, and those in the remainder of the archipelago within fifteen to thirty-five years (Weaver, 1993). A limited ecological assessment of coral reefs off the coasts of Antigua and Barbuda (Goreau and Goreau, 1996) showed that most sites were dominated by dead coral rubble and had live coral cover of only between 5% and 20%.

Overfishing is also a major problem for the Caribbean area, especially when fishing methods are used that destroy the habitat of the fish. Long line fishing, which can contribute to breakage of coral, continues to be a problem. Wire fish traps that can considerably damage a reef also continue to be widely used in the Caribbean. These fish traps are highly effective in quickly capturing large numbers of fish of various species. Ghost fish traps are those that have become separated from their lines and buoys. They continue killing hundreds of fish before they finally decompose in the sea (Island Resources Foundation, 1997). In other less destructive ways both visitors and the indigenous population contribute to the depletion of marine resources by overfishing. Many visiting pleasure boaters trade catches of fish for fuel and other supplies. The continued removal of excessive numbers of fish from reef areas could have a negative long-term effect on reef ecology (Island Resources Foundation, 1997).

A final major threat to the sustainability of coral reefs in the Caribbean is the proliferation of large cruise ships in the area that wreak incredible havoc by dropping large anchors and their chains on coral reefs. Stephen Smith, a marine ecologist at Environmental Technologies International in Honolulu, claimed that urgent action is needed to prevent serious coral loss (personal communication). Anchor-damaged reefs may never recover, and if they do, the process of recovery can take about fifty years (Allen, 1992).

Another major environmental concern in the Caribbean area is littering and inadequate solid waste management. This is evident throughout the Caribbean, especially in areas that have experienced benefit from tourism development. Litter abounds in many communities, in roads, trails and on the beaches. Inadequate garbage management in addition to a laissez-faire attitude on the part of local inhabitants may be substantially to blame for this situation. In many island and coastal environments garbage has historically been disposed of in the sea. There it was out of sight and out of mind. However, with the proliferation of packaged goods from the United States and other more developed areas, there has been an exponential explosion of discarded material ranging from gum wrappers to tin cans, to discarded and abandoned vehicles (McGregor, 1994).

The pollution of coastal waters by the dumping of raw sewage from cruise ships and other pleasure boaters is another cause of major concern. In addition to the destruction of the coral reef and the over-promotion of algal formation in harbours, the practice is making some areas unsafe for swimmers. This is especially regrettable, since the solution to this problem is relatively simple: that is, the installation of dumping stations in these areas, and the enforcement of dumping regulations (McGregor, 1994). The dumping of solid waste along shorelines also seriously threatens marine life. Many materials, including plastics, disintegrate very slowly and can exert negative impacts for many years. Marine life can ingest or become entangled in these waste products. This can lead to death or serious injury.

A final tourism threat to the sustainability of the Caribbean environment is the inefficient use of limited freshwater supplies. This area is one that truly tests the carrying capacity of Caribbean destinations. Before the onset of CMT freshwater supplies in many cases were adequate to serve the needs of the indigenous community. However, with an exponential increase in the population requiring freshwater service, problems arise. The depletion of existing freshwater supplies causes the freshwater lens to be contaminated by salt intrusion (McGregor, 1994). Often this contamination becomes a permanent condition for future generations.

ECONOMIC CONCERNS

Economic growth through the acquisition of much needed foreign exchange is the main incentive behind the promotion and acceptance of either CMT or AT development in the Caribbean. However, the accrual of economic benefits from tourism must be reexamined in light of the high economic leakage in the Caribbean from the tourist dollar. As an example, tourism industry operators, as well as the general population in the Bahamas, rely heavily on products and services imported directly from the United States. Even traditional agricultural staples that are grown in the Bahamas are imported in bulk from Florida. Estimates show that for every tourist dollar brought into the country, at least $.80 goes back out to pay for imported foodstuffs (BBC Radio).

Most tourists coming to the Caribbean originate from one of the more developed countries. Their travel arrangements are coordinated by entrepreneurs in the tourists' countries of origin. It has been estimated that the proportion of an inclusive tour price that is retained locally drops to only 22% to 25% if both the airline and the hotel used are foreign owned (Britton, 1982). Since the scarcity of capital for major tourism development is commonplace in the business community throughout the Caribbean there is a high degree of foreign investment. Caribbean governments have even supported foreign investment in their countries, over the years, in hopes of ensuring an acceptable inflow of foreign capital. However, the economic and socio-cultural threats to these destinations loom ever present, engendered by opportunistic foreign investors who seize the opportunity to milk profits from tourism businesses in these areas. They are also likely to build or purchase elaborate mansions locally and create exclusive enclaves of like-minded foreign businessmen. The profits from these businesses are repatriated out of the country.

Real estate prices in popular Caribbean destinations have become inflated beyond the means of the average low-income residents, largely because of the degree of foreign investment. Foreign holdings are in theory restricted to half an acre in urban areas, and ten acres in rural areas in Belize. It has been estimated that 90% of all coastal development in Belize is now foreign owned (Cater, 1993). This situation is too often mirrored throughout the Caribbean.

SOCIO-CULTURAL CONCERNS

In April 1997, a study by the Organization of American States for the Seventeenth Inter-American Travel Congress in San Jose, Costa Rica, outlined danger signals that heralded the saturation of a tourism destination. Adverse social impacts discussed at the conference included (1) friction and resentment between the host community and tourists and (2) social problems, such as general crime, drug abuse and prostitution (Organization of American States, 1997).

Friction and resentment between the host community and the tourist often occurs when the indigenous population perceives paying guests as hordes of well-heeled, sometimes superior, vacationers who greedily consume the limited resources of their community. These guests usually demand speedy and efficient service, especially when they pay premium rates for merchandise and service. This often clashes with the well-meaning, but slower paced, personal service that the native service person is accustomed to providing. Whereas the majority of the Caribbean population enjoys a modest living, many persons in these communities, who observe the somewhat lavish spending patterns of tourists on vacation, attempt to imitate those spenders.

They are oblivious to the fact that many of the visitors may have accumulated financial savings over long periods of time in order to reward themselves with a Caribbean vacation. Whereas these young Caribbean people could be storing up nest eggs for their future, they tend to spend inordinate amounts of hard-earned money on leisure activities, emulating the tourist on vacation. Today we no longer talk about "3S" but "4S" destinations, that is, destinations sought after by those in search of sun, sea, sand and sex. The Caribbean fills the bill as a 4S destination. Unescorted singles, especially single women on vacation, come seeking exotic experiences in a romantic setting. Their attentions are not only welcomed but encouraged by many single and not-so-single men in the population. It is little wonder that their presence is often resented by local women. Visiting single women have complained about local women "staring daggers into them" when they appear to be enjoying some dalliance with a local man.

Economic conditions indirectly create another social situation. In many smaller Caribbean communities farming and fishing are usually the mainstay. Young men typically leave school early to help augment family incomes. Although they assume significant farming roles, especially during harvest times, girls typically remain in the school system longer than boys do. Tourism development in these areas generally produces jobs for many of these young women. They become cooks, waitresses, maids, gift store clerks and so on. Although young men are increasingly employed as well in entry level and low skill positions, the proportion of native women working in the tourism industry in many locations far outweighs the number of men. These women find themselves earning much more than their fathers, brothers or spouses, who remain farmers, fishermen, or remain elsewhere on the periphery of the tourism industry. Tension ensues, causing the breakdown of the nuclear family in these traditional societies. This problem is not as prevalent today in the more developed urban areas of the Caribbean. However, as tourism development emerges in newer underdeveloped areas, this cycle repeats itself.

Drug abuse, prostitution, petty theft and other crimes have been known to follow the development of CMT everywhere. While these crimes are certainly serious they can be handled in traditional ways.

SUSTAINABLE TOURISM ENDEAVOURS

Mexico's Monarch Butterfly

Researchers from the University of Florida noticed the overwintering pattern of the Monarch butterfly some twenty-four years ago. They traced its 5,000-mile flight path from Canada to Mexico, between 1974 an 1976. This incredible phenomenon was reported in *Scientific American* and *National Geographic* magazines, which served to make the west-central area of Mexico suddenly very appealing to nature tourists. Although the existence and proliferation of this butterfly species was well known to local residents and the wider Mexican population the publication of this fact substantially altered conditions in this area (Barkin, 1996).

Although the viewing of the wintering Lepidoptera was not a planned tourism activity for the area, it nevertheless attracted hundreds of thousands of visitors to the area. The government, in an effort to preserve the goose that laid the golden egg, involved itself in establishing regulations designed to protect the butterfly and its habitat from human encroachment. Land was appropriated to create nature reserves for the butterfly. Many inhabitants of the area grew to resent this wintering visitor. Because of its annual visits their lives were increasingly regulated by the government. The socio-economic environment in the protected areas was not the best prior to the "discovery" of the winged visitor. This situation was perhaps a mirror of the larger malaise in the Mexican society. However, the conservation efforts served to exacerbate an already unsavoury situation. They made it very difficult for poor rural producers to successfully engage in traditional forestry activities. Certain important commercial areas of woodland were declared to be part of the buffer zones of the reserve. The affected communities were not remunerated for the reclassification of their lands, nor were they given alternative productive opportunities that would provide them with a living elsewhere in the region (Barkin, 1996).

Local systems of control by political bosses and economic elites were already in place before the recognition of the butterflies. Also, the industrial demand for pulp and local efforts to concentrate the wealth and opportunities were already creating pressures on the forests and pitting individuals and communities against each other. As is usually the case in this scenario, the unplanned upsurge in tourism created opportunities that were not evenly distributed throughout the communities. Only a small group of people was able to capitalize on the tourism opportunities. This situation only worsened the socio-economic condition of certain areas within the protected zone (Barkin, 1996).

This case highlights the importance of planning for sustainable development. A multidimensional approach is needed. Where a major economic activity is in place, other complementary activity should be put into place, otherwise the major activity is undermined, and the goose with the golden egg dies. In this scenario it appears that because of the economic situation and the pressure to produce pulp from foresting activity, the people in the region will continue their environmentally destructive activities, which in turn threaten the viability of the fir forests, the habitat of the Monarch butterfly (Barkin, 1996).

The Creole and Maya of Belize

Mahler (1997) examined two community tourism projects in Belize that he heralds as successful models to be emulated by other communities. One project was coordinated by a Creole community along the Belize River. The other is located in Mayan villages in southern Belize. Creole is the term used to describe Belizeans of African descent whose ancestors came to Belize, then British Honduras, as slaves or indentured servants. Another large group of Belizeans of African descent are known locally as Caribs or Garifuna. They are of West African descent as well, but they came to Belize by way of St Vincent and the Grenadines, and settled in Belize some time after the Creole population. However, for purposes of this study the differences between the Creole and the Carib population are not significant. The Creole population is the largest of the ethnic groups in Belize (Mahler, 1997).

Tourism now rivals agriculture as the leading industry in Belize. However, the tourism industry has failed to involve many Creole people in outlying areas. During the late 1980s primate specialists from the United States were drawn to a Creole settlement along the Belize River, where there was an impressive collection of black howler monkeys. The specialists were happy to see that the locals liked and respected the monkeys, which they referred to as "baboons". These monkeys, which were an endangered species, moved around freely and fearlessly among the homes and subsistence farms of the Creoles (Mahler, 1997).

The specialists suggested that the local residents create a voluntary sanctuary for the howler monkeys, and promote it as a tourist attraction. This effort would preserve the monkey population and simultaneously provide a source of income for the locals. The Community Baboon Sanctuary was born as an outgrowth of this effort. Thousands of visitors now flock to the sanctuary, which is located north-west of Belize City. Tourists now spend money on tourist guides, food, lodging and so on. (Mahler, 1997).

Creole communities that were in decline as a result of the flight of young people seeking better economic opportunities, and the decline in agricultural jobs, were being revived by the infusion of tourist money. Many families now earn a living by providing modest bed-and-breakfast services to visitors. Several full service lodges have opened up, creating work for locals as cooks, maids and the like. Even the grocery stores are able to snare a portion of the tourist dollar, selling food and cold drinks to visitors. Tour guides earn an income by guiding visitors through the jungle, identifying plants, animal tracks, and the monkeys that leap from tree to tree (Mahler, 1997).

The baboon sanctuary was originally backed by the Milwaukee Zoo, the World Wildlife Fund, the Lincoln Park Zoo, the International Primate Protection League and the Belize Audubon Society. The sanctuary now covers a 20-mile stretch of land along the Belize River, and encompasses land owned by more than one hundred individuals. The sanctuary employs several locals and maintains an impressive visitor centre and museum. Here a fee is collected from each arrival. As virtually all visitors come in contact with local residents it is the ideal place to experience both the Creole culture and nature, at the same time (Mahler, 1997).

Additional benefits from the sanctuary include stemming the exodus of young people from the area, for more urban areas, including the United States. This project has been credited for the resurgence in many wildlife species and a downturn in the number of wild animals killed by the locals for food. Scientists now come to the area to study not only the howler monkeys, but birds, turtles and other creatures that are thriving within the boundaries of the sanctuary. The protection of howler monkeys has been so successful that excess monkeys are now being captured and resettled in parts of Belize where they have become extinct (Mahler, 1997).

Mayan villagers in southern Belize have organized to promote a low-impact tourism that enables outside visitors to spend time among them, living either in guest houses built and run by their community or in the homes of individual families. Although mass tourism is not a significant threat the Mayan village leaders were afraid of the denigration of their fragile culture if a community-controlled infrastructure was not put into place. They wished to avoid the example of their neighbouring Guatemala, where tensions have flared within heavily touristed communities, where a select handful of foreign entrepreneurs reap the benefits from visitors to the area. The Maya of Belize were also concerned that their dances, festivals and art may be exploited by outsiders (Mahler, 1997).

Two locally initiated projects, the Toledo Host Family Network/Indigenous Experience Programme, and the Mayan Guesthouse and Eco-Trail Programme, seek to combine cultural tourism, sustainable agriculture and environmental conservation. For the Host Family Network experience tourists are placed in the actual homes of Mayans, where they observe and participate in daily village life. For the guesthouse programme the tourists get to visit many of the same villages that host the family network programme. In contrast though, they stay in structures specifically built for their use. In both programmes the guests eat meals prepared by and take outings guided by local residents (Mahler, 1997).

In late 1997, five communities had guesthouses in operation, and government-sponsored hospitality courses had been taken by many villagers. A rotating group of families in each community was responsible for taking care of the hospitality and tourism needs of the guests. Others in the community produced arts and crafts that the tourists could purchase. Income from the tourists is shared instead of hoarded by a small or privileged few. Under the Host Family Network programme, tourists are also distributed among a wide range of families. They are modestly remunerated for the room and board provided. All tourists pay a fee to the village council, which uses the fees for community-based projects, such as improving water systems, road repair and construction, and building schools (Mahler, 1997).

These examples from both the Maya and the Creole experience are ideal examples of what a sustainable tourism effort can produce. What is unusual about the efforts of these two indigenous Belizean groups is that their tourism projects are completely voluntary. This is a dramatic change from over fifteen years ago, when virtually nothing was being done to integrate the needs of the local people with the growing demands of tourism (Mahler, 1997). This is almost a letter-perfect example of a win–win situation for tourist and residents alike when the perfect sustainable tourism development project is enacted. This is an all too rare phenomenon.

A NATIONAL AGENDA 21 IN BARBADOS

Barbados is part of the United Nations testing programme on sustainable development indicators. It is presented in this study to show what lessons can be learned by other Caribbean states that wish to embark on a meaningful sustainable development programme. Barbados is in the process of establishing a national Agenda 21 programme for sustainable development. Sustainable tourism development is one facet of the entire programme that seeks to ensure intergenerational viability for the country.

In assessing sustainable development indicators the following areas must be examined by Agenda 21 member states:

- International cooperation and trade
- Changing consumer patterns
- Financing
- Technology
- Industry
- Transport
- Sustainable tourism

The following actions that were implemented, policies that were established or plans for future implementation have been excerpted from reports submitted to the fifth to the seventh sessions of the United Nations Commission on Sustainable Development, in April 1997, 1998 and 1999 by the Government of Barbados.

International Cooperation and Trade

No local legislation currently exists that addresses sustainable development. International trade matters are conducted by the Ministry of International Trade. Local trade matters are handled by the Ministry of Industry, Commerce and Business. Government recognizes the need for non-governmental organizations to be involved in many matters pertaining to sustainable development. The progress made by Barbados in promoting sustainable development through trade can be categorized as slow, for the following reasons (Government of Barbados, 1997–1999).

- The slow response of the international donor community in providing financial and other assistance to member states.
- A reduction in multilateral financial and technical assistance in Barbados. (Barbados has been graduated by the international funding organizations and no longer receives grants or concessional funding. Any funding Barbados receives is related to specific projects.)
- The globalization of production and finance and the creation of regional trading blocks have served to marginalize small island developing states such as Barbados.
- Domestic strain on national, human and institutional resources have hampered Barbados' efforts at implementing policies and programmes to address the area of trade and environment.

Regional and local collaboration has taken the form of: (1) joining regional partners in the Caribbean Community (CARICOM) and embarking on a program of elimination of tariff and non-tariff barriers; and (2) creation of the Association of Caribbean States (ACS) as a vehicle to assist Caribbean states in managing the globalization process.

Changing Consumption Patterns

No specific strategy or policy exists in a comprehensive framework; however, national policies regarding energy resource use, water, and so on would lead to sustainable consumption and production patterns. The following programs are in place (Government of Barbados, 1997–1999):

- The preparation of an Energy Efficiency Act for Electrical Appliances, coupled with energy efficiency labelling for electrical appliances
- The continued promotion of the implementation of the ISO 9000 and ISO 14000 Series
- Leak detection and remedy by the Barbados Water Authority
- Desalination of seawater for consumption

Further use has been made of solar energy for heating water. Tax incentives are used to promote the use of this alternative source of solar energy. Additionally, energy conservation devices continue to be used in some hotels in Barbados. Specific issues that such policies and programmes address include (Government of Barbados, 1997–1999):

- Increasing energy and material efficiency in production processes
- Reducing wastes from production and promoting recycling
- Promotion of ISO 1400 by the Ministry of Environment Division
- Energy division and encouragement of research at the University of the West Indies
- Promoting use of new and renewable sources of energy
- Using environmentally sound technologies for sustainable production
- Reducing wasteful consumption
- Increasing awareness for sustainable consumption.

Financing

The government has no specific budget for sustainable development. Development cooperation policy has not been reviewed or changed as a direct consequence of the United Nations Conference on Environment and Development (UNCED). The overall national budget addresses all national development sectors. However, specific programmes have been identified that integrate environment and development concerns. They include the following (Government of Barbados, 1997–1999):

- The Coastal Conservation Study for the South and East Coasts of Barbados (Implementation): US$7.3 million
- The South Coast Sewerage Project: US$35.0 million
- The West Coast Sewerage Study: US$2.32 million
- The West Coast Sewerage Project (Implementation): over US$35.0 million
- The Solid Waste Management Study: US$1.5 million
- The Solid Waste Management Plan (Implementation): US$25.0 million
- The Water Resources and Water Loss Study: US$1.7 million
- The National Transport Plan Study: US$0.77 million
- The Agriculture Revitalization Plan: US$10.0 million
- The Environmental Management and Land Use Planning for Sustainable Development: US$1.6 million

Technology

Presently there is no defined policy for the use of environmentally sound technologies (ESTs). Some EST devices are available in Barbados and, upon serious discussion, specific incentives and economic instruments have been applied to encourage consumption. These include water saving devices and solar water heaters. Major efforts are also underway in the legislation for the regulation and harmonization of pesticides, and the guaranteeing of environmental safety with regard to waste disposal and its environmental consequences. ESTs are most urgently needed in the areas of tourism, agriculture, health, industry and engineering (Government of Barbados, 1997–1999).

Industry

The principal threats to human health or the sustainable use of natural resources associated with industrial activity in Barbados come from the sugar industry, which generates smoke emissions from factory chimneys. Regulation and legislation pertaining to smoke emissions exist and are being enforced. Recently an overhaul of the cane transport sector has reduced emissions from all old and inefficient vehicles.

The Mobil Oil Refinery poses a potential risk of pollution in case of an accident. However, it is in the process of closing its operations. The major focus is now on ensuring the comprehensive remediation of the site so that it is suitable for future development (Government of Barbados, 1997–1999).

With regard to implementing a national policy for ecologically sustainable industrial development, efforts are being undertaken to establish a code of conduct procedure regarding environmental issues and sustainable development, to be adopted by the private sector.

Tourism is the major economic industry in Barbados and as such is a major user of freshwater resources. The scarce supply of this resource, as well as the great number of competing demands for use, could well be a constraint to future development of the tourism industry, especially if the proposed development poses greater demands on water resources (Government of Barbados, 1997–1999). No major incidents of industrial pollution have been recorded to date. However, atrazine from the agricultural sector has been detected in freshwater supplies. Efforts are under way to replace atrazine with alternative fertilizers, including organic ones.

Transport

The country is adequately supplied with maritime transport services. In this regard there is a problem with over-tonnage and high freight rates. Most maritime transport services are supplied by foreign carriers, as is most of the air transportation. It has been estimated that the average load factor is about 55%. Although this shows a degree of underutilized seat capacity, there are seasonal periods when there is a severe shortage of available space.

Among major projects and activities underway are new negotiations for both scheduled air service and chartered service. The marketing efforts of the Barbados Tourism Authority is expected to result in increased activity (Government of Barbados, 1997–1999).

INTEGRATED DECISION MAKING

The Barbados Ministry of Tourism and International Transport is responsible for sustainable tourism at the national level. At the local level, the Barbados Hotel and Tourism Association is responsible. Major groups are involved in decision making through active participation in the development of a National Tourism Policy. This is done through the submission of written comments and participation in national fora. They are also represented on committees convened by the Ministry of Tourism (Government of Barbados, 1997–1999).

The broad objective of the National Tourism Policy is to pursue sustainable tourism development through improvement and optional use of human resources and services, and through the conservation and managed use of the cultural, built, and natural heritage of Barbados, in order to ensure a product of the highest quality, while improving the life and economic development of the people of Barbados (Government of Barbados, 1997–1999).

Tourism is the major foreign exchange earner in Barbados, totalling $1.4 billion at the end of 1997. One of the negative impacts of tourism has been on the coral reefs. The carrying capacity of some reefs, especially on the south and west coasts, has been surpassed due, in part, to the concentration of both tourists and the local population in these areas. Additionally, anchoring shipping mainly for sailing vessels has contributed to degradation in some areas, particularly because of solid waste disposal (Government of Barbados, 1997–1999).

Major programmes in effect to promote sustainable tourism include:

- Subprogramme C of the Tourism Development Programme – Nature and Heritage-based Tourism
- The Water Conservation and Management Project for the Barbados Tourism Industry
- The Coastal Conservation Programme
- The Environmental Management System for Tourism Programme
- Caribbean Action for Sustainable Programmes
- The Caribbean Tourism Organisation Sustainable Tourism Plan of Action

Some constraints to pursuing sustainable tourism development in Barbados include the following:

- The lack of a national sustainable development policy
- The absence of focus on sustainable development in the national planning process
- The availability of funding and other resources

- Attitudes
- Access to appropriate training
- Bureaucracy in accessing funds from international funding sources

The Barbados Ministry of Tourism collaborates with the Barbados Tourism Authority and the Barbados Hotel Association to promote sustainable tourism, hold seminars, operate campaigns and undertake projects such as "Adopt-a-Beach". Other cooperation takes place within the framework of the following agreements:

- Agenda 21
- Agenda 21 for the Travel and Tourism Industry
- The Convention on Biodiversity
- The United Nations Framework Convention on Climate Change

The preceding example of efforts by Barbados at sustainable development was presented to show what steps could be taken in order to successfully implement a sustainable tourism development program. As is obvious Barbados did not have many of the answers to its dilemma of sustainability. However, by careful analysis of the economic, environmental and socio-cultural situation a government could devise a plan along the lines of Agenda 21, to ensure inter-generational viability, in a tourist destination.

EDUCATING THE PUBLIC TO ENSURE THE IMPLEMENTATION OF SUSTAINABLE TOURISM PRACTICES

With a clear understanding of the variety and complexity of issues threatening the sustainability of the Caribbean's tourism product we can now direct education and training programmes at the appropriate target audiences. In designing an action plan to educate for sustainable tourism practices it quickly becomes clear that no unilateral educational actions can be successful. Sustainable management of tourism resources must coexist with the economic, cultural, social, health and safety concerns of tourism destinations (Organization of American States, 1997). Therefore, a synergistic effort that harnesses the energies of the public and private sectors and is inclusive of all major stakeholders in the tourism industry is needed, in order for an education or tourism development plan to come to fruition.

Tourism planners should apply a cost/benefit analysis to tourism development to decide on what kind of, and how much, tourism development is appropriate to meet their economic and social goals. Having made this decision they must then garner the support of the general public, local government and local communities, to design a suitable tourism education programme. A tourism education programme must educate for sustainability in the environmental, economic and socio-cultural areas. It is important that tourism legislation should be enacted at the same time a programme of sustainable tourism education is undertaken. It is equally important that all tourism legislation is enforced.

Education for Environmental Sustainability

In the environmental area the tourism education programme should educate all users of the natural environment. If cruise ship traffic is allowed, then the cruise line companies should be educated as to the effect of the irreparable damage that their three- to five-ton anchors and chains do to coral reefs. In one anchoring a five-ton anchor with its chains can pulverize and decimate a coral bed the size of half a football field. Sedimentation from the mushroom clouds of pulverized coral can stress and destabilize nearby coral reefs. This destroys the feeding places of many varieties of reef fish, as well as the viewing ground of reef watching tourists and others.

Solutions to this problem could include the following:

- Provision of permanent mooring at designated locations
- Use of global positioning system (GPS), satellite-based navigational equipment, which calculates a ship's position to within a few metres. Captains can use GPS to anchor in areas devoid of reefs
- Alternatively, anchors can be hand-placed by divers to reduce potential damage to reefs

Anchoring regulations should then be enforced by stiff fines and other punitive measures. The same education that is given to cruise ship companies should be provided to all boaters in the Caribbean, and to the general public.

The sports and commercial fishing industry, as well as pleasure boaters, should be educated on the detrimental effects of over-fishing in selected areas. They should also be educated on the dangers of fishing practices that destroy reef life, such as toxic chemical usage, dynamiting, long-line fishing, and so on. Of course, regulatory legislation should be implemented and enforced as soon as the education programme is in place.

Cruise ships and pleasure boaters should be educated on the use of dumping stations for their sewage waste. Long-term dumping of raw sewage in the seas contributes directly to the destruction of reef life, as well as making swimming areas unsafe. Of course, this would mean that dumping stations would have to be installed within many harbour areas in the Caribbean. Supporting legislation to police the activity of marine waste management should also be enacted. Tour operators, including marina and dive shop operators, should all be educated about the threats to the marine ecosystems. They should also be educated about the regulations that seek to champion its sustainability. The tourists themselves need to be educated about the fragile nature of Caribbean marine ecosystems. They should not only be willing to comply with the regulations that are enforced in an effort to protect the environment, but in today's more environmentally conscious climate they are likely to applaud the conservation efforts.

With regard to on-land solid waste management, an extensive education in schools and elsewhere in the community should be undertaken, to illustrate the damaging effects of litter on the economy and the environment. As usual, in order to become effective an education programme should not be a stand-alone tactic for sustainability. It should be bolstered by effective waste management programmes carried out by the appropriate governments. The tourism industry should play an important part in the education process, initiating campaigns that show the economic importance of a clean environment, and its commitment to clean-up programmes.

Education for a Sustainable Economy

Here is an area in which government intervention must precede much of the tourism education efforts. Educational and policy-making roles should be undertaken by ministries of finance, education, tourism, agriculture and planning. A sustainable tourism policy that outlines plans for localizing many business opportunities should be initiated. Here is also where a delicate balance between the promotion of foreign investment and the encouragement of native entrepreneurship must be struck. Perhaps, the Caribbean Development Bank could play a pivotal role here. For true sustainability of the tourism product there must be substantial participation in the ownership and management of businesses, especially tourism businesses, by the indigenous population. Not only does this make good economic sense in terms of halting the leakage of the tourist dollar, but it gives the destination more character, creates more local pride and self-direction, and gives the tourist a product with the true essence of the destination. The intergenerational equity is assured when increasing percentages of the local population are driving their economic destiny.

This would suggest that the first education programme should be directed to the public sector, and probably should come from tourism planners and interest groups within the various Caribbean countries. Another effort at assuring economic sustainability must come from the collaborative effort of tourism businesses to purchase supplies locally. Some incentive to promote this activity should come from the public sector. An inventory should be taken of local crafts and cottage industry products that can be used by tourism businesses.

An education campaign to "buy locally" or "buy Caribbean" should ensue. This campaign should be spearheaded by all of the government agencies mentioned before. To further address the issue of leakage, ministries of agriculture should collaborate with the hotel industry to ensure that large quantities of locally grown produce are used in their operations. In many countries this would require the establishment of rigorous farm management and agribusiness practices to ensure that the mutual goals of farmers and consumers are met. This should reduce the amount of food being imported from the United States.

A parallel effort to initiate fish farming in the Caribbean could enlarge the local business environment, and simultaneously protect the environment from depleting its marine resources by over-fishing. Start-up costs to build the farms would be more than offset by the accrued environmental benefits, as well as the economic benefits to local businessmen.

Education for Socio-Cultural Sustainability

The Caribbean area has a rich history and diverse ethnic cultures that could be very entertaining, interesting and exciting to tourists with an affinity for cultural heritage tours. Caribbean people are naturally proud of their heritage. Ministries of education, culture or tourism should ensure that local cultural art, dance, song, folklore and craft making is preserved, promoted and maintained for future generations. Caribbean youth should receive instruction in the classroom, at civic meetings, at youth camps and on field trips, continually educating them about their cultural background and history. Contests, bazaars and festivals could be occasions to showcase local talent in cultural art activities, such as song, dance and storytelling. The presentation and interpretation of the history and culture of a destination can become a large part of the core attraction of a tourist destination. This augurs well for the sustainability of a destination.

With regard to the antisocial behaviour of the native population as tourism increases, a fundamental education programme aimed at the youth of these countries must be initiated. Acknowledging the problems that exist and analysing them is a major step toward finding solutions for them. Education programmes in the schools that explain the behaviour patterns of visitors to resort destinations will remove some of the mystique surrounding these guests. The more the guests can be portrayed as having lifestyles similar to their own when not vacationing, the less likely the population will be to ascribe some lofty status to them.

Young people in the Caribbean would be less likely to feel driven to imitate the leisure activities of the tourists, to their economic and social detriment. The innate friendliness of the native population is a boon to a sustainable tourism effort. There will always be some mutual fascination between the host and guest but if tourism education programmes are effective they could minimize the predatory "dating" activity of many local men, and minimize the resentment of local women toward visiting women.

Some Caribbean destinations already have in place well-attended education programmes aimed at making the visitor feel at home. The Bahama host programme, which was initiated many years ago, is a good example of a training programme that not only enables the tourist to have a well-rounded and meaningful vacation experience, but educates the local population about the real importance of this industry to the economic well-being of the Bahamas.

All of these educational activities are intended to mitigate the negative effect of tourism development on the sustainability of the Caribbean destination. In an ideal scenario these programmes should work perfectly. Questions arise as to what events would signal that a destination has reached its social or cultural carrying capacity. Perhaps the answer to this question will be linked with activities that also indicate that the destination has reached its saturation point in terms of crowding or pollution. One way to keep a finger on the pulse of how much tourism is too much is to have continuous involvement of the citizenry of local areas in making decisions on whether to limit or expand tourism activity.

ORGANIZATION OF AN EDUCATION PLAN

The formation of a comprehensive education programme to ensure the sustainability of tourism destination is complicated at best. This is partly because of the many populations that need education on tourism, the method of delivery of the information, and the fact that the educational process must in many instances be supported by parallel activities in order to be effective. For example, education for green management must be accompanied by policies and vehicles to accommodate recycling. Government policies must support the local use of alternate forms of energy, instead of fossil fuel.

Another dilemma that begs for a solution is who would be qualified and authorized to design and implement this education programme. A logical way to solve this dilemma is to have a tourism consultant design the education programme and play a role in the implementation process. The person (or firm) should ideally be selected by a committee from departments or ministries of education, culture, tourism, development or planning. The consulting entity should ideally have a background in both tourism education and tourism development.

The tasks for the consulting body would then be as follows:

- Prepare and present an education development plan to the committee
- Endeavour to become the central clearinghouse for sustainable tourism education
- Coordinate a community action plan, as well as an industry action plan to create understanding of environmental and social issues
- Examine and revise methods used by tour operators to reflect sensitivity and adherence to sustainable tourism development methods (with emphasis on the environment, culture and local economy)

- Initiate diploma and undergraduate courses in sustainable tourism management
- Support traditional folklore and rituals
- Educate the local community and tourism personnel about positive and negative tourism impacts, and sustainable tourism development
- Educate tourists about sustainable tourism practices, e.g., green management, ecologically sound tourism practices etc.
- Conduct workshops and training sessions for tour operators and hoteliers on the following topics:
  - Environmental management for large hotels
  - Environmental management for smaller hotels, guesthouses and cottages
  - Making use of local cottage industry items to add to the decor and ambience of your lodging
  - Utilizing food and drink containers made from local perishable material
  - Develop eco-tourist activities

CONCLUSION

Sustainable tourism development is possible only through the synergistic effort of key individuals from both the public and private sectors. No development plan can be complete without the input and ownership of the general population. The more knowledge people have about situations in which they have a present day or an intergenerational stake the more they are able to act upon that knowledge.

Throughout the Caribbean the facts about the beneficial economic impacts of conventional mass tourism have been delivered. There is still disenchantment in the local populations concerning the overall benefits that this tourism should have brought to these areas over the years. Ownership of many major tourism businesses is still in foreign hands. Inflation is high throughout the Caribbean, and there is widespread degradation of the natural resources, especially in the marine environment. Alternative tourism, including eco-tourism, has also been tried, as an environmentally sensitive answer to mass tourism. The alternative tourism concept is also not problem-free. Although success stories like the Maho Bay, Harmony and Concordia developments are present, marketing this form of tourism can be challenging. No tourism development is entirely impact free.

The answer to this dilemma is in true sustainable tourism development. This ensures that the environment, culture and economy of a tourist destination is helped and maintained by tourism development. The only way to ensure that this takes place is through a saturation of information and guidelines promoting sustainable development throughout the community, along with supporting legislative action.

REFERENCES

Allen, W.H. (1992). "Increased Dangers to Caribbean Marine Ecosystems: Cruise Ship Anchors and Intensified Tourism Threaten Reefs", *BioScience* 42 (no. 5).

Barkin, D. (1996). "Ecotourism: A Tool for Sustainable Development", abstract from Planeta.com I Exploring Ecotourism, pp. 5-6, May. http://www.green-builder.com/mader/planetalO596monarch.html.

BBC Radio. (1992). "The Economic Realities of Food for Tourism in the Bahamas", *The Food Program*, June 19 broadcast.

Britton, S. (1982). "International Tourism and Multinational Corporations in the Pacific: The Case of Fiji", pp. 252–274, in Taylor, M. and Thrift, M.J. (eds.), *The Geography of Multinationals*, Croom Helm, London.

Cater, E. (1992). "Must Tourism Destroy Its Resource Base?", pp. 309–323, in Mannion, A.M. and Bowlby, S. (eds.), *Environmental Issues in the 1990s*, Wiley, Chichester.

Cater, E. (1993). "Ecotourism in the Third World: Problems for Sustainable Tourism Development", *Tourism Management* (April).

Goreau, M. and Goreau, T.J. (1996). *Ecological Assessment of Antigua and Barbuda Reefs: Report to the Environmental Awareness Group, Antigua and Barbuda.*

Government of Antigua and Barbuda. (1998). Report to the 6th Session of the United Nations Commission on Sustainable Development, April. (Last Update: 21 October 1997.) http//www.un.orglesalagenda21/natmno/countr/antigualeco.ntm.

Government of Barbados. (1997–1999). Submission to the 5th and 7th Sessions of the United Nations Commission on Sustainable Development, April 1997, 1998 and 1999. Last Update: January, 1999. http:/www.un.org/esa/agenda2l/natlinfo/.

Island Resources Foundation. (1997). *Management Plan for the Bird Island Marine Reserve*, a management plan developed for the Organization of American States, Performance Contract # WSC14721, Organization of American States, Washington, D.C.

Mahler, R. (1997). "Communities Control their Tourism Destiny in Rural Belize", Planeta.com, pp. 1–2, November. http://www2.planeta.com/mader/planeta/l197/11 97belize.html.

McGregor, J., Ecoplan Net (1994). *The Family Islands of the Bahamas: A Sustainable Tourism Policy and Guidelines*, a study for the Organization of American States, Washington, D.C.

Organization of American States (1997). *Sustaining Tourism by Managing its Natural and Heritage Resources*, XVII Inter-American Travel Congress, April, General Secretariat of the Organization of American States, Washington, D.C., pp. 7–11.

Weaver, D.B. (1993). "Ecotourism in the Small Island Caribbean", *GeoJournal* 31 (no. 4): 457–465.

Wight, P. (1997). "Sustainability, Profitability and Ecotourism Markets: What Are they and How Do they Relate?", in *Ecotourism: Balancing Sustainability and Profitability*, Proceedings of the International Conference on Central and Eastern Europe and the Baltic Sea Region, Parnu, Estonia, September 22–23, p. 1. http://www.ee/ecotourism/wight.html

CHAPTER 22

CHALLENGES FOR ACADEMIC RESEARCH ON TOURISM IN THE CARIBBEAN

Ian Boxill

Abstract

Tourism is a major industry in the Caribbean and has significant social, economic and environmental impacts on the region. Despite the fact that it accounts for a fourth of foreign exchange earnings in the region, there is a paucity of rigorous theoretical research on tourism and tourism studies are still not seen as a legitimate discipline in the region's universities. The author makes the case for further theoretical research by describing the transition in the tourist product from "sun and fun" to eco-tourism. He argues that, although outwardly there is this shift towards conservation and protection of the environment, new tourism products such as all-inclusive hotels and water sports actually change, and in some cases destroy, the environment. He concludes by recommending that tourism studies become more focused on these burgeoning issues by drawing on the literature on development rather than the current hotchpotch of theoretical ideas from various disciplines.

INTRODUCTION

There is a great deal of research and publication on tourism by academics in the developing world. Yet Caribbean academics have conducted little systematic research on the sector. And, until recently, many Caribbeanists have been reluctant to see tourism studies as a legitimate discipline, worthy of a place in a regional university. This is surprising and unfortunate since tourism is the major foreign exchange earner in the Caribbean. It is a major source of employment and income for Caribbean people. Employment comes in various forms, from direct dependence on the tourism industry, such as working in hotels and on the beaches, to indirect involvement, for example, banking and farming. For the tourist, the Caribbean is viewed mainly as a source of pleasure, an escape from the realities of everyday life, a place that offers "sun, sea and sand". The Caribbean has attracted many visitors from all over the world to its shores, especially visitors from North America and Europe. However, for a variety of reasons, there are now questions about the sustainability of the sector in the region. To understand the importance of this issue it is necessary to have an idea of the development of the sector, its contribution to the region and its impacts on our societies.

THE DEVELOPMENT OF TOURISM IN THE CARIBBEAN

The tourism industry emerged after 1960 when many islands, burdened with economic pressures, were forced to shift from local exports to tourism as a means of earning foreign exchange. The income generated from tourism is used to service debts that these islands have with multilateral agencies and it is also used to pay for imports. Tourism has developed from a few relatives and friends arriving by boat to the islands being major ports of call for cruise ship passengers. The airline industry also has had to expand its routes to include these islands, as visitors all over the world are heavily consuming the vacation packages that the industry offers.

Tourism in the Caribbean has also developed from being merely a place of "sun and fun" to include eco-tourism, in keeping with the worldwide view that the conservation and protection of the environment is an absolute necessity. It is another type of vacation package offered to visitors, which allows them to enjoy nature in its original form. Eco-tourism is being promoted throughout the Caribbean as environmentalists have made "saving the environment" a priority. This type of tourism has been flooded with investors, as it is cheaper to establish and maintain and is easier to market in these times of environmental appreciation and awareness. Eco-tourism is still relatively new to these islands although it has the potential for growth.

Despite these attempts to protect the environment through eco-tourism, the increased numbers of all-inclusive hotels throughout the Caribbean has contributed to ecological destruction. The aim of the all-inclusive is to "create" nature, a utopia for the tourist. Man-made waterfalls and fake trees are examples of this attempted utopia. To construct perfect gardens, however, deforestation, as well as the destruction of plants, has occurred to create space for the implementation of man-made objects. Coral reefs also have been destroyed as refuse from boats attached to these hotels has been dumped into the seas. Ecological life also has been destroyed as a result of water sport activities, which the tourist enjoys in all-inclusive hotels, as well as on the public beaches.

Below is a brief treatment of the some of the environmental, social and economic impacts that tourism has throughout the Caribbean. The benefits, as well as the negative impacts of the tourism sector, will also be highlighted.

SOCIAL IMPACTS OF TOURISM IN THE CARIBBEAN

Employment

Visitor arrivals throughout the Caribbean have increased over the past number of years and, as a result, tourism is one of the primary sources of employment in the Caribbean. According to McElroy and de Albuquerque (1998), "it accounts for . . . a fifth of all jobs". In the Bahamas, for example, "total visitor arrivals during 1996 rose 5.5% to 3,415,858 from 3,239,155 during 1995". Consequently, the unemployment rate decreased from 11.1% in 1996 to 10.8% in 1997. Direct employment includes the workforce in the hotels and restaurants, as well as vendors, tour guides and taxi operators, who sell their products and services to the tourists. Tourism also affects employment within other sectors, especially agriculture and services. Farmers, storeowners and bankers depend heavily on the tourism industry for survival.

Tourism has also led to self-employment. People have been able to earn an income based on selling various products and services to the visitors. This has allowed the unemployed to use their creativity to earn an income. Popular types of self-employment are usually in the areas of craft, where local resources are used to create products that are sold to tourists.

Housing

This is an area in which tourism has impacted negatively on the society. The conflict between growth of the tourism industry and communities has resulted in a situation where hotels provide top quality accommodation for visitors but just outside these accommodations people live in abject poverty (Alleyne et al., 1994). Poverty-stricken communities have emerged in major tourist areas as a result of the mass migration of the unemployed who come into these areas with the hope of earning a living. High unemployment and inadequate housing result in the deterioration of living standards within these areas.

Health

Many of these communities are yet to acquire the services of utility companies. Therefore, the lack of water and electricity, coupled with inadequate accommodation, has led to unsanitary conditions. Health providers have to contend with diseases that are caused by these poor living conditions. Consequently, governments have had to allocate large portions of their budget to primary health care and health education so as to prevent the spread of disease.

Another negative impact of tourism within the Caribbean has been the increase in prostitution. Unemployment has forced many people into prostitution as a means of survival. However, this has resulted in the increase of sexually transmitted diseases and the spread of the HIV/AIDS virus within the Caribbean.

The use of illegal drugs has also increased in tourist areas. Jamaica, for example, has seen an increase in the amount of marijuana being used by locals, as tourists enter their shores with the preconceived notion that this drug is "legal" and is available everywhere. Another means of survival has been the selling of illegal drugs to tourists, and again this has been a catalyst for its use among locals.

Visitor Accommodation

In some islands, accommodation for the tourist has moved away from the traditional "bed and breakfast" to all-inclusive hotels, which provide for their every need. The all-inclusive hotels have developed as a result of the increase in visitor harassment. These hotels, however, have had a negative impact on both the environment and society. The absence of the tourist from the wider society has led to an increase in unemployment as the need for tour guides, taxi operators, etc., has declined. Natural settings have not constituted a part of the all-inclusive package. Therefore, these hotels have exacerbated the deterioration in the environment as attempts by the hotels to create "perfect" settings have forced them to destroy the "misfits" of nature.

ECONOMIC IMPACTS OF TOURISM IN THE CARIBBEAN

From an economic perspective, tourism has "filled the gap" in the budget that was created by other ailing sectors, such as mining and agriculture. Not only does tourism benefit the individual in terms of employment and economic gain, but it is also a major part of the foreign exchange income for many islands. According to McElroy and de Albuquerque (1998), tourism accounts for a fourth of foreign exchange earnings in the Caribbean. Growth in eco-tourism will also assist in obtaining foreign exchange for the Caribbean. In Guyana, eco-tourism "has emerged as a recognized economic activity as the sector attracts a growing proportion of international tourists" (Ganga, 1996).

The impact of tourism on gross domestic product (GDP) was demonstrated in Anguilla, where a decline in arrivals contributed to GDP contraction. GDP contracted for the second successive year after the number of visitors fell 2.7% to 37,498 in 1996. The situation is similar throughout the Caribbean, where a decline in visitor arrivals stimulates a decrease in GDP.

Although the Caribbean has experienced overall growth in this industry, some countries have experienced a decline in the number of visitors. The Bahamas, for example, experienced a 1.5% decline in 1997. One of the main reasons for this decline is the growing competition from extraregional destinations.

ENVIRONMENTAL IMPACTS OF TOURISM IN THE CARIBBEAN

McElroy and de Albuquerque (1998) cite some of the negative impacts of tourism: "filling-in of wetlands and mangrove destruction from resort construction, beach loss and lagoon pollution from sand mining, near-shore dredging, and hotel sewage dumping, and reef damage from diving, yacht and cruise ship anchoring and marina development" (p. 10). Environmentalists throughout the Caribbean have attempted to educate the population about the need to protect and preserve the environment. However, their success has been marginal as tourism officials continue to gear their packages towards the wants of the tourist and the expansion of this industry. Therefore, ships are encouraged to continue plying these routes, and officials continue in their attempt to increase the number of ships that visit. Also, attempts to create more ports and incentives to cruise ship passengers constitute a major part of this drive to increase the number of arrivals. In recent years in the

Bahamas, cruise ship arrivals rose 6.5% annually, representing a turn-around from the previous downward trend, reflecting, at least in part, the effects of package incentives (including volume discounts on the passenger head tax) made available to cruise ship lines.

Water sports have also been promoted by hotels and individuals as a means of garnering tourist interest and for economic gain. This has impacted negatively on the environment, as coral reefs have been destroyed as a result of these activities. Additionally, problems that may arise are a consequence of "the frequency of large recreational outings by tourists, often to offshore islands, and caves which disturb the wildlife and can destroy the fragile habitat of aquatic life" (Alleyne et al., 1994).

Sea pollution is another environmental concern, as many hotels do not have adequate disposal facilities and, consequently, raw sewage is flushed into the sea. Hence, "waters become polluted with faecal coliform and other pathogenic bacteria" (Alleyne et al., 1994). The destruction of the beach is further aggravated by the continuous use of motor vehicles on its shores, which destroys the sand and vegetation.

ALTERNATIVE TOURISM STRATEGIES: THE CASE OF ECO-TOURISM

In an attempt to curtail some of the damage done to nature by this industry and to assist in the alleviation of global environmental problems, eco-tourism has been introduced throughout the Caribbean. This type of tourism will not be difficult to market, as the "new" tourist is environmentally aware and interested in nature rather than the traditional attraction – "sun and fun". Packages that include nature trails, visits to indigenous communities and accommodations nestled in mountains rather than on beaches are now being marketed to the tourist.

An environmental concern that arises from the promotion of eco-tourism is that its expansion may lead to overcrowding within the natural setting, and this will lead to species loss and the destruction of vegetation. Hopefully, with the increase in environmental awareness, this destruction will be minimal.

LACK OF ACADEMIC RESEARCH ON TOURISM

Despite the importance of the tourism in the Caribbean, very little academic research has been done on this sector by Caribbean social scientists. A recently compiled bibliography on tourism research in the Caribbean shows that more than 80% of research on the sector has been done by private consultants (Boxill and Martin, 1998). Where academic research has been done, the emphasis is, primarily, on the environment (United Nations Environmental Programme, 1997). In relation to the social sciences, Caribbean social scientists and tourism researchers have tended to focus on issues such as crime (Boxill, 1994) and developing new tourism alternatives (Poon and Poon, 1993; Boxill, 1995; Dunn, 1999).

Consequently, there is very little theoretical analysis of tourism from a developmental standpoint. Caribbean social scientists have been on the periphery of tourism research and development. Thus, unlike areas such as agriculture, mining and manufacturing, there is very little scholarship on the meta-theoretical issues of tourism as the basis for a development strategy in the Caribbean. Worse yet is the appalling lack of any serious attempt to test ideas about development based on tourism strategies. There is a need to develop a body of research on tourism in the Caribbean, which focuses on the empirical, theoretical and developmental aspects of tourism as a single development strategy, or part of such a strategy.

SUGGESTIONS FOR ACADEMIC RESEARCH

Empirical Issues

There is a great deal of data on the tourism industry in the Caribbean. Most countries keep extensive databases on tourism activities and the Caribbean Tourism Organisation has its own database. However, there is a need for the systematic collection and analysis of data, which should provide a basis for addressing the question of whether tourism is a sustainable development option on its own, or part of a larger strategy for the Caribbean. By implication this research should make an important contribution to the global literature on development theory and policy analysis.

Theoretical Issues

One of the weakest areas of tourism studies as a discipline is that it lacks theoretical rigour. Again I should emphasize that, unlike other sectors, such as mining and agriculture, there are no clear theoretical frameworks that discuss tourism as a development strategy. Tourism studies are currently made up of a hotchpotch of theoretical ideas from a variety of disciplines.

As a starting point, theoretical work on tourism could draw on a number of theoretical ideas from the literature on development. Theoretical perspectives that could inform this area of the discipline include modernization, symbolic interactionism, post-fordism and dependency theories.

In regard to examining socio-cultural issues, symbolic interactionism and post-fordism could serve as useful approaches to understand the visitor–host interaction, particularly in urban environments. These approaches may also lead to an analysis of how technology affects the social construction of cultural practices within the host environment. Although some of these perspectives may, on the face of it, appear to be incompatible, the complexity of tourism research necessitates that multiple approaches be used in order to understand the relationships within the sector.

Post-fordist theory may be used to theorize the patterns of relationships between the tourism sector within a globalized world. Post-fordism is a theoretical approach that argues that the systems of production globally have transformed consumer tastes, preferences and lifestyles, making them similar across national boundaries. Additionally, according to Amin (1994), one of the characteristics of the post-fordist society is the "increasing transformation of cultural activity, especially leisure and recreation, into cultural industries, that is commodities sold in the market to individual consumers who, in turn, increasingly identify cultural gratification with consumption, rather than as an independent activity, geared towards, say, creative learning" (p. 31). If post-fordism has, through different forms of production, impacted on global demand for cultural activity and leisure, then for developing countries, which are on the receiving end of the tourism industry, this is likely to have impacts on the socio-cultural aspects of society. It is therefore important to determine the nature of these socio-cultural developments and how they impact on society.

It is also important to determine what aspects of globalization have transformed economic, ecological and social arrangements in a manner that was not possible in the "modern" period. For instance, what is the role of technology in the tourism sector in Jamaica, and how has this technology transformed relationships that retard or assist the development of the country? To what extent does this technology enhance or retard tourism's ability to develop the country in a sustainable manner? We may also ask: is there a basis for theorizing eco-tourism as a more sustainable option to mass tourism, given the developmental contradictions of mass tourism?

Modernization and dependency/plantation theories offer useful ways in which to discuss economic and social development. In relation to modernization theories, the ideas of W.A. Lewis and Max Weber, for instance, identify a number of critical variables that can be used to discuss the development of a society. Additionally, Max Weber's account of the development of industrial society may also be used as a heuristic device to explain and categorize the "tourism economies" in the region along a development continuum. Such an approach may also seek to extend/interrogate the concept of "tourism economy" and also test its legitimacy as a development model.

Dependency theory may also be useful in helping to contextualize some of the problems of tourism, especially in terms of the sector's inability to create linkages with other sectors of the society. For instance, Levitt and Best (1984) and Beckford (1972) offer creative and illuminating ways of characterizing the Caribbean economy using the concept of plantation economy. These perspectives are able to assist in trying to explain why the tourism sector has continued to develop as an enclave. The all-inclusive hotels have been shown to represent an extreme example of this enclave. However, the extent of this enclave-like structure also needs to be determined by empirical investigation.

CONCLUSION

Academic research on tourism in the Caribbean is in its infancy. This is unfortunate, given that the tourism industry is the single most important form of economic activity for the region. On the other hand, the opportunities for academic research are wide open and exciting. In my view, some of the immediate issues that require attention by academics include:

- An evaluation of tourism as a development strategy
- A framework for conceptualizing tourism as a development strategy
- An evaluation of the sector from a meta-theoretical standpoint
- An assessment of the impact of the sector from social, economic, ecological and cultural standpoints in the region
- An empirical examination of the most successful approaches to tourism in the region (e.g. community, heritage, eco- and mass)

- The creation of a framework for assessing the type of tourism most suitable for the region
- Policy recommendations for tourism development in the region

REFERENCES

Alleyne, D., Boxill, I., and Francis, A. (1994). "Economic Reform and Sustainable Development in Jamaica", Institute of Social and Economic Research, Mona, Jamaica.

Amin, A. (ed.) (1994). *Post-Fordism: A Reader*, Blackwell, Cambridge.

Beckford, G. (1972). *Persistent Poverty*, Oxford University Press, New York (reprinted 2000, Canoe Press, Mona, Jamaica).

Boxill, I. (1994). "Crime and Sustainable Tourism in Jamaica", mimeo, University of the West Indies, Mona, Jamaica.

Boxill, I. (1995). "Towards Sustainable Tourism in the Caribbean", *Caribbean Dialogue* 2 (no. 1): 17–20.

Boxill, I. and Martin, P. (1998). "Select Bibliography of Tourism Research in the Caribbean", report prepared for the World Bank, Washington, D.C.

Dunn, L. (1999). *Tourism Attractions: A Critical Analysis of this Subsector in Jamaica*, Canoe Press, Mona, Jamaica.

Ganga, G. (1996). *Eco-Tourism in Guyana*, University of the West Indies, Centre for Environment and Development, Mona, Jamaica.

Gunne-Jones, A. (1996). *Welcome to the Beachettes: A Study of the Development of Residential Tourism in Montserrat*, University of the West Indies, Centre for Environment and Development, Mona, Jamaica.

King, A. (ed.) (1991). *Culture, Globalisation and the World System*, Macmillan, New York.

Levitt, K. and Best, L. (1984), "Character of Caribbean Economy", in Beckford, G. (ed.), *Caribbean Economy*, Institute of Social and Economic Research, Mona, Jamaica.

McElroy, J. and de Albuquerque, K. (1998) "Tourism Penetration Index in Small Caribbean Islands", *Annals of Tourism Research* 25 (no. 1): 145–168.

Poon, A. and Poon, R. (1993). *The Eco-Tourism Opportunity in the Caribbean*, University of the West Indies, Centre for Environment and Development, Mona, Jamaica.

United Nations Environmental Programme. (1997). *Coastal Tourism in the Wider Caribbean: Impacts and Best Management Practices*, United Nations Environmental Programme, Kingston, Jamaica.

CHAPTER

PAST, PRESENT AND FUTURE OF TOURISM AND HOSPITALITY EDUCATION IN THE COMMONWEALTH CARIBBEAN

Ainsley O'Reilly

Abstract

This chapter reviews the importance of tourism to the Caribbean in general and the West Indies in particular, and the necessity to have a trained and qualified human resource base for the ever-growing tourism industry in the region. An analysis of the past and current status and future possibilities of tourism and hospitality education in the region is done. The chapter also reviews hotel and tourism management programmes offered at the University of the West Indies (UWI), Centre for Hotel and Tourism Management (CHTM) and recent developments in tourism and hospitality education in the region.

INTRODUCTION

For the purpose of this chapter, the Commonwealth Caribbean refers to the English-speaking countries of the Caribbean, commonly referred to as the West Indies. The current status of tourism and hospitality education in this region will be assessed, with emphasis on the work done at the Centre for Hotel and Tourism Management (CHTM), Bahamas, and the University of the West Indies (UWI), Mona campus. The importance of education and training in tourism and hospitality management is critical in the Caribbean because of the region's dependency on this sector for its economic survival. This chapter will therefore examine the past, present and future of tourism and hospitality education in the Commonwealth Caribbean while identifying the way forward for the sector.

THE IMPORTANCE OF TOURISM TO THE CARIBBEAN

Tourism has become an important economic, social and environmental factor in many, if not all, of the Caribbean nations over the last two decades. No longer are countries in the region such as the Bahamas, Puerto Rico, Jamaica and the US Virgin Islands the only ones that are embracing the tourism industry, considered the fastest growing economic sector in the world today.

Tourist accommodation has also increased considerably to meet the growing demand. There were an estimated 232,627 hotel rooms in thirty-three Caribbean countries and resort destinations at the end of 1998. This was almost 150,000 more than the number of hotel rooms registered by regional hotel associations in 1980. For example, the number of hotel rooms in Jamaica more than doubled from 10,092 in 1980 to 22,713 in 1998 and more than trebled in one of the new eco-tourist destinations in the Commonwealth Caribbean, Belize, from 1,016 to 3,921 during this period. Hotel rooms in the Dominican Republic grew more than tenfold over this period, from 3,800 in 1980 to 42,412 in 1998, making it the region's single largest destination in the region in terms of room capacity. It is followed closely by Cuba, where the number of rooms has more than quadrupled from 7,526 in 1988 to 35,708 in 1996. Ten of the thirty-one countries account for 75% of all hotel rooms: Aruba of the Dutch Antilles (7,212 rooms); Jamaica (22,713 rooms), the Bahamas (13,288 rooms) and Barbados (5,732 rooms) from the Commonwealth Caribbean; Guadeloupe (8,371 rooms) and Martinique (7,400 rooms) from the French Antilles; the US territories of Puerto Rico and the US Virgin Islands (with 11,828 and 4,929 rooms, respectively); and, from the Hispanic Caribbean, Cuba and the Dominican Republic (with 35,708 and 42,412 rooms, respectively) (Caribbean Hotel Association, 2000). Of the above grand number of 232,627 hotel rooms in the Caribbean in 1998, there were 76,496 in the Commonwealth Caribbean, representing 32.9% of total. The Spanish-speaking Caribbean, which embraces not only the larger island territories of Cuba and the Dominican Republic but also the Mexican resort destinations of Cancun and Cozumel, has by far the most hotel rooms (46.6%). The remainder of the registered rooms in the Caribbean area (about 20.5 %) are almost equally divided among the US, Dutch and French territorial groupings.

An analysis of the tourism figures from the late 1980s and the 1990s shows that stay-over tourist arrivals and cruise passenger visits grew at average annual rates of 5.5% and 6.8%, respectively, from 1988 to 1998 and have maintained their market share of around 3% of total international tourist arrivals over the 1990s. In 1998, Caribbean destinations received a total of some 31 million visitors, comprising 19.53 million tourist arrivals and 11.86 million cruise passenger visits. Gross expenditure by all visitors to the Caribbean in that year totalled approximately US$17.9 billion. As far as the West Indian grouping is concerned, tourist arrivals were also significant, representing about 31% of the total Caribbean market share and 33% of total visitor expenditure (Caribbean Hotel Association, 2000).

From the above, therefore, it is no wonder that some countries of the Caribbean, whose governments were not interested in tourism before and had considered it ephemeral and not worthy of serious thought, have now gotten into the act. For example, the government of the oil-rich Republic of Trinidad and Tobago seems to have finally considered tourism as one of its economic planks. Guyana, despite some recent political unrest, has also been trying to embrace tourism to help reconstruct its depleted economy. The government of this latter country displayed seriousness of purpose in the development of tourism by having a project study done on tourism legislation for Guyana four years ago through the Caribbean Tourism Organisation (CTO). This study examined all the legal, environmental and economic factors for the proper development of tourism in that country (Carnegie and O'Reilly, 1995).

Therefore, it can be construed that tourism is considered the lifeblood of many of the countries of the Caribbean, and a major vehicle for economic development in the region. To the West Indies and the region as a whole, tourism has been considered such an important plank of the countries' economies that the first ever Caribbean Community (CARICOM) Heads of Government Conference on tourism was held in 1992 in Kingston, Jamaica to discuss various tourism issues. A task force to monitor the industry was also created at this conference by the Caribbean Hotel Association (CHA), representing private sector interests, and the CTO, representing the public sector. This task force was chaired by no less a figure than the charismatic former prime minister of Jamaica, the late Michael Manley. The importance of tourism to the region in the future (based on past performance) can be summed up, therefore, as follows:

Future predictions are that the Caribbean's dependence on tourism will become even greater. This is a function both of the reality that tourism has become the world's fastest growing industry and that several of the Caribbean's other economic sectors are either in decline or under threat. (Holder, 1996)

EMPLOYMENT IN THE TOURISM SECTOR

The Need for Education and Training

Tourism is also a great generator of employment in the region. Throughout the Caribbean, up to one in six workers finds direct employment in tourism, more than in any other region of the world, according to the World Travel and Tourism Council. The hotel sector generally hires the largest number of employees in the tourism industry. However, the employment multiplier is very evident in this industry, as a number of other employment sections are necessary to completely service it. These include airline personnel, tour operators, taxi drivers, restaurant and bar workers, casino workers, craft vendors, hair braiders, security personnel, tour guides, retail store personnel, and public servants employed in various ministries and departments of government, such as tourism, customs and immigration. Therefore,

> When all of these workers are aggregated, it becomes evident that a large proportion of the region's labour force is directly or indirectly dependent on tourism for their livelihood. This gives the tourism industry the potential of being the largest single employer of people in the region. (Charles, 1997)

> The increase in world tourism (and tourism to the region), the tourist demand for quality goods and services and the increasing capacity of tourism enterprises require professionally trained and educated personnel for the variety of jobs that will be created in the industry during the next decade. . . . Its [tourism's] continued growth in the region, with projected flows of 20 million arrivals by the end of the century, will create new jobs, requiring appropriate education and training at all levels. (Brathwaite et al., 1990)

The above quote, taken from the lead research paper done by the UWI's Centre for Hotel and Tourism Management for the first Caribbean Conference on Tourism Education, organized by the CTO in Barbados in October 1990, still holds true and may even be considered more important today. Education and training are vital to the development and sustainability of the tourism industry in the region, especially as more countries want a share of the tourist dollar and more development in this sector has become much more evident, as shown earlier.

The Past

In an effort to gradually diminish their countries' high unemployment rates, the governments of Barbados and Jamaica, which were two of the countries that were the most socially advanced in tourism development in the West Indies in the 1960s, saw the need from as early as that time to train their nationals especially for entrance-level positions in hotels. Hotel schools were set up in these countries in the mid- to late-1960s to train young Barbadians and Jamaicans in basic hotel skills.

The Jamaica Hotel School, located at the Hotel Casa Monte in Stony Hill, Kingston, Jamaica, was set up in 1968 by the government to teach young men and women skills in the front office, housekeeping, dining room and kitchen departments. Students had a twenty-room hotel as their laboratory, and lived in dormitories provided by the government on site.

This small facility, located in a beautiful, wooded setting overlooking Kingston, became a very popular dining spot for the inhabitants of Kingston and its environs and also a quiet retreat for tourists, many of whom became return guests. This hotel school proved to be a very good laboratory for students, and became the prototype for other hotel schools in the region, such as the Trinidad and Tobago Hotel School (started in the early 1970s) and the Bahamas Hotel Training College (started in 1975). However, these two schools, which are still in existence, do not have hotels attached to them for training purposes. The demise of the Jamaica Hotel School in the 1970s, however, was inevitable, because of the democratic-socialist political thinking of the day. The existing hotel school in Jamaica, started in the early-1980s on the north coast at Runaway Bay, seems to have been formulated exactly after the "Casa Monte" concept, with its own hotel laboratory and beautiful surroundings. The Barbados Hotel School, a department of the Barbados Community College, on the other hand, began its operations in 1966 basically as a culinary school, but has been extended into a full-blown facility by the Government of Barbados, having its own hotel attached to it as a teaching laboratory.

The Present

There are currently in the Caribbean approximately twenty-four schools and programmes within schools that have hospitality and tourism studies as their major concentration. These schools and programmes range widely in their focus, many of them purely trade schools. A few, such as the Centre for Hotel and Tourism Management of the UWI, the joint degree programme offered by the UWI and the University of Technology, Jamaica, several programmes offered by universities in Puerto Rico, the Dominican Republic and in Latin America, and the diploma programmes at Bermuda College, offer degree-level education in hospitality and tourism studies (Conlin, 1993).

However, most of these schools have not been developed properly, have poor facilities and are generally under-funded. John Bell, executive vice president of the CHA, based in Puerto Rico, echoes the thinking of many involved in human resource development within the industry when he states:

> Despite the labour intensive nature of the hotel and tourism sector, and the many technical and practical skills involved, those hotel training schools, invariably government-owned, that do exist within the region are horribly under-funded, under-established and in general treated like low grade technical schools for the students who cannot make it into other careers. (Bell, 1991)

According to Conlin:

> What is required in hospitality and tourism education in the region is institutional strengthening. This is necessary to allow the schools and programmes to command the respect of their institutions and governments in order to access the necessary resources they need to upgrade their physical plants, their programmes, and their faculties. (Conlin, 1993)

But how can institutional strengthening be done without the necessary funding to obtain professional teachers and state-of-the-art plants and equipment? Many of the hotel schools in the region, especially those in the smaller territories, have found it very difficult to operate due to lack of funding from the governments, resulting in poor teaching and laboratory facilities.

This subject of human resource development in the hospitality and tourism sector has been discussed to little or no avail in many regional fora, even at the highest levels. For example at the CARICOM Summit on Tourism held in Kingston in 1992, referred to earlier, this topic was discussed at length. The Summary and Conclusions contained the following:

> Agreed . . . that in respect of human resource development, and availability of skills, Governments would make every effort to upgrade or facilitate the upgrading of their national hotel schools, the Caribbean Hotel Training Institute (CHTI), the University of the West Indies Centre for Hotel and Tourism Management. To facilitate this, Governments would consider seeking resources from donor sources such as the European Community (EC) or the Inter-American Development Bank (IDB). (CARICOM, 1992)

However, despite this "agreement", although some progress has been made in upgrading some facilities in the region, in Barbados, the Bahamas, Jamaica and Trinidad, a lot remains to be done in this regard, especially in the countries that make up the Organisation of Eastern Caribbean States.

THE CENTRE FOR HOTEL AND TOURISM MANAGEMENT

History and Development

In recognition of the importance of tourism to the Caribbean region as an earner of foreign exchange and creator of employment opportunities, the UWI began pursuing the possibility of setting up a hotel management programme at the university level in the 1970s. In 1971, the UWI, with the support of appropriate contributing governments, obtained financial assistance from the Inter-American Development Bank (IDB) to undertake feasibility studies relating to possible expansion in a number of areas of education and training, including tourism and hotel management. A special committee, comprised of faculty representatives from the Faculty of Social Sciences, directors of tourism of some of the major destinations in the West Indies, and external consultants from Florida International University and Switzerland, was appointed. Its terms of reference included the testing of training in tourism and hotel management at the university level, with special attention to the academic content of the programme, and practical training involving attachments to hotels. Other factors that were considered were preparation of a scheme for staff development, recruitment of staff, development of appropriate teaching materials and preparation of cost estimates for alternative locations of the programme.

The committee found that there was a need for the education and training of local managers for the regional hotel and tourism industry and that the UWI should play a major role in satisfying this need. The committee recommended that the first objective of the programme should be to provide a broad education for potential entrants to the industry, to enable them to bring some influence to bear on the development of the industry in accordance with the environmental, social, economic and cultural needs of the Caribbean. At the same time, the programme should train students in certain specific skills, to prepare them to assume management responsibilities and equip them to perform certain specific functions in the various sectors of the industry. Hence, the programme would aim at producing graduates capable of performing at high standards, while having a strong Caribbean orientation and flavour in its approach. Thus, the programme should be (and was) developed to embrace the following:

- Social science and environmental studies (social, political, economic and physical)
- Basic tool courses designed to develop the intellectual capacity and the analytical and decision-making abilities of the students
- Courses intended to facilitate articulation, expression and communication of ideas orally and in writing
- Technical areas of study focused specifically on tourism, travel and hotel operations (UWI, 1971)

Out of the deliberations of the special committee, and after a gestation period of seven years, in 1977 the UWI established in Jamaica a Hotel Management degree programme, which, as its name suggests, concentrated mainly on the hotel management aspect of tourism education. At the same time, a diploma in Hotel Management was introduced for students with a first degree in management studies or business administration. The programme operated out of the Department of Management Studies at UWI, Mona and courses were taught both in the Faculty of Social Sciences and at the Jamaica Hotel

School, which was referred to above. However, it was transferred in 1978 to the Bahamas as the country with the best-developed plant in the West Indies and, hence, the greatest potential for effective university–industry interface (O'Reilly and Charles, 1990). However, the UWI did not carry out any research as to the suitability of having the programme in a non-campus territory such as the Bahamas, where there was little or no infrastructure for establishing it.

The name of the institution was changed in 1983 to the Centre for Hotel and Tourism Management, to reflect the introduction of a bachelor's degree in Tourism Management, and it became a full-fledged department of the Faculty of Social Sciences of UWI in 1985. The CHTM, therefore, is a specialist department (within the Faculty of Social Sciences) offering BSc degrees in Hotel Management and Tourism Management, as well as, currently, postgraduate diplomas in these two disciplines. Following the British tradition, after which the UWI was patterned, the bachelor's programmes are of three years duration and the diploma programmes sixteen months. Year one of the bachelor's degree programme is done at any of the three campuses in Jamaica, Barbados or Trinidad and comprises a broad educational foundation in the social sciences and management. In order to facilitate applicants from the Bahamas, which, for the most part, follows the American system of education, it was agreed that graduates of the College of the Bahamas might be admitted to the degree programmes with an Associate of Arts degree in Business or Tourism. All specific hospitality and tourism-related courses are pursued at the CHTM in Nassau in the second and third years. These two years are, therefore, very intensive.

In addition to the academic programmes offered, the CHTM also conducts special in-house management/supervisory development and training courses for client organizations in the industry in the region and has acted in an advisory capacity on tourism-related matters to CARICOM governments. The three-month internship, held between December and March of years two and three, is a very critical aspect of the education process in the programme and affords an opportunity for greater interface between the university and the industry that it serves. Effective use of computer technology for decision making, problem solving and research is an integral part of many of the courses offered in the programme. The department currently has a state-of-the-art computer centre, with several PCs and its own Web page and an Intranet to better serve its clientele. The department is also equipped with a modern kitchen and restaurant laboratory.

Students, with guidance from faculty, manage this facility, which is open to the public and serves four-course lunches and dinners every Friday during the semester. Public feedback has been very positive over the years of the facility's existence.

Student intake has increased considerably over the past five academic years. The programme was started in 1978 in Nassau with only 13 students. This number more than doubled in the 1980s, to an average of 30 students (in both second and third years) per year, with approximately 14 students graduating each year. In the early 1990s, this number doubled to 60 students per year. Since the academic year 1999/2000, there have been about 130 students registered.

From 1979 to 2000, over 500 students graduated from the CHTM. More than half (55%) of these graduates are from Jamaica, followed by the Republic of Trinidad and Tobago (17%), Barbados (14%), the OECS countries, the Turks and Caicos Islands and the British Virgin Islands (8%) and the Bahamas (6%). The majority of the graduates have done well over the years in the hotel, tourism and allied industries in the Caribbean. It has been found that hotels and other businesses of today prefer to start a young graduate as a management trainee or as a supervisor/department head at the middle-management level. The CHTM maintains contacts with hotels, tourist boards, airlines and other hospitality facilities in the region through the annual internship programme, and contacts with regional and international hotel chains are made by the CHTM and the Placement Services Department of the UWI to arrange interviews for graduates.

The Future

The Office of the Board for Undergraduate Studies (OBUS) of the UWI, in a paper entitled "New Directions in Tourism Education: A Rationale", wrote that the UWI is attempting to respond to the requests from the region for an improved human resource base for the tourism sector. The intention is to give students the necessary tools with which they can improve the regional tourism product. (OBUS, 1998). This project, spearheaded by OBUS, involves the forging of partnerships with several tertiary institutions, colleges and a university in the region, which the CHTM will supervise for the UWI. To date, partnerships have been formed with the University of Technology (UTech), Jamaica, the Antigua State College (ASC), the Barbados Community College (BCC) and the Trinidad campus of the Trinidad and Tobago Hospitality Training Institute (TTHTI). UWI will offer five areas of concentration. These are:

- Hotel and resort management
- Food and beverage and catering management
- Events and entertainment management
- Tourism product management
- Eco-tourism site management

The programmes in Jamaica, Antigua and Barbados started in 1998. The TTHTI/UWI programme got underway in 2001. The joint UWI/UTech programme in Jamaica has four areas of specialization: hotel and resort management, food and beverage management, tourism management and culinary services. The ASC programme, on the other hand, is a feeder programme. Students, after successful completion of the two years at ASC, can transfer to the CHTM or the St Augustine campus in Trinidad. At the CHTM, students can pursue the "traditional" specializations mentioned above. At St Augustine, students can study the "non-traditional" components, such as eco-site management and events management. The UWI/BCC and the UWI/TTHTI are also feeder programmes where the student, after successfully completing two years at the community college or the hotel school in the specialized areas of hotel and food and beverage will transfer to the UWI Cave Hill or St Augustine campus to pursue the more general courses.

It is the consensus of CHTM Faculty that the four-year bachelor's degree programmes with their various specialized areas will allow for much greater depth. There will be great concentration placed on foreign language training. Internships, a necessary element of the package, will be done during the summer period of the second, third and final years. It has been agreed, in principle, that placements will be done in all language groupings and in a wide range of facilities, including heritage sites and protected parks.

The CHTM is also currently engaged in delivering distance-teaching modules for a diploma programme in Hospitality and Tourism Management, to be offered to thirty-five middle managers in the hospitality and tourism industries in the region. The programme is financed through the European Union and is one of two programmes in Hospitality and Tourism Human Resource Development funded by the European Union, the other being the MSc in Hospitality and

Tourism Management, which started on the UWI Mona campus in September 1999 with a student intake of twenty-six.

CONCLUSION

Tourism and hospitality education and training are indeed necessary for the continued growth of tourism in the region. There must be a properly trained and educated cadre of management trainees who will become the leaders of the industry in the next decade and beyond. A start has been made through the CHTM. However, with the UWI joining hands with the state schools in the region, in addition to retaining its own programmes in Nassau, the numbers of management trained personnel in the West Indies will naturally increase. On the other hand, there must also be a continuous reservoir of trained staff that will help to take our industry to higher levels. The regional hotel schools must be in a position to provide these numbers. Although some of the hotel schools are well equipped to do the job, there are others whose governments, with the help of the hospitality sector, still need to provide the proper facilities for training in the hospitality industry.

The CARICOM Summit on Tourism in 1992 also made the following recommendation, to "encourage the establishment of a Regional Tourism Education Council, which would have among other functions the co-ordination of training programmes and the accreditation and articulation of programmes" (CARICOM, 1992). These objectives can be accomplished with these new models in which the UWI/CHTM and the wider university are involved. This will naturally create a holistic approach in the offerings of tourism and hospitality education in West Indian countries, thus helping to create improvement in and sustainability of the product as more programmes come on stream.

REFERENCES

Bell, J. (1991). "Caribbean Tourism Realities", *World Travel and Tourism Review* 1: 111–114.

Brathwaite, R.D., Charles, K.R., Hall, J.A., and O'Reilly, A.M. (1991). "The Status of Tourism Education in the Caribbean – Primary, Secondary, and Tertiary", pp. 5–23, in Hall, J.A. et al. (eds.), *Tourism Education and Human Resource Development for the Decade of the 90s: Proceedings of the First Caribbean Conference on Tourism Education*, University of the West Indies, Mona, Jamaica.

Caribbean Hotel Association. (2000). *Caribbean (CHA) Hotel Association 2000 Handbook,* Caribbean Publishing Co., Miami, FL, pp. 41–47.

Caribbean Tourism Organisation. (1995). *Caribbean Tourism Statistical Report,* Caribbean Tourism Organisation, Bridgetown, Barbados.

CARICOM. (1992). *Summit on Tourism, Summary of Conclusions,* CARICOM, Georgetown, Guyana.

Carnegie, A.R. and O'Reilly A.M. (1995). *Guyana Tourism Legislation Project Report,* Caribbean Tourism Organisation, Bridgetown, Barbados.

Charles, K.R. (1997). "Tourism Education and Training in the Caribbean: Preparing for the Twenty-first Century", *Progress in Tourism and Hospitality Research* 3: 189–197.

Conlin, M. (1993). "The Caribbean", pp. 147–160, in Baum, T. (ed.), *Human Resource Issues in International Tourism,* Butterworth-Heinemann, Oxford.

Holder, J.S. (1996). "Regional Solutions to Caribbean Tourism Sustainability Problems", *Proceedings from the Caribbean Conference on Sustainable Tourism,* Punta Cana Beach Resort, Dominican Republic, 1995, CTO.

Office of the Board for Undergraduate Studies (OBUS). (1998). "New Directions in Tourism Education – a Rationale", unpublished document, Office of the Board for Undergraduate Studies, Mona, Jamaica.

O'Reilly, A.M. and Charles, K.R. (1990). "Creating a Hotel and Tourism Management Programme in a Developing Country: The Case of the University of the West Indies", *Hospitality and Tourism Educator* 18: 47–49.

Pattullo, P. (1996). *Last Resorts: The Cost of Tourism in the Caribbean,* Ian Randle Publishers, Kingston, Jamaica.

University of the West Indies (UWI). (1971). "Report of the Special Committee on Tourism and Hotel Management", unpublished report, University of the West Indies, Mona, Jamaica.

World Tourism Organization. (1998). *Tourism Highlights 1997,* World Tourism Organization, Madrid, Spain.

World Tourism Organization. (1999). *Compendium of Tourism Statistics 1993–1997,* World Tourism Organization, Madrid, Spain.

CHAPTER 24

A SEAMLESS EDUCATION AND TRAINING SYSTEM FOR CARIBBEAN TOURISM HUMAN RESOURCE DEVELOPMENT

Carolyn E. Hayle

Abstract

Until recently tourism education has not been viewed as a scholarly subject and traditional employers have preferred to hire based on personal ties rather than on the basis of formal training and education. More recently, however, new entrants to the business have begun to challenge the old way of thinking. Governments in the Caribbean too have recognized the need to formalize training in the tourism sector and have responded by creating two entities – the Caribbean Tourism ands Education Council (CTEC) and the Association of Caribbean Tertiary Institutions (ACTI). These organizations have focused on two main concerns – developing flexible and responsive educational systems and creating a seamless system for training and education. Although these initiatives have been useful there is need for further industry participation, particularly in curriculum development and in the development of a labour market information system.

THE LINK BETWEEN SUSTAINABILITY AND TOURISM

Sustainability for Caribbean tourism can be grouped into two main issues: the preservation of its environment and the development of its people. Millions of visitors come to the region each year to experience blue seas and lush vegetation, and to enjoy the interaction with its warm, friendly people. At present, there is an abundant supply of all three ingredients. The question is how to preserve these elements to ensure a sustainable future for Caribbean tourism.

In 1992, 182 countries of the world met in Rio de Janeiro, Brazil, to discuss the state of the environment. At the end of those deliberations a comprehensive programme of action known as Agenda 21 was developed. In a document developed by the World Travel and Tourism Council entitled "Agenda 21 for the Travel and Tourism Industry Toward Environmentally Sustainable Development", the following nine areas were highlighted for governments and national tourism organizations:

1. Assessing the capacity of the existing regulatory, economic and voluntary framework to bring about sustainable tourism
2. Assessing the economic, social, cultural and environmental implications of the organization's operations
3. Training, education and public awareness
4. Planning for sustainable tourism development
5. Facilitating exchange of information, skills and technology relating to sustainable tourism between developed and developing countries
6. Providing for the participation of all sectors of society
7. Design of new tourism products with sustainability at their core
8. Measuring progress in achieving sustainable development
9. Partnerships for sustainable development (World Travel and Tourism Council, 1995)

These areas were determined by the World Travel and Tourism Council as areas of great relevance to the sustainability of tourism. Similar priorities were developed for the private sector. In this chapter, however, items 3, 5 and 9 above are of particular interest, as they focus on education and training, information and partnership as tools for sustainability. This chapter reviews past developments and proposes a plan of action and a system for treating with tourism education and training in the region.

THE NEED FOR A CHANGE

In reviewing education and training for tourism, it is important to analyse the needs and wants of the customer. The Florida Caribbean Cruise Association, for example, in numerous presentations to the Caribbean tourism sector has stated that their customers are interested in heritage, culture and shopping and that most destinations have been unable to fill these needs. This void translates into economic loss for the region.

The profile of "the visitor" has changed considerably over the last decade. Most visitors are now well aware of their responsibility to preserve and respect the environment and the culture of others. To underscore this point, in an airport exit interview conducted on behalf of an environmental organization in Jamaica, 70% of those visitors interviewed exhibited a willingness to pay to ensure that the environmental conditions in the island were maintained (Natural Resources Conservation Authority, 1995). In at least one instance, in another study conducted in 1996 in Jamaica, 11% of the visitors said they would not return to the island because of environmental problems (Dunn and Dunn, 1994). Some of those interviewed made reference to the socio-economic conditions of the local people, which these visitors viewed as depressing.

These types of data coupled with data from the industry form the basis on which strategic planning for tourism ought to be undertaken. There is a notion, however, that tourism stands by itself. This type of thinking has gone a long way in alienating the local people from tourism, and the industry from the nation. For the economy to survive, an integrated approach to nation building and national planning, inclusive of tourism and its contribution to the general economy, needs to become the norm. Policies in education are central to the development of the type of citizen necessary to make the country competitive not only in terms of tourism, but also in every other sector of the economy. Subjects such as social studies and principles of business seem central to the development of a cadre of individuals with a wide understanding of global issues. These subjects, at present, are electives and are rejected by most teachers and students. Tourism, unfortunately, falls within the purview of social studies and so it too gets cast aside. Ironically, tourism is the major industry for the region.

For many years, it has been generally accepted that education and training are the vehicles through which the peoples of the region, especially the less affluent members of society, are likely to achieve upward mobility. However, tourism represents a dichotomy. Until recently, tourism was not taken seriously in determining the wealth of nations. As a result, it was viewed as the playground of the rich but not so scholarly. Therefore, until about twenty to thirty years ago no serious education or training programmes for tourism were put in place in the Caribbean. To get a job in tourism it was common to find a "friend" in the business. This trend, while decreasing slightly, continued until recently and is substantiated by a 1993 study on the hospitality sector in Jamaica, in which it was revealed that only 30% of those interviewed for the study had a formal interview, job specifications and job description (Hamilton and Associates, 1993).

In more recent times, tourism has taken its rightful place on the economic agenda. The time period between the early beginnings of tourism and more recent times of "acceptance" has yielded an odd mix of people. The stage is full of recent entrants to the business who are well trained and well educated. There are other, more experienced, players with clout of one sort or another but lack technical competence and the exposure that would allow them to take tourism to a highly sophisticated competitive market environment. These two groups compete with each other for centre-stage. The result is an uneven platform, uneven results and rivalry between groups. Hence, the new "breed" of managers and entrepreneurs compete with the "old" breed for the attention of the policy makers, instead of utilizing each other's strengths to move the industry forward. Insecurities and threats to positions, real or imagined, creep into the work setting. This does not foster a productive and motivated workforce for the region's most lucrative business.

To further compound the problem, tourism is a multifaceted industry. At the top end of the spectrum are the mega-room facilities while at the lower end, there are "mom and pop" operations, including taxi drivers, attraction owners, craft vendors and water sports operators, to name a few. Yet, each notch on the continuum services its own appropriate niche with varying degrees of success. Again a dichotomy exists, as both need each other to survive, but the notion of inclusion and participation – basic principles of sustainable development – are foreign to the average Caribbean entrepreneur.

To add to the problem, in many countries of the region there is a large pool of dropouts from the education system. These dropouts can be loosely defined as individuals who either went through the school systems but learnt very little, or individuals who left the school system at a very early age. In both instances, self-esteem tends to be low and society on the whole finds ways of marginalizing them.

This group poses the greatest challenge to tourism, as it is often ignored but is the most volatile of all elements. These dropouts end up working either for or against tourism, depending on the approach used towards them by individuals within the private sector or governments. Lack of attention to programmes such as remedial education, counselling, personal development and conflict resolution has serious negative impact on the tourism sector. In fact, these are areas in which the universities and the sector can be used to form partnerships to build the industry at the community level.

In order to achieve sustainability, the following points must be addressed by the education and training system:

- It must support a dynamic socio-economic system
- There must be the development of a viable education and training system
- It must generate a correlation between skills requirement and labour force resources
- It must give assistance in identifying and implementing strategies/projects/programmes and consolidating the contributions of all who are concerned with developments in technical and vocational education and training

Entrepreneurs external to tourism identified the need for training programmes aimed at the many target groups. On the public sector side, a number of trainers and training institutions appeared, yet there was no clear path developed to formally address these training needs.

The changing nature of the visitors, the industry and the global environment re-emphasize the need for change within the region. The Caribbean tourism industry in the twenty-first century faces certain threats and opportunities. In an article entitled "Mastering Change in a Turbulent Environment" (IJHRD, 1994), the author outlines the following process for mastering change:

- Environmental scanning
- Establishing mega trends
- Identifying the direction of change and discontinuities
- Estimating the magnitude of change
- Assessing the impact of change
- Scenario building
- Strategy formulation
- Contingency preparation

These are the strategies that need careful review and analysis in reshaping the Caribbean tourism product for the next twenty years. These elements pose a challenge to the education and training system. The role of education and training is to create the type of individual who can make a difference in positioning the region to compete globally.

THE CARIBBEAN CONTEXT

In March 1993, the vice chancellor of the University of the West Indies (UWI), having regard for the importance of tourism to the economies of the Caribbean Community (CARICOM), established a committee to advise on needs for training in hotel and tourism management in the region; to indicate the types and levels of training programmes required to fill management and other positions; to examine the capability of the UWI's Centre for Hotel and Tourism Management in Nassau and to recommend what steps needed to be taken to satisfy the needs for training in the region.

The composition of the committee reflected the significance of the following statement made by its chairman, Ambassador Don Bryce:

> Given the linkages to virtually every other sector of the economies of the region, a vibrant tourist industry imparts momentum to activity in construction, manufacturing, agriculture, banking and finance, tour and travel services and other related areas. Conversely, it has been repeatedly demonstrated that a downturn in the tourist industry usually heralds a downturn in the economy as a whole. (University of the West Indies, 1995)

The Bryce Committee recognized the impact of human resource development on tourism when it stated:

> The product being marketed is of paramount importance, and while the physical attributes of the tourism product undoubtedly rate high in the product mix, the deciding factor as often as not rests with the human element, as tourism is essentially a service industry. The degree of sophistication and standards of service undoubtedly influence the perceptions of the travel trade and the growth of a healthy repeat visitor business. (University of the West Indies, 1995)

In August 1995, the Summit of the Heads of State and Governments of the Association of Caribbean States (ACS) on Tourism, Trade, and Transport was held in Port of Spain, Trinidad. At that meeting, specific decisions were taken with respect to education and training for tourism. Members of the Council of Ministers adopted, *inter alia*, the following conclusions, as they relate to tourism:

- The establishment of a Caribbean Regional Tourism Development Fund
- The establishment of a Caribbean Tourism Education and Training Council and the Regional Programme for Education, Training and Research in Sustainable Tourism

The Council of Ministers also agreed to a meeting of the relevant agencies and interest groups on January 15, 1996 in Chetumal, Quintana Roo, Mexico (Ministry of Foreign Affairs, 1996a).

Item two is of particular relevance to this chapter. The ACS made, *inter alia*, the following recommendations:

With respect to Human Resources:

(xiv) Accept the offer of the Government of Mexico to establish a Regional Programme for education, training and research in sustainable tourism, based at the Universidad de Quintana Roo (Mexico), aimed at widening efforts to develop human resources that will increase competitiveness and quality of tourist services in the Caribbean region;

(xv) create within the next three months a Caribbean Tourism Education and Training Council, with the following terms of reference:

    (a) to examine the manpower needs of the region and review the number and type of public and private sector institutions in the ACS region which are currently involved in tourism training;

    (b) to ascertain what certification in tourism is available at all tourism training institutions throughout the ACS region and the extent to which they are acceptable and transferable between the various States, Countries and Territories and to create a directory of ACS wide travel and tourism institutions and professionals;

    (c) to consider the adoption of the recommendations of the University of the West Indies report on tertiary education in tourism, with respect to expansion and rationalisation of institutions, transferability of credits, postgraduate training in the region, language training and certification and the provision of financial support required and implementation;

(d) to find a co-ordination mechanism between the institutions
    of higher education to deal with setting and monitoring of
    educational standards and levels of certification, within the
    colleges and universities in the region;

(e) to establish job performance standards leading to the certifi-
    cation of knowledge and skills of professionals, which is rec-
    ognised throughout the region and which will facilitate the
    free movement of tourism professionals, in accordance with
    the legislation currently in force in each country;

(f) to examine the offer from the Government of Mexico with
    a view to ensuring that it complements existing pro-
    grammes. (Association of Caribbean States, 1995)

INTERVENTIONS OVER THE PAST DECADE

In a report prepared by the Association of Caribbean Tertiary Institutions (ACTI) for the Tenth Meeting of the Standing Committee of
Ministers Responsible for Education in 1994, some of the problems
facing the region were expressed this way:

> One of the issues of concern to educators in the Caribbean has been
> the absence of a regional mechanism to determine equivalency of
> educational qualifications, particularly in the face of the proliferation
> of private and public institutions, especially at the tertiary level. Some
> of the resulting problems included the difficulties students experience
> as they seek transfers from one institution to another, and the prob-
> lems faced by employers in the public and private sector as they
> attempt to determine the equivalency of educational credentials.

ACTI fully supported the recommendation for the establishment of
a coherent training system, closely developed with industry to ensure
an appropriate education and training system from vocational to
graduate levels.

ACTI was recently endorsed by the Heads of Government as the
regional mechanism for coordination of tertiary education and training and has developed a regional accreditation system. This ought to
facilitate the systematic development of human resources within the
Caribbean region. Members of ACTI are the University of the West
Indies, University of Guyana, University of the Virgin Islands, University College of Belize, University of Technology, College of Bahamas,
Barbados Community College, Sir Arthur Lewis Community College,

Antigua State College, the community colleges of Jamaica, the Cultural Training Centre (Jamaica), National Institute of Higher Education, Research, Science and Technology (NIHERST), teacher training colleges in the region, national or state colleges, and several private tertiary educational institutions.

ACTI has two standing committees: the Accreditation, Equivalency and Articulation Committee and the Programmes and Institutional Development Committee. Both of these committees have worked together to fulfil the mandate given to ACTI by the Standing Committee of Ministers of Education in 1994. The mandate was to make ACTI the primary implementation agency for a Regional Mechanism for Equivalency, Articulation and Accreditation.

In order to understand the importance of creating a seamless system throughout the region, it is equally important to understand the distinction between equivalency, articulation and accreditation. These three elements, along with modularized curricula, have a central role to play in creating flexibility for education and training.

- *Equivalency* (used interchangeably with validation) is a process by which the content level of a programme or course is approved as being a given standard by an institution recognized as a validating institution.
- *Accreditation* is a principle in which a programme of study is assessed for its value and given official recognition.
- *Articulation* facilitates the movement from one institution to another without a break or loss of time for the students. Institutions that deliver the programmes, which are similar in nature, are allowed to link in a stepwise process. It facilitates entry into another institution or transfer of credits toward a programme of study and at a higher level.

Realizing the significance of equivalency, articulation and accreditation and standardization, ACTI suggested, in 1994, that agreement be reached on the following:

1. A common credit system in which 15 hours = 1 credit hour be accepted
2. An acceptable credit system which would take into consideration:
   - The competency domains
   - A building block accumulation of credit points

- A sequential movement (vertical and horizontal) from one level of qualification to the next
- Assessment of work experience
3. A comparison between academic and competency-based systems
4. Acceptance of the position put forward by the OECS with respect to technical and vocational education and training
5. The role of the associate degrees
6. Account be taken of the Caribbean Examination Council within the system

A National Equivalency Personnel workshop held in Trinidad and Tobago, in July 1994, highlighted the fact that in a regional survey of the policies and procedures used in determining equivalencies of educational credentials the following were identified:

1. The need for consistency in evaluating non-traditional courses
2. The need to evaluate for consistency those for which no local benchmarks exist
3. The need to design appropriate programmes for training and retooling of staff
4. The need to make it easier to access resource material
5. The need to establish closer linkages between ministries and other agencies that evaluate educational credentials

The creation of a regional mechanism in the form of ACTI has addressed most of these concerns and laid the foundation for the movement and development of the people of the region.

The technical vocational institutions, which are also a part of ACTI, have further organized themselves under one umbrella. CINTERFOR is the coordinating nucleus and driving force for a system of cooperation among training institutions in the countries of the Americas. It was born out of the Seventh Conference of American International Labour Organization (ILO) Member States in Buenos Aires in 1961, in response to a proposal made to the ILO at that time to establish a centre for exchanging experiences, based on research, documentation and dissemination of vocational training activities. It undertakes studies and research and contributes to the preparation of personnel required for training tasks. It is headquartered in Montevideo, Uruguay.

Within the Caribbean, the vocational institutions interface with each other through a CINTERFOR Regional Sub-Committee on Technical Vocational Education and Training (TVET). In addition, the Eastern Caribbean countries are represented on that committee, jointly and severally, by the OECS.

ELEMENTS OF A NEW SYSTEM

The arrangements for education and training for the region in general also apply to tourism. However, there are two important components in designing an education and training system for this sector: (1) industry must drive the process, and (2) flexibility must be ensured.

In 1993 in an analysis of manpower and strategies for the Jamaican hospitality industry, it was determined that twenty-six functional areas were considered critical success skills for the hospitality sector. These are:

Textile/fabric care	Food preparation	Food hygiene
Sanitation	Service quality	Food storage
Food grading	Purchasing	Store recording
Human relations	Communications	Sales/marketing
Cost control	Office practices	Financial administration
Customer relations	Plumbing	Electrical
Safety procedures	Security procedures	Foreign language
Supervision	Drink preparation	Mechanical
First aid	Report writing	

While the elements outlined above refer specifically to skill areas, the underlying principle belies the shift required for improvement in product quality. The study also serves to underscore the importance of creating a seamless educational system throughout the region that will facilitate not only the movement of people but will provide new job opportunities for people. ACTI is a major part of that process.

The second component in creating this seamless system is flexibility. The paradigm has shifted. Physical space and time of day are no longer constraints. For example, with the assistance of technology, the UWI is now able to train supervisors for the industry via the Internet. This training can be done at the convenience of the student. In other words, a supervisor in a property in Tobago will be able to enrol in a course in supervisory management with UWI and complete that course without having to attend classes in Nassau, the actual location at which the course is taught. The quality of the content is equal to that of a course taught on any of the UWI campuses. The customer is now in control. This is part of the shift in the paradigm. Students are indeed customers. Institutions merely facilitate the process of education and training. The country is the ultimate beneficiary.

Along with the creation and acceptance of a regional mechanism to oversee education and training, within the last decade a number of things have happened in the education and training arena, the most significant of which is the acceptance of technical vocational training as having an integral part to play in the development of the region. The other significant issue is the acceptance of a five-level system which addresses issues of equalization of occupational standards and curriculum within skill areas. This flexibility allows for the pursuit of courses over time and in ways that are convenient to the student rather than to the institution.

In Jamaica, for example, the National Council for Technical and Vocational Education and Training (NCTVET) has not only designed a five-level programme that encompasses both the UWI and OECS approach, but also includes the training of trainers and teachers, as well as automotive training and agriculture. The NCTVET system has progressed to the point where an accreditation and certification process has been worked out. The NCTVET level definitions are as follows:

Level 1. Routine/entry-level/supervised work
Level 2. Technical/broad-based/semi-supervised
Level 3. Applied skills/pre-professional/unsupervised
Level 4. Master 1. Managerial/professional
Level 5. Master 2. Master craftsman/professional/managerial

This system has been endorsed on the international stage and creates a competitive advantage for industries in general, and tourism in particular.

THE STATE OF THE DEBATE

In 1996, when the research for this chapter was originally conducted, many organizations were beginning to see the need for one central system. The purpose of the research at that time was to rationalize what was happening in regional tourism with respect to education and training and to make recommendations for its improvement. At that time, there were fragments of systems for education and training. It was then proposed that a system that incorporated elements of several systems be adopted. With much effort and cooperation a regional system does appear to be emerging.

To further assist the process, several international agencies have pumped millions of dollars into the region's education and training systems in an effort to improve the human resource stock. CARICOM has created the regional mechanism that will address issues of equivalency, articulation and certification. In this system a student can enter the system at primary school level, through appropriate exposure and guidance counselling and by following a predetermined path he or she can exit the system several years later at the doctoral level.

In response to the mandate from the ACS, the Caribbean Tourism Organisation created a Human Resource Council on which members of both the public and private sectors sit to oversee the development of education and training for the region. Of even greater significance is the fact that this body has made tangible inputs into the development of training material for the system and into the training of teachers of tourism. Education and training are beginning to play a significant role in shaping the development of the human resources in the Caribbean.

At the UWI a number of new initiatives for tourism have been included in its teaching programme. The university has accepted that tourism requires a multidisciplinary approach and has included most of its faculties in the development of and discussions on new programmes for this sector. For example, it is now possible to enter the UWI tourism programme in several ways:

1. A levels and the completion of one year in the Faculty of Social Sciences
2. Five CXCs and by joining at one of the UWI-approved tertiary level institutions leads to an associate degree or diploma, depending on the institution
3. Five CXCs and by joining in the joint degree programme offered by the UWI/University of Technology (in Jamaica)
4. Upper-second-class honours degree with one year of postgraduate experience in the tourism sector and by joining in the master's degree programme in Tourism and Hospitality Management

PARTNERSHIPS

Understanding the global economy as well as the local scene is of critical significance, not only to the private sector but also to the training system. A regional partnership that collects and analyses labour market information is essential. Information, a major component of Agenda 21, is the basis on which sound decisions are made. This is true not only for the private sector to have a competitive edge, but also for institutions to maintain programmes of relevance and national/regional focus.

Industry participation in the training system can take other forms, such as input in curriculum development. This, in the context of the NCTVET system, is by way of a lead group concept. What this means is that representatives selected by industry sit with job analysts and curriculum developers to determine elements that feed into curricula. This process more or less guarantees a close fit between industry needs and the output of educators and trainers. Feedback mechanisms designed to keep universities current should also be a part of the process. A partnership between the private sector, the public sector and the universities is of paramount importance if the tourism products offered by the region are to remain competitive in the global arena.

Flexibility and partnership in the process can be achieved by accrediting suitable tourism facilities (hotels, attractions, etc.) to act as training institutions. To designate well-operated facilities as training institutions could be one of the methods used to increase competitiveness among entities, thus improving the quality of the product offering. Additionally, staff within these institutions would benefit from interaction with educators and trainers and vice versa. Improved access for instructors, teachers and trainers to tourism facilities would assist in validating and/or upgrading their own skills. This is important because it makes for better delivery. This has been a major deficiency in the current system. The Caribbean Tourism Organisation Human Resource Council has agreed to oversee a regional internship programme which should further assist with partnership building.

WHAT IS MISSING

While much progress has been achieved, there is still room to accommodate more innovation in the system. Some possible strategies that can be employed are:

- The creation of a unit that focuses on a labour market information system. This unit could be owned and operated by an independent third party. It would keep up-to-date records fed into it by national hotel associations and public sector organizations. This information would include the number and type of job vacancies, the number and type of positions, and projected new areas of product expansion. The existing labour market information system currently being piloted by the ILO, by agreement, could be incorporated into this system. The ILO office has also put together a directory of occupations for Trinidad and this can, therefore, be expanded to include the rest of the region. The ILO and CHA could work closely with the NCTVET to develop a comprehensive system.
- International funds would have to be sought to finance the labour market information system, the registration process, research and development, and continuous professional development programmes for the trainers and administrators of institutions.
- To maintain the integrity of the system all tourism trainers would be registered with the labour market information system database unit. This would allow for the compilation of a directory of professionals in the sector.
- This registration process will allow for periodic upgrading of the trainers by requiring that a specified number of hours be spent in industry every three years (time period would have to be determined by experts). This forces the trainers to remain current and purges the system of those who do not meet this requirement.
- Community outreach programmes, including remedial and prevocational programmes, need to be implemented throughout the region to foster a spirit of participation.
- Prior to the implementation of the regional programmes, national tourism councils need to be created, each charged with responsibility for overseeing the strategic inputs for its country.
- Inputs from these national councils could be fed to the Caribbean Tourism Organisation's Human Resource Council on which all regional educational institutions are represented.

- An apprenticeship system needs to be used more extensively to fill technical needs. This could be merged with the current Internship Programme being fostered by the Human Resource Council.
- Accreditation of some tourism entities as centres of learning would serve as an excellent tool for staff development.

CONCLUSION

Education and training are essential elements in the sustainability drive of the tourism industry. The Caribbean, at this juncture, faces stiff competition from the rest of the world. The best marketing strategy lies in the development of the human resource potential in the region. An integrated approach to planning, steeped in the principles of sustainable development, will lead to a better understanding of ourselves as people, and to the development of a legacy befitting those who may follow. A seamless system for education and training must have at its core accommodation for the diversity of backgrounds, experiences and desires of people from separate yet similar cultures. The warmth and friendliness of the Caribbean people go unchallenged. A well-educated and trained citizenry is the ultimate weapon in a differentiation strategy designed for the sustainability of Caribbean tourism.

REFERENCES

Association of Caribbean States. (1995). "Plan of Action on Tourism", Association of Caribbean States, Port of Spain, Trinidad, Annex 2, p. 1.

Association of Caribbean Tertiary Institutions. (1994). Paper V, paper presented at meeting of officials preparatory to the Tenth Meeting of the Standing Committee of Ministers Responsible for Education, Association of Caribbean Tertiary Institutions, Barbados.

Dunn, L.L. and Dunn, H.S. (1994). "Visitor Harassment and Attitudes to Tourism and Tourists in Negril", Jamaica Tourist Board, Kingston, Jamaica.

Hamilton, T. and Associates. (1993). "Study on Human Resource Development for the Hospitality and Tourism Sector, Hamilton and Associates, Kingston, Jamaica.

"Mastering Change in a Turbulent Environment". (1994). *International Journal of Human Resource Development and Management* 1: 30.

Ministry of Foreign Affairs. (1996a). Excerpts from document circulated by Ministry of Foreign Affairs, Kingston, Jamaica.

Ministry of Foreign Affairs. (1996b). Paper summarizing the Association of Caribbean States Summit, Ministry of Foreign Affairs, Kingston, Jamaica.

Natural Resources Conservation Authority. (1995). Unpublished report, Natural Resources Conservation Authority, Kingston, Jamaica.

University of the West Indies. (1995). Report of the Committee on Training in Hotel and Tourism Management in the Region, University of the West Indies, Mona, Jamaica, pp. 3–4.

World Travel and Tourism Council. (1995). Agenda 21 for the Travel and Tourism Industry Toward Environmentally Sustainable Development, Executive Summary, World Travel and Tourism Council, London, p. 5.

Contributors

Chandana Jayawardena, DPhil, FHCIMA, CHE, is a research fellow, senior lecturer and the academic director – MSc in Tourism and Hospitality Management, University of the West Indies. He has published five books, ten book chapters and twenty-six papers. He is also the regional editor and research director for the Caribbean of WHATT E-journal.

Allison Atkinson, MBA, is the administrative assistant for the MSc in Tourism and Hospitality Management Programme, University of the West Indies, Mona campus. She has had seven years working experience in the travel, airline and hotel industries.

Ian Boxill, PhD, is a senior lecturer in Sociology at the University of the West Indies (UWI). He also lectures in the graduate tourism programme at UWI. He coordinated the sustainable tourism programme at the UWI Centre for Environment and Development and has researched and published extensively on tourism issues across the Caribbean. He recently co-edited the book *Tourism in the Caribbean*.

Maxine Campbell, MBA, is a quality management consultant who has a proven track record of achievement in the field of quality management and ISO 9000 implementation. As managing director of Maxine Campbell and Associates Limited she guided the first hotel in the Caribbean to achieve ISO 9002 certification.

Susan M. Carter, MEd, CBVE, is the former deputy director – Tourism for Dominica, a senior instructor in hotel management and tourism and training consultant currently working with regional projects focusing on the development of ecotourism, environmental and occupational performance standards, training, certification, branding, quality inspection and eco-accreditation systems.

Kwame R. Charles, PhD, is a director of Quality Consultants Ltd, a regional management and information technology consulting firm. He also teaches at the University of the West Indies Institute of Business, Trinidad and Tobago, the University of the West Indies Centre for Management Development, Barbados and the School of Business, Nova Southeastern University, Florida, USA.

Hugh Cresser, MA, is currently attached to the Jamaica Hotel and Tourist Association. He introduced the Environmental Audits for Sustainable Tourism (EAST) Project as the project coordinator.

Anthony Clayton, PhD, is the Alcan Professor of Caribbean Sustainable Development at the University of the West Indies. He is also an Honorary Fellow in the Faculty of Science and Engineering and an Advisory Board member of the Centre for the Study of Environmental Change and Sustainability at the University of Edinburgh, UK.

Anne P. Crick, PhD, is a lecturer in Organizational Behaviour at the University of the West Indies, Mona campus. Her main research interest is personalized service. She has published articles on the role of human resource development in the delivery of personalized service, and on the opportunities that personalized service offers to small hotels.

Rae Davis, PhD, is the president of the University of Technology, Jamaica. He played a vital role in upgrading the former College of Arts, Science and Technology (CAST). He is a graduate of the University of the West Indies and has three postgraduate degrees from Loughborough University, UK and Johns Hopkins University, USA.

Guillermo J. Graglia, MBA, is the head of the Hotel Management Department, Pontifica Universidad Católica Madre y Maestra (PUCMM), Dominican Republic. He is also regional manager for the Tourism Internship Exchange System (TIES) for the Caribbean. He is currently completing a MS in Service Management. He is a member of the Caribbean Tourism Organisation's Caribbean Tourism Human Resources Council.

J. Anthony Hall, MA, CHA, is a tourism and human resources development consultant. Currently, he is the director of the Inter-American Development Bank/Jamaica Hotel and Tourist Association (IDB/JHTA) Human Resources Management Information System Project in Jamaica. A former lecturer in Tourism at the University of the West Indies Centre for Hotel and Tourism Management in the Bahamas, he has published several papers on regional and international tourism.

Kenneth O. Hall, PhD, is pro vice chancellor and principal of the University of the West Indies, Mona campus. A historian and former deputy secretary-general of CARICOM, he has recently published three books on Caribbean regional integration. He is chairman of the

Scholarship Committee of the Caribbean Tourism Organisation Michael Manley Scholarship Fund.

Carolyn E. Hayle, MBA, is a senior project officer at the University of the West Indies. She lectures on Sustainable Tourism and Marketing in the MSc Tourism and Hospitality Management degree programme at UWI. She is currently pursuing a doctoral degree in Sustainable Development with an emphasis on tourism.

Ralph L. Higgs is an assistant director of Tourism with the Turks and Caicos Island Tourist Board and shares responsibility for marketing the destination with the director of Tourism. He obtained an honour diploma in Tourism Studies from Calgary's Career College in Canada.

May Hinds is a former managing director and senior consultant, Hotel Management Services Ltd, Barbados, a consultancy firm specializing in the development of small hotels. She is currently trading as May Hinds Consulting and serves as a training consultant to lead tourism agencies. She has a diploma in Hotel Middle Management.

Michelle McLeod, BSc, AHCIMA, is the tourism development officer of the Tourism and Industrial Development Company of Trinidad and Tobago Ltd. She graduated from the University of the West Indies Centre for Hotel and Tourism Management with honours in 1991 and subsequently obtained a diploma in Tourism Management with distinction from the Institute of Tourism and Hotel Management, Salzburg, Austria.

Lindsey Musgrove, BSc, is one of two assistant directors of Tourism employed by the Turks and Caicos Tourist Board. Currently, he manages the Tourist Board's office in Providenciales with primary responsibility for product development. He is currently completing a master's degree in Hotel, Restaurant and Tourism Administration.

Ainsley O'Reilly, MSc, MHCIMA, is a senior lecturer and former director of the Bahamas-based Centre for Hotel and Tourism Management of the University of the West Indies, which he helped to set up with the Cornell School of Hotel Administration in 1978. He has published one book and twenty-six papers.

Godfrey A. Pratt, EdD, CTC, is co-director of the Hospitality Management Programme at Morgan State University. He is a twelve-year veteran of the Bahamas Ministry of Tourism, and was a special projects manager with Maryland's Office of Tourism for five years. He is an avid researcher of Caribbean tourism topics.

Naline Ramdeen-Joseph, MSc, is the head of Customer Services, Grenada Board of Tourism. She is a former department head and lecturer at the T.A. Marryshow Community College, Grenada. She was in the first cohort of the MSc programme in Tourism and Hospitality Management at the University of the West Indies.

Sophia A. Rolle, PhD, is currently the head of department of the Hospitality and Tourism Management Programme in the School of Hospitality and Tourism Studies at the College of the Bahamas. She also lectures part-time at the University of the West Indies Centre for Hospitality and Tourism Management in the Bahamas.

Ava Sewell, MSc, is a lecturer in the School of Hospitality and Tourism Management at the University of Technology, Jamaica. She was in the first cohort of the MSc programme in Tourism and Hospitality Management at the University of the West Indies.

Donald Sinclair, MPhil, is coordinator and programme convenor of Tourism Studies at the University of Guyana. He has written a number of articles on the subject of tourism and has served for three years as chairman of the Guyana Tourism Advisory Board.

John M. Skippings, BSc, is the director of tourism for the Turks and Caicos Islands. During his directorship, the destination has seen a 34% increase in visitor arrivals and the commencement of service by two major international airlines.

Marcia Taylor-Cooke, MBA, is a senior lecturer, former programme coordinator, the joint BSc degree, and former acting head of the School of Hospitality and Tourism Management, University of Technology, Jamaica. She is currently completing her doctoral dissertation in Strategic Management at Virginia Polytechnic Institute and State University of Virginia.

Sharret Yearwood, MSc, is a lecturer at the University of Belize. A member of the first cohort of the MSc programme in Tourism and Hospitality Management at the University of the West Indies, she is currently working on a proposal for a BSc programme in Tourism for the University of Belize.

Ayanna Young, LLB, is an attorney-at-law. She is presently pursuing her MSc degree in International Business at the University of the West Indies.